# Codeless Time Series Analysis with KNIME

A practical guide to implementing forecasting models for time series analysis applications

**Corey Weisinger**

**Maarit Widmann**

**Daniele Tonini**

BIRMINGHAM—MUMBAI

# Codeless Time Series Analysis with KNIME



**Group Product Manager**: Reshma Raman
**Publishing Product Manager**: Reshma Raman
**Senior Editor**: Nithya Sadanandan
**Technical Editor**: Pradeep Sahu
**Copy Editor**: Safis Editing
**Project Coordinator**: Deeksha Thakkar
**Proofreader**: Safis Editing
**Indexer**: Manju Arasan
**Production Designer**: Prashant Ghare
**Marketing Coordinator**: Priyanka Mhatre

First published: July 2022

Production reference: 1220722

Published by Packt Publishing Ltd.
Livery Place
35 Livery Street
Birmingham
B3 2PB, UK.

ISBN 978-1-80323-206-5

www.packt.com

*Thanks to my colleagues at KNIME for the technical support and encouragement, especially to Andisa Dewi and Tobias Kötter for the Taxi Demand Prediction application, and Rosaria Silipo, Phil Winters, and Iris Adä for the Anomaly Detection application.*

*– Maarit Widmann*

*I would like to thank the KNIME team for including me in this great project. Especially thanks to Rosaria Silipo, for her trust and support, and to my co-authors Maarit and Corey, for taking this long journey with me.*

*– Daniele Tonini*

# Contributors

## About the authors

**Corey Weisinger** is a data scientist with KNIME in Austin, Texas. He studied mathematics at Michigan State University focusing on actuarial techniques and functional analysis. Before coming to work for KNIME, he worked as an analytics consultant for the auto industry in Detroit, Michigan. He currently focuses on signal processing and numeric prediction techniques and is the author of the *From Alteryx to KNIME guidebook*.

**Maarit Widmann** is a data scientist and an educator at KNIME: the instructor behind the KNIME self-paced courses and a teacher of the KNIME courses. She is the author of the *From Modeling to Model Evaluation* eBook and she publishes regularly on the KNIME blog and on Medium. She holds a master's degree in data science and a bachelor's degree in sociology.

**Daniele Tonini** is an experienced advisor and educator in the field of advanced business analytics and machine learning. In the last 15 years, he designed and deployed predictive analytics systems, and data quality management and dynamic reporting tools, mainly for customer intelligence, risk management, and pricing applications. He is an Academic Fellow at Bocconi University (Department of Decision Science) and SDA Bocconi School of Management (Decision Sciences & Business Analytics Faculty). He's also an adjunct professor in data mining at Franklin University, Switzerland. He currently teaches statistics, predictive analytics for data-driven decision making, big data and databases, market research, and data mining.

## About the reviewers

**Miguel Infestas Maderuelo** has a Ph.D. in applied economics and has developed his career around data analytics in different fields (digital marketing, data mining, academic research, and so on). His last project is as a founder of a digital marketing agency, applying analytics on digital data to optimize digital communication.

**Rosaria Silipo**, Ph.D., now head of data science evangelism at KNIME, has spent 25+ years in applied AI, predictive analytics, and machine learning at Siemens, Viseca, Nuance Communications, and private consulting. Sharing her practical experience in a broad range of industries and deployments, including IoT, customer intelligence, financial services, social media, and cybersecurity, Rosaria has authored 50+ technical publications, including her recent books *Guide to Intelligent Data Science* (Springer) and *Codeless Deep Learning with KNIME* (Packt).

# Table of Contents

3

## Preparing Data for Time Series Analysis



4

## Time Series Visualization

# 5

## Time Series Components and Statistical Properties



# Part 2: Building and Deploying a Forecasting Model

# 6

## Humidity Forecasting with Classical Methods



# 7

## Forecasting the Temperature with ARIMA and SARIMA Models

8

## Audio Signal Classification with an FFT and a Gradient-Boosted Forest



9

## Training and Deploying a Neural Network to Predict Glucose Levels

# 10

## Predicting Energy Demand with an LSTM Model



# 11

## Anomaly Detection – Predicting Failure with No Failure Examples

# Part 3: Forecasting on Mixed Platforms

## 12

## Predicting Taxi Demand on the Spark Platform



## 13

## GPU Accelerated Model for Multivariate Forecasting



## 14

## Combining KNIME and H2O to Predict Stock Prices

## Answers



## Index

## Other Books You May Enjoy

# Preface

This book gives an overview of the basics of time series data and time series analysis and of KNIME Analytics Platform and its time series integration. It shows how to implement practical solutions for a wide range of use cases, from demand prediction to signal classification and signal forecasting, and from price prediction to anomaly detection. It also demonstrates how to integrate other tools in addition to KNIME Analytics Platform within the same application.

The book instructs you on common preprocessing steps of time series data and statistics and machine learning-based techniques for forecasting. These things need to be learned to master the field of time series analysis. The book also points you to examples implemented in KNIME Analytics Platform, which is a visual programming tool that is accessible and fast to learn. This removes the common time and skill barrier of learning to code.

## Who this book is for

This book is for data analysts and data scientists who want to develop forecasting applications on time series data. The first part of the book targets beginners in time series analysis by introducing the main concepts of time series analysis and visual exploration and preprocessing of time series data. The subsequent parts of the book challenge both beginners and advanced users by introducing real-world time series analysis applications.

## What this book covers

*Chapter 1, Introducing Time Series Analysis*, explains what a time series is, states some classic time series problems, and introduces the two historical approaches: statistics and machine learning.

*Chapter 2, Introduction to KNIME Analytics Platform*, explains the basic concepts of KNIME Analytics Platform and its time series integration. This chapter covers installation, an introduction to the platform, and a first workflow example.

*Chapter 3, Preparing Data for Time Series Analysis*, introduces the common first steps in a time series analysis project. It explores different sources of time series data and shows time alignment, time aggregation, and missing value imputation as common preprocessing steps.

*Chapter 4, Time Series Visualization*, explores time series visualization. It provides an exploration of the most common visualization techniques to visually represent and display the time series data: from the classic line plot to the lag plot, and from the seasonal plot to the box plot.

*Chapter 5, Time Series Components and Statistical Properties*, introduces common concepts and measures for descriptive statistics of time series, including the decomposition of a time series, autocorrelation measures and plots, and the stationarity property.

*Chapter 6, Humidity Forecasting with Classical Methods*, completes a classic time series analysis use case: forecasting. It introduces some simple yet powerful classical methods, which often solve the time series analysis problem quickly without much computational expense.

*Chapter 7, Forecasting the Temperature with ARIMA and SARIMA Models*, delves into the ARIMA and SARIMA models. It aims at predicting tomorrow's temperatures with the whole range of ARIMA models: AR, ARMA, ARIMA, and SARIMA.

*Chapter 8, Audio Signal Classification with an FFT and a Gradient Boosted Forest*, introduces a use case for signal classification. It performs the classification of audio signals via a Gradient Boosted Forest model and the FFT transforms the raw audio signals before modeling.

*Chapter 9, Training and Deploying a Neural Network to Predict Glucose Levels*, gives an example of a critical prediction problem: predicting the glucose level for a timely insulin intervention. This chapter also introduces neural networks.

*Chapter 10, Predicting Energy Demand with an LSTM Model*, introduces recurrent neural networks based on **Long Short Term Memory** (**LSTM**) layers, which are advanced predictors when temporal context is involved. It tests whether the prediction accuracy improves considerably from an ARIMA model when using a recurrent LSTM-based neural network.

*Chapter 11, Anomaly Detection – Predicting Failure with No Failure Examples*, tackles the problem of anomaly detection in predictive maintenance by introducing approaches that work exclusively on the data from a correctly working system.

*Chapter 12, Predicting Taxi Demand on the Spark Platform*, implements a solution to the demand prediction problem via a Random Forest to run on a Spark platform in an attempt to make the solution more scalable.

*Chapter 13, GPU Accelerated Model for Multivariate Forecasting*, extends the demand prediction problem to a multivariate by taking into account exogenous time series as well, and scalable, by training the recurrent neural network on a GPU-enabled machine.

*Chapter 14, Combining KNIME and H2O to Predict Stock Prices*, describes the integration of KNIME Analytics Platform with H2O, another open source platform, to implement a solution for stock price prediction.

## To get the most out of this book

This book will introduce the basics of the open source visual programming tool KNIME Analytics Platform and time series analysis. Basic knowledge of data transformations is assumed, while no coding skills are required thanks to the codeless implementation of the examples. Python installation is required for using the time series integration in KNIME.

| Software/hardware covered in the book | Operating system requirements |
|---|---|
| KNIME Analytics Platform 4.6 | Windows, macOS, or Linux |
| Python 3.8 | Windows, macOS, or Linux |

The installation of some use case-specific extensions and integrations will be indicated and instructed in the respective chapters. We will introduce KNIME Server for enterprise features in *Chapter 2, Introduction to KNIME Analytics Platform*, but all practical examples are implemented in the open source KNIME Analytics Platform.

**If you are using the digital version of this book, we advise you to type the code yourself or access the code from the book's GitHub repository (a link is available in the next section). Doing so will help you avoid any potential errors related to the copying and pasting of code.**

## Download the example code files

You can download the example code files for this book from GitHub at `https://github.com/PacktPublishing/Codeless-Time-Series-Analysis-with-KNIME` and `https://hub.knime.com/knime/spaces/Codeless%20Time%20Series%20Analysis%20with%20KNIME/latest/~GxjXX6WmLi-WjLNx/`. If there's an update to the code, it will be updated in the GitHub repository.

We also have other code bundles from our rich catalog of books and videos available at `https://github.com/PacktPublishing/`. Check them out!

## Download the color images

We also provide a PDF file that has color images of the screenshots and diagrams used in this book. You can download it here: `https://packt.link/2RomT`.

## Conventions used

There are a number of text conventions used throughout this book.

`Code in text`: Indicates code words in text, database table names, folder names, filenames, file extensions, pathnames, dummy URLs, user input, and Twitter handles. Here is an example: "For example, the `../sales.csv` workflow relative path reads the `sales.csv` file located in the same workflow group as the executing workflow."

**Bold**: Indicates a new term, an important word, or words that you see onscreen. For instance, words in menus or dialog boxes appear in **bold**. Here is an example: "If you want to do that, you will need to unlink it via the component's context menu by selecting **Component | Disconnect Link**."

> **Tips or Important Notes**
> Appear like this.

## Get in touch

Feedback from our readers is always welcome.

**General feedback**: If you have questions about any aspect of this book, email us at `customercare@packtpub.com` and mention the book title in the subject of your message.

**Errata**: Although we have taken every care to ensure the accuracy of our content, mistakes do happen. If you have found a mistake in this book, we would be grateful if you would report this to us. Please visit `www.packtpub.com/support/errata` and fill in the form.

**Piracy**: If you come across any illegal copies of our works in any form on the internet, we would be grateful if you would provide us with the location address or website name. Please contact us at `copyright@packt.com` with a link to the material.

**If you are interested in becoming an author**: If there is a topic that you have expertise in and you are interested in either writing or contributing to a book, please visit `authors.packtpub.com`.

## Share Your Thoughts

Once you've read *Codeless Time Series Analysis with KNIME*, we'd love to hear your thoughts! Scan the QR code below to go straight to the Amazon review page for this book and share your feedback.

`https://packt.link/r/1803232064`

Your review is important to us and the tech community and will help us make sure we're delivering excellent quality content.

# Part 1: Time Series Basics and KNIME Analytics Platform

By the end of this part, you will know what a time series is, how to preprocess, visualize, and explore it, and how to configure and use KNIME Analytics Platform for time series analysis. The following are the chapters included in this part:

# 1

# Introducing Time Series Analysis

In this introductory chapter, we'll examine the concept of time series, explore some examples and case studies, and then understand how **Time Series Analysis** (**TSA**) can be useful in different frameworks and applications. Finally, we'll provide a brief overview of the forecasting models used over the years, highlighting their key features, which will be further explored in the following chapters.

In this chapter, we will cover the following topics:

- Understanding TSA and its importance within data analytics
- Time series properties and examples
- TSA goals and applications
- Overview of the main forecasting techniques used over the years

By the end of the chapter, you will have a good understanding of the key aspects of TSA, gaining the foundation to explore the subsequent chapters of the book with greater confidence.

## Understanding TSA

When analyzing business data, it's quite common to focus on what happened at a particular point in time: sales figures at the end of the month, customer characteristics at the end of the year, conversion results at the end of a marketing campaign, and more. Even in the development of the most sophisticated ML models, in most cases, we collect information that refers to different objects at a specific instant in time (or by taking a few snapshots of historical data). This approach, which is absolutely valid and correct for many applications, not only in business, uses cross-sectional data as the basis for analytics: data collected by observing many subjects (such as individuals, companies, shops, countries, equipment, and more) at one point or period of time.

Although the fact of not considering the temporal factor in the analysis is widespread and rooted in common practice, there are several situations where the analysis of the temporal evolution of a phenomenon provides more complete and interesting results. In fact, it's only through the analysis of the temporal dynamics of the data that it is possible to identify the presence of some peculiar characteristics of the phenomenon we are analyzing, be it sales/consumption data, rather than a physical parameter or a macroeconomic index. These characteristics that act over time, such as trends, periodic fluctuations, level changes, anomalous observations, turning points, and more can have an effect in the short or long term, and often, it is important to be able to measure them precisely. Furthermore, it is only by analyzing data over time that it is possible to provide a reliable quantitative estimate of what might occur in the future (whether immediate or not). Since economic conditions are constantly changing over time, data analysts must be able to assess and predict the effects of these changes in order to suggest the most appropriate actions to take for the future.

For these reasons, TSA can be a very useful tool in the hands of business analysts and data scientists when it comes to both describing the patterns of a phenomenon along the time axis and providing a reliable forecast for it. Through the use of the right tools, TSA can significantly expand the understanding of any variable of interest (typically numerical) such as sales, financial KPIs, logistic metrics, sensors' measurements, and more. More accurate and less biased forecasts that have been obtained through quantitative TSA can be one of the most effective drivers of performance in many fields and industries.

In the next sections of this chapter, we will provide definitions, examples, and some additional elements to gain a further understanding of how to recognize some key features of time series and how to approach their analyses in a structured way.

# Exploring time series properties and examples

A general definition of a time series is the following:

> *A Time Series is a collection of observations made sequentially through time, whose dynamics are often characterized by short/long period fluctuations and/or long period direction.*

This definition highlights two fundamental aspects of a time series: the fact that observations are a function of time and that, as a consequence of this fact, some typical *temporal features* are often observed. The fluctuations and the long period direction of the series are just some of these features, as there might be other relevant aspects to take into consideration such as **autocorrelation**, **stationarity**, and the **order of integration**. We will explore these aspects in more detail in future chapters. In this section, we will focus on the distinction between discrete time series and continuous time series, on the concept of independence between observations, and finally, we will show some examples of real-world time series.

## Continuous and discrete time series

A **Time Series** is defined as **continuous** when observations are collected continuously over time, that is, there can be an infinite number of observations in a given time range. Typically, continuous time series data is sampled at irregular time intervals. Consider the measurement of a patient's blood pressure in a hospital done at varying time points during the day, not equally spaced. This happens because, in some settings, regular monitoring at fixed intervals is not possible. For instance, in *Figure 1.1*, there are four medical continuous time series, relative to the health parameters of four patients:

- Mean blood pressure
- Heart rate
- Temperature
- Glucose data

As evident from the graphs, there are some temporal ranges where the measures are not present, for example, the temperature and glucose between approximately 20 hours and 30 hours of the monitoring period. There are other time points where data is collected more frequently than in other periods. These time series features are due to the fact that the data has been collected manually by the physician or by the nurse, not at fixed moments of the day. Therefore, this type of time series is inherently irregularly sampled:

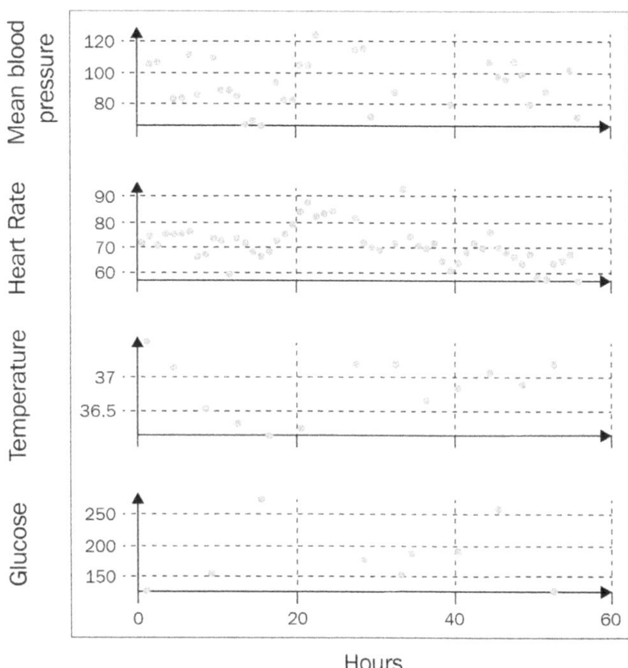


Figure 1.1 – Four continuous, irregularly sampled, medical time series

A time series is defined as **discrete** when observations are collected regularly at specific times, typically equally spaced (that is, hourly, daily, weekly, and yearly data points).

A time series of this type can be *natively* discrete, such as the annual budget data of a company, or it can be created through the aggregation or accumulation of a numerical variable in equal time intervals. For example, the monthly sales of a supermarket or the number of daily passengers in a train station. A continuous time series can be *discretized* by binning/grouping the original data and, eventually, obtaining a discrete time series.

Classical TSA focuses on discrete time series because they are more common in real-world applications and easier to analyze. Therefore, in this book, we mainly deal with discrete time series, where observations are collected at equal intervals. When we consider irregularly sampled time series, first, we will try to transform them into regularly sampled data points.

## Independence and serial correlation

One of the most distinctive characteristics of a time series is the mutual dependence between the observations, generally called **serial correlation** or **autocorrelation**.

In many statistical models, observations are assumed to be generated by a random sampling process and to be independent of each other (consider the *linear regression model*). Typically, this assumption turns out to be inconsistent with time series data, where simply collecting the data sequentially, along the time axis, generally produces observations that are not independent of each other.

Think of the daily sales of an e-commerce company. It's reasonable to imagine that today's sales are somehow related to the previous day's sales: successive observations are dependent. However, in this context, which clearly can create some problems in using classical statistical tools, it is however possible to exploit the temporal dependence of observations to improve the forecasting process. If today's sales are related to yesterday's, and we can consistently estimate this relationship, then we can improve the forecast of tomorrow's sales based on today's result.

## Time series examples

Interesting examples of time series can be collected in a multitude of information domains: business/economics, industrial production, social sciences, physics, and more. The time series obtained from these fields might be profoundly different in terms of statistical properties and the granularity of the available data, yet the methodologies of descriptive analysis and forecasting are essentially the same.

Here, we will explore a **line chart** (also called a **time plot**) of some representative discrete time series, with the aim of showing how it is possible to observe very different dynamics, depending on the type of data and the field of reference. *Figure 1.2* shows the pattern of two annual time series, that is, the *Number of PhDs awarded in the US*, split between the subjects of engineering and education:

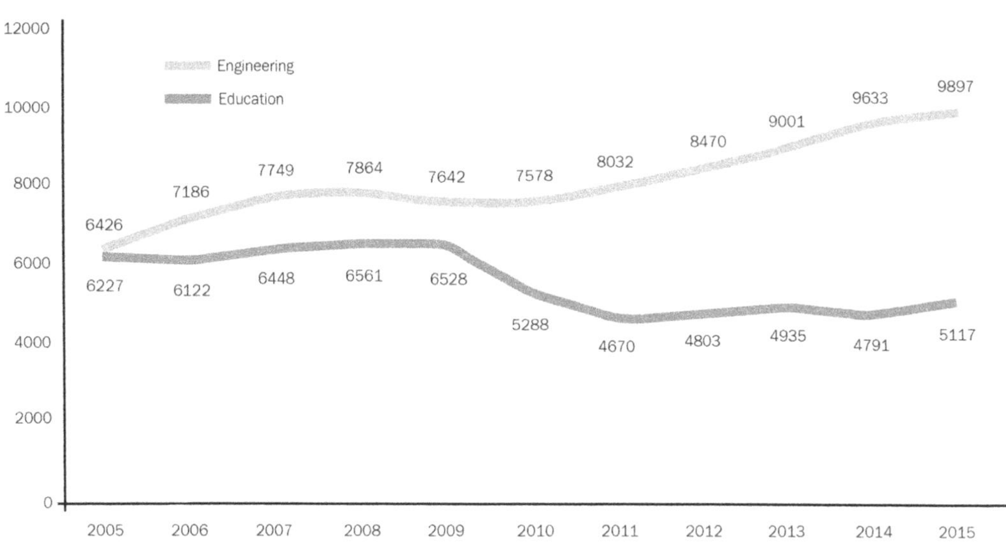


Figure 1.2 – Time series example 1: number of PhDs awarded in the US, showing the annual data for Engineering versus Education

In the preceding graph, we can see that both time series do not show periodic fluctuations, and this is typical of annual data. The engineering doctorate series appears to be increasing over time, especially in the last 5 years presented, while the education doctorate series shows a flatter trend, with a level shift between 2010 and 2011.

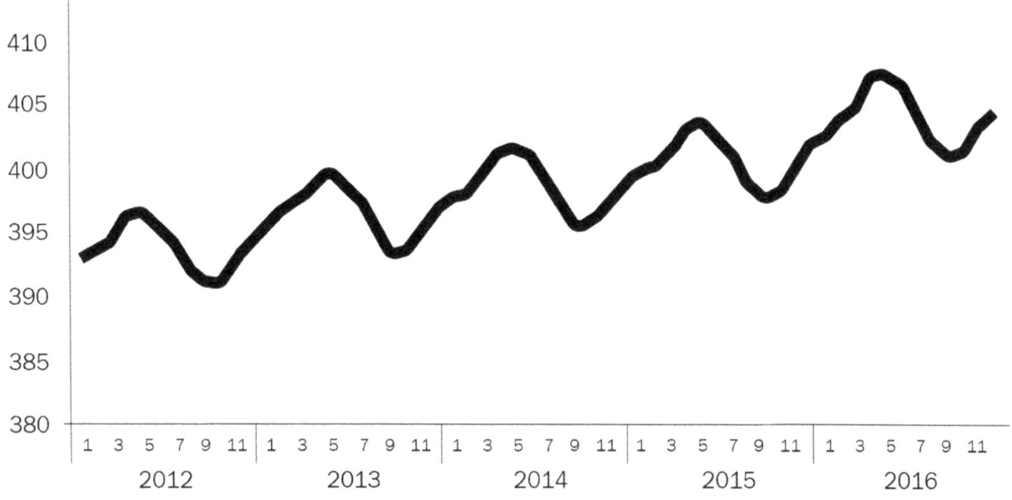


Figure 1.3 – Time series example 2: monthly carbon dioxide concentration (globally averaged from marine surface sites)

Focusing on a different series, the *Monthly carbon dioxide concentration* in *Figure 1.3* shows a completely different pattern than the previous series. In fact, the dynamics of this monthly time series are dominated by periodic fluctuations, which are repeated consistently every year. In addition, we observe the constant growth of the level of the carbon concentration, year after year. In summary, this series shows an increasing oscillatory pattern that appears to be quite stable and, therefore, easily predictable.

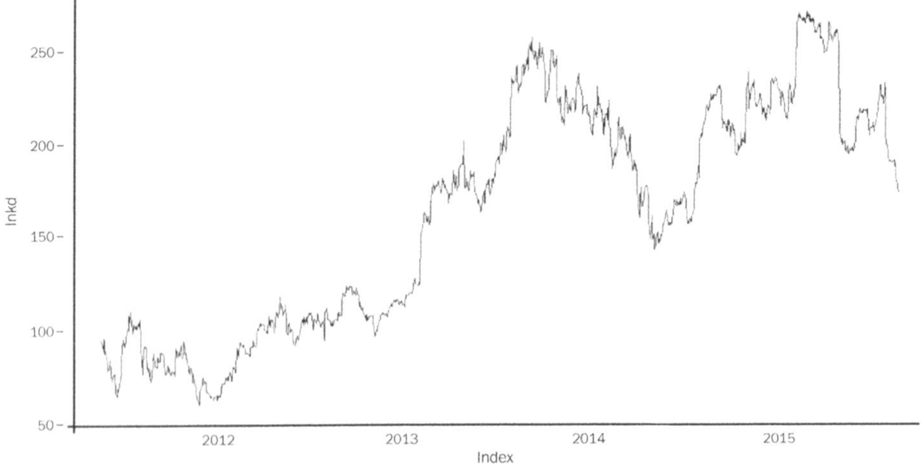


Figure 1.4 – Time series example 3: LinkedIn's daily stock market closing price

In contrast, the evolution of the time series shown in *Figure 1.4* seems to be much more unpredictable. In this case, we have daily data points of *LinkedIn's stock market closing price*. The pattern during the 5 years of observation seems to be very irregular, without periodic fluctuations, with sudden changes of direction superimposed on an increasing trend in the long run.

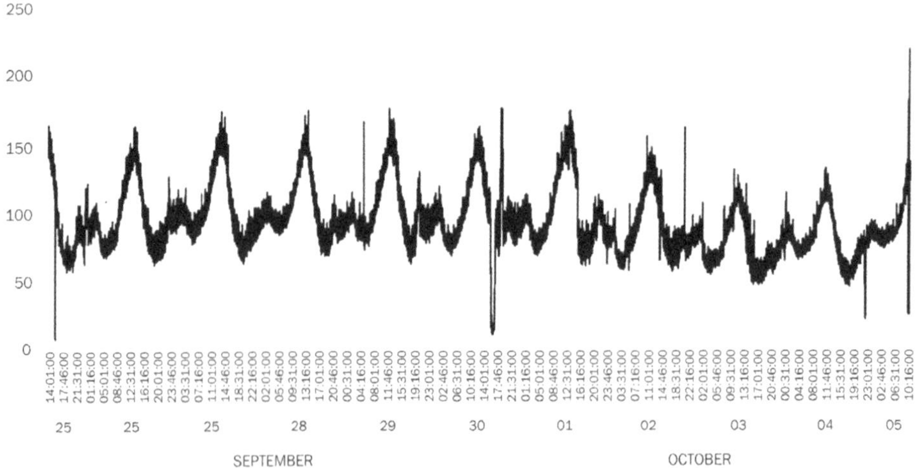


Figure 1.5 – Time series example 4: number of photos uploaded onto Instagram every minute (regional sub-sample)

Considering another example in the social media theme, we can look at *Figure 1.5*, in which the plot shows the *Number of photos uploaded onto Instagram every minute (regional sub-sample)*. In this case, the granularity of the data is very high (one observation every minute) and the dynamics of the time series show both elements of *regularity*, such as constant fluctuations and peaks that are observed in the early afternoon of each day. At the same time, there are also *discontinuities* such as the presence of some anomalous observations.

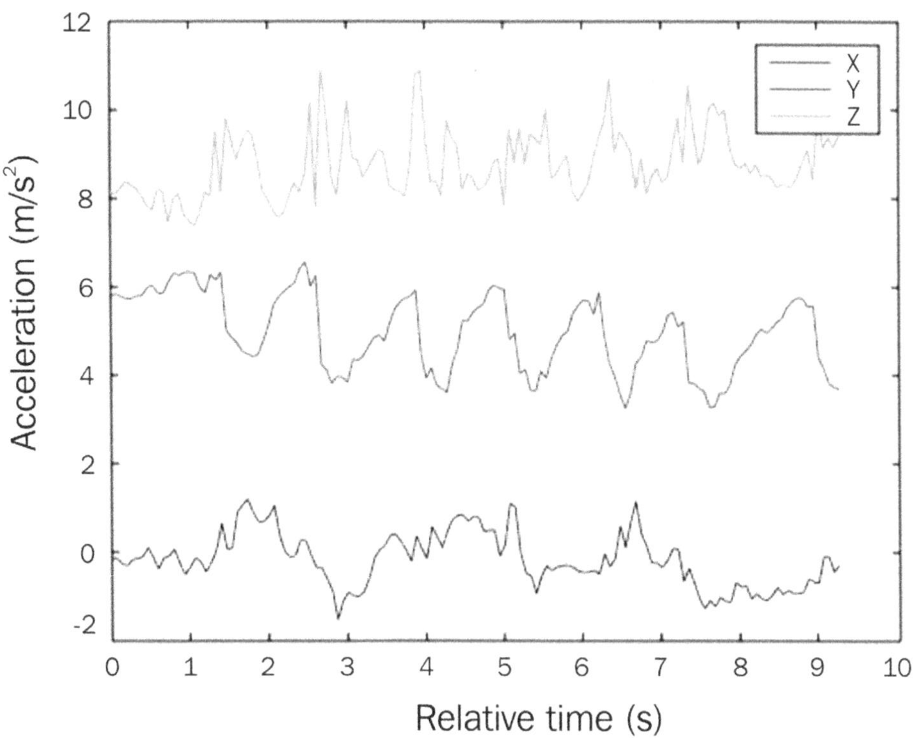


Figure 1.6 – Time series example 5: acceleration detected by smartphone sensors during a workout session (10 seconds)

Finally, the analysis of the three time series shown in *Figure 1.6*, highlights how, for the same phenomenon (a *workout session*), both regular and irregular dynamics can be observed, depending on the point of observation. In this case, the three accelerometers mounted to the wearable device show fairly constant peaks along one spatial dimension and greater irregularity on the others.

In conclusion, from the examples that we have shown in this section, we notice that time series might have characteristics that are very different from one another. Determining aspects such as the origin of the data and the reference industry, the granularity of the data, and the length of the observation period can drastically influence the dynamics of the time series, revealing really heterogeneous patterns.

# TSA goals and applications

When it comes to analyzing time series, depending on the industry and the type of project, different goals can be pursued, from the simplest to the most complex. Likewise, multiple analytical applications can be developed where TSA plays a crucial role. In this section, we will look at the main goals of time series analysis, followed by some examples of real-world applications.

## Goals of TSA

In common practice, TSA is directly associated with *forecasting*, almost as if it were a synonym for this task. Although the objective of predicting the data for a future horizon is probably the most common (and challenging) goal, we should not assume TSA is only that. Often, the purpose of the analysis is to obtain a correct representation of data over time: think of the construction of a tool for data visualization and business intelligence or analyzing the data of a manufacturing process to detect possible anomalies.

Therefore, there are different objectives in the analysis of time series that can be listed in the following four points:

- **Exploratory analysis and visualization**: This consists of the use of descriptive analytics tools dedicated to the summary of data points with respect to time. Through these analyses, it's possible to identify the presence of specific temporal dynamics (for example, trends, seasonality, or cycles), detect outliers/gaps in the data, or search for a specific pattern. In business intelligence, it is critical to correctly represent time series within enterprise dashboards in order to provide immediate insights to business users for the decision-making process.
- **Causal effect discovery and simulation**: In many sectors, often, it is useful to verify how one or more exogenous variables impact a target variable. For example, how advertising investments on different channels (whether digital or not) impact the sales of a company or how some environmental conditions impact the quality of the industrial production of a particular product. These types of problems are very common and, in data analytics, are frequently addressed through the estimation of multiple regression models (adapted to work well with time series data). Once possible causal relationships are identified, it is possible to simulate the outcome of the objective variable as a function of the values assumed by the exogenous variables.
- **Anomaly detection and process control** (*Figure 1.7*): We can use TSA to prevent negative events (such as failures, damage, or performance drops):

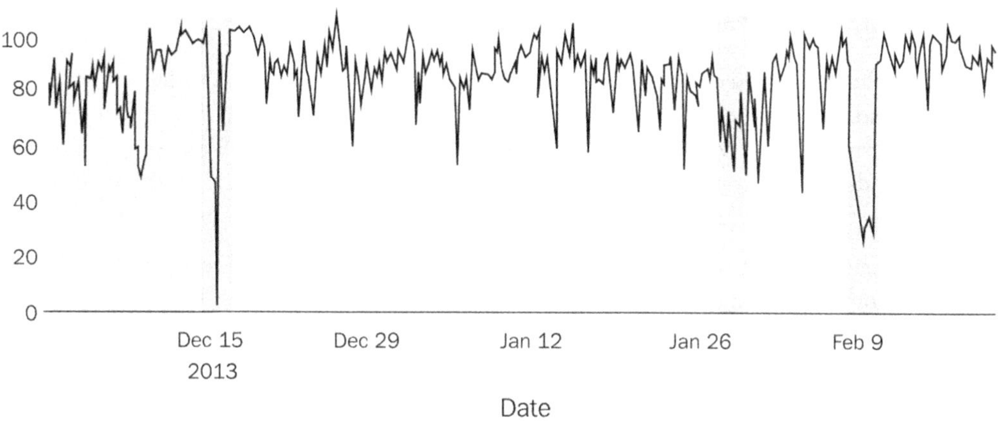


Figure 1.7 – Anomaly detection using time series

The main idea is to promptly detect an anomaly during the operation of a device or the behavior of a subject, even if the specific anomaly has never been observed before. For many companies, reducing anomalies and improving quality is a key factor for growth and success; for example, reducing fraud in the banking sector or preventing cyber attacks in IT security systems. In manufacturing, process engineers use *control charts* to monitor the stability of a production process and also a measurement system. Typically, a **control chart** is obtained by plotting the data points of a time series related to a specific parameter of the manufacturing process (for example, wire pull strength, the concentration of a chemical, oxide thickness, and more) and adding some *control limits*, which is useful to identify possible process drifts or anomalies.

- **Forecasting**: This definitely constitutes the main objective of time series analysis and consists of predicting the future values of a time series observed in the past. The forecasting horizon can be short-term or long-term. There are many methods used to obtain the predicted values; we will discuss these aspects in more detail in the Exploring *Time series forecasting techniques* section.

## Domains of applications and use cases

The fields of application of TSA are numerous. **Demand Forecasting and Planning** is one of the most common applications, as it's an important process for many companies (especially retailers) to anticipate demand for products throughout the entire supply chain, especially under uncertain conditions. However, from industry to industry, there are many more interesting uses of TSA. Right now, it would be almost impossible to list all applications where the use of TSA plays an important role in creating business solutions and assets; therefore, we will limit ourselves to a few examples that might give you an idea of the heterogeneity of use cases in the field of TSA.

For instance, consider the following list of examples:

- **Workforce planning**: For a company operating in the logistics and transportation industry, it is crucial to predict the workload so that the right number of staff/couriers are available to handle it properly. In a workforce planning context, correctly forecasting the volume of parcels to be handled can help to effectively allocate effort and resources, which means eventually improving the bottom line for companies with, typically, low-profit margins.
- **Forecasting of sales during promotions**: E-commerce, supermarkets, and retailers increasingly use promotions, discount periods, and special sales to increase sales volume; however, stock-out problems are often generated, resulting in customer dissatisfaction and extra operative costs. Therefore, it is essential to use forecasting models that integrate the effects of promotions into sales forecasting in order to optimize warehouses and avoid losses, both economic and reputational.
- **Insurance claim reserving**: For insurance companies, estimating the claims reserve plays an important role in maintaining capital, determining premiums, and being in line with requirements imposed by the policyholder. Therefore, it is necessary to estimate the future number and amount of claims as correctly as possible. In recent years, actuarial practitioners have used several time series-based approaches to obtain reliable forecasts of claims and estimate the degree of uncertainty of the predictions.
- **Predictive maintenance**: In the context of the Internet of Things, the availability of real-time information generated by sensors mounted on devices and manufacturing equipment enables the development of analytics solutions that can prevent negative events (such as failures, damage, or drops in performance) in order to improve the quality of products or reduce operating costs. Anomaly detection based on TSA is one of the most widely used methods for creating effective predictive maintenance solutions. In *Chapter 11, Anomaly Detection – Predicting Failure with No Failure Examples*, we will provide a detailed use case in this area.
- **Energy load forecasting**: In deregulated energy markets, forecasting the consumption and price of electricity is crucial for defining effective bidding strategies to maximize a company's profits. In this context, TSA is a widely used approach for day-ahead forecasting.

The applications just listed provide insight into how the application of TSA and forecasting techniques form the core of many processes and solutions developed in different industries.

## Exploring time series forecasting techniques

Within the data science domain, doing time series forecasting first means extending a KPI (or any measure of interest) into the future in the most accurate and least biased way possible. And while this remains the primary goal of forecasting, often, the activity does not boil down to just that as it's sometimes necessary to include an assessment of the uncertainty of forecasted values and comparisons with previous forecasting benchmarks. The approaches to time series forecasting are essentially two, listed as follows:

- **Qualitative forecasting** methods are adopted when historical data is not available (for example, when estimating the revenues of a new company that clearly doesn't have any data available). They are highly subjective methods. Among the most important qualitative forecasting techniques, it is possible to mention the Delphi method.
- **Quantitative forecasting** techniques are based on historical quantitative data; the analyst/data scientist, starting from this data, tries to understand the underlying structure of the phenomenon of interest and then uses the same data for forecasting purposes. Therefore, the analyst's task is to identify, isolate, and measure these temporal dynamics behind a time series of past data in order to make optimal predictions and eventually support decisions, planning, and business control. The quantitative approach to forecasting is certainly the most widely used, as it generates results that are typically more robust and more easily deployed into business processes. Therefore, from now on (including in the next chapters), we will focus exclusively on it.

In the following section, we will explore the details of quantitative forecasting, focusing on the basic requirements for carrying it out properly and the main quantitative techniques used in recent years.

## Quantitative forecasting properties and techniques

First and foremost, the development of a quantitative forecasting model depends on the available data, both in terms of the amount of data and the quality of historical information. In general, we can say that there are two basic requirements for effectively creating a reliable quantitative forecasting model:

- Obtain an **adequate number of observations**, which means a sufficient depth of historical data, in order to correctly understand the phenomenon under analysis, estimate the models, and then apply the predictions. Probably one of the most common questions asked by those who are facing the development of a forecasting model for the first time is *how long does the Time Series need to be to obtain a reliable model*, which, in simple terms, means *how much past do I need?* The answer is not simple. It would be incorrect to say *at least 50 observations are needed* or that *the depth should be at least 5 years*. In fact, the amount of data points to consider depends on the following:
    - The complexity of the model to be developed and the number of parameters to be estimated.
    - The amount of randomness in the data.
    - The granularity of the data (such as monthly, daily, and hourly) and its characteristics. (Is it intermittent? Are there strong periods of discontinuity to consider?)
    - The presence of one or more seasonal components that need to be estimated in relation to the granularity of the data (for example, to include a weekly seasonality pattern of hourly data in the model, at least several hundred observations must be available).
- Collect information about the «**time dimension**» of the time series in order to determine the starting/ending points of the data and a possible length for the seasonal components (if present).

Given a set of sufficient historical data, the basis for a quantitative forecasting model is the assumption that there are factors that influenced the dynamics of the series in the past and these factors continue to *bring similar effects in the future, too.*

There are several criteria used to classify quantitative forecasting techniques. It is possible to consider the historical evolution of the methods (from the most *classical* to the most *modern*), how the methods use the information within the model, or even the domain of method development (purely statistical versus ML). Here, we present one possible classification of the techniques used for quantitative forecasting, which takes into account multiple relevant elements that characterize the different methods. We can consider these three main groups of methods as follows:

1. **Classical univariate forecasting methods**: In these statistical techniques, the formation of forecasts is only based on the same time series to be forecast through the identification of structural components, such as trends and seasonality, and the study of the serial correlation. Some popular methods in this group are listed as follows:

    - **Classical decomposition**: This considers the observed series as the overlap of three elementary components (trend-cycle, seasonality, and residual), connected with different patterns that are typically present in many economics time series; classical decomposition (such as other types of decomposition) is a common way to explore and interpret the characteristics of a time series, but it can certainly be used to produce forecasts. In *Chapter 5, Time Series Components and Statistical Properties*, we will delve deeper into this method.
    - **Exponential smoothing**: Forecasts produced by exponential smoothing methods are based on weighted averages of past observations, with weights decaying exponentially as the observations get older; this decreasing weights method could also take into account the overlap of some components, such as trends and seasonality.
    - **AutoRegressive Integrated Moving Average** (**ARIMA**): Essentially, this is a regression-like approach that aims to model, as effectively as possible, the serial correlation among the observations in a time series. To do this effectively, several parameters in the model can handle trends and seasonality, although less directly than decomposition or exponential smoothing.

2. **Explanatory models**: These techniques work in a multivariate fashion, so the forecasts are based on both past observations of the reference time series and external predictors, which helps to achieve better accuracy but also to obtain a more extensive interpretation of the model. The most popular example in this group is the ARIMAX model (or regression with ARIMA errors).
3. **ML methods**: These techniques can be either univariate or multivariate. However, their most distinctive feature is that they originated outside the statistical domain and were not specifically designed to analyze time series data; typically, they are artificial neural networks (such as multilayer perceptron, long-short memory networks, and dilated convolutional neural networks) or tree-based algorithms (such as random forest or gradient boosted trees) originally made for cross-sectional data that can be adapted for time series forecasting.

A very common question asked by students and practitioners who are new to TSA is whether there is one forecasting method that is better than the others. The answer (for now) is no. All of the models have their own pros and cons. In general, exponential smoothing, ARIMA, and all the classical methodologies have been around the longest. They are quite easy to implement and typically very reliable, but they require the verification of some assumptions, and sometimes, they are not as flexible as you would like them to be. In contrast, ML algorithms are really flexible (they don't have assumptions to check), but commonly, you need a large amount of data to train them properly. Moreover, they can be more complicated (a lot of hyperparameters to tune), and to be effective, you need to create some extra-temporal features to catch the time-related patterns within your data.

But what does *the best forecasting model* mean? Consider that it's never just a matter of the pure performance of the model, as you need to consider other important items in the model selection procedure. For instance, consider the following list of items:

- Forecast horizon in relation to TSA objectives: Are you going to predict the short term or the long term? For the same time series, you could have a model that is the best one for short-term forecasts, but you need to use another one for long-term forecasts.
- The type/amount of available data: In general, for small datasets, a classical forecasting method could be better than an ML approach.
- The required readability of the results: A classical model is more interpretable than an ML model.
- The number of series to forecast: Using classical methods with thousands of time series can be inefficient, so in this case, an ML approach could be better.
- Deployment-related issues: Also, consider the frequency of the delivery of the forecasts, the software environment, and the usage of the forecasts.

In summary, when facing the modeling part of your time series forecasting application, don't just go with one algorithm. Try different approaches, considering your goals and the type/amount of data that you have.

## Summary

In this chapter, we introduced TSA, starting by defining what a time series is and then providing some examples of series taken from various contexts and industries. Next, we focused on the goals that are typically related to TSA and also provided some examples of applications in real-world scenarios. Finally, we covered a brief review of the main forecasting methods, providing a taxonomy of methodologies and generally describing the characteristics of the main models, from the most classic to the most modern.

In this chapter, the basic concepts provided are of great importance for approaching the subsequent chapters of the book in a structured way, having the concepts of time series and forecasting clear in your head.

In the next chapter, we'll cover the basic concepts of KNIME Analytics Platform and its time series integration, introducing the software and showing a first workflow example.

# Questions

The answers to the following questions can be found in the *Assessment* section at the end of the book:

1. What is a discrete Time Series?

   A. A collection of observations made continuously over time.

   B. A series where there can be an infinite number of observations in a given time range.

   C. A collection of observations that are sampled regularly at specific times, typically equally spaced.

   D. A series where observations follow a Bernoulli distribution.

2. Which of the following is not a typical goal pursued in Time Series Analysis?

   A. Causal effect discovery and simulation.

   B. Function approximation.

   C. Anomaly detection and process control.

   D. Forecasting.

3. Which is a basic requirement to develop a reliable quantitative forecasting model?

   A. Obtain an adequate number of historical observations.

   B. Collect time-independent observations.

   C. Collect a time series that shows a trend.

   D. Obtain a time series without gaps and outliers.

4. Which of the following is not a group of methods typically used in quantitative Time Series Forecasting?

   A. Classical univariate methods.

   B. Machine learning techniques.

   C. Explanatory models.

   D. Direct clustering algorithms.

# 2
# Introduction to KNIME Analytics Platform

In this chapter, we will introduce KNIME Analytics Platform—your tool for *codeless time series analysis*. We will explain different features of the KNIME software and the basic concepts of visual programming. We will also guide you through installing KNIME Analytics Platform, building your first workflow, and configuring the time series integration. These topics are covered in the following sections:

- Exploring the KNIME software
- Introducing nodes and workflows
- Building your first workflow
- Configuring the time series integration

You will learn basic visual programming skills and install the necessary software for time series analysis in KNIME.

# Exploring the KNIME software

In this first section, we will introduce you to the features of the **KNIME software**, which covers two products: the open source KNIME Analytics Platform, and the KNIME Server commercial product. Together, these two products enable all operations in a data science application, from data access to modeling and from deployment to model monitoring.

We will first introduce you to KNIME Analytics Platform.

## Introducing KNIME Analytics Platform for creating data science applications

**KNIME Analytics Platform** is an open source tool for **creating data science applications**. It is based on **visual programming**, making it fast to learn, accessible, and transparent. If needed, you can also integrate other tools—including scripts—into your visual workflows.

In visual programming, each individual task is indicated by a colored block, which in KNIME Analytics Platform is called a **node**. A node has an intuitive name describing its task and a **graphical user interface** (**GUI**). Individual nodes are connected into a pipeline of subsequent tasks, which we call a **workflow**. In a workflow, the connection lines from node to node emulate the flow of data. A node is the counterpart of a line of code in scripting languages, while a workflow is the counterpart of an entire script. We will tell you more about nodes and workflows in the *Introducing nodes and workflows* section.

The following diagram shows an example of a KNIME visual workflow:

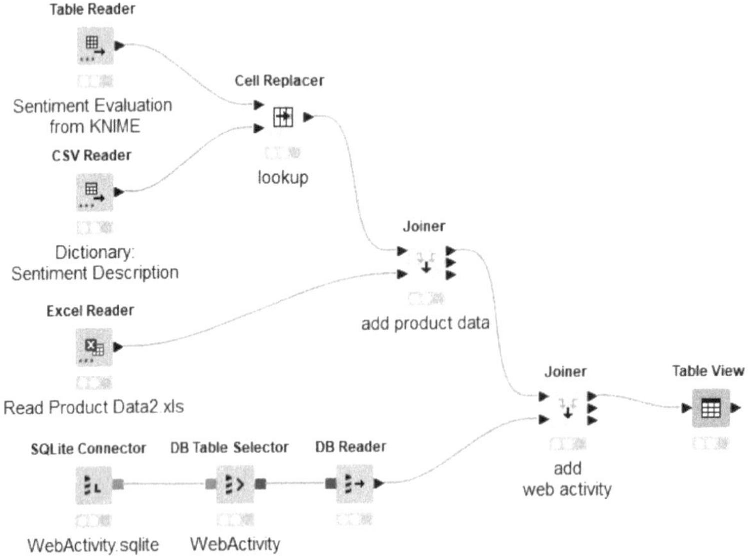


Figure 2.1 – An example of a visual workflow

The workflow reads data in different file formats and from a database, blends them, and displays them in an interactive browser-based table. As you can already see from this simple workflow, KNIME Analytics Platform is open to different file formats and sources, platforms, and external tools. You can access data from any source—database software, cloud environments, big data platforms, and different file types. You can also use scripting languages such as Python, access open source **machine learning** (**ML**) libraries such as H2O, and connect to reporting tools such as Tableau via **KNIME integrations**.

In the following subsection, we will show how to install KNIME Analytics Platform.

### *Installing KNIME Analytics Platform*

KNIME Analytics Platform is **open source**, and you can install it right away by following these steps:

1. Go to `https://www.knime.com/downloads` and fill in your name, email address, and—if you want—some additional information. This step (signing up) is voluntary but recommended to get started quickly with just a few introductory emails and to keep up to date about new resources. After that, click **Next**.
2. Select KNIME Analytics Platform for Windows, Linux, or macOS according to your operating system.
3. Optionally, click **Next**, and learn more about KNIME via the beginners' guide, videos, and other learning material.
4. After downloading the installation package, start it, and follow the instructions on your screen.
5. Finally, start the application from the desktop link/application/a link in the **Start** menu, or the appropriate folder. When you do, a dialog box opens asking for the **KNIME workspace**. This is a folder on your machine to store all workflows, data files, and other items related to your workflows. You can accept the default folder called `knime-workspace`. Furthermore, the first time you launch KNIME Analytics Platform, a dialog opens asking whether you want to consent to send anonymized usage data. If you opt in, you will reciprocally get access to node recommendations from the KNIME community to speed up your work.

In the next subsection, we introduce elements of the KNIME workbench.

## Exploring the KNIME workbench

The **KNIME workbench** contains all the resources that you will need to build your workflows. You can see an illustration of this in the following screenshot:

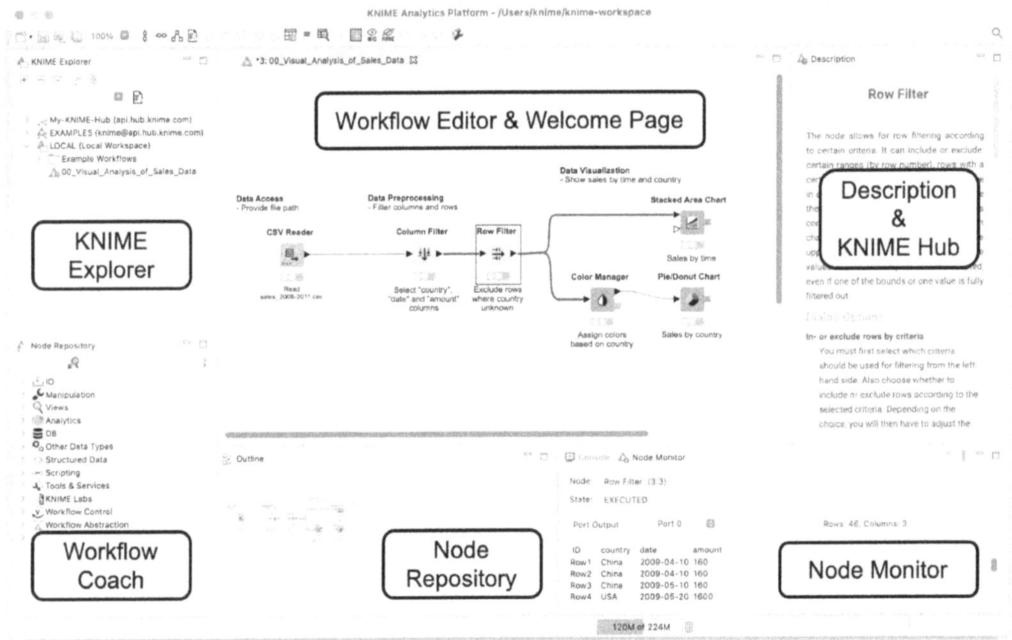


Figure 2.2 – The KNIME workbench

The main panels of the KNIME workbench are annotated in *Figure 2.2*. Next, we summarize their functions, as follows:

- **Welcome page**: When you launch KNIME Analytics Platform, you will see a welcome page in the middle of the workbench. This contains links to useful information, such as recent updates, upcoming events, news, and tips and tricks.
- **Workflow editor**: The workflow editor appears in the same place as the welcome page. In the workflow editor, you will build and inspect your workflows.
- **KNIME Explorer**: The KNIME Explorer manages your workflows and KNIME Server connections. A folder in the KNIME Explorer is called a **workflow group**, and it can contain workflows, data files, shared components, and other workflow groups. The KNIME Explorer can contain multiple **mountpoints**—that is, uppermost folder levels for different workflow repositories. The possible mountpoints are listed here:
    - **My-KNIME-Hub** for public and private workflows on the KNIME Hub

    - **EXAMPLES** for example workflows on a public server hosted by KNIME
    - **LOCAL** for workflows in your local workspace
    - **KNIME Server** for workflows on other KNIME servers (if available)
- **Node repository**: The node repository contains all nodes that you can use in your workflows, organized under categories such as **Manipulation** and **Mining**. You can search for nodes via the search box and add a node into your workflow by dragging and dropping or by a double-clicking.
- **Workflow coach**: The workflow coach lists suggestions for the next node in your workflow based on KNIME community usage statistics. Notice that this panel is only active if you consented to the collection of anonymous usage statistics when launching the application for the first time.
- **Description**: The description panel provides additional information on nodes and workflows. If a node is selected in the workflow editor or node repository, the description explains the node's task, setting options, and **input and output** (**I/O**). If no individual node is selected, it shows a description of the currently active workflow. You can also edit the description of a workflow via this panel.
- **KNIME Hub**: The KNIME Hub panel allows for searching and importing nodes, workflows, and other resources shared by KNIME and the KNIME community on the KNIME Hub. The KNIME Hub is also accessible via `https://hub.knime.com`.
- **Node monitor**: The node monitor displays a preview of the output table of the node that is currently selected in the workflow editor.

In KNIME Analytics Platform, you have everything you need within the same tool as a single data scientist. However, for enterprise purposes, the KNIME Server commercial product provides a flexible and protected collaboration environment with production functions. We will introduce KNIME Server in the next subsection.

> **Note**
>
> A KNIME Server license is not required in any of the practical exercises in this book. Instead, we introduce the enterprise features of KNIME Server to give you an idea of how to use your time series applications effectively in the real world.

## Introducing KNIME Server for productionizing data science applications

In this subsection, we will give an overview of KNIME Server for **collaborating** and **productionizing data science applications**. We will explain how the **Integrated Deployment** and **KNIME data apps** make productionizing **infallible**, **fast**, and **accessible**.

In a nutshell, KNIME Server is a secure collaboration environment that enables all users to access workflows from within their local installation of KNIME Analytics Platform and to harness the execution power of the remote server. Furthermore, KNIME Server also allows for **automated execution**, **versioning**, **permission handling**, and **recovery**.

Moving a data science application into production means that we move it out of an experimental setting into the real world. When we do this for a model (a time series forecasting model, for example), moving into the real world is called model **deployment**. The integrated deployment extension makes this step especially easy and reliable. It allows for capturing any workflow sequence(s) in the training workflow and exporting it into a deployment workflow. The first benefit is that the required data preprocessing and model application steps need to be built only once in the training workflow and they don't need to be repeated manually in the deployment workflow. Another benefit is that the deployment workflow's configuration will correspond to the latest configuration of the training workflow.

While integrated deployment smooths out the actual process from creation to deployment, another KNIME Server feature called KNIME Data Apps smoothens communication between the humans at both ends. Building and using KNIME data apps requires no KNIME skills from the domain expert nor any frontend language skills from the data scientist. Furthermore, a data app can be accessed as an analytical application via any **web browser**.

A KNIME data app could be, for example, one of these:

- A **guided analytics application** to access, visualize, and explore data.
- A **dashboard** of business **key performance indicators** (**KPIs**). See the following screenshot for an example of this:

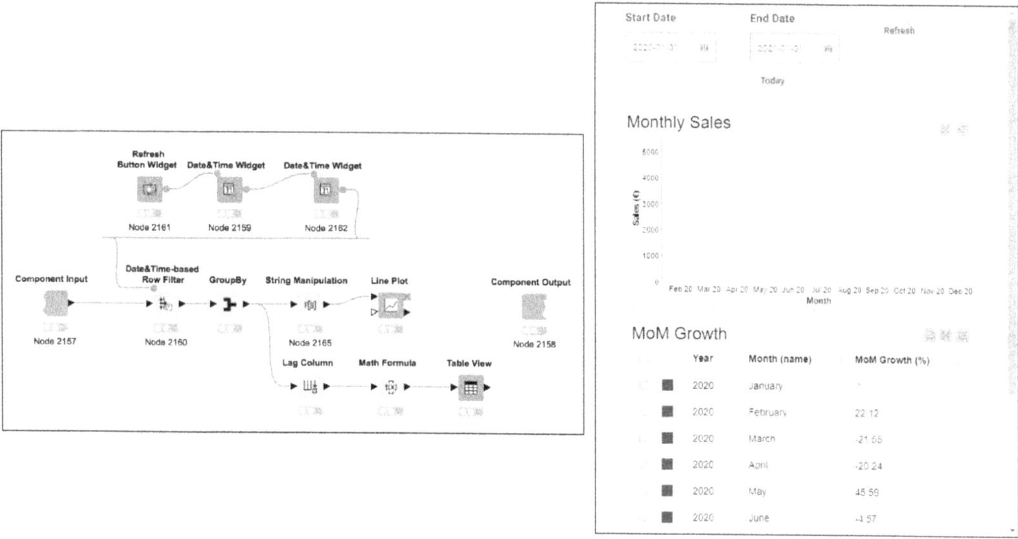


Figure 2.3 – An example of an interactive dashboard as a KNIME data app and the workflow behind it

*Figure 2.3* shows the workflow executing on KNIME Server and the dashboard shown to the business analyst on a web browser. The time period shown on the dashboard can be customized by changing the start and end date via the date widgets.

The data app is available via a secure **WebPortal**, or via a shareable and embeddable link. Business analysts can steer the execution of the workflow via selected **touchpoints**—for example, select a start date and end date via the respective **widgets**. At the same time, they do not need to know the logic of the workflow executing under the hood.

In the next section, we will introduce the functionalities of nodes, workflows, and the KNIME Hub.

# Introducing nodes and workflows

In this section, we go through the different parts of a node, explain operations on nodes, and show how to connect nodes to workflows. We also introduce **metanodes** and **components**. Finally, we will see how to find and share these resources on the KNIME Hub.

## Introducing nodes

A **node** is responsible for one task and it is the smallest processing unit in KNIME: the Row Filter node, which filters rows, the CSV Reader node, which reads a **comma-separated values** (**CSV**) file, and the Bar Chart node, which builds a bar chart are a few examples. Although nodes can perform very different tasks, they all look similar and have similar operations.

### *Different parts of a node*

A node is a visual block with a **name**, **I/O ports**, **annotation**, and a **traffic light**. The following diagram shows these parts of a node for the CSV Reader node as an example:

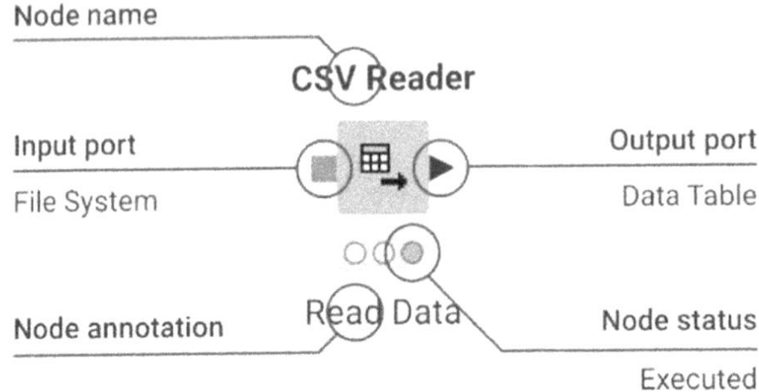


Figure 2.4 – The different parts of a node

The node parts are explained in detail as follows:

- **Node name**: A descriptive name of the node's task. You can search for nodes by their name in the node repository and on the KNIME Hub.
- **I/O ports**: A node receives data to process via its input port and provides the processed data in its output port, which can be of different types such as *data table*, *model*, or *filesystem connection*. Each port type is denoted by a different symbol: black triangles for data tables and blue rectangles for filesystems, for example. Only ports of similar type can be connected.
- **Node status**: The node status is indicated by the color of the traffic light below the node, as detailed next:
    - Red for **Not configured**: The node's task has not been defined yet.
    - Yellow for **Configured**: The node is ready to be executed.
    - Green for **Executed**: The node's task was executed successfully.

- Red cross for **Error**: Something went wrong with the execution. Reconfigure the node before re-executing.

- **Node annotation**: A custom description of the node's task. Double-click the annotation to edit the description.

In the next subsection, we will explain node operations.

### *Node operations*

**Node operations** are—for example—configuring and executing a node's task, and inspecting the output. You can perform all these tasks via the node's **context menu**, which opens by right-clicking the node, as illustrated in the following screenshot:

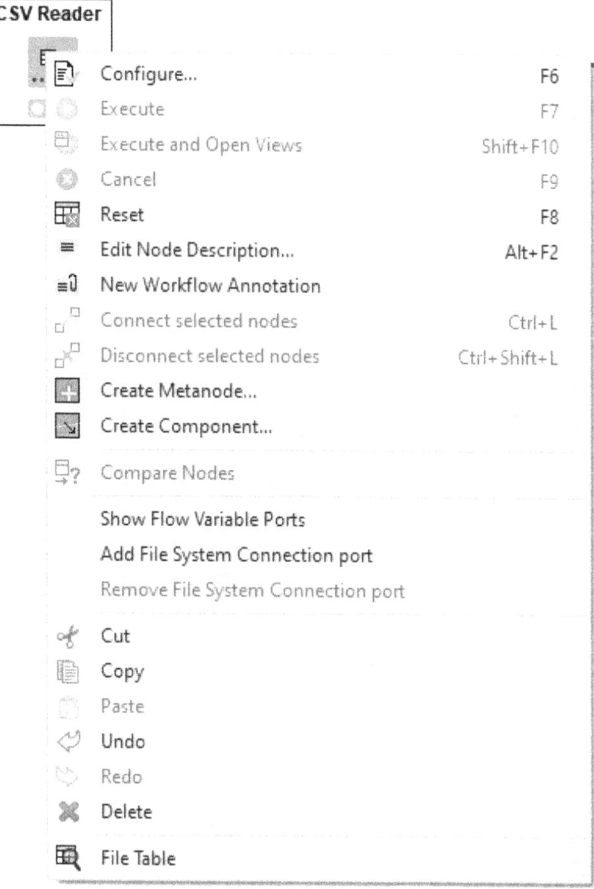


Figure 2.5 – The context menu of a node

Next, we introduce the four most common node operations available in the context menu:

- **Configure...**: This opens the node's configuration dialog to define the node's task. The configuration dialog of the CSV Reader node is shown in the following screenshot, with options to define a file path and a table structure:

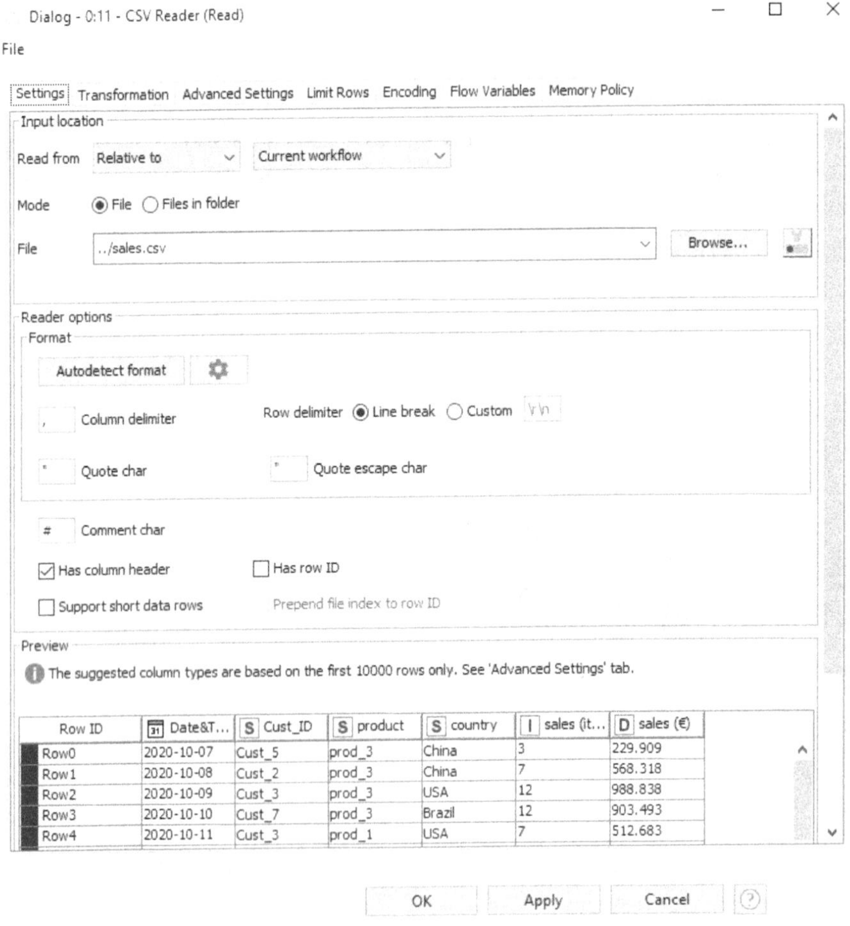


Figure 2.6 – The visual configuration dialog of a node

- **Execute**: This executes the task of a configured node. For example, executing the CSV Reader node accesses data from the CSV file and outputs it as a KNIME data table in the node's output.
- **Reset**: This switches the node's status from executed back to configured.
- The last option shown in *Figure 2.5*, **File Table**, opens the KNIME data table output of the node.

> **Note**
> Data in workflows is organized as KNIME data tables, which have unique row **identifiers (IDs)** and column headers.

In the next subsection, we will demonstrate how to connect nodes to workflows.

## Introducing workflows

A **workflow** contains multiple nodes that perform their tasks sequentially in one branch or simultaneously in parallel workflow branches. In this subsection, we show how to create workflows, how to structure them with metanodes, and how to package them into components.

### *Connecting nodes to workflows*

Let's start with how to build workflows. You can connect nodes to workflows in three ways, as outlined here:

- Drag and drop the node into the workflow canvas. Connect it to the previous node by **dragging a connection line** from the output port to the input port.
- Or, select the previous node in the workflow and **double-click the next node** in the node repository. This will automatically connect the two nodes.
- Or, **drag a node onto the existing connection line** and release it when the connection line turns red.

You can perform tasks on individual nodes (configure, execute, inspect the output, and so on) at any point in your workflow. Notice, though, that executing (resetting) a node also executes (resets) the upstream (downstream) nodes.

In the next subsection, we explain how to structure your workflows with metanodes.

### *Structuring workflows with metanodes*

A **metanode** captures a part of a workflow into a **sub-workflow**. A sub-workflow encapsulates any nodes, yet often those that are performed simultaneously or that follow each other in the sequential logic of the workflow. Metanodes make workflows easier to interpret and tidier to present. Notice, though, that a metanode is not a functional unit in your workflow but solely a container for nodes to clean up and **structure your workflow hierarchically**.

Follow these steps to create a metanode:

1. Select nodes on the workflow canvas by doing one of the following:
   - Pressing *Ctrl* and clicking the nodes one by one
   - Drawing a rectangle over the nodes
2. Right-click the selection and select **Create Metanode...** in the context menu, as illustrated in the following screenshot:

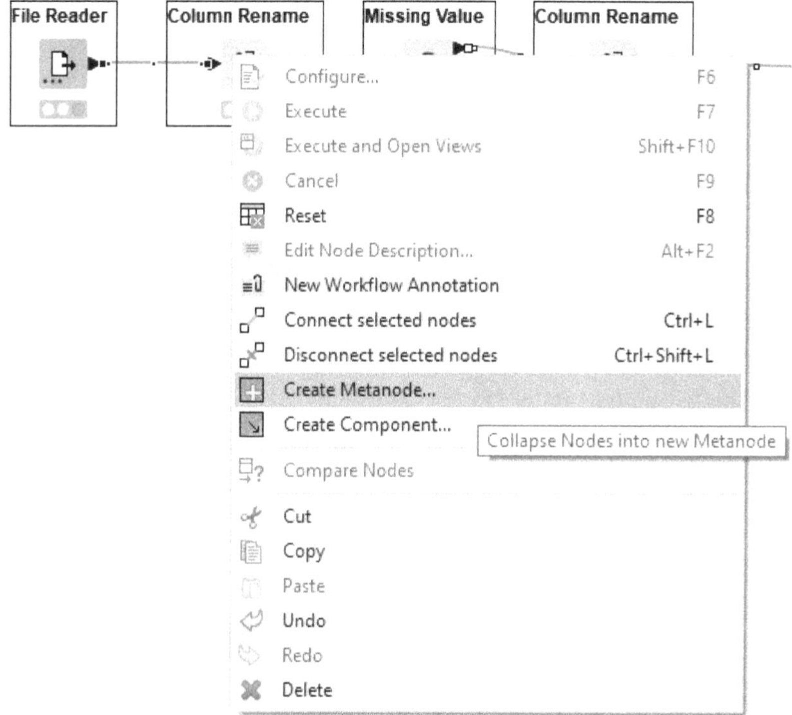


Figure 2.7 – Creating a metanode

3. In the dialog that opens, give the metanode a descriptive name and click **OK**.

At any point, you can inspect and reconfigure a workflow inside a metanode by double-clicking on the metanode and reviewing it in a separate workflow tab that opens. Furthermore, you can change the name of a metanode and add I/O ports by clicking **Metanode | Reconfigure...** in the metanode's context menu, as illustrated in the following screenshot:

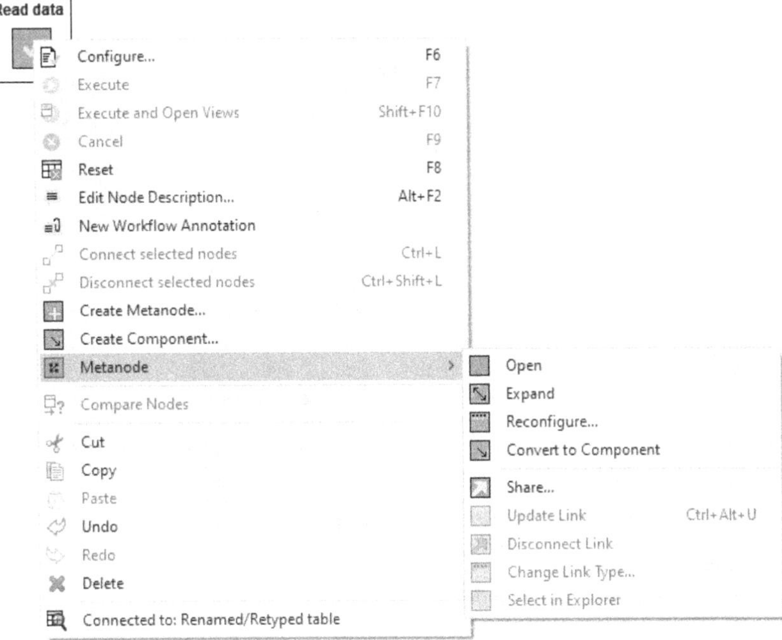


Figure 2.8 – Navigating a metanode's context menu

In the next subsection, we explain how to package workflows into components.

### *Packaging workflows into components*

A **component** is a node that encapsulates a KNIME workflow segment for a pre-defined functionality that can be reused in multiple workflows. Next, we list the most common use cases of components:

- **Creating and reusing custom tasks**: If a task can only be implemented by a sequence of nodes, you can wrap the sequence of nodes into a component and reuse it like a KNIME node in different workflows.
- **Sharing functionalities**: You can save a component in the KNIME Explorer panel in the same way as a workflow and share it via KNIME Server or the KNIME Hub.
- **Hiding complexity**: If you want to highlight only the necessary options for executing a component's task, you can build a custom configuration dialog via the dedicated *Configuration* nodes for input, selection, and filtering.

- **Creating custom interactive views**: A component can have an interactive composite view that displays all single views of nodes inside a component. You can also create interaction points in a view via dedicated *Widget* nodes for input, selection, and filtering.
- **Building web pages in a data app**: Each web page in a KNIME data app corresponds to a component in the workflow that is executing in the background.

## Creating and sharing a component

You can create a component in the same way as a metanode, as introduced in the *Structuring workflows with metanodes* subsection. Furthermore, you can **share** a component under any mountpoint in KNIME Explorer. To do so, follow these steps:

1. Create a **description** and add an **icon** to the component, as follows.
2. Open the component in a separate workflow tab by pressing *Ctrl* and double-clicking the component.
3. Write a description of the component in the **Description** panel.
4. Share the component, as follows by right-clicking the component. Select **Component | Share...**, as illustrated in the following screenshot:

Figure 2.9 – Sharing a component via its context menu

5. In the dialog that opens, select a destination, and click **OK**.
6. Reuse the component by dragging and dropping it from KNIME Explorer into your workflow, as illustrated in the following screenshot:

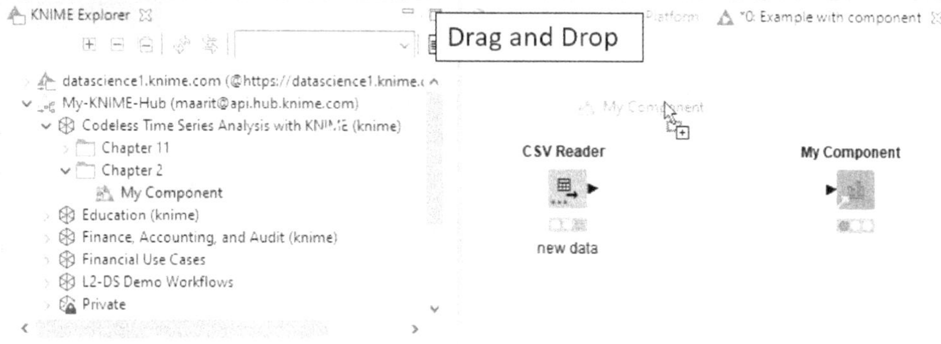


Figure 2.10 – Using an instance of a shared component in a workflow

Notice that all instances of a shared component are linked to their original location. If the shared component is updated, updates are triggered in the instances of it in all workflows. Therefore, you cannot edit the workflow inside an instance of a shared component. If you want to do that, you will need to unlink it via the component's context menu by selecting **Component** | **Disconnect Link** (see *Figure 2.9*).

## Introducing KNIME verified components

Components developed and shared by KNIME are called **verified components**. You can find them from the *EXAMPLES* server and the KNIME Hub (available at `https://kni.me/s/pG7mP5BmhFevTUR0`). They are also introduced on the *KNIME Verified Components* web page (`https://www.knime.com/verified-components`).

Particularly, most of the time series functionalities in KNIME are available as verified components. The time series components use functions from the Python `statsmodels` package, yet the components encapsulate the Python script behind a GUI, allowing for codeless time series analysis.

We conclude this section about nodes and workflows by introducing the KNIME Hub in the next subsection.

## Searching for and sharing resources on the KNIME Hub

The KNIME Hub (`https://hub.knime.com/`) is a public repository for **workflows**, **nodes**, **components**, and **extensions** provided by KNIME and the **KNIME community**. We will demonstrate next how to use nodes, import workflows, install extensions, and share resources on the KNIME Hub.

### *Using nodes and workflows from the KNIME Hub*

Once you have found the node or component you need, you can add it to your KNIME Analytics Platform installation by dragging and dropping it from the KNIME Hub web page, as seen in the following screenshot:

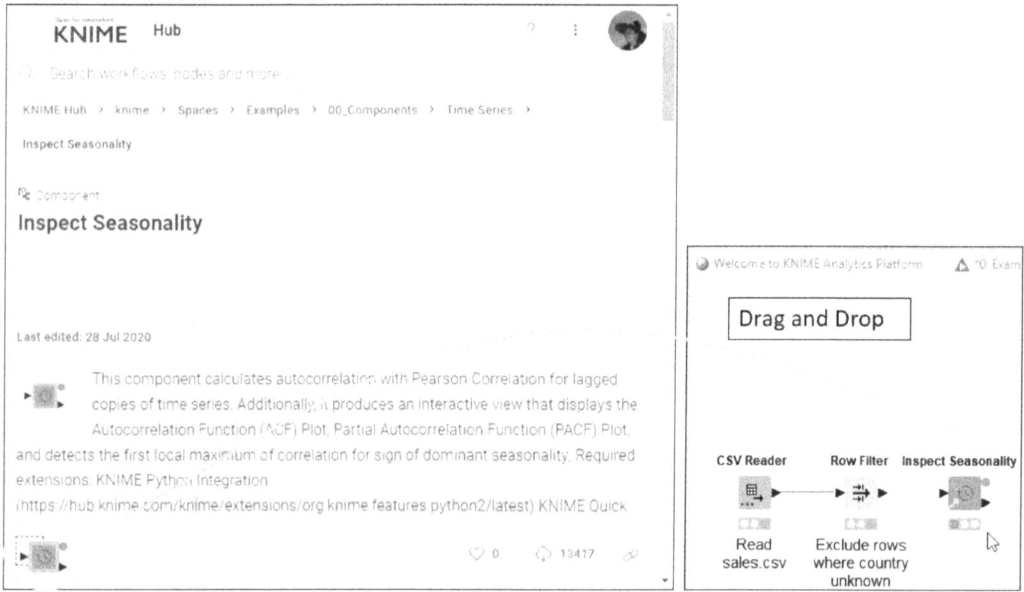


Figure 2.11 – Adding a resource from the KNIME Hub to KNIME Analytics Platform

In the same way, you can also add workflows to your KNIME Explorer installation, by dragging and dropping them into the destination workflow group.

### *Installing extensions*

Extensions provide additional functionalities and tools to KNIME Analytics Platform and therefore more nodes in the node repository. For example, *KNIME Python Integration* includes nodes with a Python script editor inside, and *KNIME Plotly Integration* includes additional view nodes. You can install extensions either from KNIME Analytics Platform or from the KNIME Hub by following the next steps:

From KNIME Analytics Platform, proceed as follows:

1. Click **File** | **Install KNIME Extensions…**.
2. Select an extension to install in the dialog. Click **Next** >. The process is illustrated in the following screenshot:

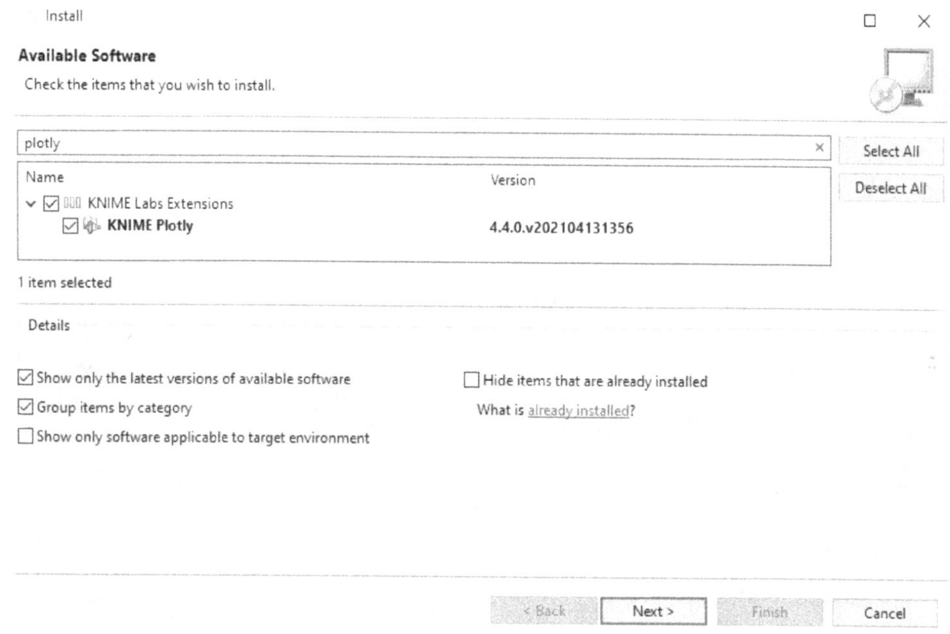


Figure 2.12 – Installing KNIME extensions from KNIME Analytics Platform

3. On the next page, accept the terms of the license agreements. Click **Finish**.
4. Restart KNIME Analytics Platform.
5. From the KNIME Hub, proceed as follows:

   A. Visit the KNIME Hub page of the KNIME extension—for example, `https://kni.me/e/NXfbxRi-JV1Tt7yC` for the KNIME Plotly integration.

B. Drag and drop the extension into your KNIME workbench.

C. Accept the terms of the license agreements and restart KNIME Analytics Platform.

> **Note**
>
> If you drag and drop a node from the KNIME Hub, it will prompt the installation procedure if the extension has not yet been installed. The same happens if you open a workflow that contains nodes from missing extensions. To review which extensions have already been installed, click **Help | About KNIME Analytics Platform**.

### *Sharing resources on the KNIME Hub*

Resources on the KNIME Hub are organized into **spaces**. For example, the workflows introduced in this book are in a space called *Codeless Time Series Analysis with KNIME*, accessible via `https://kni.me/w/GxjXX6WmLi-WjLNx`. You can also create your own spaces, which can be **public** or **private**. You can create and manage the workflows in your space via the *My-KNIME-Hub* mountpoint in KNIME Explorer.

In this section, we have introduced nodes, workflows, metanodes, components, and extensions. In the next section, we complete a simple workflow as a practical example.

## Building your first workflow

In this section, we show you how to build your first workflow for **data access**, **data preprocessing**, and **visualization**. You will learn all the necessary workflow-building skills to follow along with the more complex analysis tasks in the upcoming chapters.

The instructions are divided into the following subsections:

- Creating a new workflow (group)
- Reading and transforming data
- Filtering rows
- Visualizing data
- Building a custom interactive view
- Documenting workflows

The result, your first workflow, is shown in the following diagram:

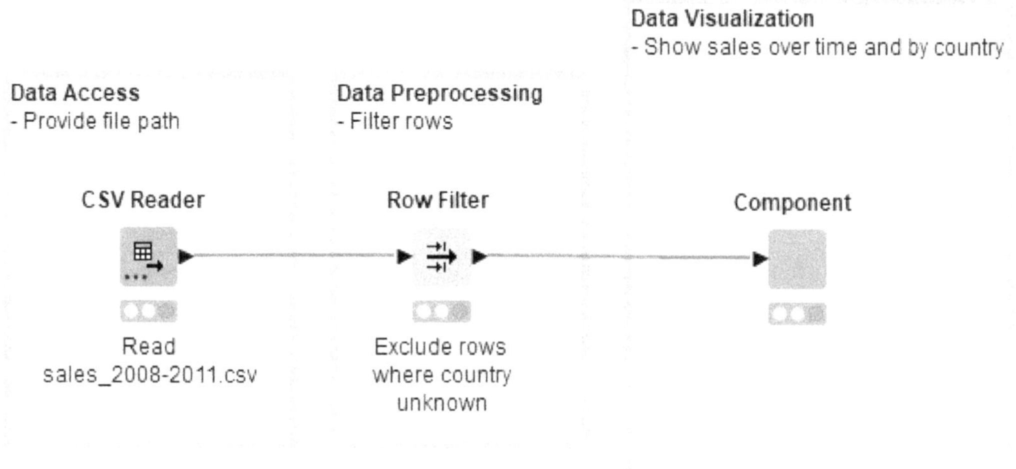


Figure 2.13 – Example workflow for accessing, preprocessing, and visualizing data

The workflow accesses data with information about ordered products: order dates and countries, customer IDs, and sales amount and quantity. Next, it preprocesses the data by filtering unnecessary rows and columns. Finally, it creates an interactive dashboard of the sales metrics.

## Creating a new workflow (group)

In this subsection, we will show how to create an empty workflow canvas as a starting point for your visual workflow. We will also show how to organize workflows in **workflow groups**. A workflow group is a folder in KNIME Explorer that can contain workflows, shared components, data files, and other workflow groups.

Your task is to create a new workflow group called `Chapter 2` and a new workflow called `My First Workflow`. You can either create an empty workflow group or import an existing workflow group. Both ways are described next:

1. Create an **empty workflow group**, as follows:

2. Right-click the **LOCAL** mountpoint, or a workflow group under it, and select **New Workflow Group...** in the menu, as illustrated in the following screenshot:

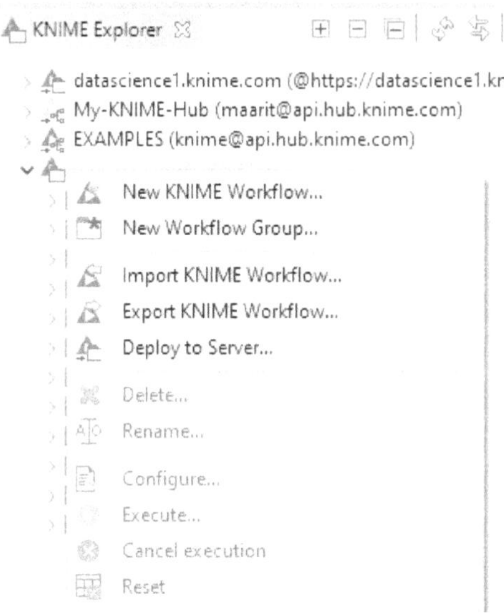


Figure 2.14 – Creating a new workflow group from KNIME Explorer

3. In the dialog that opens, write `Chapter 2` as the name of the workflow. If you want, you can still change the location of the new workflow at this point by clicking **Browse...** and selecting another destination in KNIME Explorer. Click **Finish**. The process is illustrated in the following screenshot:

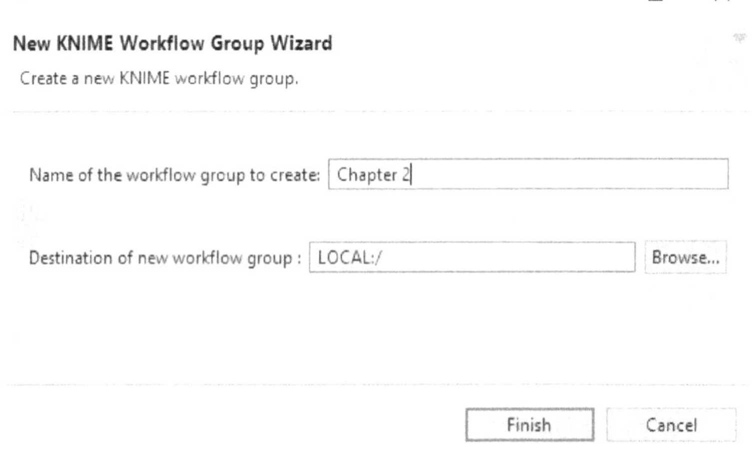


Figure 2.15 – Defining the name and destination of a new workflow

4. Or, drag and drop a workflow group from the KNIME Hub into your local workspace. For example, you can drag and drop the `Chapter 2` workflow group from the KNIME Hub space of this book (under `https://kni.me/s/GxjXX6WmLi-WjLNx`) into your local workspace, as illustrated in the following screenshot:

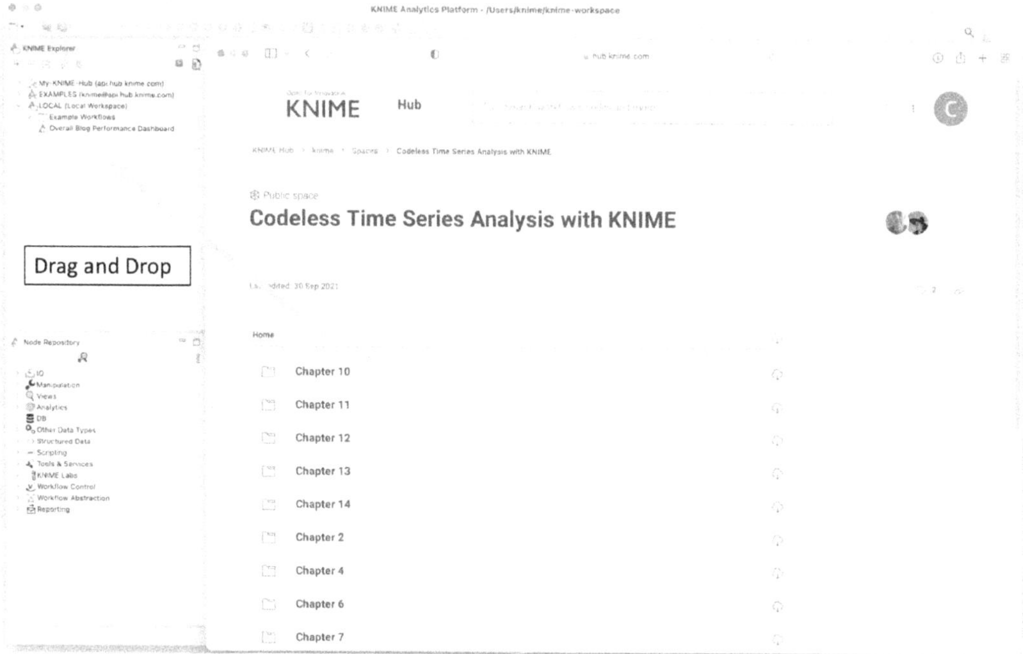


Figure 2.16 – Dragging and dropping a workflow group from the KNIME Hub into KNIME Explorer

5. Or, import a `.knar` file into your KNIME Explorer installation by selecting **Import KNIME Workflow...** (see *Figure 2.14*) in the right-click menu. **KNIME Archive file** (`.knar`) is the KNIME dedicated file format for workflow groups.

Furthermore, as with creating workflow groups, you have three ways of creating workflows, as follows:

1. Via the right-click menu in KNIME Explorer or via the toolbar (see *Figure 2.14*)
2. Via dragging and dropping from the KNIME Hub
3. Via importing a **KNIME Workflow file** (`.knwf`), which is the dedicated file format for single workflows

By now, you should have a `Chapter 2` workflow group in your local workspace, and a new empty workflow inside it. If you dragged and dropped or imported the workflow group from the KNIME Hub, you should also have the `sales.csv` file within it.

In the next subsection, you will read a CSV file as the first task in your workflow.

## Reading and transforming data

Your first task is to read the `sales.csv` file, which is available on the KNIME Hub (`https://kni.me/s/Vdv1OOqFVz5UNC4Z`). If you imported the workflow group from the KNIME Hub in the previous step, then you can already find the file in KNIME Explorer. Otherwise, you can download it from the KNIME Hub.

If the file is in KNIME Explorer, the fastest way of reading a file from there is to *drag and drop the data file* onto your workflow canvas. This action also creates the right node to read the file: a CSV Reader node for CSV files, an Excel Reader node for Excel files, and so on. If the file is located somewhere else, you can create an appropriate reader node from the node repository and navigate to the file location from its configuration dialog. The first option automatically populates the file path option in the reader node's configuration dialog. The latter option requires defining the file path manually, as we explain next.

### Defining the location of a file

All reader nodes have the same **Input location** setting in their configuration dialogs, as illustrated in the following screenshot:

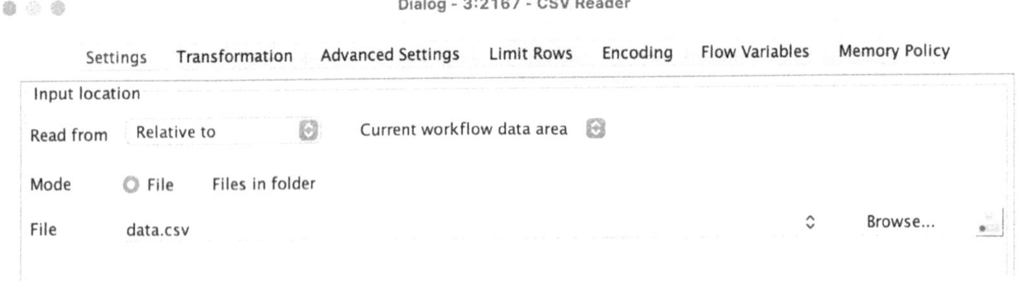


Figure 2.17 – The Input location setting of a reader node

The **Input location** setting consists of three fields to define, which we explain next:

- Filesystem type, which can be one of the following:
  - **Local**: A path on the local machine
  - **Mountpoint:** A path in KNIME Explorer under a selected mountpoint
  - **Relative to:** A path relative to the currently active mountpoint, workflow, or workflow group
  - **Custom/KNIME URL**: A **Uniform Resource Locator** (URL) address

  - Specifier, which provides additional information to the **Mountpoint** and **Relative to** filesystem types, as outlined next:

    - For the **Mountpoint** path type, the specifier can be one of the following:

      - The LOCAL mountpoint
      - A named *KNIME Server* mountpoint
      - The *My-KNIME-Hub* mountpoint

    - For the **Relative to** path type, the specifier can be one of the following:

      - **Current mountpoint**: The path starts from under the currently active mountpoint. For example, the `Chapter 2/sales.csv` mountpoint relative path accesses the `sales.csv` file in the `Chapter 2` workflow group under the currently active mountpoint, such as *LOCAL*.
      - **Current workflow**: The path starts from the location of the executing workflow. Two dots indicate a movement to an upper folder level. For example, the `../sales.csv` workflow relative path reads the `sales.csv` file located in the same workflow group as the executing workflow.
      - **Current workflow data area**: Reads a file from a **data** folder that is stored inside the workflow. Copying, moving, and deleting the workflow applies to the data file as well.

- **File path**, which navigates to the data file within the location specified by the preceding settings. You can populate the file path via the **Browse...** button in the configuration dialog.

Once you have successfully accessed the file, the configuration dialog shows a preview of the file, as shown in *Figure 2.6*. After that, you can perform transformations on data already in the reader node. We show you how to do that in the next subsection.

### *Performing data transformations in reader nodes*

You can find a **Transformation** tab in all reader nodes. This allows for applying the following transformations to the data that you are reading:

- **Resorting columns**: Move columns either by dragging and dropping or via the **Move up** and **Move down** buttons.
- **Removing unnecessary columns**: Uncheck columns in the table.
- **Renaming columns**: Write a new name in the **New name** column.

- **Converting column types**: Select a new data type in the menu in the **Type** column.

The following screenshot shows an example of transformations being applied:

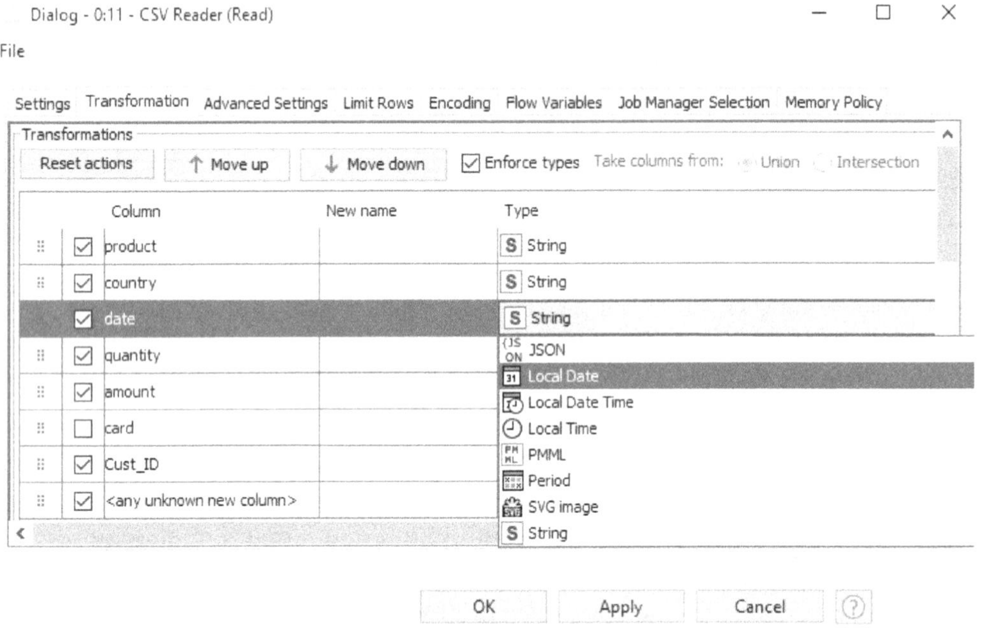


Figure 2.18 – Applying transformations to data tables directly in the reader node

In your first workflow, in the CSV Reader node that you just added, you are supposed to exclude the **card** column by unchecking it and change the data type of the **date** column from **String** to **Local Date**, as shown in *Figure 2.18*.

After that, you can move on to filtering rows in the next subsection.

## Filtering rows

You can perform row filtering with—for example—the **Row Filter** node, which you can find in the **Manipulation** category in the node repository, along with many other nodes for data manipulation.

Your task is to filter out rows where the country is unknown. The required configuration is to select **country** as the column to test and **unknown** as the pattern, and enable the **Exclude rows by attribute value** radio button in the configuration dialog of the **Row Filter** node, as illustrated in the following screenshot:

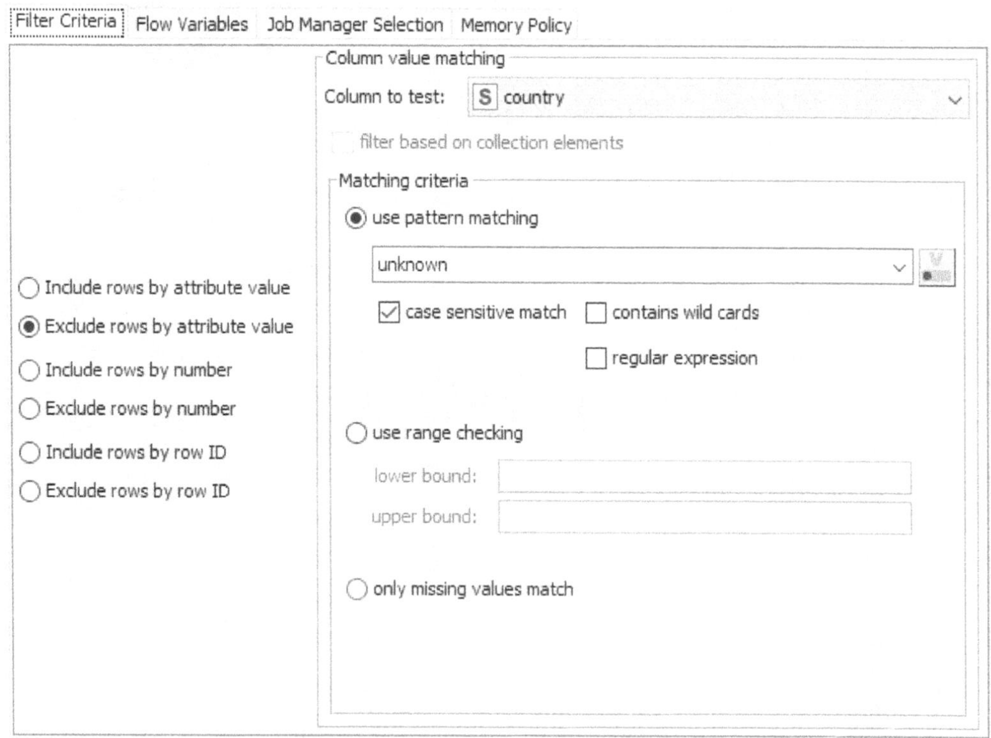


Figure 2.19 – Configuring the Row Filter node

Notice that with the Row Filter node, you could also include and exclude rows by **value**, **row index**, or **row ID**. These options correspond to the other radio buttons on the left side of the configuration dialog. Here, however, we move on to the next step, which is data visualization.

## Visualizing data

**Data visualization** varies from univariate to multivariate views that show characteristics and relationships in the data beyond plain numbers. For example, in an interactive table, you can search for entries and sort columns; in a line plot, you can detect a trend; in a scatter plot, you can detect a linear correlation; and so on. You can find visualization nodes in the **Views** | **JavaScript** category in the node repository. All nodes in this category—**Line Plot**, **Bar Chart**, **Histogram**, and so on—create **interactive views**. In addition, nodes in the **KNIME Labs** | **JavaScript Views (Labs)** | **Plotly** category create interactive views from Plotly's data visualization library.

As an example, your task is to visualize the number of ordered items over time in a line plot. The following screenshot shows the corresponding configuration of the **Line Plot (Plotly)** node:

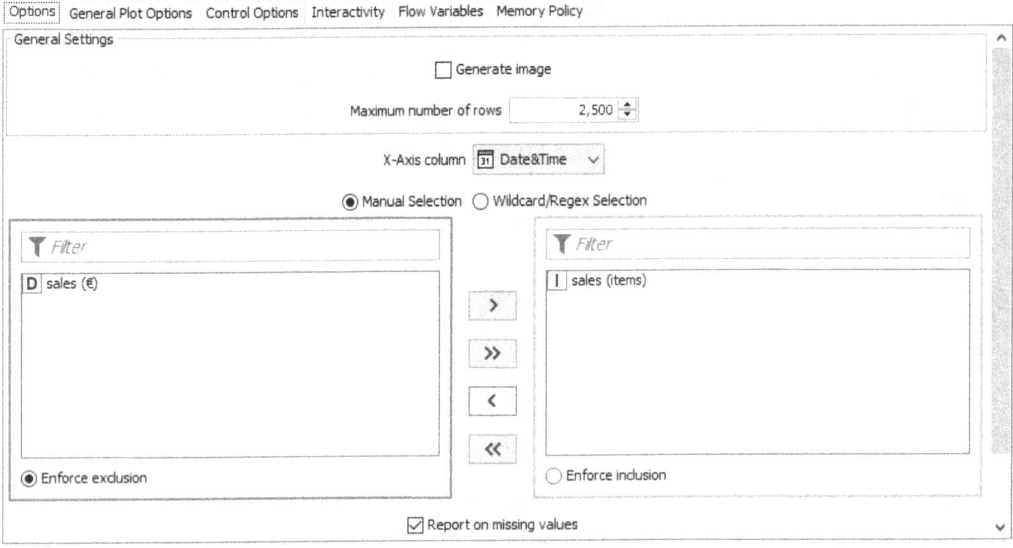


Figure 2.20 – Configuring the Line Plot (Plotly) node

The necessary configuration is to select the *x*-axis column (here, **Date&Time**) and the *y*-axis column (here, **sales (items)**). The output view is shown in the following screenshot:

Figure 2.21 – A line plot showing the number of ordered items over time

> **Note**
>
> To open the interactive view output of the node (*Figure 2.21*), select **Execute and Open Views...** at the top of the node's right-click menu. If the node is already executed, select **Interactive View: Line Plot** in the middle of the menu.

In the output view, the **user control buttons** in the top left allow for zooming in and out, moving the plot, selecting a subset of the data, and downloading the currently active area as a **Scalable Vector Graphics** (**SVG**) image. The **menu button** at the top right allows for changing axis columns, disabling tooltips, and managing other interactivity options (introduced in the next subsection). The interactive menu of the line plot is shown in the following screenshot:

Figure 2.22 – Customizing a node view via its interactive menu

Furthermore, you can edit the visual appearance of a view—for example, change the view title and axis labels—in the **General Plot Options** tab in the configuration dialog (see *Figure 2.20*).

In the next subsection, we show how to combine multiple views into one interactive view.

## Building a custom interactive view

A custom **interactive view** of a component includes multiple views that are produced by nodes that reside inside the same component.

Your practical exercise is to continue your workflow by creating a custom interactive view. You can create one with two views—the line plot from the previous subsection, and a bar chart—by following these steps:

1. Add the **Bar Chart node** to the workflow. In the configuration dialog, select the **country** column as the category column and **sales (items)** as the *y*-axis column. In addition, select **Sum** as the aggregation method for the *y*-axis column. This bar chart will show the total number of ordered items by country.
2. Encapsulate the view nodes into a component, as shown in the *Packaging workflows into components* subsection.
3. Execute the component and open its interactive view. The following screenshot shows the expected result:

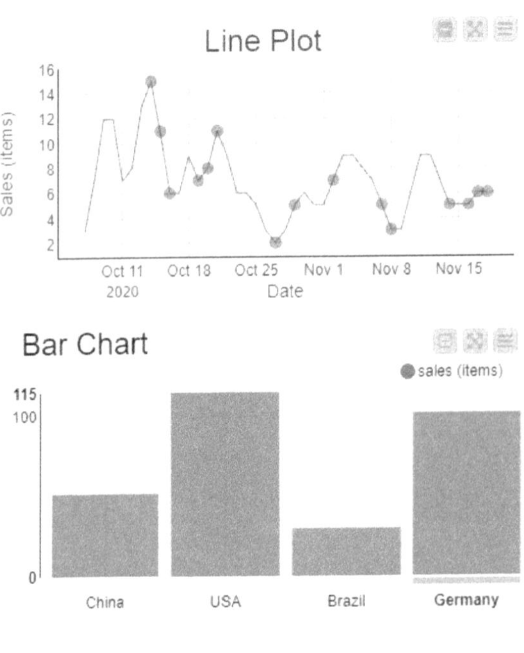


Figure 2.23 – A component's interactive view containing all interactive views produced within it

The interactive view shows both views from inside the component—a line plot and a bar chart. You can select a subset of the data in one view, such as the bar for **Germany** in *Figure 2.23*. When you do, the bar chart **publishes** the **selection**, and the line plot **subscribes** to the selection event by highlighting dates when there were sales from Germany. You can disable and enable the publishing/subscribing of filtering/selection events via the menu button at the top right (see *Figure 2.22*).

If you want, you can also change the layout of the interactive view in the **Visual Layout Editor** of the component, which you can open by clicking the visual layout editor button in the toolbar, as illustrated in the following screenshot:

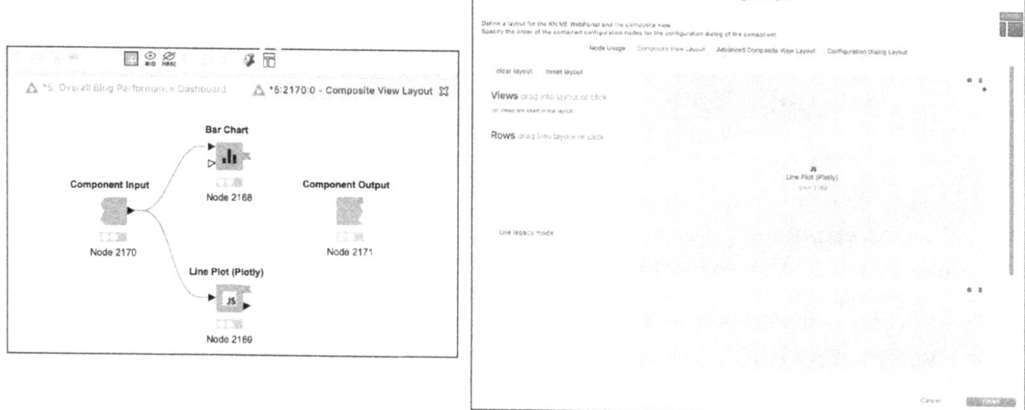


Figure 2.24 – Organizing the layout of a custom interactive view in the visual layout editor

The visual layout editor shows all views and widgets produced by the nodes inside the component, which you can organize by dragging and dropping them into the columns and rows in the layout editor.

At this point, you have finished building and configuring your first workflow. Before you move on to the next subsection about documenting your workflow, check that you have completed the following steps:

1. Reading the `sales.csv` file
2. Removing the **card** column and changing the data type of the **date** column
3. Removing rows where *country* is unknown
4. Visualizing sales over time in a line plot and sales by country in a bar chart
5. Encapsulating the line plot and bar chart into a custom interactive view

## Documenting workflows

**Documenting a workflow** means describing what the workflow and individual nodes are doing.

In the previous sections, we already mentioned two ways of documenting workflows: **node annotations** and **workflow descriptions**. A third way of documenting your workflow is adding **workflow annotations**—colored boxes with text to describe the entire workflow or a part of it.

You can add an annotation to your workflow by right-clicking on the workflow canvas and selecting **New Workflow Annotation** in the menu, as illustrated in the following screenshot:

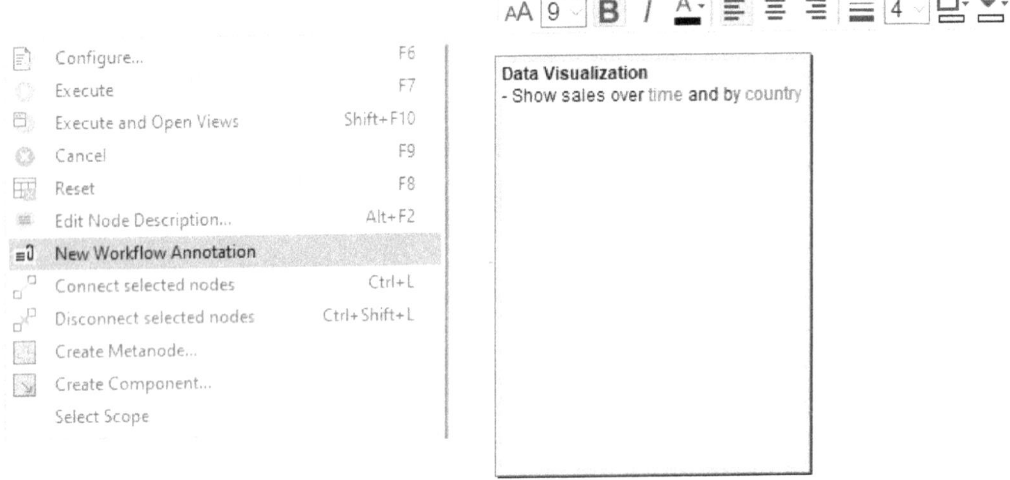


Figure 2.25 – Creating and editing a workflow annotation

You can then activate the **text editor** by double-clicking in the top-left corner. In the text editor, you can change the visual appearance of the annotation—for example, the font, text color, annotation width, and annotation color.

Finally, when you have documented your workflow, save the workflow by clicking the **Save** button in the toolbar, as illustrated in the following screenshot:

Figure 2.26 – Saving the workflow via the toolbar

You have now finished your first workflow. Congratulations! The next section concludes the chapter by demonstrating the required one-time setup for time series analysis in KNIME. If you want to practice more with basic workflows, the *Beginners Space* on the KNIME Hub (accessible via `https://kni.me/s/Ln1fgQnWKKeRceeP`) contains simple examples for accessing, manipulating, and analyzing data.

# Configuring the time series integration

In this section, we will give an overview of **time series components** in KNIME and guide you through the installation of **KNIME Python Integration**.

## Introducing the time series components

The time series components in KNIME implement various preprocessing and modeling tasks that are specific to time series analysis, such as time-aligning the data, aggregating by time granularities, and training a **Seasonal Autoregressive Integrated Moving Average** (**SARIMA**) model for forecasting.

You can find the time series components from the *Examples* space on the KNIME Hub (`https://kni.me/s/1415IA5ZFtVXlwg_`) and from the *EXAMPLES* server under **00_Components** | **Time Series**, as shown in the following screenshot:

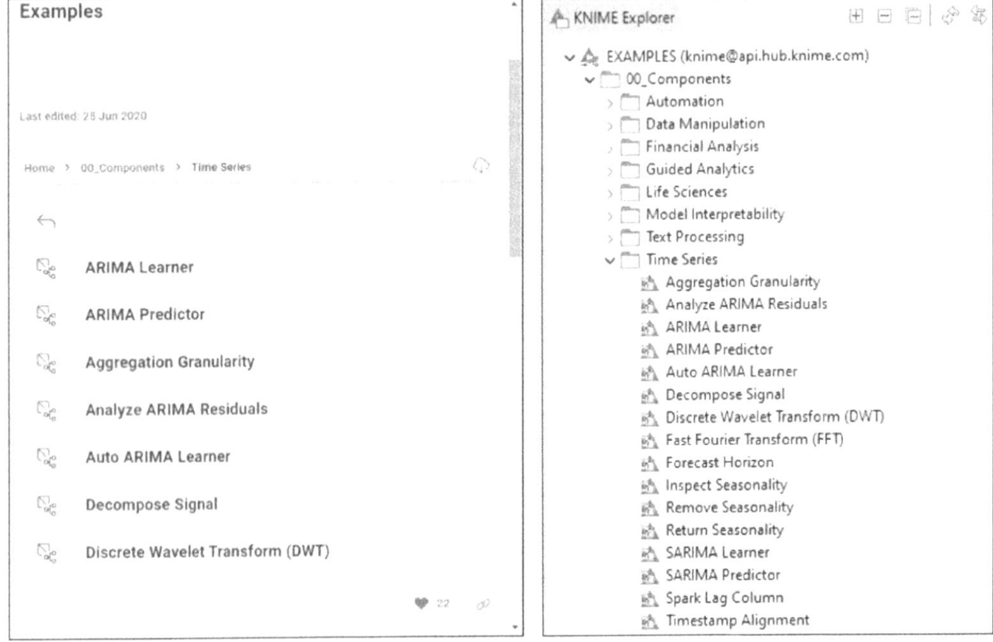


Figure 2.27 – Time series components on the KNIME Hub and on the EXAMPLES server

From both the KNIME Hub and *EXAMPLES* server, you can drag and drop components into your workflows.

Most of the time series components encapsulate a Python node with a script inside. The following screenshot shows the workflow inside the *SARIMA Learner* component as an example:

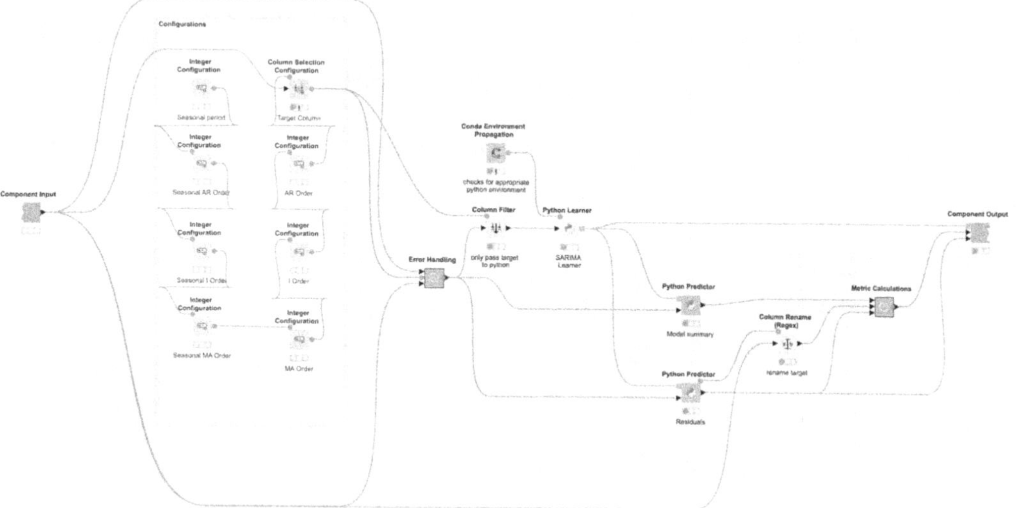


Figure 2.28 – A KNIME workflow inside a time series component

In the workflow inside the component, the configuration nodes define the setting options in the custom configuration dialog. The KNIME nodes transform the I/O. The **Python Learner** and **Python Predictor** nodes execute the actual task—training and predicting with a SARIMA model.

The following screenshot shows the Python script for training a SARIMA model in the script editor of the Python Learner node:

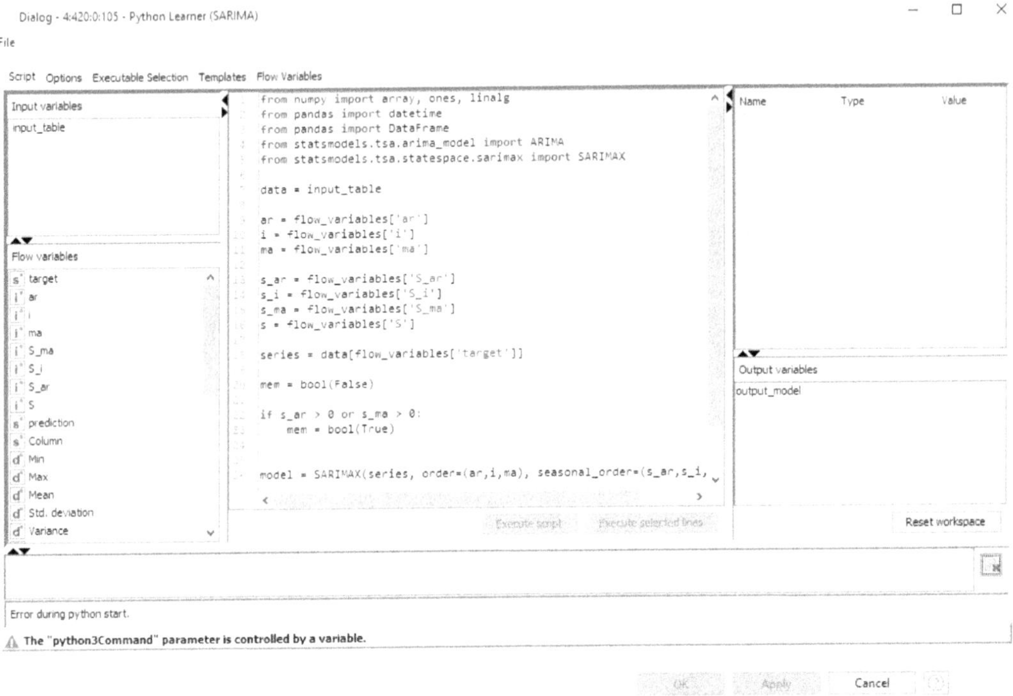


Figure 2.29 – Python script for training a SARIMA model inside the Python Learner node

This script is only executing in the background, while you can define model parameters via the component's configuration dialog shown in the following screenshot:

Figure 2.30 – The configuration dialog of the SARIMA Learner node

The **visual configuration dialog** of the **SARIMA Learner component** contains a setting for each model parameter—`p`, `d`, `q`, `P`, `D`, `Q`—and the seasonal period. Configuring the component will customize the Python script accordingly. The component's output is then the corresponding SARIMA model and the model summary that both originate from the respective Python script inside.

Due to the Python script executing inside the time series components, executing them requires a local Python installation.

In the next subsection, we will show how to install Python and configure Python in KNIME.

## Configuring Python in KNIME

Follow these steps to install Python on your local machine:

1. **Download Anaconda**, as follows:
2. Go to `https://www.anaconda.com/distribution/` and download Anaconda for Python 3.8.

3. Run the installer.
4. **Install the required extensions**, as follows:
5. Go to **File | Install KNIME Extensions**. Select **KNIME Python Integration, KNIME Deep Learning – Keras Integration, and KNIME Deep Learning – TensorFlow Integration**. Follow the instructions in the dialog to finish the installation.
6. Restart KNIME Analytics Platform.
7. **Configure KNIME**, as follows:
8. Go to **File | Preferences | KNIME | Python.**
9. Click **Browse** and navigate to the folder where you installed Anaconda.
10. Click **New environment…** next to **Python 3**.
11. Create a new environment and give it a name without any spaces.
12. Click **Apply and Close**.

The process is illustrated in the following screenshot:

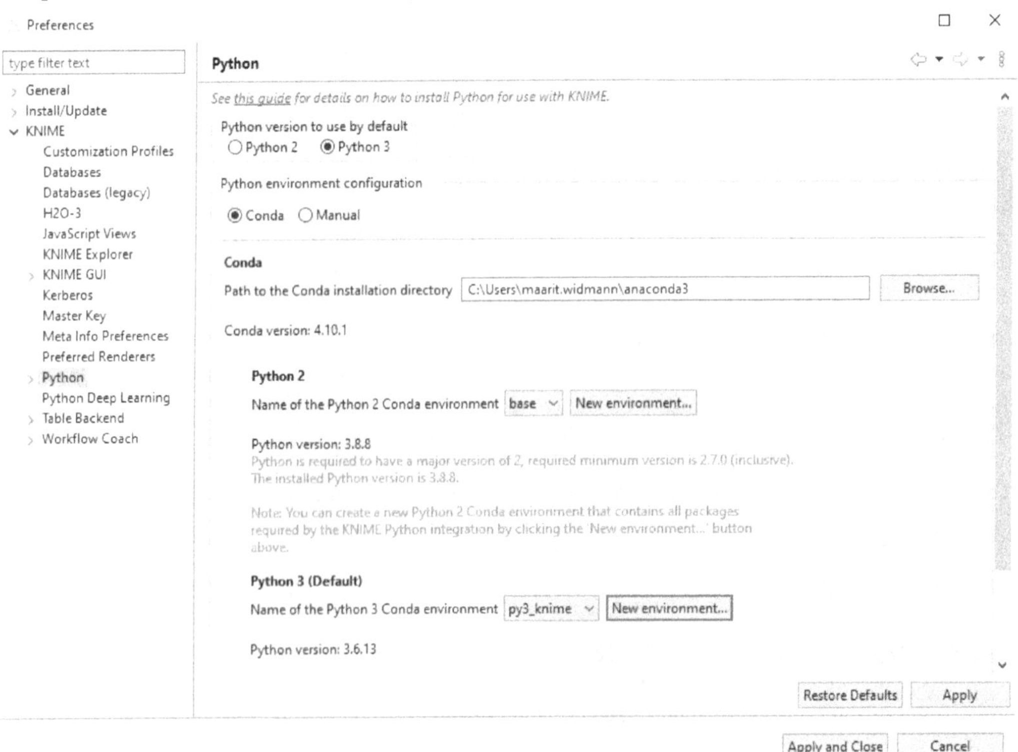


Figure 2.31 – Configuring Python in KNIME

13. Go to **File | Preferences | Python Deep Learning**. Select **Use configuration from the "Python" preference page**. Click **Apply and Close**.
14. Install additional Python packages, as follows:
15. Open **Anaconda Prompt** by typing `Anaconda` in the taskbar (Windows) or by opening the Terminal (Mac).
16. Type `conda install -n [your environment name] statsmodels=0.11.1`, as illustrated in the following screenshot:

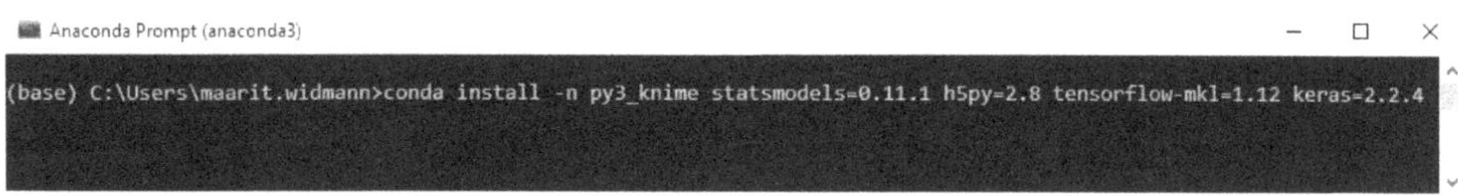


Figure 2.32 – Installing additional packages via Anaconda Prompt

17. Restart KNIME Analytics Platform.

With the Python installation running under the hood, you're ready to start with codeless time series analysis in KNIME. You can build, find, and share visual workflows using the skills that you acquired in this section. In particular, you can use the components for time series analysis as pre-packaged building blocks in your time series workflows.

# Summary

In this chapter, we have taken a tour of the KNIME software and introduced the basic skills of visual programming. In addition, we have shown the required setup for time series analysis in KNIME.

Throughout the chapter, you familiarized yourself with the KNIME workbench and the basic concepts of nodes and workflows. You completed your first workflow, learned about the time series components, and configured Python in KNIME.

You gained all the skills you will need to follow along with the practical use cases in this book and KNIME workflows in general.

In the next chapter, we will introduce common data preparation steps in time series analysis. Let's get going!

## Questions

1. Which of the following descriptions defines a node?

    A. The smallest processing unit in KNIME

    B. A subset of data

    C. A remote data storage

    D. A task implemented via an integrated tool

2. Which of the following operations can you NOT perform on workflows?

    A. Structure hierarchically

    B. Reuse as single functionalities

    C. Edit outside the KNIME workbench

    D. Share publicly

3. How does the time series integration in KNIME function?

    A. The tasks are implemented with the KNIME native nodes and packaged into components for simplicity

    B. The tasks are implemented via single Python nodes which you can reuse in your workflows

    C. The tasks are implemented using functionalities from Python libraries and combining them with the KNIME native nodes

    D. The tasks are implemented by the KNIME Community using KNIME native nodes, Python libraries, and possibly other tools

# 3
# Preparing Data for Time Series Analysis

In this chapter, we will introduce the common first steps in a time series analysis project. We will explore different sources of **time series data** and show you how to clean the raw data through equal spacing, missing value imputation, and time aggregation.

After preparing the data using these steps, we can proceed with visualization, descriptive analysis, and modeling of time series data.

Additionally, we will introduce preprocessing techniques in the upcoming sections:

- Introducing different sources of time series data
- Time granularity and time aggregation
- Equal spacing and time alignment
- Missing value imputation

You will learn about the common first steps of almost all time series applications. Also, you will learn about the different techniques used at each preprocessing step and gain an understanding of how to select the best approach for your data and application. Finally, you will also learn how to implement these techniques on **KNIME Analytics Platform**.

In the *Introducing different sources of time series data* section, we'll give examples of time series data from different sources and with different characteristics.

## Introducing different sources of time series data

In this section, we'll introduce real-world sources of time series data that represent a wide range of possible characteristics of time series data.

Time series data contains, besides the physical dimension of time, measurements of a quantitative variable such as temperature, a financial KPI, or sales. In the *raw data*, the progress of this variable can be reported at **regular** or **irregular** intervals. In regular time series, the sampling frequency is predefined and constant, whereas, in irregular time series, the timestamps are generated based on the occurrences of random events.

For example, if we record the total sales at the end of each day, we produce a time series with regular, daily intervals. If we, instead, record the sales generated by each customer in a day, we produce a time series with irregular intervals and possibly multiple values for the same timestamp. However, both time series can be analyzed by time series analysis techniques after some preprocessing, such as time aggregation and timestamp alignment.

The third type of time series is *signal*, which represents a physical event, such as a sound, by amplitude and frequency. The signal processing by **Fast Fourier Transformation** (**FFT**) is introduced in *Chapter 8, Audio Signal Classification with an FFT and a Gradient Boosted Forest.*

These different types of time series can be collected from many, traditional and modern sources. The sources of time series data have increased in variety and size together with the advancement of technology and the ability to store and analyze large amounts of data. The data collected from smart homes or health tracking are examples of modern sources of time series data.

The following are some other examples of sources of time series data:

- **Meteorology**: Temperature, humidity, and precipitation
- **Medicine**: Glucose level and the progress of a disease
- **Economics and finance**: The **Gross Domestic Product** (**GDP**) of a country, quarterly sales, **Annually Recurring Revenue** (**ARR**), and stock prices
- **Social sciences**: Literacy in population and population growth
- **Epidemiology**: The spread of infection
- **Physical sciences**: Traffic data, audio signals, and sensor data for mechanical maintenance

Despite the wide spread of the sources of the data, the time series analysis techniques apply universally. Within these fields, we apply time series analysis to describe and understand the patterns and their underlying causes, which is known as **exploratory analysis**. We *forecast* future values and create *simulations*.

In exploratory analysis and forecasting, we can utilize classic time series analysis techniques that consider time series-specific characteristics such as autocorrelation, stationarity, and seasonality. Additionally, these characteristics might only appear after preprocessing via aggregation and time alignment. Furthermore, these preprocessing steps are specific to time series data, which, otherwise, violates many of the assumptions of the comparable statistical methods on cross-sectional data, such as the independent sampling of observations.

In this chapter, we will introduce common preprocessing steps of time series data as determined by the source, shape, and further analysis of the data. In the next section, we will introduce a preprocessing step called **time aggregation**.

# Time granularity and time aggregation

In this section, we will introduce the concepts of **time granularity** and **time aggregation**. We will show examples of time series with different granularities. Additionally, we will show you how to aggregate time series in KNIME. We will cover these topics in the following subsections:

- Defining time granularity
- Finding the right time granularity
- Aggregating time series data

## Defining time granularity

**Time granularity** refers to the time interval between the observations within a time series. For example, if we record a financial KPI at the end of each year, then the granularity of the time series is yearly. If a glucose monitor reports the glucose level every minute, then the granularity of the time series is by the minute. In general, time granularity can be any time interval: daily, weekly, monthly, quarterly, and more.

To illustrate how time granularity determines the dynamics of a time series, the following screenshot shows two line plots of the same time series (taxi trip counts) at different granularities:

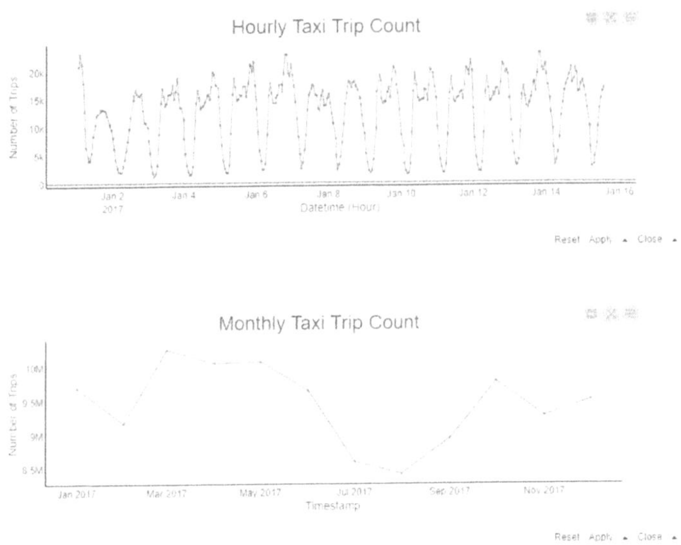


Figure 3.1 – Two time series with different granularities

The top line plot shows a more detailed time series where a trip count is reported at every hour. The bottom line plot shows a smoother time series where the trip count is reported for each month. Both time series originate from the same raw data, which reports the taxi trips and their timestamps at irregular intervals.

> **Important Note**
> The line plot is a common visualization technique that is used to compare the dynamics of two time series. The visualization techniques for time series data are introduced in *Chapter 4, Time Series Visualization*.

The granularity of time series is often changed from the original sampling frequency to fit the purpose of the application. In the next subsection, we explain how to find the right time granularity.

## Finding the right time granularity

Finding the right granularity is an important preprocessing step for effective and expedient analysis.

Firstly, time granularity determines the *volume* of the data. The volume of the time series data increases with more detailed granularity if we keep considering the same time period because the shorter the time interval between the subsequent observations, the more data will be collected or stored over the same period. For example, if we work with the taxi trip counts for every hour versus for every day, we will end up with 24 times as many observations in the first case versus the latter case.

Secondly, the granularity determines the *level of detail* in the dynamics that we can observe in the time series. If the purpose of the application is to generate hourly predictions, then the hourly granularity is appropriate and necessary. Whereas for daily or monthly predictions, the hourly fluctuation and redundant repetitions of observations would increase the computing time needlessly and possibly introduce noise that biases the algorithm.

In *Figure 3.1*, you can see the differences in the volumes of the line plots. The top line shows a half month from January 1 to January 15 with 350 data points, whereas the bottom line plot shows a whole year with only 12 data points.

Instead, a frequency that is too coarse can fail to show the dynamics of the time series. The hourly trip counts might be needed, for example, in city planning to recognize rush hours repeating from day to day, as you can see from the repeating peaks in the top line plot in *Figure 3.1*. This information would not be visible in daily or monthly data where the daily fluctuation has been eliminated.

Finally, the **forecasting horizon** also determines the appropriate granularity of the data. If the data are random with frequent changes, such as stock market data, then we are often interested in short-term forecasts. Then, we also don't aggregate the data, because by doing so, we would hide these short-term dynamics of interest. Instead, if the data shows a **seasonal pattern** and, thus, enables long-term forecasting, then we most likely benefit from aggregating the data to eliminate the random short-term fluctuation.

The right granularity for such data is also related to the length of the seasonal pattern. The appropriate granularity displays enough seasonal cycles in the training data efficiently. For example, if we want to observe yearly seasonality, we need data from several years to confirm that the yearly pattern is repeating. Therefore, if we have daily data, we will need 365 observations to complete one seasonal cycle and about $4 * 365 = 1460$ data points to confirm – and for the algorithm to learn – that it is repeating the pattern. Whereas if we work with monthly data, we can observe the same, repeating yearly patterns with only $4 * 12 = 48$ data points.

In the next subsection, we will introduce ways of aggregating time series data.

## Aggregating time series data

When we perform time aggregation, we reduce the granularity of a time series into a time series of summary metrics at a coarser granularity. We can perform the aggregations based on the date and time fields and fixed window size.

### *Aggregating time series by time granularity*

When we aggregate time series by date and time fields, we consider, for example, all observations from one hour, day, month, week, and more for one metric. The size of each time window is not necessarily the same in observations, but it is the same in calendar terms, for example, one full month.

For the time-based aggregations, KNIME Analytics Platform provides a component called **Aggregation Granularity**. This component extracts the selected granularity from the timestamp column in the input data and calculates the mean, mode, sum, minimum, maximum, count, or variance of the selected numeric column over each time field. We can select any output granularity that is coarser than the input time series; if the input data is daily, it can be aggregated to monthly and yearly. If the input data is hourly, it can be aggregated to daily, monthly, yearly, and more.

The tables in the following screenshot show an example of the input and output data of the component:

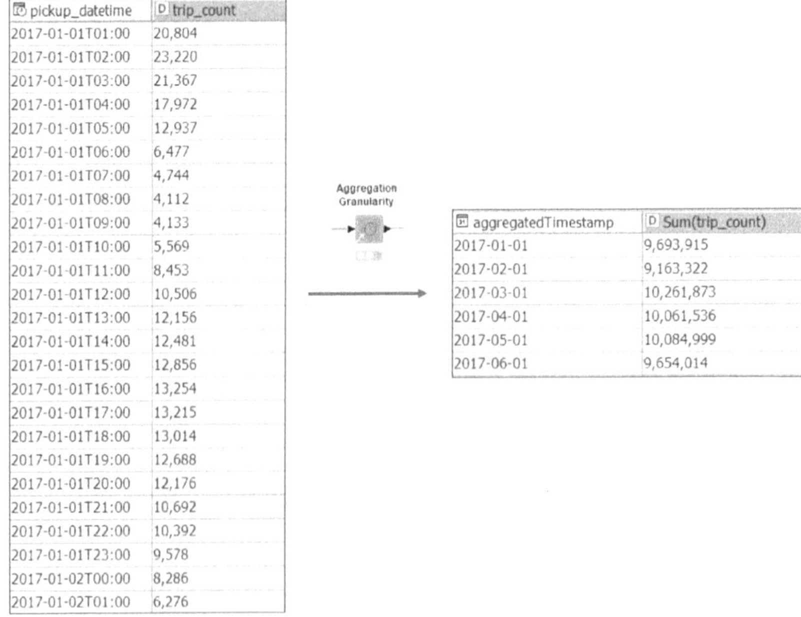

| pickup_datetime | trip_count |
|---|---|
| 2017-01-01T01:00 | 20,804 |
| 2017-01-01T02:00 | 23,220 |
| 2017-01-01T03:00 | 21,367 |
| 2017-01-01T04:00 | 17,972 |
| 2017-01-01T05:00 | 12,937 |
| 2017-01-01T06:00 | 6,477 |
| 2017-01-01T07:00 | 4,744 |
| 2017-01-01T08:00 | 4,112 |
| 2017-01-01T09:00 | 4,133 |
| 2017-01-01T10:00 | 5,569 |
| 2017-01-01T11:00 | 8,453 |
| 2017-01-01T12:00 | 10,506 |
| 2017-01-01T13:00 | 12,156 |
| 2017-01-01T14:00 | 12,481 |
| 2017-01-01T15:00 | 12,856 |
| 2017-01-01T16:00 | 13,254 |
| 2017-01-01T17:00 | 13,215 |
| 2017-01-01T18:00 | 13,014 |
| 2017-01-01T19:00 | 12,688 |
| 2017-01-01T20:00 | 12,176 |
| 2017-01-01T21:00 | 10,692 |
| 2017-01-01T22:00 | 10,392 |
| 2017-01-01T23:00 | 9,578 |
| 2017-01-02T00:00 | 8,286 |
| 2017-01-02T01:00 | 6,276 |



| aggregatedTimestamp | Sum(trip_count) |
|---|---|
| 2017-01-01 | 9,693,915 |
| 2017-02-01 | 9,163,322 |
| 2017-03-01 | 10,261,873 |
| 2017-04-01 | 10,061,536 |
| 2017-05-01 | 10,084,999 |
| 2017-06-01 | 9,654,014 |

Figure 3.2 – Performing time aggregation with the Aggregation Granularity component

This component's input table contains the hourly taxi trip counts of 6 days altogether. *Figure 3.2* shows the first 26 observations covering one day and the first 2 hours of the next day. The output table only contains six observations, as many as there are days in the input data, and shows the total trip count for each day.

In the example, in *Figure 3.2*, the selected granularity was **daily**, and the selected aggregation method was **sum**, but we could also calculate, for example, the average weekly trip count with the same component. The appropriate metric depends on the type of data and analysis purpose. For example, when aggregating sales values, summing up the single sales values produces the total sales value, which is a meaningful metric to analyze. Whereas when aggregating temperature values, calculating the average, maximum, or minimum produces a more meaningful metric than the total temperature.

Besides the date and time fields, we can also aggregate time series data by the number of data points within a time window. We will introduce this approach next.

### Aggregating time series by a moving window

Aggregating by a time window means including a *fixed number of subsequent observations* in the calculation of an aggregated value. The following formula shows the calculation of a forward simple **moving average**:

$$MA_i = \frac{1}{k}\sum_{t=(i-1)*k+1}^{i*k} x_t,$$

Formula 3.1

Here, $k$ is the window length, $t$ is the index of a single observation, and $i$ is the index of the aggregated value.

For example, we can use a window of $k=60$ subsequent values to calculate the moving average over 60 subsequent observations, such as 60 days or 60 seconds. Then, the first aggregated value ($i=1$) is calculated over the first 60 observations, the second ($i=2$) over the observations from 61 to 120, and so on.

Instead of the mean, we could also perform other calculations, such as the sum, over the time window. In general, this operation is called **moving aggregation**. Moving aggregation is useful to *smooth the data* and *provide a reference value* to replace missing values or check how the individual observations relate to a longer time average.

To illustrate this, *Figure 3.3* shows a line plot with daily signal amplitude values together with the moving average over 30 past observations:

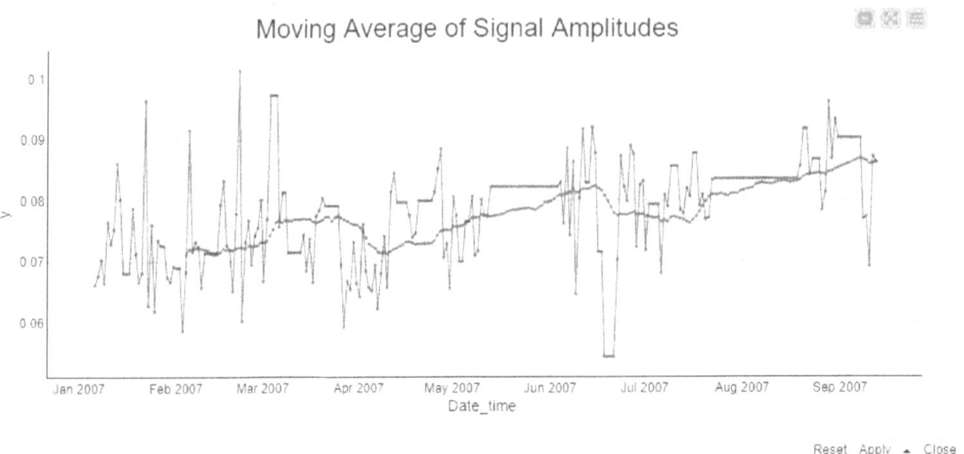


Figure 3.3 – A time series with signal amplitudes and its moving average

The moving average is shown by the *smoother* line that cuts the *fluctuating* line of the original signals. The moving average line shows movements up or down only if the original signals keep on a high or low level for a long time or if a single signal has an exceptionally high or low value.

You can calculate the moving average over a selected window length with the **Moving Average** node. *Figure 3.4* shows this node and its configuration dialog:

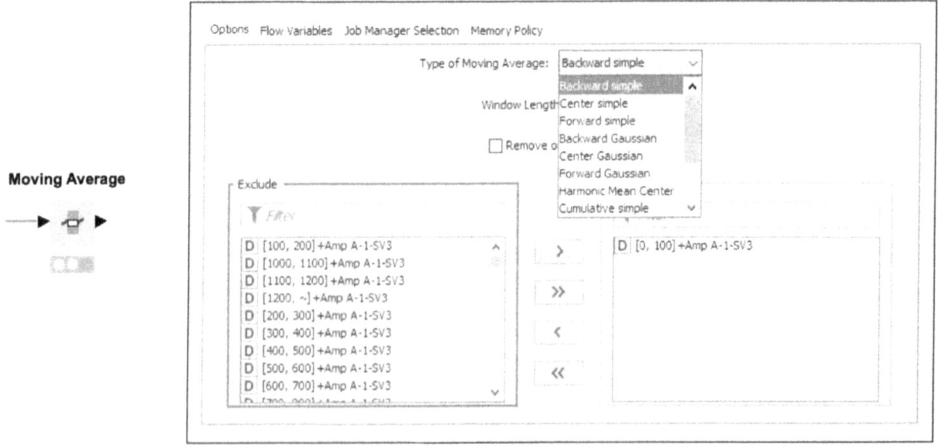


Figure 3.4 – Configuring the moving average node

In the configuration dialog of the **Moving Average** node, you can select between different methods of calculating the average. These methods differ in two ways. Firstly, whether you should calculate the aggregated value on past values, future values, or centered values. And secondly, whether you should weigh the data points differently depending on their position in the window. The **backward/center/forward simple** types consider all values in the window equally, while the **Gaussian** and **exponential** means give more weight to close observations. The **Harmonic mean** gives less weight to outliers.

> **Important Note**
>
> The formulas for calculating the different mean metrics are stated in the node description of the **Moving Average** node.

For aggregation methods, other than the average, you can use the **Moving Aggregation** node, as shown in the following screenshot:

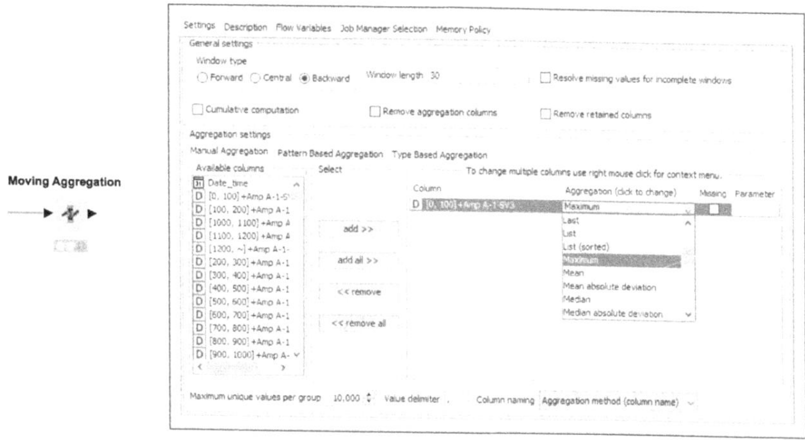


Figure 3.5 – Configuring the Moving Aggregation node

The preceding node can perform multiple aggregations at the same time over a window of a selected size that you can specify as a forward window, a central window, or a backward window. The available aggregation methods range from the sum, the minimum, and the maximum to the missing value count, variance, and many other functions. Also, this node allows you to perform a **cumulative calculation** by checking the **Cumulative computation** option.

In a cumulative computation of an aggregated metric, the window length is determined by the number of past values and is the same as the index of each observation. For example, the cumulative mean of the first value is the value itself. The cumulative mean of the second observation is the mean over the first two values, and so on. The cumulative mean of the last observation is the mean over all of the past data.

> **Important Note**
>
> You can calculate the *simple* moving average together with other aggregations using the Moving Aggregation node, but if you want to apply a different method, such as *backward Gaussian*, you'll need to use the Moving Average node.

After time aggregation, we move on to time alignment, which we will introduce next.

# Equal spacing and time alignment

In this section, we explain what an **equally spaced time series** is and show you how to make time series equally spaced by time alignment. We will cover these topics in the following subsections:

- Introducing the concept of equal spacing
- Performing time alignment for equally spaced time series

## Explaining the concept of equal spacing

An **equally spaced time series** has equal time intervals between the subsequent observations. For example, in daily data, equal spacing means that all days between the first day and the last day in the time series are present. This is often not the case in raw time series, where, for example, a holiday makes a gap in the daily sales data and a system breakdown impedes the sending of signals.

> **Important Note**
>
> The regular sampling intervals do not necessarily reflect regular intervals in terms of the physical time but can also be determined by, for example, trading days in stock market data.

Raw time series data can be *unevenly spaced by nature*, or gaps might be a *result of the data collection* procedure. For example, data unevenly spaced by nature could represent the visiting times of customers. If we instead follow a predetermined sampling frequency and collect, for example, daily electricity consumption data from smart meters, we will produce equally spaced raw data with daily granularity. However, it might be that one day the smart meter breaks and fails to produce an entry until the next day, which produces a missing value in the otherwise equally spaced time series.

In the next subsection, we will first focus on how to time-align the regularly sampled data.

### Time aligning regularly sampled time series

Time aligning regularly sampled time series means introducing the missing timestamps in-between, for which we can use the **Timestamp Alignment** component. This component takes the time series data with missing values as input and produces an equally spaced time series as its output. *Figure 3.6* shows an example input and output of the component:

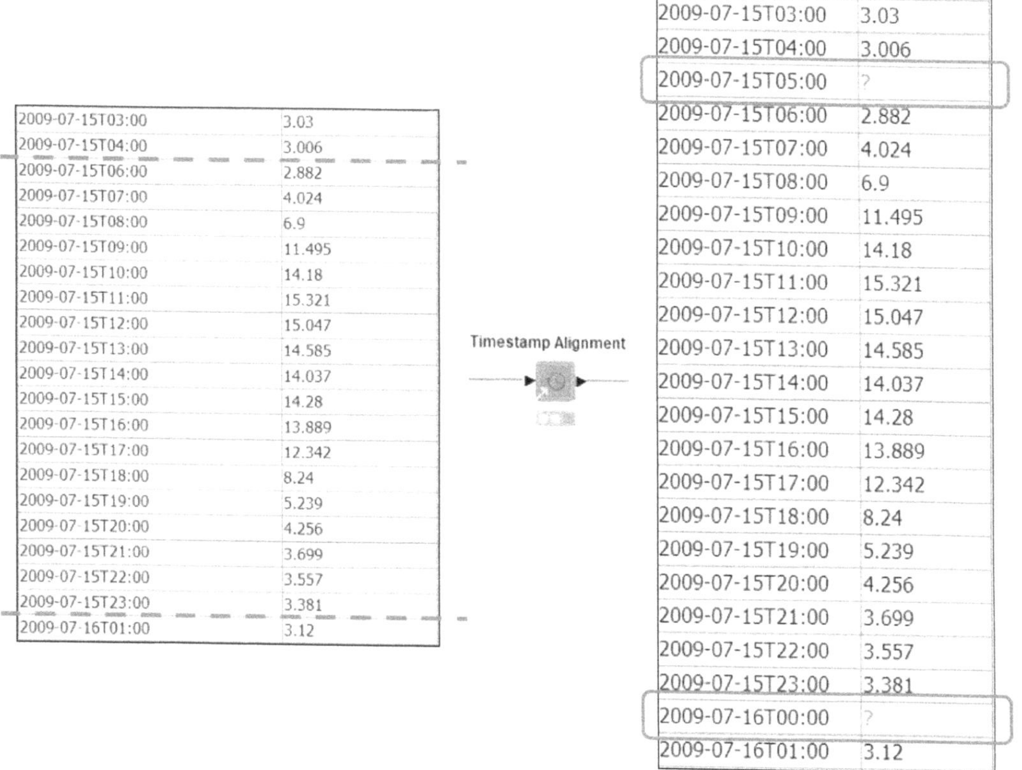

| | |
|---|---|
| 2009-07-15T03:00 | 3.03 |
| 2009-07-15T04:00 | 3.006 |
| 2009-07-15T06:00 | 2.882 |
| 2009-07-15T07:00 | 4.024 |
| 2009-07-15T08:00 | 6.9 |
| 2009-07-15T09:00 | 11.495 |
| 2009-07-15T10:00 | 14.18 |
| 2009-07-15T11:00 | 15.321 |
| 2009-07-15T12:00 | 15.047 |
| 2009-07-15T13:00 | 14.585 |
| 2009-07-15T14:00 | 14.037 |
| 2009-07-15T15:00 | 14.28 |
| 2009-07-15T16:00 | 13.889 |
| 2009-07-15T17:00 | 12.342 |
| 2009-07-15T18:00 | 8.24 |
| 2009-07-15T19:00 | 5.239 |
| 2009-07-15T20:00 | 4.256 |
| 2009-07-15T21:00 | 3.699 |
| 2009-07-15T22:00 | 3.557 |
| 2009-07-15T23:00 | 3.381 |
| 2009-07-16T01:00 | 3.12 |



| | |
|---|---|
| 2009-07-15T03:00 | 3.03 |
| 2009-07-15T04:00 | 3.006 |
| 2009-07-15T05:00 | ? |
| 2009-07-15T06:00 | 2.882 |
| 2009-07-15T07:00 | 4.024 |
| 2009-07-15T08:00 | 6.9 |
| 2009-07-15T09:00 | 11.495 |
| 2009-07-15T10:00 | 14.18 |
| 2009-07-15T11:00 | 15.321 |
| 2009-07-15T12:00 | 15.047 |
| 2009-07-15T13:00 | 14.585 |
| 2009-07-15T14:00 | 14.037 |
| 2009-07-15T15:00 | 14.28 |
| 2009-07-15T16:00 | 13.889 |
| 2009-07-15T17:00 | 12.342 |
| 2009-07-15T18:00 | 8.24 |
| 2009-07-15T19:00 | 5.239 |
| 2009-07-15T20:00 | 4.256 |
| 2009-07-15T21:00 | 3.699 |
| 2009-07-15T22:00 | 3.557 |
| 2009-07-15T23:00 | 3.381 |
| 2009-07-16T00:00 | ? |
| 2009-07-16T01:00 | 3.12 |

Figure 3.6 – Introducing missing timestamps in time series with the Timestamp Alignment component

The input data contains hourly electricity consumption values. The dashed lines point to hours where the measurements are missing, for example, the 05:00 hour of July 15th in 2009 and the 00:00 hour of July 16th. The **Timestamp Alignment** component introduces these missing values into the output data and fills the numeric column with missing values for these rows, as highlighted in the table on the right-hand side. The only thing we need to configure in the component is to define the granularity of the time series, which, in this case, is **hour**.

> **Important Note**
>
> This component only introduces the missing values in between the data and does not introduce the missing hours from the beginning of the first day nor the end of the last day.

Next, we'll introduce techniques for time aligning irregularly sampled time series.

### *Time aligning irregularly sampled time series*

The time alignment of irregularly sampled time series is possible via **time aggregation**. If we are dealing with event-based data with arbitrary timestamps, first, we can extract a *time* field from the timestamps. However, at that point, we will have multiple values for the same timestamp; hour for example. Therefore, second, we will need to aggregate them into one value by timestamp.

Time aggregation can also be used to *synchronize time series* that are reported at different timestamps. For example, if we have two sensors that produce data minute-by-minute, one every 13th second of a minute and one every 28th second, then we can take the most granular time field that represents both signals—which, in this case, is minute—and report the signals' values at the same timestamp.

Notice that the time alignment by introducing the gaps and by synchronizing two timestamps does not discard any numeric values. Instead, as shown in *Figure 3.6*, the time alignment enriches the data by introducing the missing timestamps. Only in the time alignment of event-based data do we decrease the granularity and aggregate the signal values and, thus, lose the information of the original timestamps and values of the single entries.

To complete the data preprocessing, we handle the missing values, which we will introduce next.

# Missing value imputation

In this section, we will show you how to impute the missing values in the numeric column. Missing values might exist in the raw data, or they can be introduced in the data during the time alignment. We will introduce the **missing value imputation** in the following subsections:

- Defining different types of missing values
- Introducing missing value imputation techniques

First, we will investigate the different types of missing values.

## Defining the different types of missing values

In KNIME, you can recognize a missing value from a *red question mark* in the data. Furthermore, many nodes, such as the line plot for visualizing time series, provide the option to either remove the missing values or leave them in before performing their tasks. Also, you can inspect the number of missing values in the data in the **No. Missing** column in the output view of the **Statistics** node:

Numeric | Nominal | Top/bottom

| Column | Min | Mean | Median | Max | Std. Dev. | Skewness | Kurtosis | No. Missing | No. +∞ | No. -∞ | Histogram |
|---|---|---|---|---|---|---|---|---|---|---|---|
| cluster_26 | 2.4576 | 7.2032 | ? | 23.2739 | 4.9938 | 1.1176 | -0.1194 | 644 | 0 | 0 | 2 |

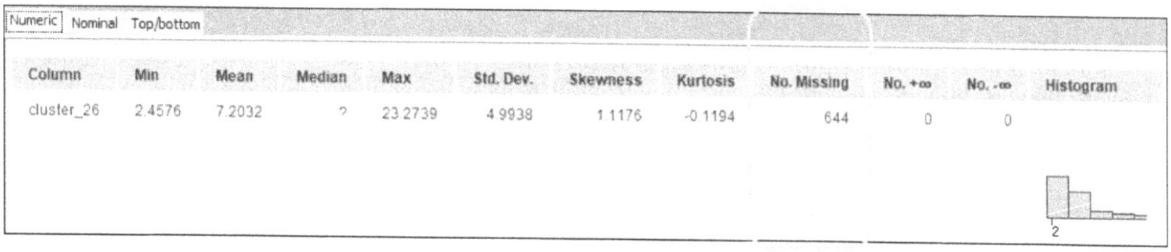

Figure 3.7 – Displaying the number of missing values in the output view of the statistics node

The output view of the statistics node shows the number of missing values in the input column along with other statistical metrics and a histogram of the data.

The missing values can have one of the following three types depending on how the missing values are introduced into the data:

- **Missing completely at random**
- **Missing at random**
- **Not missing at random**

These three types of missing values can appear in the same data. Using the electricity consumption data as an example, a completely random missing value could appear due to the accidental deletion of a data row in the data wrangling process. A random missing value could appear due to a power outage, which is related to an exogenous variable such as temperature, but not the electricity consumption values themselves. A non-random missing value could occur if the smart meter did not produce data until a certain threshold for electricity consumption was exceeded.

Additionally, the type of the missing value determines the appropriate imputation technique. In the next subsection, we will introduce different missing value imputation techniques and show you how to perform them in KNIME Analytics Platform.

## Introducing missing value imputation techniques

In this subsection, we will introduce the techniques for handling missing values in time series. Because each missing value has a time index in time series data, deleting the rows is not an option. Instead, the best approximation of the missing value is often one of the following:

- An **existing value**, such as the previous value or a fixed value
- A **statistical value**, such as the column mean
- A **predicted value**, such as an in-sample forecast

Each of these approaches covers multiple strategies. The following is a list of some common strategies for time series and example use cases:

- **Previous/next value**: A daily temperature value is missing and can be approximated by the temperature of the day before/after.
- **Seasonal lag**: The sales value of a Saturday is missing, and it is estimated by the sales value from the Saturday of the previous week, that is, by the past value at lag seven.
- **Fixed value**: A product was not on the market yet and could not generate any sales. The sales value is set to `0`.
- **Linear interpolation**: The number of customers is missing for one day and is estimated by the average of the previous day's and the next day's customer count.
- **Moving average**: This estimates the irregular dynamics of IoT data.
- **In-sample forecasting**: This replaces missing values in stationary training data for better forecasting performance.

In most cases, the **Missing Value** node is all you need for missing value handling. The node can perform the missing value imputation by either the column type or the column name. The selected strategy by column name will overwrite the strategy set by the column type. *Figure 3.8* shows the corresponding tabs in the configuration dialog of the **Missing Value** node:

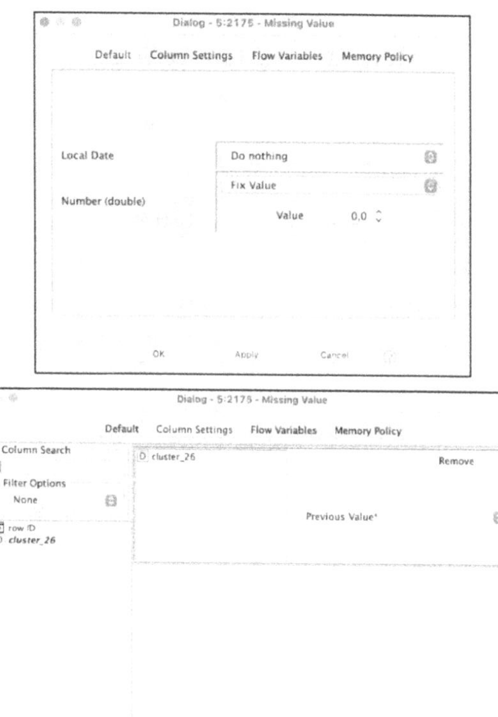


Figure 3.8 – Defining the missing value handling in the Missing Value node

The available missing value replacements are either fixed or statistical values. Some of the most common strategies for time series data are listed as follows:

- **Mean**
- **Previous Value**
- **Next Value**

- **Linear Interpolation**
- **Fixed value** such as 0

The **Missing Value** node outputs the data with missing values handled accordingly. Furthermore, the node produces the **transformation model** in its **Predictive Model Markup Language (PMML)** model output. Via this model output, the same missing value handling can be applied to new data, for example, the test set, using the same transformation strategy as in the training data. The node to apply the transformation is called **Missing Value (Apply)**.

> **Important Note**
> PMML is a format for interchanging predictive and statistical models between applications.

Finding the best missing value imputation strategy comes down to, first, knowing the type of the missing value, and second, knowing the data source to find the best approximation of it. Beyond the **Missing Value** node, the predictor nodes of forecasting algorithms and the **Moving Average** node can also be used for missing value imputation. Also, it is possible to train the same model on multiple training sets, each one with a different missing value handling strategy, and check which one performs the best on the test data.

## Summary

In this chapter, we introduced common sources of time series data and given examples of the different types of time series that they generate. We introduced time aggregation, time alignment, and missing value handling as common preprocessing steps of time series data. Also, we demonstrated how to perform these preprocessing steps in KNIME Analytics Platform.

These preprocessing steps shape the raw time series data from various sources to fulfill the requirements of classic time series analysis methods, create insightful visualizations, and perform efficient and unbiased analysis. As you continue reading this book, you will realize that we refer to the preprocessing steps introduced here frequently. And when you start building your own time series analysis applications, you will likely start with the steps explained in this chapter.

If you're interested in a workflow example of the preprocessing techniques, you can look at an example workflow on the KNIME Hub (which is accessible via `https://kni.me/w/Ae0lo0oIiFtWZWxO`) that cleans and explores the energy consumption data.

In the next chapter, *Time Series Visualization*, you will learn how to discover different characteristics of time series visually.

# Questions

1. What is time granularity?

   A. The time interval between subsequent observations

   B. The number of missing values in time series data

   C. The number of single entries in time series data

   D. The length of a seasonal pattern

2. Which of the following is *not* a purpose of time aggregating data?

   A. To discard redundant information

   B. To discover patterns of interest

   C. To reduce the size of the data

   D. To replace missing values not missing at random

3. How many observations do you get if you time-align daily data from February 1 to January 1?

   A. Less than 365

   B. More than 365

   C. 365

4. Which of the following missing values is *not missing at random*?

   A. Sales data is missing on December 25.

   B. Website traffic data is missing because a log file has been overwritten accidentally.

   C. Temperature data is missing because the thermometer breaks at minus temperatures.

   D. Sales data is missing because the online shop was temporarily closed.

# 4
# Time Series Visualization

In a time series analysis application, visualization often follows data preprocessing, which we introduced in the previous chapter. Data preprocessing cleans the data and puts it into the right size and level of detail for effective visualization and modeling.

This chapter is dedicated to **time series visualization** to see the kind of time series we are dealing with. It will provide an exploration of the most common visualization techniques to visually represent and display time series data: from a classic line plot to a lag plot; from a seasonal plot to a box plot.

By visualizing time series, we can gain first insights into the data and the analytical problem and increase its *accessibility* and *understandability*. Visual data exploration of time series can thus be the goal of the analysis, or it can justify further preprocessing steps and selected analysis methods.

In this chapter, we will introduce visualization techniques on energy consumption data in the following sections:

- Introducing an energy consumption time series
- Introducing line plots
- Introducing lag plots
- Introducing seasonal plots
- Introducing box plots

The thorough explanation of the different visualization techniques in this chapter will help you to gain essential insights from time series visualizations. You will also learn which visualization to look at to obtain the desired information. Finally, you will also learn how to build these visualizations in KNIME Analytics Platform.

## Technical requirements

The workflow that creates the visualizations introduced in this chapter is available on KNIME Hub at `https://kni.me/w/8geg5u6HpiDC4YGi` and on GitHub at `https://github.com/PacktPublishing/Codeless-Time-Series-Analysis-with-KNIME/tree/main/Chapter04`.

## Introducing an energy consumption time series

In this section, we'll introduce the energy consumption time series that we'll use to demonstrate visualization techniques of time series data. The data is characterized by seasonal patterns and autocorrelation, about which the line plot, lag plot, seasonal plot, and box plot show different details.

The regular behavior of the time series is exposed to the raw energy consumption data by preprocessing and clustering it, as we'll explain in the following subsections.

### Describing raw energy consumption data

The raw energy consumption data originates from 6,000 households and businesses in Ireland, and it was collected by smart meters that record energy consumption every *half an hour* in **kilowatts** (**kW**) between July 2009 and August 2010. The original data contains three columns: a timestamp, an **identifier** (**ID**) of the household, and the energy consumption.

Since the data was collected from very different buildings—including homes, offices, commercial stores, and so on—we'll split the time series into clusters that contain buildings that behave very similarly in terms of their energy consumption. In the end, we'll only need to analyze one time series representing the cluster center (the average of the smart meter data in the cluster) instead of multiple time series produced by individual smart meters.

In the next subsection, we'll describe the clustering procedure.

### Clustering energy consumption data

We cluster the time series of energy consumption from individual smart meters through the **k-means clustering** algorithm, which creates *convex-shaped* clusters of similar size based on the *Euclidean distance* in a feature space of numeric columns. The number of clusters must be defined beforehand, and we set it to `30`.

> **Important Note**
>
> A convex shape does not have inside curvatures larger than 180°; for example, the maximum inside curvature of a square is 90°, and it is a convex shape. Instead, the inside curvatures of a star are greater than 180°, and it is a non-convex (concave) shape.

The input columns to the algorithm are generated from the original time series by calculating the following **key performance indicators** (**KPIs**):

- Percentage energy consumption on each weekday versus the week in total
- Percentage energy consumption within a day segment versus the day in total
- Average energy consumption within a day, month, week, hour, year, business day, and weekend, respectively
- Total energy consumption over the whole time period

Altogether, 42 columns (KPIs) were used for the clustering, and the number of clusters was set to 30. We expect this number of clusters to capture the most similarities among the buildings. The resulting clusters vary in their size from tens of buildings to several hundreds of buildings. Each cluster characterizes a type of building and its usage is based on, for example, how concentrated energy consumption is at certain parts of the day and how high total energy consumption is.

Out of the 30 clusters produced by the k-means algorithm, we will introduce the visualization techniques using *cluster 26* as an example. This cluster represents 83 buildings that are characterized by *high average daily and hourly energy consumption* and the *concentration of energy consumption values into business hours*, implying buildings for large businesses.

**Important Note**

The implementation of clustering is explained in detail in the white paper available at `https://www.knime.com/sites/default/files/inline-images/knime_bigdata_energy_timeseries_whitepaper.pdf`. The workflow for creating clustering columns is available on KNIME Hub at `https://kni.me/w/9pHnxeJUp8aueCJT`.

In the next section, we'll start the visual exploration of the data with a line plot.

## Introducing line plots

In this section, we will introduce a **line plot**, which is a widely used plot to display time series data. A line plot shows the observed values on the vertical axis (*y* axis) against time on the horizontal axis (*x* axis). The consecutive values are joined by straight lines to emphasize the continuity of the data over time and the chronological order of the observations.

In the following subsections, we will explain which characteristics of a time series a line plot can show and how to interpret a line plot. We will also show how to build a line plot in KNIME Analytics Platform.

## Displaying simple dynamics with a line plot

A line plot displays the entire sequence of a time series. It is especially useful for displaying simple dynamics in a time series, such as a trend or a seasonal pattern. The following screenshot shows the average hourly energy consumption within *cluster 26* in a line plot:

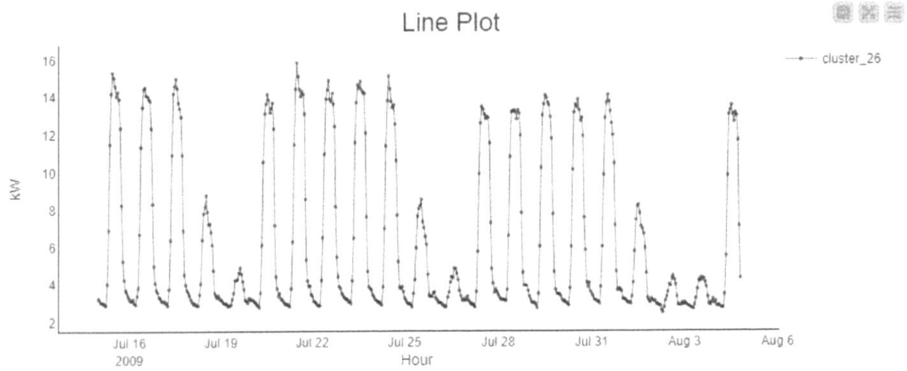


Figure 4.1 – Example of a line plot

The line plot shows each hour between July 15 and August 6 on the *x* axis and the hourly energy consumption values in kW on the *y* axis. The hourly values repeat similar values every 24 observations, which indicates *daily seasonality*. In addition, the daily pattern repeats itself with two low peaks and five high peaks, which indicates *weekly seasonality*. The data is highly regular because the seasonal cycles repeat almost identically from day to day and week to week. Within a short time period, the data doesn't show any trend.

A line plot is also useful to compare multiple time series, such as clusters of large versus small businesses, original versus smoothed values, or actual values versus the trend line. A line plot is thus useful to compare relationships *between* time series, while many other visualizations of time series compare relationships *within* time series. A line plot is often used as the *first visualization of the time series*, and after that, the data exploration is elaborated with other techniques based on the insights from the line plot.

In the next subsection, we will introduce in detail the characteristics of a time series that a line plot can display.

## Interpreting the dynamics of a time series based on a line plot

A line plot reveals the long-term behavior of the time series, indicates the quality of the data, and points to exceptional events that we should handle or investigate further. Here, we name and explain the characteristics that you can possibly find in a line plot:

- **Trend**: A trend refers to values that decrease or increase over time. A trend can be linear, with a constant rate, or non-linear, such as exponential.
- **Seasonal patterns**: Seasonal patterns show as regularly repeating peaks and lows in the line plot. The range of the *x* axis must be large enough to cover multiple seasonal cycles and, further, confirm that the pattern is repeating.
- **Long-term cycle**: A long-term cycle can only be visible in a line plot if it covers a long period of time. It shows a repeating pattern with a long seasonal cycle.
- **Sharp changes**: Sharp changes indicate events that change behavior at once—for example, when a pandemic reduces traffic dramatically.
- **Gaps**: Gaps result from (a series of) missing values in the time series. These might be interesting, such as—for example—indicating the period when a smart meter was broken. If values should be replaced, a line plot can help to determine the best replacement of a missing value.
- **Outliers**: Outliers are exceptionally high or low values on the *y* axis and thus deviations from regular dynamics. Detecting and handling outliers is required for an accurate analysis. Outliers might also be the actual values of the analysis that you're interested in to detect—for example—signs of a deteriorating rotor in mechanical maintenance.
- **Turning points**: Turning points indicate the change of a trend in the time series—for example, when a new competitor enters the market.

Just as an example, we show in the following screenshot a line plot with some of these characteristics, visualizing **fast Fourier transform** (**FFT**) amplitude values from a sensor monitoring a rotor:

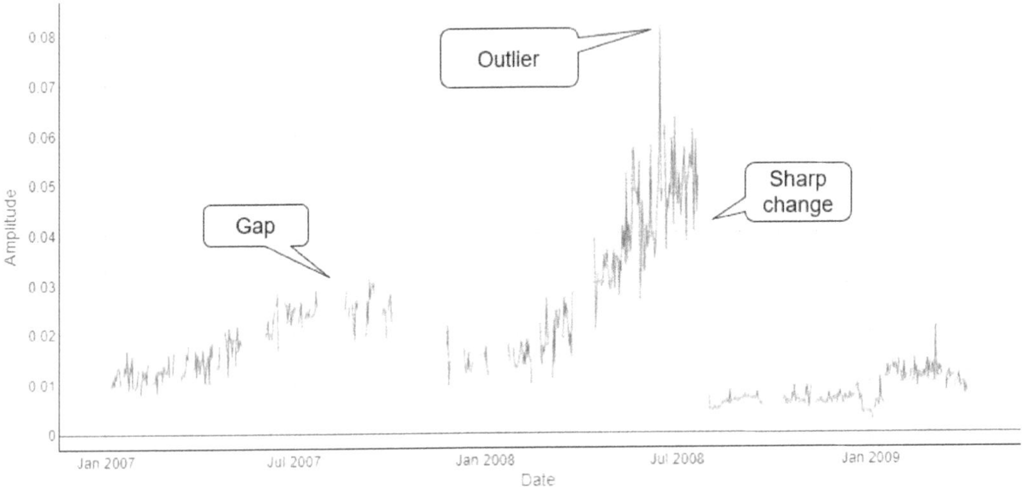


Figure 4.2 – Characteristics of time series in a line plot

The line plot shows a sharp change in July 2008, indicating the time when the rotor breaks. Before and after that event—with old and new rotor pieces—the amplitude values are considerably different. Furthermore, every now and then, the line plot shows a gap, which indicates a missing signal value. Finally, the line plot shows *outliers* before the rotor breakdown when the amplitude values are exceptionally high. The line plot doesn't show a *trend* or *seasonal pattern*.

In the next subsection, we will see how to build a line plot in KNIME.

## Building a line plot in KNIME

You can build a line plot in KNIME with the **Line Plot** and **Line Plot (Plotly)** nodes, which create line plots in an interactive view. In this subsection, we will see the configuration of the Line Plot (Plotly) node, which generates an interactive view based on the **Plotly JavaScript** graphing library.

In the next subsection, we'll first show how to configure axis columns.

### *Configuring axis columns*

The required configuration of a line plot is to define *x*-axis and *y*-axis columns. The following screenshot shows these options in the configuration dialog of the Line Plot (Plotly) node:

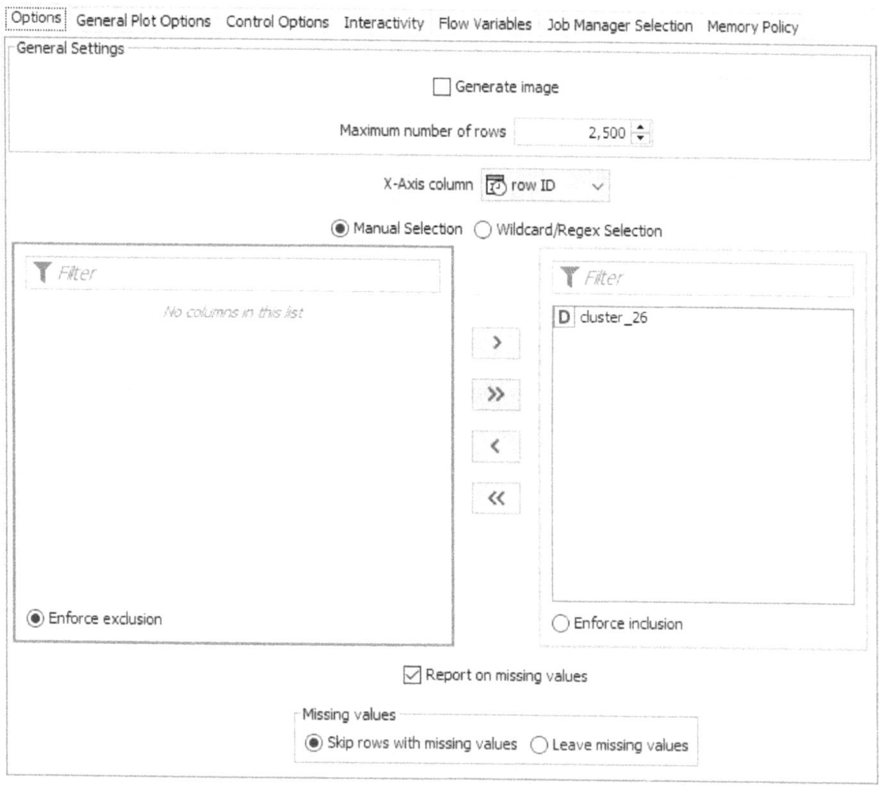


Figure 4.3 – Configuring axis columns in the Line Plot (Plotly) node

Axis columns are defined in the **Options** tab of the configuration dialog. Next, we explain these and the optional settings in this tab, as follows:

- **Maximum number of rows**: This setting determines how many single values are shown in the line plot, starting from the top of the input table. By default, only the first **2,500** rows will be shown. If the table contains more observations, the number must be updated; otherwise, the remaining rows will be discarded. Notice that increasing the maximum number of rows might slow down the execution time and is often not necessary.
- **X-Axis column**: This setting shows a drop-down menu to select a timestamp column, which can be a timestamp in the dedicated **Date&Time** column type, or for example, the **row ID** column.
- **The exclude-include framework**: This setting shows all numeric columns in the input data. By default, they appear in one of the two panels. The columns in the include panel are the columns selected for the line plot. These columns should have the same range because the *y* axis will have only one range that is automatically adjusted according to the columns' domains.

- **Missing values**: Via the radio buttons, you can select how to handle missing values in the data. The possible options are connecting the available data points with a straight line (the **Skip rows with missing values** option) and introducing them as gaps in the line plot (the **Leave missing values** option).

The output line plot will look like the line plots shown in *Figure 4.1* and *Figure 4.2*. However, as you can see, a line plot also has a title, axis labels, grid lines, and other visual properties. In the next subsection, we will see how to configure the visual appearance of a line plot.

### Configuring the visual appearance of a line plot

The configuration dialog of the Line Plot (Plotly) node contains the **General Plot Options** and **Control Options** tabs to—firstly—change the *visual appearance* of the line plot and—secondly—disable or enable the *reconfiguration* of the line plot in the interactive view.

The following screenshot shows the settings in the **General Plot Options** tab of the Line Plot (Plotly) node:

Figure 4.4 – Defining additional settings in the General Plot Options tab

In the three fields at the top, you can write a custom title and axis labels. By default, the column headers of the axis columns will be used as axis labels.

At the bottom of the tab, you can decide whether you want to display a legend and show horizontal and vertical grid lines in the line plot. You can also define the following color options:

- **Data color**, which is the color of the dots connected in the line plot. Notice that this setting only applies if you check the **Override colors** checkbox.
- **Background color**, which is the area outside the axes.
- **Data area color**, which is the area inside the axes.
- **Grid color**, which is the color of the grid lines.

The image settings in the middle will only apply if you want to produce a line plot as a static image in the image output port of the node.

Next, the following screenshot shows the settings in the **Control Options** tab to enable and disable interactivity in the view:

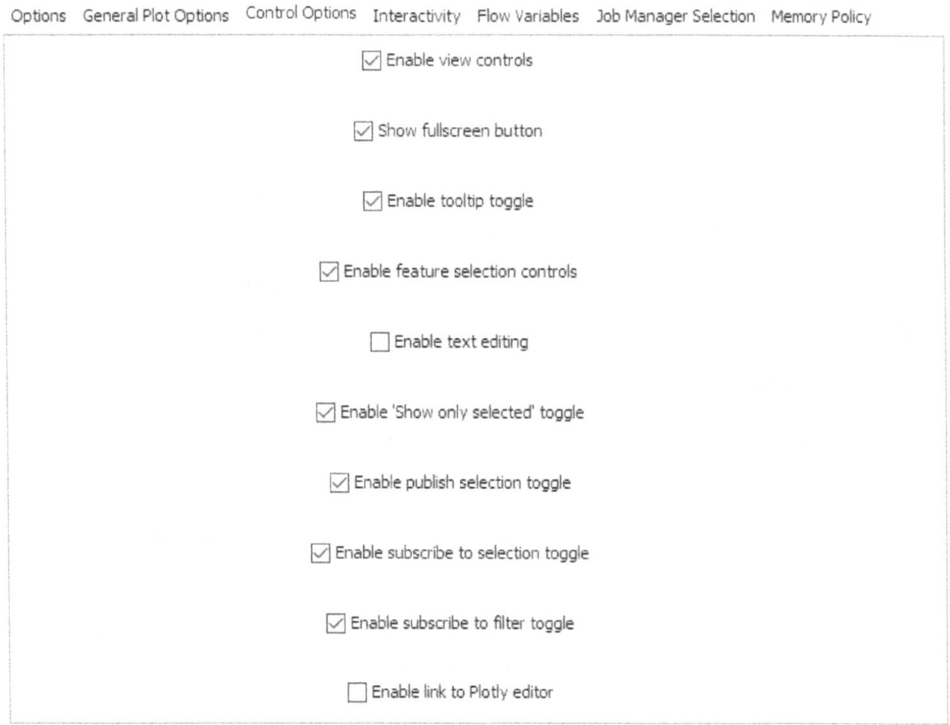


Figure 4.5 – Defining interactivity options in the Control Options tab

The topmost setting, **Enable view controls**, enables all interactivity in the view. Furthermore, you can enable individual interactivity options by using the checkboxes below this—for example, checking the **Enable feature selection controls** box enables you to change the *x*-axis and *y*-axis columns directly in the view. Checking the **Enable text editing** box allows you to change the title and axis labels directly in the view.

For the line plot shown in the following screenshot, we illustrate how the settings introduced in this subsection appear in the interactive view:

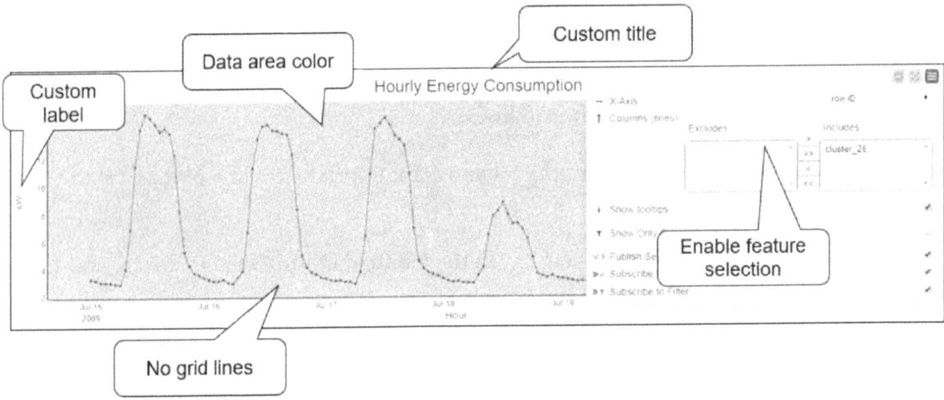


Figure 4.6 – Interactivity options in the interactive line plot view

The view reflects the following custom settings:

- Custom data area color (*light gray*) and no grid lines
- Custom y-axis label (**kW**), which can be edited by double-clicking the label
- Custom title (**Hourly Energy Consumption**), which can be edited by double-clicking the label
- Menu for changing the axis columns in the top-right corner

All the actions that we apply in the menu will change the view immediately. However, if you want to apply edits until the next reset of the node, you need to click **Apply** in the bottom-right corner before you close the view and select **Apply settings temporarily** in the dialog that opens. If you want to apply edits in the view as a new default, then select **Apply settings as new default** in that dialog.

In this section, we introduced line plots as a common visualization technique of time series data and explained the configuration options to build an interactive line plot in KNIME. The interactivity options are similar in the other views that we introduce in the following sections.

In the next section, we explain how to visually explore time series data in a lag plot.

# Introducing lag plots

A **lag plot** is a scatter plot showing currently observed values on the *y* axis versus their lagged values on the *x* axis.

While the scatter plot is a **bivariate analysis** of two numeric variables, it is also possible to add color to the dots in a scatter plot to represent a third—numeric or nominal—variable. The most common lag plot shows the values at lag 1, which is also called a **first-order lag plot**.

In the following subsections, we will explain the insights and usage of a lag plot and see how to build a lag plot in KNIME.

## Introducing insights derived from a lag plot

A lag plot shows the persistence of values at the selected lag: the more concentrated the data points on the diagonal of the scatter plot are, the stronger the **autocorrelation** at the selected lag. If the data points are concentrated above the diagonal, the lagged values are lower than the current value, and if they are concentrated below the diagonal, the lagged values are higher than the current values. Because a lag plot compares current and lagged values of the same time series, it is used to analyze *within* time series relationships.

The following screenshot shows a lag plot between energy consumption in the current hour (*y* axis) and energy consumption in the previous hour (*x* axis):

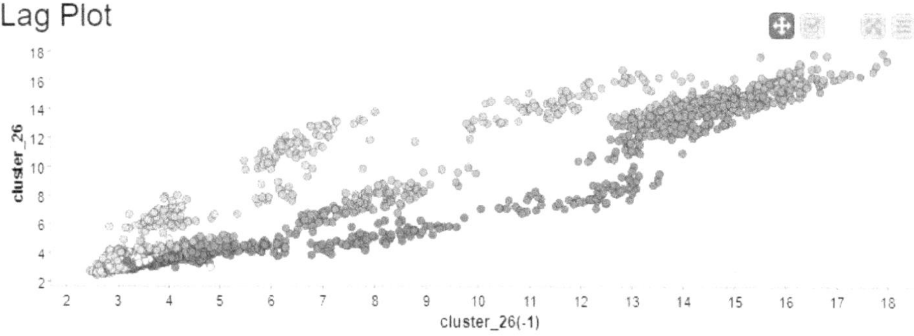


Figure 4.7 – Lag plot displaying the relationship between energy consumption in the current versus the previous hour

The energy consumption depicted here shows strong positive autocorrelation between the current and lagged values because the observations appear close to the diagonal. However, the observations appear in groupings and are not equally distributed along the diagonal. Therefore, we have colored the dots based on the hour of the day—*light gray dots* corresponding to the early morning hours and *dark gray dots* corresponding to the late evening hours. The color-coding shows that in the morning, the values increase hour by hour, as shown by the lighter dots above the diagonal. In the evening, the values decrease hour by hour, as shown by the darker dots below the diagonal.

To summarize, a lag plot provides the following insights:

- Shows whether the autocorrelation is different in groups defined by a third feature
- Shows model fit of an **autoregressive** (**AR**) model
- Shows the level of randomness between past and current values

In the next subsection, we will show you how to build a lag plot in KNIME.

## Building a lag plot in KNIME

You can build an interactive lag plot with the **Scatter Plot** node and use the **Lag Column** node to create a column with past values at the selected lag. If you want, you can add a third feature to the lag plot by color-coding the data points with the **Color Manager** node.

In the next subsection, we show you how to configure the Scatter Plot node.

### *Configuring the Scatter Plot node*

The Scatter Plot node displays a scatter plot based on the pairs of values in two numeric columns that make the *x* and *y* axes. In the case of a lag plot, these values are current and past values created with the Lag Column node.

The following screenshot shows the configuration dialog of the Scatter Plot node:

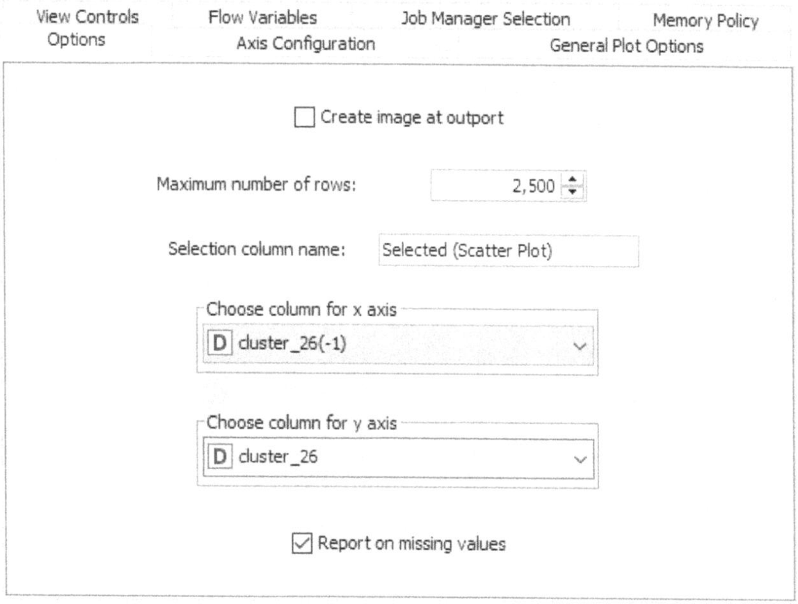

Figure 4.8 – Configuring the Scatter Plot node to build a lag plot

The **Options** tab of the configuration dialog shows the settings necessary to build a lag plot. These settings are the two drop-down menus shown in *Figure 4.8* to determine the *x*-axis and *y*-axis columns. Furthermore, you can define axis labels, title, colors, and other additional settings in the remaining tabs of the configuration dialog. These options are similar to configuring a line plot, as explained in the *Introducing line plots* section.

In the next subsection, we'll finish this section about lag plots by showing you how to configure the Color Manager node.

### *Introducing colors to a lag plot with the Color Manager node*

The **Color Manager** node introduces colors to data rows based on their value in a selected nominal or numeric column. The row colors then become visible in a view that displays individual observations, such as a scatter plot.

The following screenshot shows the configuration dialog of the Color Manager node:

Figure 4.9 – Assigning colors to rows with the Color Manager node

You can select a column whose values map colors in the drop-down menu under **Select one Column**. If the selected column is a **Nominal** column, then the color palettes below this activate. You can assign different colors to different nominal values, either automatically by selecting an entire palette or manually by clicking **Custom** and writing—for example—the **red, green, and blue** (**RGB**) codes of the colors. If you instead select a numeric column, such as **Hour** in *Figure 4.9*, you can define two colors that indicate the minimum and maximum of that column.

In this section, we introduced lag plots to inspect the relationship between current and past values. In the next section, we'll introduce seasonal plots to inspect the relationships between seasonal patterns over time.

# Introducing seasonal plots

A **seasonal plot** is a line plot with a separate line for each **seasonal cycle**. For example, for data with daily seasonality, a seasonal plot can show daily seasonal cycles in parallel in different weeks, months, or years.

In the following subsections, we will introduce insights you can gain from a seasonal plot and show how you can build a seasonal plot in KNIME.

## Comparing seasonal patterns in a seasonal plot

Since a seasonal plot compares different seasonal cycles that follow each other in the same time series, this visualization technique compares relationships *within* the time series.

In a seasonal plot, you can see the seasonality as a *collection of similarly behaving lines* over a single seasonal cycle. The *x* axis shows the progression of the seasonal cycle—for example, from hour 0 to hour 24—while the *y* axis shows aggregated values by units within the seasonal cycle.

The following screenshot shows an example seasonal plot with 24 hours of a day on the *x* axis and average energy consumption by hour on the *y* axis:

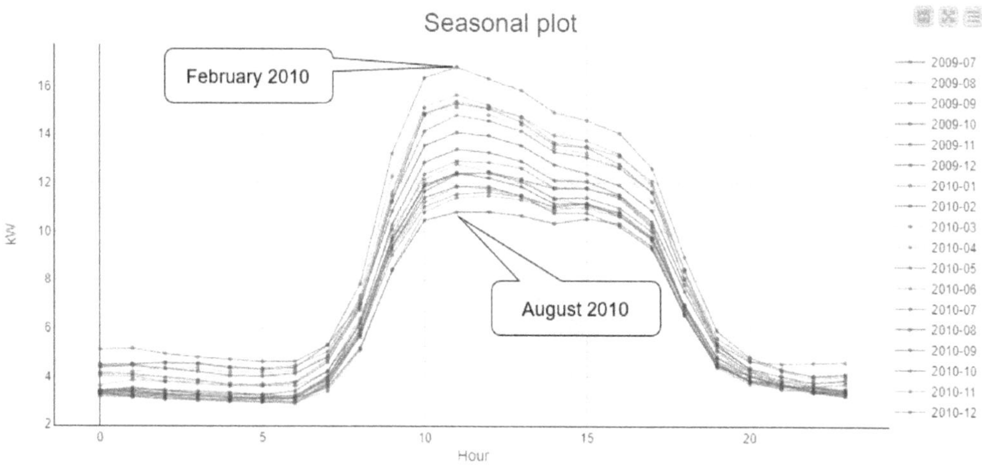


Figure 4.10 – Comparing daily seasonality in different months in a seasonal plot

The lines for each month follow the same pattern where energy consumption increases toward noon and afternoon and decreases toward evening and night, as is the daily seasonal pattern. However, as highlighted in *Figure 4.10*, the daily maximum values are much higher in February and other winter months compared to August and other summer months. This could be due to holidays and reduced use of office buildings in the summer and colder outside temperatures and increased heating in the winter.

In the next subsection, we will show you how to build a seasonal plot in KNIME.

## Building a seasonal plot in KNIME

In KNIME, you can build a seasonal plot with the **Pivoting** and **Line Plot** nodes. The Pivoting node is needed to transform the time series into a data table with the units in the single seasonal cycle as row IDs, the compared time periods as column headers, and the aggregated values as cell values. For example, to build the seasonal plot shown in *Figure 4.10*, we have transformed the time series into a pivot table with hours 0-23 as row IDs, months from **2009-07** to **2020-12** as column headers, and average energy consumption values by hour and month as cell values.

Besides a line plot, we can also build a radar plot that shows the single seasonal cycle as a circle rather than a horizontal line. In that case, we use the **Radar Plot (Plotly)** node, which creates a radar plot, shown as follows:

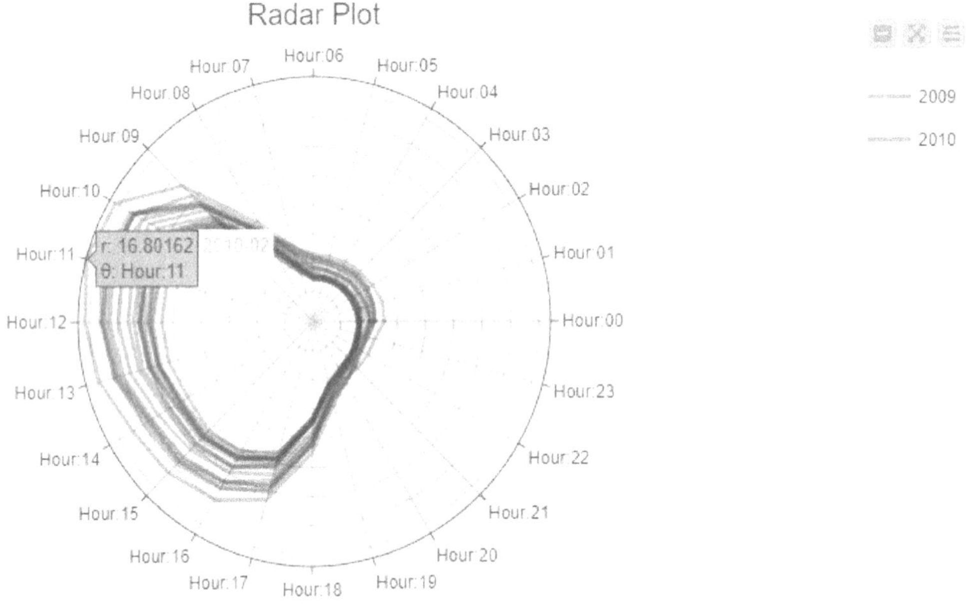


Figure 4.11 – Comparing seasonality in a radar plot

The radar plot shows all hours within a daily seasonal cycle as **spokes** starting from the middle of the radar plot. The energy consumption values are then shown by the position of the lines at the spokes around the circle. The radar plot in *Figure 4.11* reaches the farthest point from the center at **Hour: 10** and **Hour: 11** because energy consumption is the highest in the middle of a business day. We also compare seasonal cycles between months by showing multiple lines in the radar plot. The line for February reaches the farthest from the center, as shown by the annotation. Finally, we also group lines by a third feature—the year—and show only a subset of lines at a time.

When building a radar plot, each row in the input table will make a line and each selected column will make a spoke in the radar plot. In our case, these lines will correspond to separate months and the spokes will correspond to hours of the day. Thus, we create a pivot table with the months as the row IDs, the hours as the column headers, and the aggregated energy consumption values as the cell values. After that, we configure the Radar Plot (Plotly) node, as shown in the following screenshot:

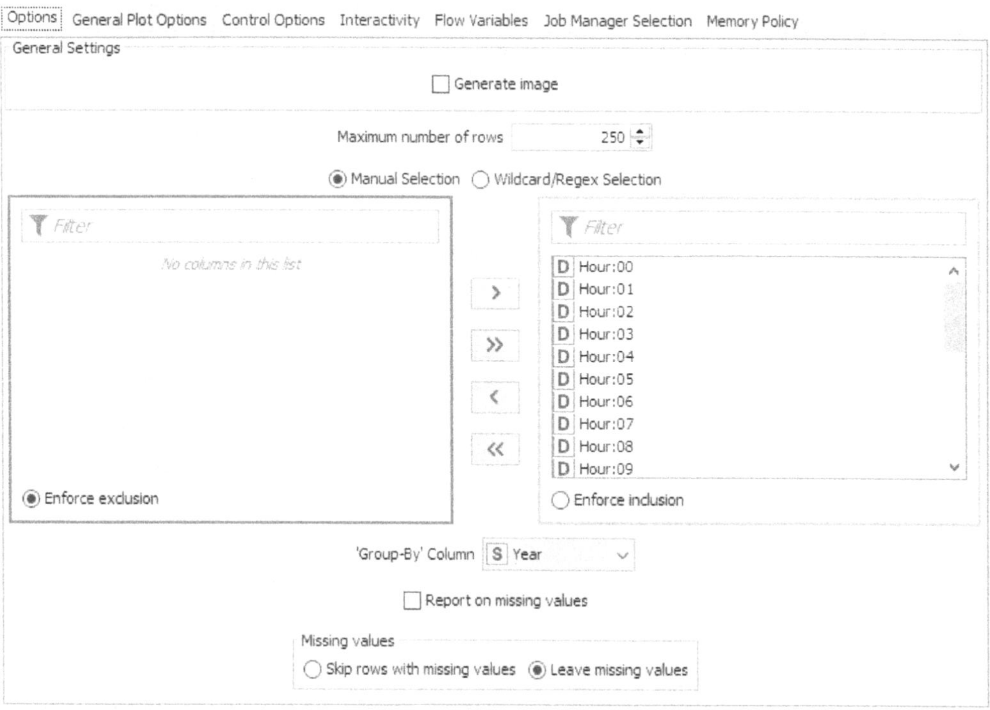


Figure 4.12 – Configuring the Radar Plot (Plotly) node

In the configuration dialog, we select hourly values in the include-exclude framework. In addition, we select **Year** for the **'Group-By' Column** field to be able to filter lines by the year value.

In this section, we introduced seasonal plots to compare seasonal cycles through a time series. In the next section, we will introduce box plots to evaluate the variability of time series.

# Introducing box plots

A **box plot** shows the distribution of a numeric column without assuming any parametric distribution of the data. A parametric method would be—for example—the **z-score method**, which calculates how far in the tails of a **Gaussian distribution** a data point appears. A box plot instead reports **sample quantiles** of the data and shows the variability of the data relative to the range between the first and third quartiles. It is also possible to report variability by groups using a **conditional box plot**.

In the following subsections, we will explain how you can use a box plot to visually explore time series data and how you can build a (conditional) box plot in KNIME.

## Inspecting variability of data in a box plot

A box plot shows the first quartile (*Q1*), **median** (*Q2*), and third quartile (*Q3*) that make the box-plot body, and in addition, the **whiskers** that determine the range of normal variation. The upper whisker is calculated by adding to Q3 the length of the **interquartile range** (**IQR**) (*IQR=Q3 - Q1*) multiplied by a selected multiplier, often 1.5. The lower whisker is calculated by subtracting it from Q1. The following screenshot shows a box plot of hourly energy consumption data:

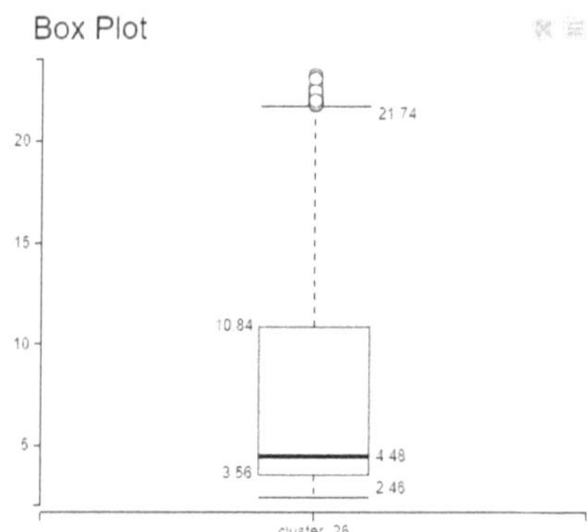


Figure 4.13 – A box plot showing the distribution of hourly energy consumption

The median energy consumption lies at **4.48** kW per hour, as indicated by the line in the middle of the box plot body. The first and third quartiles lie at **3.56** and **10.84**, respectively. Furthermore, there is not much variation below the first quantile because energy consumption cannot be negative. Thus, the lower whisker shows the minimum value in the data—in this case, **2.46**. Instead, the upper whisker is at **21.74**, which is the upper limit for normal fluctuation of hourly energy consumption. All energy consumption values above that are outliers, and their values are shown separately by the dots above the upper whisker.

A box plot shows the variability of data—in other words, how large the *range* between the minimum and maximum is, and how *dense* the data is. The narrower the box plot body, the more concentrated the data is around the median. Furthermore, the narrower the box plot body, the shorter the whiskers, and the less deviation from the median is considered normal. In addition, if the median is not in the middle of the box plot body, the data is not symmetric around the median, meaning that there is more variability upward than downward or vice versa.

A box plot has a few benefits as a visual exploration technique. Firstly, it takes less space compared to—for example—histograms, and secondly, a conditional box plot can illustrate variability within a time series. With a conditional box plot, you can—for example—compare medians through the months of a year and inspect yearly seasonality. The following screenshot illustrates this:

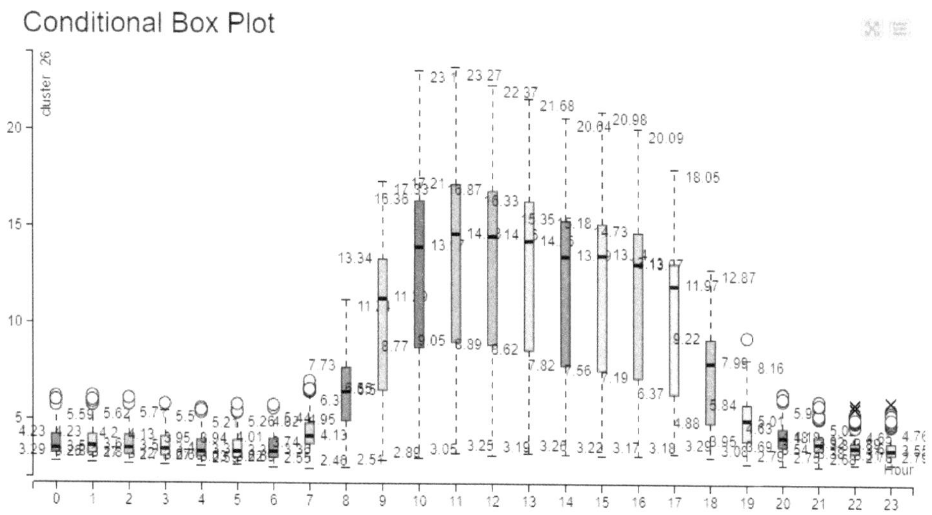


Figure 4.14 – Displaying variation within a seasonal cycle with a conditional box plot

The conditional box plot shown in *Figure 4.14* shows variation in energy consumption at different hours. The medians in the box plot are higher during working hours compared to evening and night hours. Furthermore, there is much more variability in energy consumption during working hours, as indicated by the wider box plot bodies at these hours. During working hours, the fluctuation also happens both upward and downward, while in the other hours, there is more fluctuation upward than downward. This conditional box plot also shows some outliers, which only occur during evening and night hours when the range of normal energy consumption is narrower.

In the next subsection, we will show how to build a (conditional) box plot in KNIME.

## Building a box plot in KNIME

To build a simple box plot, you can use the **Box Plot** node, and to build a conditional box plot, you use the **Conditional Box Plot** node. In the following screenshot, we show the configuration dialog of the Conditional Box Plot node:

Figure 4.15 – Configuring the Conditional Box Plot node

In the configuration dialog, the **Category Column** option determines the groups for which the box plot will be built separately. We have selected the **Hour** column to show one box plot per hour, as in *Figure 4.14*. In addition, in the include-exclude framework, you can select the numeric column that is shown in the box plot, which in our case is the **cluster_26** column.

The node's output—the interactive view, as shown in *Figure 4.14*—has the same interactivity options as explained in the *Introducing line plots* section. Also, notice that the configuration of the Box Plot node works much the same way, just without selecting **Category Column**, and it also produces an interactive view.

With the box plot, we have now finished our introduction to visual exploration techniques of time series. A (conditional) box plot complements line plots, lag plots, and seasonal plots by exploring how much variation there is in a time series and which extremes are reached at the peaks and lows of a seasonal cycle.

You can inspect all the visualizations introduced in this chapter via the *Additional Visualizations* workflow (available on KNIME Hub at `https://kni.me/w/8geg5u6HpiDC4YGi`) shown in the following screenshot:

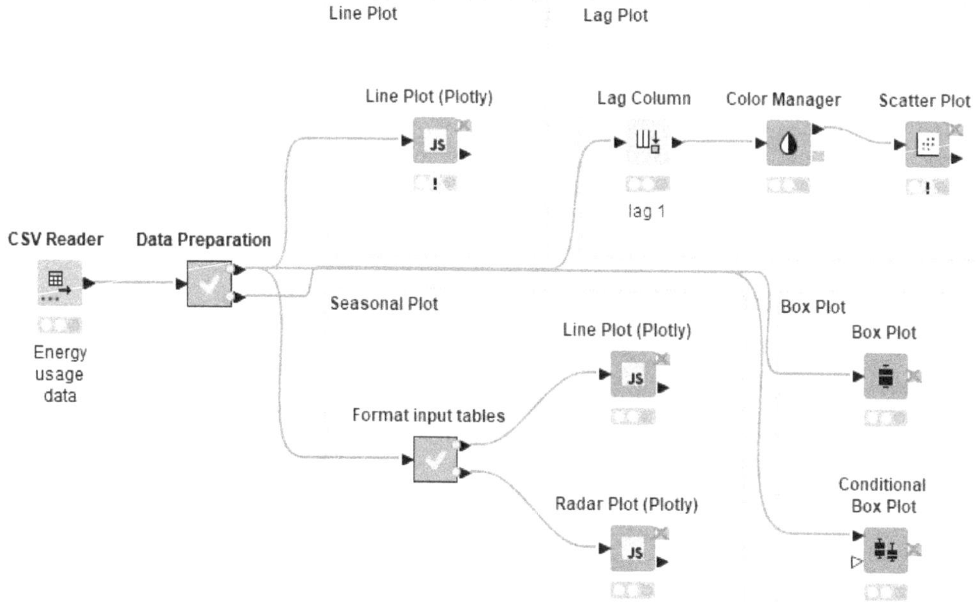


Figure 4.16 – Workflow implementing visual exploration techniques of time series

The workflow accesses the energy consumption data, preprocesses the data as required by the four visual exploration techniques introduced in this chapter, and finally creates visualizations—that is, a line plot, lag plot, seasonal plot, and box plot.

# Summary

In this chapter, we introduced popular techniques for the visual exploration of time series data. We started from a line plot, which shows simple dynamics of time series, and moved on to a lag plot to explore the relationship between past and current values. After that, we compared seasonal cycles in parallel in a seasonal plot, and finally, we inspected the variability of a time series in a box plot.

You learned how to interpret the dynamics in these plots and how they enrich your understanding of time series. You also learned how to implement these visualization techniques in KNIME Analytics Platform.

These visualizations appear in the data exploration phase of most time series analysis applications. You will need them to inspect whether the time series is periodic or shows a trend, to evaluate the model fit of an AR model, to obtain the best seasonal lag for prediction and missing value replacement, to assess the type of seasonality, and to visually evaluate the stationarity of data, just as a few examples.

In the next chapter, Chapter 5, *Time Series Components and Statistical Properties*, you will learn about the descriptive analysis of a time series by its statistical properties.

# Questions

1. How does the clustering of raw data contribute to a more insightful visual exploration of the data?

    A. It allows for displaying fewer data columns.

    B. It allows for displaying fewer data rows.

    C. It helps to detect outliers.

    D. It allows for modeling differently behaving time series at once.

2. Which of the following plots can compare relationships *between* different time series?

    A. Seasonal plot

    B. Box plot

    C. Line plot

    D. Lag plot

3. Which of the following plots can distinguish between a *multiplicative* or *additive* seasonality?

   A. Seasonal plot and lag plot

   B. Line plot and lag plot

   C. Line plot and seasonal plot

   D. Only line plot

# 5

# Time Series Components and Statistical Properties

In the introductory chapters, we defined some basic features of the Time Series and learned how to describe them graphically. Now, before going into the challenging methodologies used to build a real forecast based on algorithms of different types, it is necessary to cover some properties of Time Series in detail—properties that will be important to better apply and understand the forecasting models of the following chapters.

As you may have guessed in the previous pages of the book, learning to use data from a Time Series and, above all, creating a reliable forecast of the same for the future, depends heavily on the ability to fully understand the temporal dynamics of the process underlying the data. What is the non-random structure that can be extracted from the observations? What are the measurable regularities over time? What is the relationship between the observation at time $(t)$ and the observation at time $(t - k)$? These are the fundamental questions that require a minimum of formalization to fully understand and answer.

The aspects of Time Series that we are going to cover in detail in this chapter, from both a theoretical and an applied point of view, are the following:

- Trend and seasonality components
- Autocorrelation
- Stationarity

There are other common features of Time Series that would be useful to explore, for example, conditional heteroskedasticity, aberrant observations (such as additive/innovative outliers or level shifts), or nonlinearities. However, we will focus on the ones listed because they are the most important for the models and applications we will see in the following chapters.

By the end of the chapter, you will have learned the main characteristics of a Time Series, including those aspects that are fundamental to correctly interpreting data over the time dimension and setting the foundations for a complete and reliable forecasting process.

## Technical requirements

As prerequisites for this chapter, you need KNIME Analytics Platform with the following additional extensions:

- KNIME JavaScript Views
- KNIME Plotly
- KNIME Timeseries nodes

All workflows introduced in the chapter are available on the KNIME Hub at the following link: `https://kni.me/s/GxjXX6WmLi-WjLNx`.

## Trend and seasonality components

If we consider the graphical analysis presented in the previous chapter to describe a Time Series, it is evident that there are different patterns that characterize the temporal dynamics of the data. We have already spoken, several times, in the book about trend or seasonality; however, it is necessary to go into more detail about these components in order to subsequently understand how to treat them within a forecasting model. Let's start with trends.

### Trend

**Trend** can be described as the *direction in which the Time Series is running during a long period.* So, in general, a trend exists when there is a long-term increase (that is, the upward trend) or decrease (that is, the downward trend) in some Time Series data. Typically, it's difficult to formally define "trend" because its characteristics depend on the framework where the trend is analyzed. For instance, the formal definition of trend could be different depending on the method we are using to model it (for instance, ARIMA, exponential smoothing, or other univariate methods).

A trend does not have to be necessarily linear; it could be exponential or assume other functional forms. When examining the time plot of the historical series, it is quite easy to recognize the presence of a trend in the data and identify some of its characteristics.

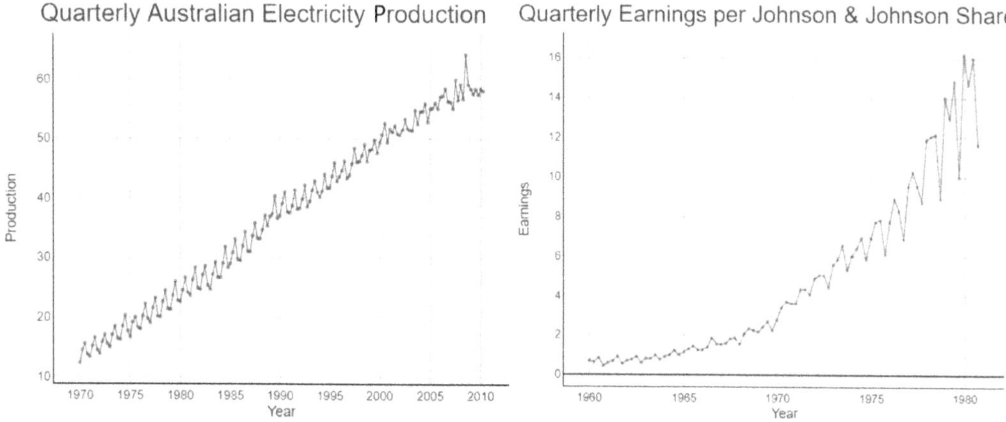


Figure 5.1 – Trend comparison: Linear (left) versus exponential-like (right)

For example, looking at *Figure 5.1*, on the left it is easy to recognize an approximately linear trend in the Time Series of **Australian electricity production** (quarterly data, 1970 to 2010), whereas, in the right plot, the Time Series of **earnings per Johnson & Johnson share** (quarterly data, 1960 to 1980) shows a nonlinear exponential-like growth.

It's fundamental in the analysis of the Time Series to try to identify the characteristics of the trend before developing any forecasting model. A trend, in fact, is a component that, if present, can contribute significantly to the medium-long term forecasts (but it is absolutely not to be underestimated even in short-term forecasts). In addition, in the presence of a trend, as we will see later in the chapter, the Time Series is, by definition, not stationary as its average changes constantly over time; this aspect must be considered for the development of specific models. Finally, with an upward trend, it is easy to show that the forecast variance also increases over time, strongly impacting the out-of-sample forecast error.

Summing up, the identification and measurement of a trend can be extremely useful in a process of analysis of Time Series for the following two main reasons:

- After having correctly measured the trend component, it is possible to *remove it* from the Time Series, creating a so-called **detrended** series. This allows us to observe how the series moves around a constant average, better identifying the characteristics of possible residual fluctuations.
- Incorporating the trend inside a forecasting model allows us to obtain a better forecast of the future values of the Time Series. In this case, instead of removing the trend from the series, we focus on its modeling.

Trend modeling (and removal) can be done in several ways; the most commonly used methods are presented in the following sub-sections.

### Curve fitting (linear or nonlinear)

This method consists of estimating a polynomial regression model where the Time Series to be analyzed is expressed as a function of time *t*. For example, in the case of a linear model, the estimated equation is as follows:

$$y_t = \beta_0 + \beta_1 t + \varepsilon_t$$

Formula 5.1

Where:

- $y_t$ is the target Time Series of length *n*.
- *t* is the time periods variable so that $t=1,2,3,\ldots n$.
- $(\beta_0, \beta_1)$ are the coefficients (constant and slope, respectively) of the regression line to be estimated using, for instance, the ordinary least squares method.
- $\varepsilon_t$ is the random error of the model, and that could be white noise or an ARMA process (we'll learn more on ARMA models in *Chapter 7, Forecasting the Temperature with ARIMA and SARIMA Models*).

If the dynamics of the trend seem to be nonlinear, it is possible to modify the preceding equation by inserting other terms (quadratic, cubic, or higher-order), or by modifying the functional form of the same, for example, by considering a logistic or exponential function.

In KNIME, it is fairly straightforward to apply this trend estimation and removal approach through the use of the Polynomial Regression Learner node. *Figure 5.2* shows how it is possible to estimate a nonlinear trend using a *third-degree polynomial*. Obviously, to estimate a linear trend, it is sufficient to request a first-degree polynomial from the Polynomial Regression node or alternatively use the Linear Regression Learner node.

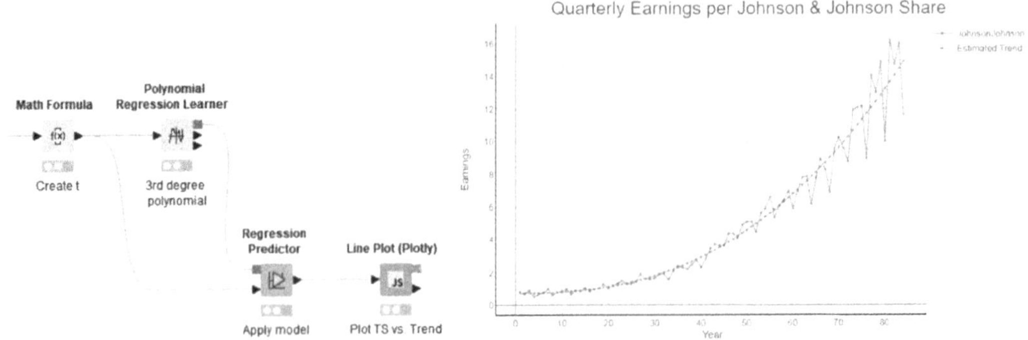


Figure 5.2 – Nonlinear trend estimation in KNIME via Polynomial Regression

Be aware that estimating the trend using the curve-fitting method implicitly assumed that the trend component remains constant over time. The Time Series for which this assumption constitutes a good approximation of the reality are in fact called *trend-stationary*, or we can say that they contain a *deterministic trend*. We will return to this aspect later in this chapter.

### Filtering (moving average smoothing)

A second method for estimating the trend component is to apply a linear filter that converts the original series into a transform of the same that *smoothes* the fluctuations and irregularities of the series, making the trend more visible. Often this kind of filtering procedure is called *moving average smoothing*. The typical application of the moving average is when we calculate, at each point in time, the averages of the observed values (possibly weighted) that surround a particular time point.

Generally, to remove fluctuations from a series so that we can better see the trend, we would use a **moving average** (**MA**) with a length equal to the frequency of the seasonal period (see the following section for more details). The filter equation that can be applied to smooth the Time Series is, in general, as follows:

$$MA_t = \sum_{r=-q}^{+s} a_r y_{t+r}$$

Formula 5.2

Where:

- $y_t$ is the target time series of length $n$.
- $MA_t$ is the filtered time series.
- $a_r$ is a set of weights (where $\sum a_r = 1$).

Commonly, in the equation in *Formula 5.2*, the filter is made symmetric by setting $s$=$q$ and $a_j = a_{-j}$, obtaining a moving average that is centered in the middle of the values being averaged. Typically, to highlight the trend when the Time Series shows strong seasonal fluctuations, we have to use specific centered moving average smoothing that is dependent on the type of seasonal period. For instance, a typical moving average applied to quarterly data is the following:

$$w_t = \frac{1}{8}y_{t-2} + \frac{1}{4}y_{t-1} + \frac{1}{4}y_t + \frac{1}{4}y_{t+1} + \frac{1}{8}y_{t+2}$$

Formula 5.3

Using the Moving Average node in KNIME (*Formula 5.3*), it is possible to calculate different types of moving averages (forward, backward, exponential, and so on), specifying the length of the moving window in the configuration dialog; however, it's not possible to directly obtain a centered moving average such as the one presented in *Formula 5.3*. In the *Seasonality* section of this chapter, we will return to this point and be more precise about how to use the moving average smoothing, showing all of the mathematical expressions behind *Formula 5.3* and the steps in KNIME to obtain a centered moving average.

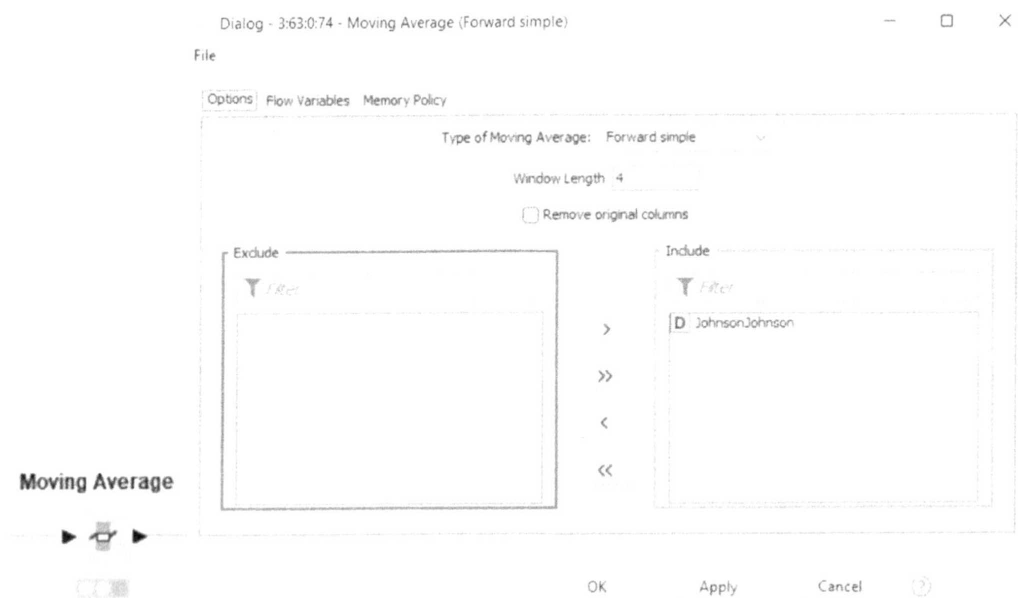


Figure 5.3 – KNIME Moving Average node configuration dialog

In the following figure, we used KNIME to create the centered moving average of the equation (*Formula 5.11*) in order to remove the annual seasonal fluctuations and estimate the trend (go to the *Seasonal filtering* part of the *Seasonality* section to see the details):

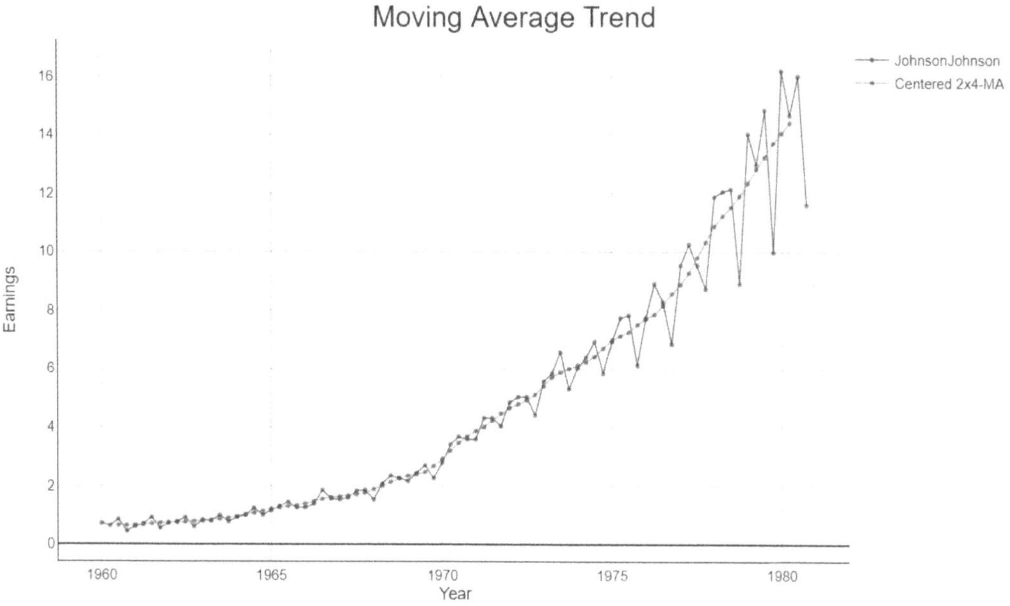


Figure 5.4 – Trend estimation in KNIME – Moving average smoothing

Note that the transformed series after applying a moving average smoothing always has fewer observations than the original time series. In the case of the example presented in the preceding figure, there are two missing data at the beginning of the series and two at the end.

There are other types of filters that can be applied to the series to highlight the trend other than the moving average. For example, the popular *exponential smoothing* approach.

## Differencing

Differencing can be thought of as a particular type of filter useful to remove the trend (but not only) from a time series. It is a very simple operation that consists of subtracting a past value from each observation of the Time Series (that is, computing the differences between two observations laying at different time points).

The most common type of difference is *first-order differencing*, which generates the transformed series $y'_t$ and is obtained from the differences between two consecutive observations in the original time series $y_t$ as follows:

$$y'_t = y_t - y_{t-1}$$

Formula 5.4

The differentiated series will contain one value less than the original series. First-order differencing generally succeeds in removing the trend from a time series, but sometimes the resulting series is still trending. In this case, it may be necessary to apply again the differencing operation to completely remove the trend. This operation is called *second-order differencing* and is obtained as follows:

$$y''_t = y'_t - y'_{t-1} = (y_t - y_{t-1}) - (y_{t-1} - y_{t-2})$$

Formula 5.5

Second-order differencing is able to remove the *changes in the changes* present in the original set. Typically, it is not necessary to go beyond second-order differencing to completely remove the trend.

*Figure 5.5* shows how the application of first-order differencing is able to remove the trend completely from the original time series. Obviously, the constant fluctuations associated with the seasonal pattern are still well present.

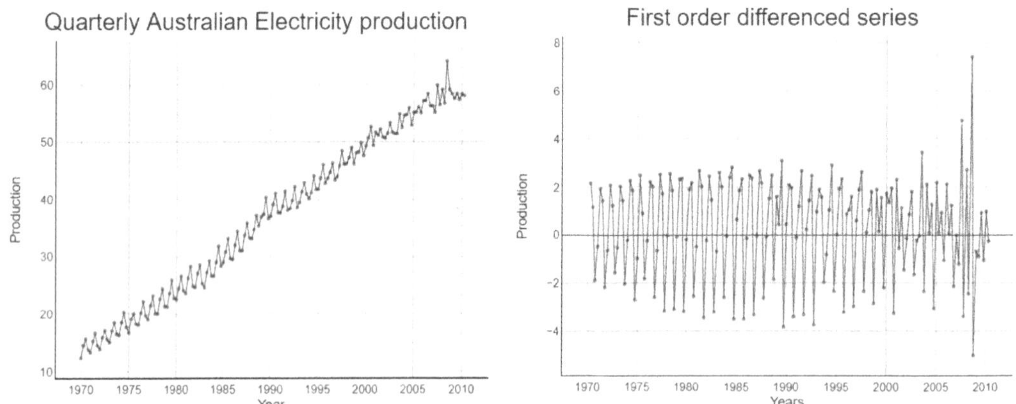


Figure 5.5 – First-order differencing example

The differentiation operation will be better explained in *Chapter 7, Forecasting the Temperature with ARIMA and SARIMA Models*, in the context of (S)ARIMA models where its usefulness and usage will be better understood.

Before moving on to the analysis of the seasonality component, it is necessary to make a final remark about the trend component. Very often you hear about the difference between a **deterministic trend** and a **stochastic trend**.

If the series has a stable long-term trend and the values of the series tend to return to the trend line after a shock, then we are seeing a *deterministic trend*, which can typically be modeled with the first method presented, namely the curve-fitting method.

However, sometimes detrending with the curve-fitting method fails to be effective in removing the trend because the trend component cannot be described simply by a constant function of time (linear or otherwise), but it varies continuously. This situation typically indicates the presence of a *stochastic trend* in the Time Series, which is a trend that changes continuously over time, in an unpredictable way, and where a shock has permanent effects. In this case, the use of the differencing operator is more appropriate to remove/model the trend. To recognize the presence of a stochastic trend rather than a deterministic one (for example, using the so-called *unit root* tests) is very important for the correct specification of a forecasting model.

## Seasonality

Many time series are characterized by persistent fluctuations in their observations over time. These fluctuations are very recognizable, for example, when observing an economic Time Series (monthly or quarterly) over several years. When these fluctuations turn out to be regular over time, it is said that the Time Series is affected by **seasonal factors**, such as the time of year, the day of the week, or the time of day. It is easy to imagine how the number of visitors to a seaside resort will be higher each year during the summer than during the winter, or how the number of people commuting in a train station will be systematically higher in the early morning hours or around 5 to 7 p.m., corresponding to working hours. However, there are other situations where recognizing a seasonal pattern is more complex. The fact that a time series is affected by seasonal factors indicates the presence of the **seasonal component** in it.

So we can define seasonality as *the short-term fluctuations that occur regularly in a time series.* Seasonality is always of a specific and known period. This period is typically known as the *frequency* of the seasonal component. We will return to the frequency topic later.

The seasonal component could be additive or multiplicative with respect to the other components of the time series (especially the trend) as follows:

- When the seasonality is **additive**, the seasonal variation stays roughly the same magnitude regardless of the level of the time series. For instance, an increase in the values of the time series over time due to the trend component will not cause an increase in the size of seasonal fluctuations. This is because with additive seasonality, the seasonal effect and the trend effect are independent of one other. In *Figure 5.6*, we can see two examples of seasonal patterns that appear to be additive.

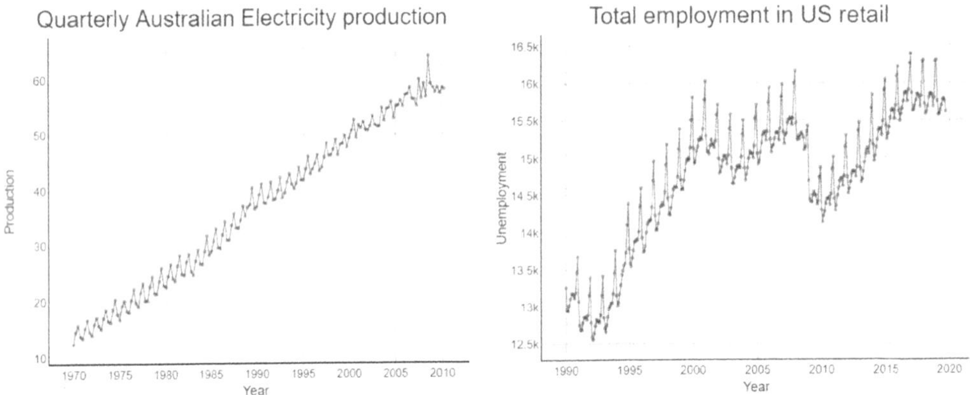


Figure 5.6 – Examples of Time Series with additive seasonality

- Having a **multiplicative** seasonality means that the amplitude of the seasonality increase (decrease) with an increasing (decreasing) trend, therefore, contrary to the additive case, the two components are not independent of each other. When the dynamics of the seasonal component (or the variation of the time series around the trend) seem to be proportional to the level of the time series, we are facing a multiplicative seasonality, as shown in *Figure 5.7*.

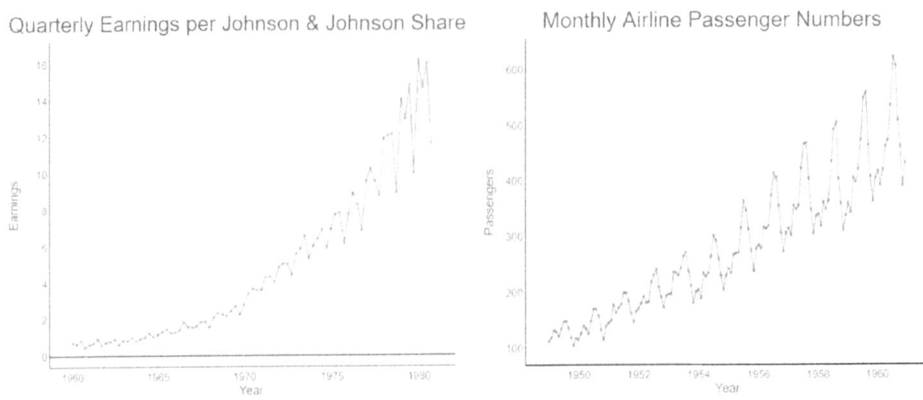


Figure 5.7 – Examples of Time Series with multiplicative seasonality

Seasonality is not the only type of fluctuation that can be observed in a time series. In fact, sometimes, if we have a long enough series, we might see long-term irregular fluctuations that are distinct from seasonal fluctuations. This component is called the time series **cycle**. It is necessary to avoid confusing the cycle with seasonality; the former is totally unrelated to fixed effects connected to the *calendar*, that is, the month of the year or the day of the week. Furthermore, while seasonality generally occurs annually, the cycle can occur at irregular intervals that are typically wider (even 5/10 years). Ultimately, by considering a time series snapshot shorter than the duration of the entire cycle, and increasing or decreasing the movement of the cycle can easily be modeled as a simple trend.

A final important aspect of seasonality to consider, before moving on to its measurement/removal, is the *frequency* (or the *length*) of the seasonality. The frequency can be defined as the number of observations for each seasonal period. For instance, in the case of monthly data and considering an annual seasonality, the frequency is equal to 12. In the case of taking daily data and considering a weekly seasonal period, the frequency is equal to 7. We use the capital letter "S" to define the seasonal frequency of a time series.

According to data granularity, it is important to consider the right seasonal frequency in order to correctly model this component. There are no issues if our data points are years, quarters, months, or weeks. In this case, we will typically need to consider the annual seasonality only; but if the data granularity is shorter than a week, the situation is more complicated as we can observe *multiple seasonal patterns overlapping*. For example, hourly data might have a daily seasonality *(S=24)*, a weekly seasonality *(S=24×7=168)*, and an annual seasonality *(S=24×365.25=8766)*. In the following table, you'll find that it's possible to see the different frequencies according to the considered seasonal period and specific data granularity.

| **Frequency values** | | **Seasonal period** | | | |
|---|---|---|---|---|---|
| | | **Hour** | **Day** | **Week** | **Year*** |
| **Data granularity** | Annual | | | | 1 |
| | Quarterly | | | | 4 |
| | Monthly | | | | 12 |
| | Weekly | | | 1 | 52.18 |
| | Daily | | 1 | 7 | 365.25 |
| | Hourly | 1 | 24 | 168 | 8766 |
| | Minutes | 60 | 1440 | 10080 | 525960 |

*Every year, on average, is made up of 365 days and 6 hours (allowing for a leap year every fourth year) → so 365.25 days and 365.25/7=52.18 weeks is the corresponding average frequency.

Table 5.1 – Examples of Time Series with multiplicative seasonality

It's crucial to underline that before applying any technique to model seasonality, it's good practice to correctly identify the presence, type, frequency, and intensity of the seasonal component through a careful *exploratory data analysis*. The indications derived from the examination of the descriptive tools presented in the preceding paragraph (time plot, seasonal plot, lag, plot, and so on) should be used to guide the analysis of the seasonal component. For example, in the case of data that could potentially contain multiple overlapping seasonal components (daily or hourly data), it would be necessary to understand what the dominant seasonal pattern is and how it relates to the others in order to properly include all seasonal dynamics in the forecasting model.

The techniques used to measure and remove seasonality are related to the trend modeling methods we faced earlier. In particular, to measure the seasonal factors, it is necessary to start from a series without trend (or where it is of little importance) or from a series where the trend has been properly removed. The following are some of the most popular methods to deal with seasonality.

### Conditional means (differences or ratios)

Considering a time series *without a trend*, it's possible to calculate the seasonal factors starting from *simple conditional means for each term of the seasonal period*. For example, in the case of monthly data, we calculate the averages of all of the available months of January, then of all Februarys and so on, obtaining 12 average values. Then, we can estimate the *seasonal factors*, as in the seasonal effect of each element of the period (month, day of the week, hour of the day, and so on), taking the difference (or the ratio) between each conditional mean and the global mean. With no trend or little trend, the seasonal component will typically be additive. Take, for example, *Figure 5.8*.

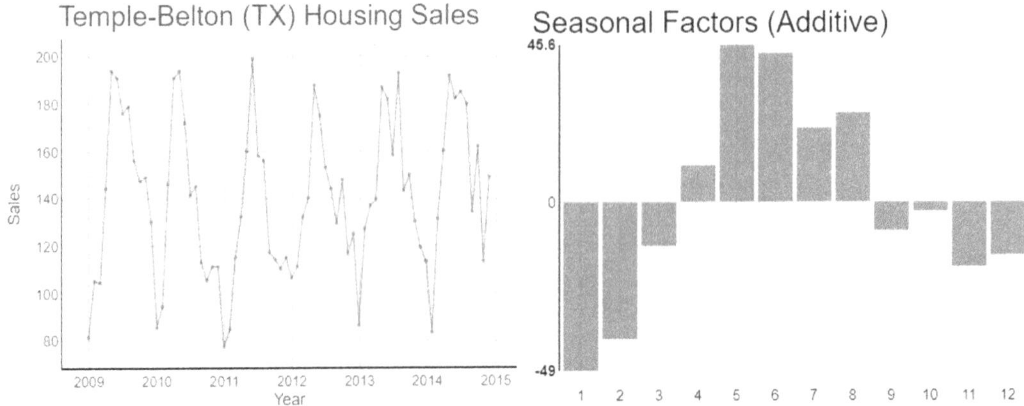


Figure 5.8 – Computing seasonal factors via conditional means differences

By looking at the time plot (left graph), the monthly series of housing sales in Temple-Belton (TX) does not show a relevant trend over the period considered, but there are obvious seasonal fluctuations. Calculating the conditional means of sales with respect to the month of the year and then taking the difference from the overall sales provides an estimate of seasonal factors (right graph). If one wants to seasonally adjust the time series, we could simply calculate the difference between the value of each month in the original series and the corresponding seasonal factor.

## Regression with dummies

When the time series presents an evident trend, it's necessary to consider it when estimating the seasonal factors, so the standard conditional means approach is not applicable (except with some modification). To include the trend in our analysis, we can try either to model it together with the seasonality or to remove it before computing the seasonal factors.

Following the modeling approach, the first possible method to measure the seasonal component is to estimate a *regression model* for the time series that includes both trend and seasonal terms. A common technique is to take the regression equation (*Formula 5.1*) and add *seasonal dummies*.

In general, dummy variables are a representation of one (or more) categorical variables of interest. The idea is to code each category of the variable with a binary `0/1` variable, where the `1` value means the presence of that category in a specific observation of the data. So, for example, we can recode the `FRAUD (YES/NO)` variable with a dummy variable where `1` = `YES FRAUD` and `0` = `NO FRAUD`. The usefulness of dummy variables lies in the fact that they offer the possibility to include categorical predictors in models where it's not directly feasible, for example, in the linear regression model.

For instance, thinking about time series, consider the following dummy variable encoding of the quarter of the year.

Seasonal dummies

| S year | S quarter | D elec_cons | I Q1 | I Q2 | I Q3 | I Q4 |
|---|---|---|---|---|---|---|
| 1970 | Q1 | 12.328 | 1 | 0 | 0 | 0 |
| 1970 | Q2 | 14.493 | 0 | 1 | 0 | 0 |
| 1970 | Q3 | 15.664 | 0 | 0 | 1 | 0 |
| 1970 | Q4 | 13.781 | 0 | 0 | 0 | 1 |
| 1971 | Q1 | 13.299 | 1 | 0 | 0 | 0 |
| 1971 | Q2 | 15.23 | 0 | 1 | 0 | 0 |
| 1971 | Q3 | 16.667 | 0 | 0 | 1 | 0 |
| 1971 | Q4 | 14.484 | 0 | 0 | 0 | 1 |
| 1972 | Q1 | 13.838 | 1 | 0 | 0 | 0 |
| 1972 | Q2 | 15.919 | 0 | 1 | 0 | 0 |
| 1972 | Q3 | 17.149 | 0 | 0 | 1 | 0 |
| 1972 | Q4 | 15.564 | 0 | 0 | 0 | 1 |
| 1973 | Q1 | 15.024 | 1 | 0 | 0 | 0 |
| 1973 | Q2 | 17.064 | 0 | 1 | 0 | 0 |
| 1973 | Q3 | 18.512 | 0 | 0 | 1 | 0 |
| 1973 | Q4 | 16.467 | 0 | 0 | 0 | 1 |
| 1974 | Q1 | 16.249 | 1 | 0 | 0 | 0 |

Figure 5.9 – Quarterly seasonal dummies

Notice that we actually need three seasonal dummies to completely encode the quarter of the year. This is due to the fourth quarter category being captured when the first three dummy variables are all set to zero. So, the rule of thumb is to use one less dummy variable than the number of terms of the seasonal period. For quarterly data, such as the preceding example, we will use three dummies. For monthly data, given a seasonal period of 12 months, we're going to use 11 dummy variables, and for daily data (considering a weekly seasonality), we use six dummies, and so on.

Now let's use the dummy variables in a regression model to include the seasonal dynamic in the data. Starting from a time series characterized by a trend and a seasonality of frequency *S*, we can write the following linear regression model to capture all of the components:

$$y_t = \beta_0 + \beta_1 t + \beta_2 D_2 + \beta_2 D_3 + \cdots + \beta_S D_S + \varepsilon_t$$

Formula 5.6

Notice we are using *S-1* dummies in the regression (here we have excluded $D_1$), because we also included the constant in the equation. This is to avoid the so-called **dummy variable trap**. When the intercept is present in the equation, together with all the dummies, there will be one too many parameters to estimate and the regression will fail. Therefore, you can either remove one dummy or exclude the constant from the equation. The interpretation of the single coefficient of each dummy variable is that it's the estimated effect of that category relative to the omitted category.

For example, if we now apply the model expressed in the equation in *Formula 5.6* to the **quarterly Australian electricity production** presented previously in *Figure 5.1*, we can see how this model is able to fit the data pretty well because of the constant dynamic of the series over time. The trend is roughly linear and of the same slope during the 30 years and the seasonal component is clearly additive and stable.

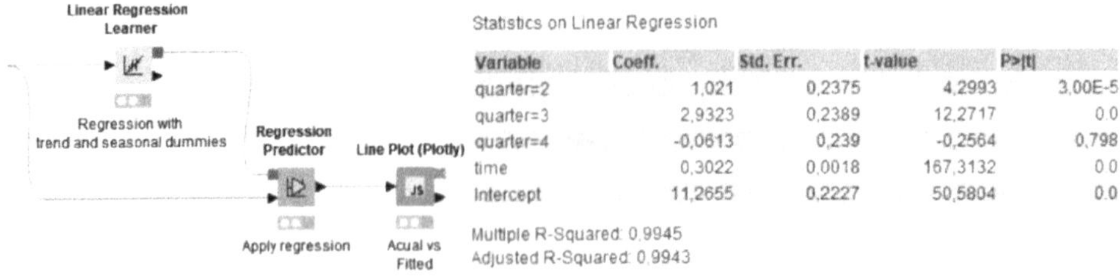


Statistics on Linear Regression

| Variable | Coeff. | Std. Err. | t-value | P>\|t\| |
|---|---|---|---|---|
| quarter=2 | 1,021 | 0,2375 | 4,2993 | 3,00E-5 |
| quarter=3 | 2,9323 | 0,2389 | 12,2717 | 0.0 |
| quarter=4 | -0,0613 | 0,239 | -0,2564 | 0,798 |
| time | 0,3022 | 0,0018 | 167,3132 | 0.0 |
| Intercept | 11,2655 | 0,2227 | 50,5804 | 0.0 |

Multiple R-Squared: 0.9945
Adjusted R-Squared: 0.9943

Figure 5.10 – Regression with trend and seasonal dummy results (quarterly Australian electricity production)

In *Figure 5.10*, you can see the application of the linear model with seasonal dummies in KNIME. This is the interpretation of the estimated coefficients as follows:

- There is an average upward trend of 0.3022 per quarter (as in, every quarter the electricity production increases, on average, by 0.3022 billion kWh).
- On average, the second quarter has a production of 1.021 billion kWh higher than the first quarter, the third quarter has a production of 2.9323 billion kWh higher than the first quarter, and the fourth quarter has a production of 0.0613 billion kWh lower than the first quarter. This last effect is not statistically significant (high p-value).

The R squared is equal to 0.99, suggesting a very high percentage of explained variance of the original time series.

Consider that the regression of the equation (*Formula 5.6*) is appropriate only in the case of a linear deterministic trend and a stable additive seasonality. For instance, when you have a more complex trend (for example, stochastic), it could be more suitable to estimate a regression model on the *differentiated* time series that also includes the seasonal dummies.

## *Seasonal filtering*

In the previous section on trend, we discussed filtering through moving average calculations to estimate the trend component. In this section, we continue and expand on this topic for a different purpose. We use filtering as an intermediate step to detrend the time series and allow better identification of seasonal factors.

First, let's rewrite the equation in *Formula 5.2*, considering the special case of a simple (symmetric) moving average where all of the terms in the average have the same weight $a_r = 1/(2q+1)$ as follows:

$$MA_t = \frac{1}{2q+1}\sum_{r=-q}^{+q} y_{t+r}$$

Formula 5.7

In this case, the *length* (or the *order*) of the moving average is expressed by $L=(2q+1)$. In general, we write *[L-MA]* to indicate a simple moving average of length *L*. For example, a *[7-MA]* has seven terms: three to the right side, four to the left side, and one central observation corresponding to $y_t$. Please note that to have an integer $q$, $L$ must be an odd number.

This type of moving average has the advantage of being able to smooth the fluctuations/irregularities in the time series and also of being centered on the values that you want to smooth (because it does not generate a "shift" of the average tendency of the series over time, as backward or forward-moving averages do). But what does this have to do with identifying seasonal factors? Simply, in the case of Time Series that show both trend and seasonality, you can use the moving average to estimate the seasonal component following these steps:

1. Remove the seasonality and estimate the trend using the simple moving average of the same length of the seasonal frequency $(L=(2q+1)=S)$.
2. Detrend the time series by doing the following:

- Subtracting the trend estimates from the series when the seasonality is **additive**
- Dividing the series by the trend values when the seasonality is **multiplicative**

3. Calculate the seasonal factors on the detrended series following the same procedure of the conditional means indicated earlier.

This process works smoothly when the frequency of the time series is odd (for example, daily data considering a weekly seasonality, so $S=7$), but in the case of *even* seasonal frequency ($S=4$, $S=12$, $S=24$, and so on), the moving average of the equation (*Formula 5.7*) should be adjusted. In fact, notice that when $L$ is even, $q$ is not an integer anymore. The procedure to compute the centered moving average when the seasonal frequency is even is the following:

- When $S$ is even, using the equation in *Formula 5.7* and setting $L=S$, we have two possible MAs that are "almost" centered, but not completely, because one side of the MA is longer than the other by one observation; these two moving averages can be defined as follows:

$$MA_{t-0.5} = \frac{1}{L} \sum_{r=-(L/2)}^{+(L/2)-1} y_{t+r} \;\; ; \;\; MA_{t+0.5} = \frac{1}{L} \sum_{r=-(L/2)+1}^{+(L/2)} y_{t+r}$$

- Taking the mean of these two moving averages, we have a result that is centered at time *t*:

$$MA_t^* = \frac{MA_{t-0.5} + MA_{t+0.5}}{2}$$

- So taking a *[L-MA]* followed by a *[2-MA]* gives a centered moving average, typically written as *[2XL-MA]*.

For example, consider quarterly data with a seasonal frequency of 4 (so *L=S=4*). We have the following:

$$MA_{t-0.5} = \frac{y_{t-2} + y_{t-1} + y_t + y_{t+1}}{4}; MA_{t+0.5} = \frac{y_{t-1} + y_t + y_{t+1} + y_{t+2}}{4}$$

$$MA_t^* = \frac{1}{2}\left(\frac{y_{t-2} + y_{t-1} + y_t + y_{t+1}}{4} + \frac{y_{t-1} + y_t + y_{t+1} + y_{t+2}}{4}\right) = \frac{1}{8}y_{t-2} + \frac{1}{4}y_{t-1} + \frac{1}{4}y_t + \frac{1}{4}y_{t+1} + \frac{1}{8}y_{t+2}$$

So a *[4-MA]* followed by a *[2-MA]* gives a *[2X4-MA]* that is a centered moving average when *S=4*. This result corresponds to *Formula 5.3* that was presented earlier in the chapter and it is clearly connected to a weighted moving average of order 5, but considering a case where the weights for each period are not equal. In general, a *[2XL-MA]* is equal to a weighted MA of order *L+1* with weights *1/L* for all of the terms except for the first and last observations in the average, which have weights *1/((2L))*.

| S year | S quarter | D JohnsonJohnson | D 4-MA | D Centered 2x4-MA |
|---|---|---|---|---|
| 1960 | 1 | 0.71 | ? | ? |
| 1960 | 2 | 0.63 | 0.657 | ? |
| 1960 | 3 | 0.85 | 0.632 | 0.645 |
| 1960 | 4 | 0.44 | 0.647 | 0.64 |
| 1961 | 1 | 0.61 | 0.665 | 0.656 |
| 1961 | 2 | 0.69 | 0.693 | 0.679 |
| 1961 | 3 | 0.92 | 0.72 | 0.706 |
| 1961 | 4 | 0.55 | 0.74 | 0.73 |

Figure 5.11 – Calculation of a centered moving average for quarterly data (F=4)

In the preceding figure, you can see how the centered moving average is applied to the Time Series of *earnings per Johnson & Johnson share* (quarterly data).

In order to create a centered moving average in KNIME (such as the one presented in *Figure 5.11*), you have to proceed with the following steps:

1. Calculate a forward MA of the same length of the seasonal period (here it's 4 as we have quarterly data). Use the KNIME Moving Average node, selecting the **Forward simple** type and a window length of 4 as shown in *Figure 5.12*.

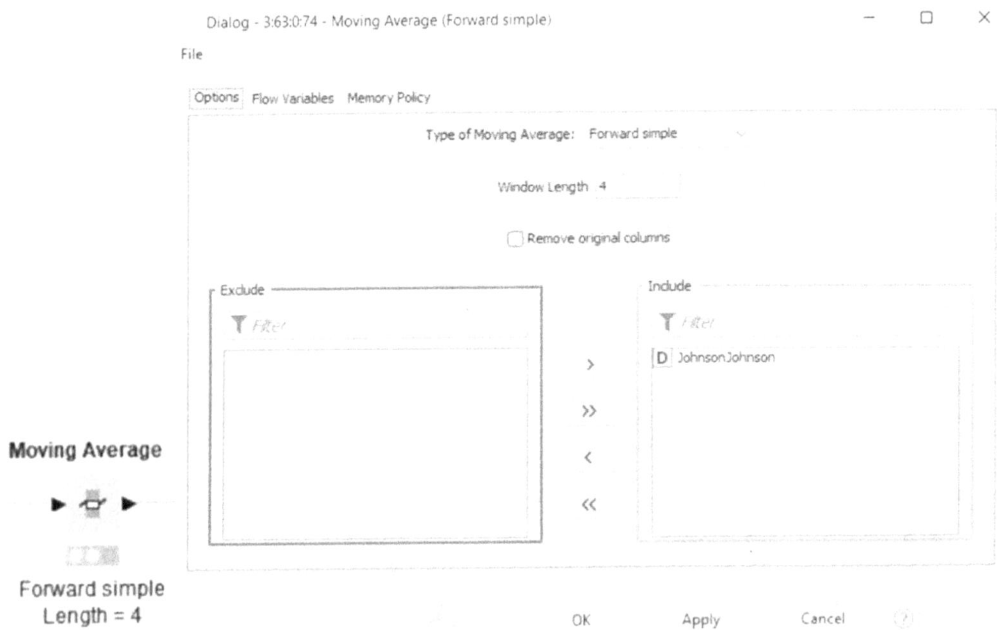


Figure 5.12 – Forward simple MA of length equal to the seasonal period

2. Use the Lag Column node to "shift" downward the obtained MA column by the *[(S/2)-1]* rows. That means, for example, shifting by one row in the case of quarterly data (where *S=4*) or five rows in the case of monthly data (where *S=12*). Looking at *Figure 5.13*, where the configuration dialog of the Lag Column node is presented, the amount of rows you want to shift is defined by the **Lag interval** option.

**STEP 2**

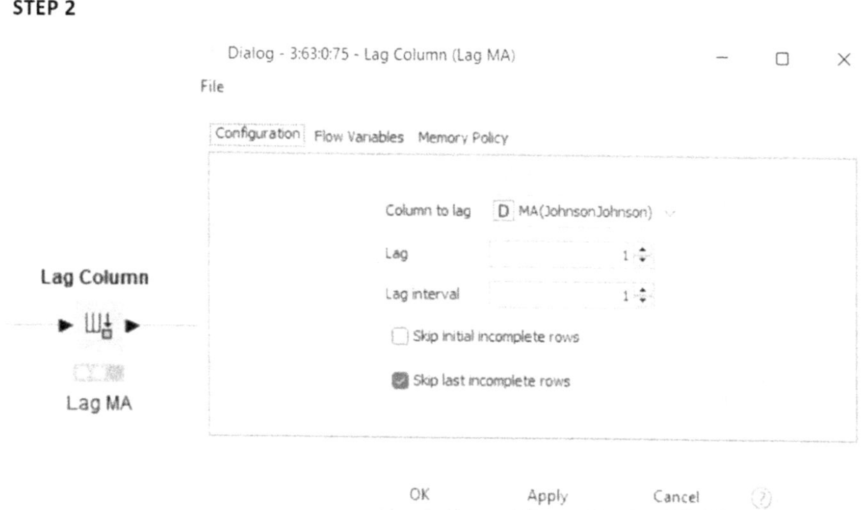


Figure 5.13 – "Lagging" the MA column obtained in the first step

3. Use the Moving Average node again to calculate a backward simple moving average with a window length of 2 (note: always use a length of 2 here, regardless of the seasonal period of your time series) as shown in *Figure 5.14*. This last step will basically calculate the mean of the two MAs the presented earlier.

**STEP 3**

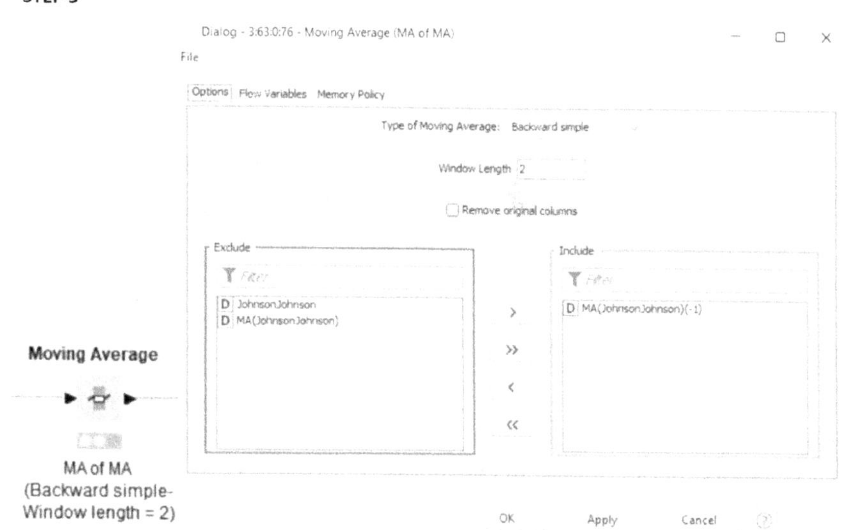


Figure 5.14 – Backward simple MA of length equal to 2

Once we calculate the trend through the moving average smoothing, it's possible to proceed as described earlier in order to detrend the original series (through difference or ratio, in the function of the type of seasonality) and subsequently calculate the seasonal factors through the conditioned means.

For example, in the case of the earnings series for Johnson & Johnson shares (*Figure 5.15*), since seasonality is multiplicative, we will proceed to calculate the ratio between the original series and the trend (estimated with the moving average method) to obtain the detrended series. Then, finding the conditional means for each quarter of the detrended series, it's possible to obtain the seasonal factors, as seen in the following figure.

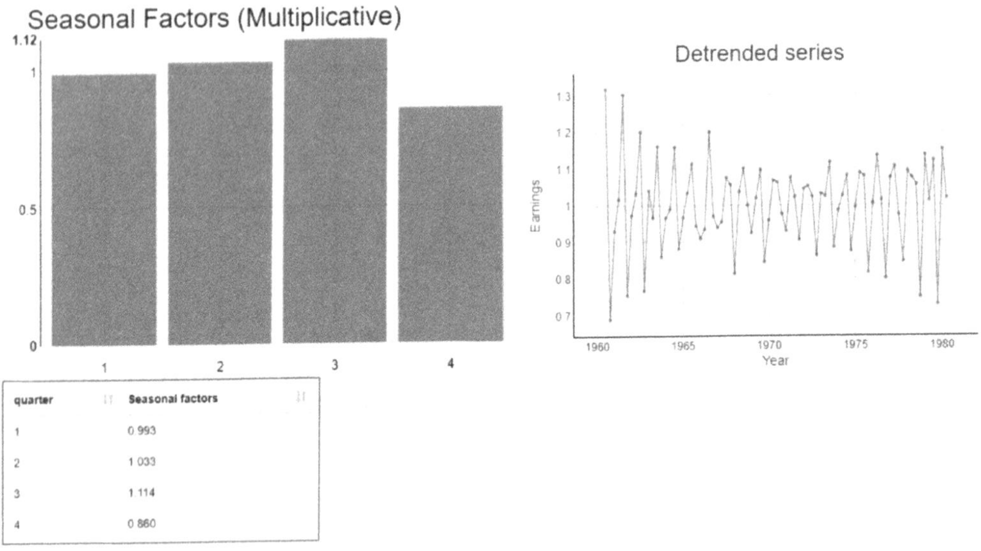


| quarter | Seasonal factors |
|---|---|
| 1 | 0.993 |
| 2 | 1.033 |
| 3 | 1.114 |
| 4 | 0.860 |

Figure 5.15 – Calculation of a centered moving average for quarterly data (F=4)

The seasonal filtering is therefore an alternative tool to the regression with dummies, which in many cases is more flexible because it is able to identify (and remove) more complex seasonal patterns.

## Seasonal differencing

The seasonal effect can be eliminated (or greatly reduced) through the *seasonal differencing* operation. This operation is entirely similar to that seen earlier for trend removal.

In the case of seasonal differencing, we also proceed by subtracting a past observation from each observation of the Time Series, but in this case, the past value is relative to the seasonal period, meaning it will always be a multiple of the seasonal frequency *S*:

$$y'_t = y_t - y_{t-S}$$

Formula 5.8

For example, in the case of monthly data, the first seasonal difference will be equal to $y_t - y_{t-12}$.

## Decomposition

In the previous sections, we discussed how you can measure (or remove) trend and seasonality components in a time series. These procedures are typically included in an integrated approach to time series analysis called *decomposition*.

Decomposition methods are often used to extract the components we have discussed so far, namely trend and seasonality, from a Time Series. More complex decompositions might also include long-run cycles, holiday effects, other complex factors, and so on. In this section, we consider only those decompositions that involve trend and seasonality. One of the main goals of a decomposition procedure is to estimate seasonal effects that can be used to create the so-called *seasonally-adjusted* series. In a seasonally-adjusted series, the seasonal pattern is removed so that the other temporal dynamics (particularly the trend) are made more immediately visible.

In this chapter, we have already discussed the patterns that are generally present in a Time Series, namely trend, seasonality, and long-term cycles, and we have considered them as distinct elements. However, very often in decomposition procedures, the trend and cycle are considered together, creating a single trend-cycle component. In summary, in time series decomposition, we can think of a time series ($y_t$) as composed of three components: a *trend-cycle component* ($T_t$), a *seasonal component* ($S_t$) and a *residual (or remainder) component* ($R_t$) that includes everything that is not considered by the other two elements. So, in the decomposition, we assume the following:

$$y_t = f(T_t, S_t, R_t)$$

Formula 5.9

If the dynamics of the time series are completely described by the trend-cycle and seasonality components, we expect that the residual part will be totally random (that means a white noise process). In order to put together these three different components, it's possible to choose between the following two models:

- *Additive decomposition model*:

$$y_t = T_t + S_t + R_t$$

Formula 5.10

- *Multiplicative decomposition model*:

$$y_t = T_t \times S_t \times R_t$$

Formula 5.11

As we have already shown in the *Seasonality* section, the additive decomposition model is best suited if the magnitude of the seasonal fluctuations (around the mean or around the trend) does not change with the level of the time series. On the other hand, when the seasonal dynamics appear to be proportional to the level of the time series, then it is preferable to use a multiplicative decomposition model. Alternatively, if the series shows a multiplicative seasonality, it's sufficient to first apply a logarithmic transformation to the data and then use the additive decomposition model.

There are several approaches to decomposition (there is no single universal method) that differ primarily in how individual components are extracted from the data. We can mention classical decomposition, which was the first widely used approach, or the STL and X11 decomposition methods. In general, decomposition follows the following four steps:

1. **Trend estimation**: The trend is measured through one of the methods discussed earlier, in particular through a centered moving average or curve-fitting. More advanced decomposition methods may use more sophisticated estimation methodologies.
2. **Calculation of the detrended series**: In the additive decomposition model, the trend is subtracted from the original series, whereas in the multiplicative decomposition model, the original series is divided by the trend.

   *Additive Model* $Detrendedseries: Dt = Yt - Tt = St + Rt$

   *Multiplicative Model* $Detrendedseries: Dt = \frac{Yt}{Tt} = St \times Rt$
3. **Calculation of seasonal factors**: The most common method for estimating these effects is to average the detrended values for a specific seasonal term (that is, month, week, day, and so on); this is the conditional means method presented earlier. The seasonal factors are typically adjusted so that they average to 0 in the additive decomposition model or they average to 1 in the multiplicative one.
4. **Determination of the residual component**: Also in this step, depending on whether the model is additive or multiplicative, a difference or ratio is calculated to determine the remainder.

   *Additive Model* $Residualcomponent: Rt = Yt - Tt - St$

   *Multiplicative Model* $Residualcomponent: Rt = \frac{Yt}{Tt \times St}$

In *Figure 5.16*, you can see the results of the whole decomposition process, from the original time series to the estimation of trend and seasonal components.

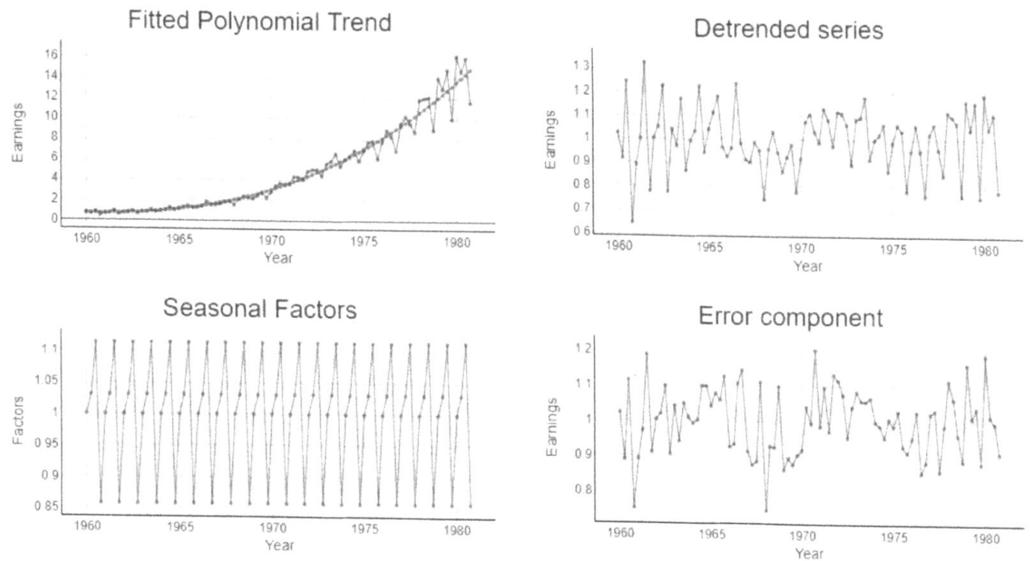


Figure 5.16 – Complete decomposition of earnings per Johnson & Johnson share (quarterly data)

To recap, the decomposition of time series is still an important element to include in the toolbox of those who approach Time Series Analysis at any level. In fact, the extraction of key features through decomposition can be used both as an initial descriptive analysis to understand the dynamics of data and to generate features to be included in more complex forecasting models.

## Autocorrelation

One of the most distinctive characteristics of a time series is the mutual dependence between the observations. In fact, it's important in Time Series Analysis to focus on the relationship between the *lagged values* of a time series.

In bivariate statistics, to analyze the relationship between two numerical variables, the Pearson linear correlation index is probably the most used (and abused) association metric. The correlation index is a relative (symmetric) measure of the linear relationship existing between two quantitative variables, X and Y, and it's calculated as follows:

$$r = \frac{s_{XY}}{s_X s_Y}$$

Where:

- $s_{XY}$ is the sample covariance between X and Y($s_{XY} = [1|(n-1)]\sum_{i=1}^{n}(x_i - \overline{x})(y_i - \overline{y})$).

- $s_X$ and $s_Y$ are the sample standard deviation of X and Y.

Just as the correlation index measures the linear relationship between two variables X, the **autocorrelation** index measures the linear relationship between the *lagged values* of a time series. As the standard deviation and the mean of $y_t$ are approximately equal to the standard deviation and the mean of $y_{t-k}$ (when the time series length $T$ is large and $k \ll T$ ), it's possible to calculate $r_k$, the value of the autocorrelation index between $y_t$ and $y_{t-k}$, as follows:

$$r_k = \frac{\sum_{t=k+1}^{T}(y_t - \bar{y})(y_{t-k} - \bar{y})}{\sum_{t=1}^{T}(y_t - \bar{y})^2}$$

Formula 5.12

Where:

- $k$ is the lag order.
- $\bar{y}$ is the sample mean of $y_t$.
- $T$ is the length of the time series.

The concept of autocorrelation, its analysis, and its use within forecasting models will be discussed in more detail in the following chapters where the **autocorrelation function** (ACF) of the **partial autocorrelation function** (PACF) will be discussed.

## Stationarity

**Stationarity** is a mathematical concept connected to stochastic processes, and so it's a broader concept as it's not only related to Time Series Analysis. Here, we don't focus on the mathematical definition (also because we have different types of stationarities in mathematics and so many definitions), but we explain what a stationary time series is.

The most simple definition of stationarity is the following: stationarity indicates that fundamental statistical properties of the Time Series, such as its mean and its variance, do not change over time. However, this does not imply that the Time Series does not change at all over time. We can still observe time-dependent dynamics and autocorrelation in a stationary time series, but the mean, the variance, and the autocorrelation structure of a stationary time series will be roughly constant over time.

So, the main characteristics of a stationary time series are the following:

- The values oscillate frequently around the mean, independent of time.
- The variance of the fluctuations remains constant over time.
- The autocorrelation structure is constant over time and no periodic fluctuations exist.

So, a Time Series that shows trend or seasonality is not stationary.

Whenever a shock occurs (for example, a sudden "disturbance" in the pattern of the series), a stationary process is said to be *mean-reverting*, meaning that the effect of the shock is only temporary and the Time Series will converge back to its mean in the short run. In non-stationary processes, on the other hand, shocks have a permanent impact on the mean, which is sustainably changed and does not converge back to the pre-disturbance value.

Why is the concept of stationarity important? First, because stationary processes are easier to analyze; they are more stable and under control. Therefore, having the ability to transform the Time Series so that it becomes stationary can simplify subsequent analyses. Second, stationarity is a common assumption for many practices and tools of time series analysis, such as the SARIMA models that we will discuss in *Chapter 7*.

# Summary

In this chapter, we have introduced some key concepts that will form the components of the analyses shown in the following chapters. First, we learned how to isolate and recognize the trend and seasonality of a time series, either through techniques dedicated to the estimation of individual components or by using a joint approach, such as decomposition. Finally, we introduced the concepts of autocorrelation and stationarity, which are the foundations on which ARIMA models are built.

Regardless of the industry in which one finds oneself working and the type of time series one wants to predict, knowing the statistical properties of the target series and how to correctly identify trends and seasonality can help any business analyst be more effective in isolating patterns of interest, whether for descriptive or predictive purposes. The first building block of Time Series analysis is always the ability to correctly decompose a Time Series, and, in this chapter, we have provided, step by step, all of the elements to do so effectively.

In the following chapters, we will focus on how to build a forecasting model, both through classical methodologies and based on machine learning methods.

# Questions

1. Which is not a method useful to identify and remove a trend from a time series?

    A. Curve fitting.

    B. Applying the logarithmic transformation.

    C. Filtering with moving average smoothing.

    D. Differencing.

2. What is a limit of moving average smoothing compared to curve fitting for trend estimation?

    A. Once the moving average is applied, the resulting time series will have less observations than the original series.

    B. Moving average smoothing is less powerful than curve fitting to detect irregularities in the trend.

    C. Moving average smoothing cannot be used when the time series shows seasonality.

    D. Moving average smoothing is a more complicated method compared to curve fitting.

3. Which are the two main types of seasonal component, considering the relationship of this component with the level/trend of the time series?

    A. Additive and stochastic seasonality.

    B. Multiplicative and deterministic seasonality.

    C. Additive and multiplicative seasonality.

    D. Linear and quadratic seasonality.

4. Which is not a method used to identify and remove seasonality from a time series?

    A. Regression with dummies.

    B. Seasonal filtering.

    C. Applying the Box-Cox transformation.

    D. Seasonal differencing.

5. Which are the steps to be followed to decompose a time series?

    A. Trend estimation, calculation of seasonal factors, determination of the residual component.

    B. Trend estimation, calculation of the seasonally adjusted series, determination of the residual component.

    C. Trend estimation, calculation of the detrended series, calculation of seasonal factors, calculation of the predicted series.

    D. Trend estimation, calculation of the detrended series, calculation of seasonal factors, determination of the residual component.

# Part 2: Building and Deploying a Forecasting Model

In this part, we enter the world of predictive modeling applied to time series. We proceed with practical examples in a crescendo of technical difficulty, starting from statistics-based and finishing with machine learning-based forecasting. The following are the chapters included in this part:

# 6
# Humidity Forecasting with Classical Methods

In this chapter, we will build the first forecasting model ready for deployment, looking at how data can be recorded from sensors attached to an Arduino controller.

You'll learn how KNIME Analytics Platform, as well as KNIME Server, can connect to sensors via REST endpoints, the basics of time series data cleaning and pre-processing, the different options for data granularity levels, and several classic and easy-to-use models that can be used for forecasting. Finally, we'll look at some simple ways the model can be deployed for real-world applications with KNIME, such as writing model predictions to databases or saving trained models and workflows for later use.

We will cover the following main topics in the chapter:

- The importance of predicting the weather
- Streaming humidity data from an Arduino sensor
- Resampling and granularity
- Training and deployment

By the end of this chapter, we will have completed our first project with a forecasting use case. You will understand when simple classical solutions are better than more complex algorithms and when you may need to move to more advanced techniques such as those covered in later chapters. The pipeline for moving data from external sources to modeling and deployment will be first covered here as well.

## Technical requirements

The following are the prerequisites for this chapter:

- KNIME Analytics Platform installed
- Optional – KNIME Server to enable REST endpoints, not required for analysis

All workflows introduced in the chapter are available on the KNIME Hub at `https://kni.me/s/GxjXX6WmLi-WjLNx`.

## The importance of predicting the weather

Forecasting the weather is something people have been doing for nearly forever, with a huge amount of different approaches. For this chapter, we use humidity as an accessible and relatable example. The most sophisticated modern methods for forecasting the weather, temperature, and humidity use complicated physical simulations alongside data science techniques, and we can't really hope to outperform them for long-term forecasts.

Despite this, we will see that with a concisely defined purpose, even the simplest models can prove useful. In this chapter, we will focus on generating forecasts only a few units (in our case, hours) into the future. If the humidity is in the process of spiking, we will want to bring our sensors, and whatever they are attached to, inside before it rains. In later chapters, we will extend the forecast horizon to predict days or weeks into the future.

> **Building Concise Data Science Projects**
>
> When building a data science project, you'll always see the most success when plenty of time is taken to define the business need, the available inputs, and the outputs that will be helpful.
>
> For example, I keep my window open at the office, but I don't want my desk to get wet when it rains. If I go away and try and build a full-bodied weather forecasting tool complete with tomorrow's high and low temperatures, I'll find my chance of successfully solving the original problem has dropped substantially. Simply building a tool that knows whether it is currently raining or is likely to rain in the next few minutes will give us a much higher chance of completing the project successfully.

What are some other sensors we may consider plugging into when forecasting the weather? Enriching our Time Series data with additional Time Series such as the following can be helpful.

### Other IoT sensors

Often, we try to exclude extra data that correlates strongly with existing columns. This can be useful when trying to reduce the dimensionality of input data to a model in traditional classification or regression use cases, but with Time Series, sometimes choosing data that correlates strongly and building a multivariate model will allow us to generate better predictions.

So, what kinds of sensors might correlate with humidity?

- **Temperature sensor**

  Humidity is measured as the ratio of water vapor in the air versus the total amount possible before it would precipitate. We can intuitively expect the temperature to correlate strongly with humidity, thus a temperature sensor would be a good sensor to add to the system.

- **Clock**

  Just as humidity is directly tied to temperature, the temperature is tied to the time of day. Perhaps it is most humid in the morning just as the sun rises or in the evening right after it sets.

- **Ambient light sensor**

  When I think of humid days, I think of overcast skies, and when I think of dry days, I think of clear skies with plenty of sunlight. This could be helpful, noticing the skies darken before a rainstorm, especially when paired with a clock time.

- **Sensors at different locations**

  Many modern forecasting systems are not built strictly of data from one sensor location but from many sensors scattered across the city, country, and world. Beyond that, even satellite readings are used to augment local data for weather forecasts. Now, we're not going to be launching a satellite just to decide whether I need to close my office window...but we could add one to the roof or the opposite side of the same building.

Remember that our goal is simple, and that building a convoluted project only hurts our chances of success. Let's look at what we can do with just Arduino, KNIME, and some basic models.

## The use case

In the example for this chapter, we've used an Arduino board to record sensor readings from outside an office window. While we will talk a bit about what an Arduino board is, how it works, and how to use it, it is not the topic of this chapter. So, I encourage you to check out the Arduino website to learn more about it: `https://www.arduino.cc`.

The Arduino we're using is the *MKR WIF 1010 Module*, in part because it was on hand and in part because it is Wi-Fi compatible. This comes in very handy when sending the sensor data to our KNIME workflow, as you'll see in the coming sections when we talk about REST services.

To actually record the humidity, we needed to attach a sensor to the Arduino board; we chose the Arduino *MKR IoT Carrier* because it's readily compatible with the baseboard and has multiple sensors besides just humidity. In the following figure, you can see how all the different systems will come together in this chapter:

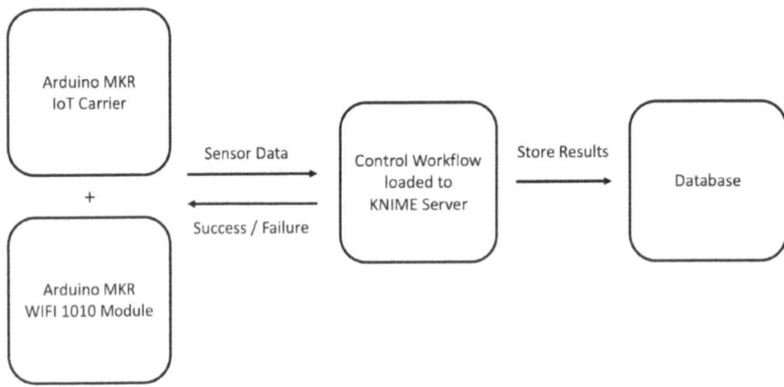


Figure 6.1 – Architecture diagram for Arduino/KNIME web service

At the top left, we have the **Arduino MKR IoT Carrier**; this is where humidity in the air is converted to an electrical voltage and our digitization begins. This sensor is connected to the **Arduino MKR WIFI 1010 Module**; this tiny computer converts the sensor voltage readings to digital data points, doubles, and integers, for example, which we'll conduct an analysis on. However, this board has almost no storage space to record long periods of data! For this reason, we regularly send these readings to our KNIME workflow over the internet via REST. From here, we can aggregate and store the data for later analysis and modeling in a database.

With an overview of our plan complete, we'll start with the first step: how do we get data from the sensors on the Arduino board to KNIME? In the next section, we'll talk about the control workflow referenced in the center of *Figure 6.1*.

## Streaming humidity data from an Arduino sensor

The first stage of the process when building an application on top of IoT data is gaining access to the sensors. This process will look quite a bit different depending on the sensor you're connecting to and where it is located. Since our sensor is located on an Arduino board with Wi-Fi connectivity, we choose to send it over the internet via REST. Conveniently, any workflow loaded to the KNIME Server automatically has REST endpoints generated for it. We'll get to those and how to find them shortly.

First, a bit more background about the Arduino; we'll need this knowledge to design an appropriate workflow to accept its data.

## What is an Arduino?

We've used the name a bit already but as we get into this section on setting up the Arduino board and retrieving our sensor data, it's important we recap what exactly we're working with. Arduino is an open source software and hardware company. They produce microcontrollers and other devices that attach to these controllers, for example, the Arduino MKR IoT Carrier that we're using. To use an Arduino, you'll have to do a bit of coding, but they're very intuitive to use and they have great educational materials available through their website.

> **Arduino Sketches**
>
> The blocks of code run on Arduino are called **sketches**; they inform the Arduino how to initialize itself upon startup and what to do upon execution. The setup portion of the sketch details what devices are connected to the Arduino and the execution portion of the sketch, which is typically a loop, informs the Arduino what to do with the connected devices.

If you choose to use a different Arduino microcontroller than the one we used, be sure to choose one that is Wi-Fi capable, either with a built-in Wi-Fi card or with the ability to connect to one. This is necessary when sending data to KNIME Server.

To make the Arduino microcontroller useful, we need to attach a sensor to it as the base microcontroller can't do too much on its own. The Arduino MKR IoT Controller we've attached to it can buzz, light up, and, as we're most interested in, sense air temperature, pressure, and humidity.

## Moving data to KNIME

To get our data from the Arduino, we will go through the internet and a **REST** connection on the KNIME Server. Since the Arduino we're using is Wi-Fi enabled, we can establish that connection and consume a web service through an HTTPS connection. The web service we'll be reaching out to will be our KNIME workflow!

Using a KNIME Server in this way is very straightforward; there are no obnoxious API keys, tokens, or the like, and the connection is established with a basic OAuth authorization. Once a connection is established, a JSON containing the sensor data can be sent to the proper address, the REST endpoint, and the rest is handled inside the KNIME workflow.

> **Building a JSON**
>
> **JSON** stands for **JavaScript Object Notation**; it is a standard file format for transferring data between applications. Its applications in web services are everywhere. Because we're parsing the JSON into a data table inside of our KNIME workflow, we have the freedom to construct it in whichever way is most convenient.

To find the REST endpoints for the KNIME workflow that our Arduino sketch will send the JSON data to, we first need to load the workflow to a KNIME Server. To do this we can right-click on a workflow or workflow group and select **Deploy to Server**, as you can see in the following screenshot. To do this, you'll need to purchase a KNIME Server license as it is not open source, as Analytics Platform is:

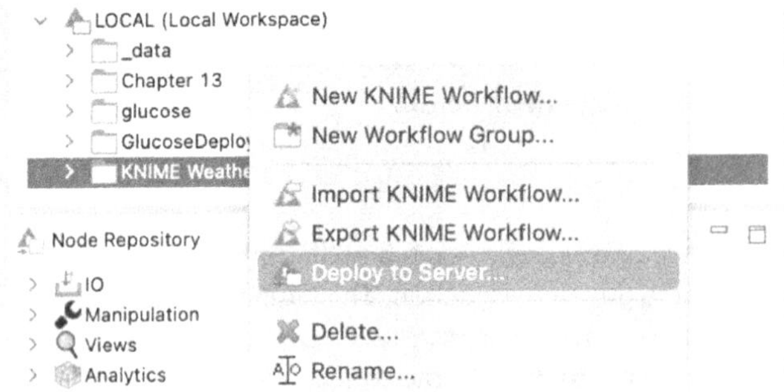


Figure 6.2 – Right-click to deploy to the server

After selecting **Deploy to Server**, as in *Figure 6.2*, you will be prompted to browse to the location on a KNIME Server you are connected to that you want to save your workflow or workflow group to.

After your workflow has been deployed to a KNIME Server, it will automatically have REST endpoints generated for it. These REST points can be seen by right-clicking on the workflow, which is now on the KNIME Server, and selecting **Show API definition**. You can see what this looks like in the following screenshot:

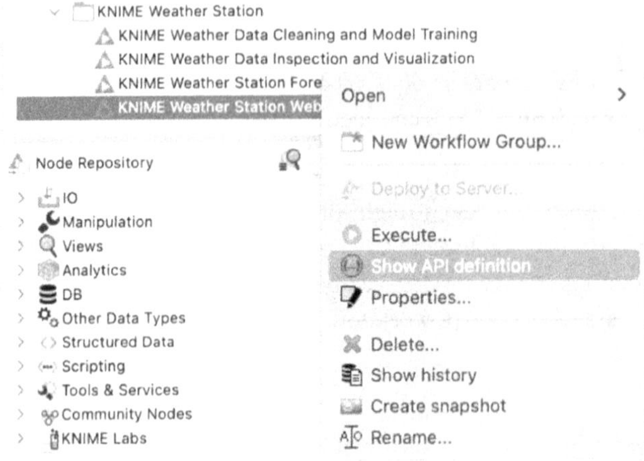


Figure 6.3 – Right-click to show API definition

Selecting **Show API definition** will launch a web browser and pull up a web page detailing the swagger definition of your specific workflow. From here, you can see the different types of requests you can send to the endpoints and the format to compose JSONs in. In the following figure, we see what this API definition looks like after opening it in the browser:

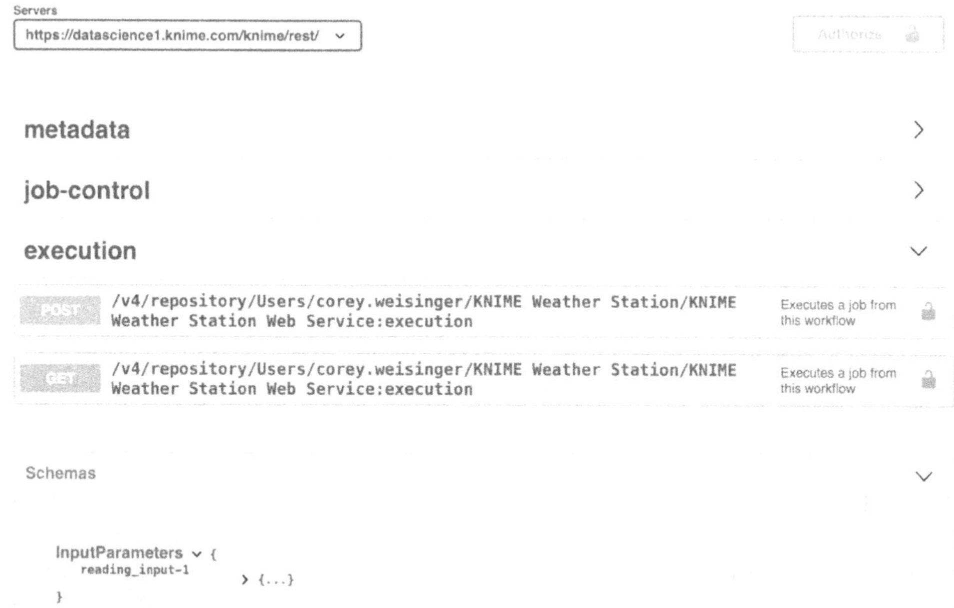


Figure 6.4 – KNIME workflow REST endpoint swagger definition

Looking back at the swagger definition shown in *Figure 6.4*, we see several different categories, each allowing the REST endpoint user to access different aspects of the workflow, from metadata extraction to execution triggers to input and output schemas. Let's review the different sections available when reviewing the REST endpoint swagger definition on the page you saw in *Figure 6.4*:

- **metadata**

  There is one REST endpoint available in this category; it will respond with meta-information about the workflow when hit but will not accept data or trigger an execution of the workflow.

- **job-control**

  Jobs are separate executions of a workflow on the KNIME Server. In this category, you can see a list of jobs, active or completed executions of the workflow, or create a new one. Creating a new one triggers a fresh execution of the workflow.

- **execution**

  From here, you can create a new job, just as with the **job-control** endpoint, and execute the workflow.

- **Schemas**

  The **Schemas** section details the JSON shape the workflow expects to receive and what shape it expects to respond with.

For our task, connecting the Arduino to the KNIME Server REST endpoints, we will take advantage of the **Schemas** section to make sure our JSONs are in the correct shape, and the **execution** section to see the address we need to send the REST request to.

> Try It Out!
>
> By clicking on the **POST** or **GET** button you see on the swagger definition page in *Figure 6.4*, and again on the **Try it out** button, you can submit `Get` or `Post` requests to the KNIME workflow in real time to see how it will respond and verify everything is working as intended.

Once the Arduino is speaking with the KNIME workflow via the REST endpoints, we need to figure out what to do with the data. We're not sending enough data in an individual submission to train a model or conduct much analysis right away. So, first, we need to stockpile some data for this purpose.

## Storing the data to create a training set

There are many different file types, cloud storage systems, and databases that KNIME Analytics Platform can connect to, and for that reason, we have many options for where and how to store the data we receive from the Arduino sensor, but there are some key features good choices will have in common. Let's review some of them:

- We want to be able to append data to whatever storage format we choose; it will be much easier than reading and overwriting a flat file such as a CSV file.
- We want this file to be cloud-based so it is easy to access from the KNIME Server and from local workflows when the time comes to train a model.
- A free solution is always nice!

With all these features in mind, we've chosen to simply log our sensor readings into a Google sheet. Other good options that may perform better at scale would be loading the readings into a database such as Oracle or Snowflake.

### Connecting to Google Sheets

Connecting to **Google Sheets** with KNIME is very easy with the Google Authentication and suite of Google Sheets manipulation nodes. You can read and write sheets of course, but you can also update the sheet, which allows us to change individual records in the table or append records to the end of existing sheets.

Figure 6.5 – Google Sheets connectivity nodes

Interacting with the Google suite requires the use of a couple of nodes in sequence but will be very straightforward:

1. The Google Authentication node to connect to your Google account will open a web browser prompting you to log in.
2. The Google Sheets Connection node to move to the Google Sheets framework. There is nothing to configure in this node.
3. Use the Google Sheets Reader or Google Sheets Writer node just like you would other reader and writer nodes to connect to different sheets. There's also the Google Sheets Appender node for adding rows to an existing Google sheet.

We tie this all together in a KNIME workflow to receive the JSON data from our Arduino and append it to a Google sheet for later analysis with the methods we'll introduce in the remainder of the chapter.

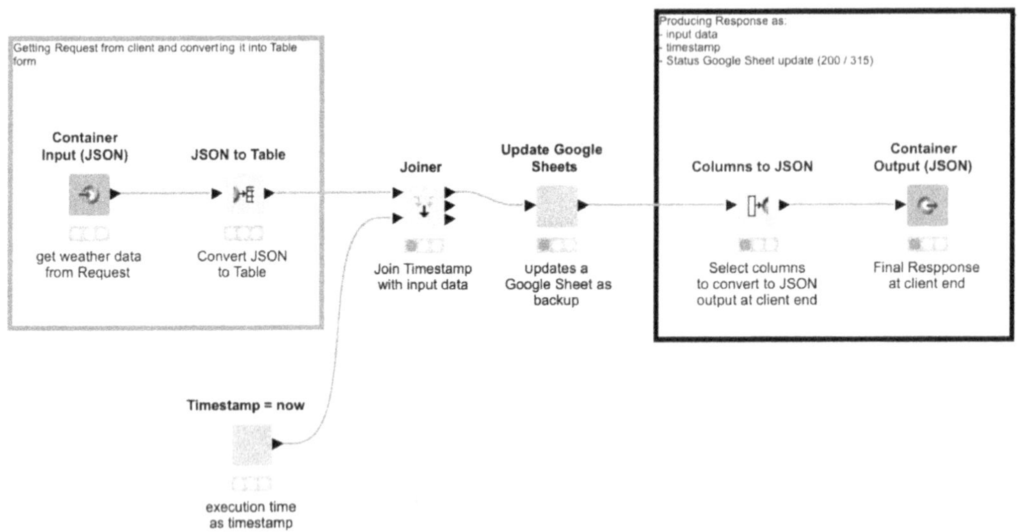


Figure 6.6 – Web service workflow

*Figure 6.6* shows the web service workflow that accepts JSON data via the Container Input (JSON) node, converts it to a table format, loads the records to Google Sheets, and responds to the Arduino via the Container Output (JSON) nose to verify the data was logged. This is all done through the automated REST endpoints of the KNIME Server.

With this, the construction of the control workflow we first mentioned way back in *Figure 6.1* is complete. Our data is now being parsed from the sensors on the Arduino and logged into a table. Next, we will discuss how to work with this newly acquired Time Series data and perform our analysis and forecasting on it.

# Resampling and granularity

Time series data has its own set of common data cleansing and preprocessing steps, and these are especially important when working with IoT data. Sensors often produce data with gaps, outliers, or missing values. It's not necessarily because sensors are less reliable than other data sources, but the sheer frequency with which we receive data points means we're more likely to have these types of errors.

In the next few sections, we'll recap some of the most common techniques we apply when preparing our Time Series data for analysis and modeling: aligning timestamps, correcting missing values, and aggregating.

## Aligning data timestamps

The most common issue I've run into when analyzing IoT, specifically when plugging directly into a sensor, is *irregularly spaced timestamps*. For some types of analysis, this may not be a problem. Some of the methods in this chapter (**mean value forecast**, **naïve forecast**, and **linear regression**) can handle irregular spacings when used properly. Other models, such as neural networks, ARIMA, and SARIMA from later in this book, however, will not.

I still advise aligning your timestamps to fix any irregular spacing as a best practice. It gives us insight into any possible mistakes in our data gathering process and keeps the data in a consistent format. To align timestamps in KNIME Analytics Platform, we use the **Timestamp Alignment** component. You can find this component on the KNIME Examples server under **00_Components** | **Time Series**. Configuring the **Timestamp Alignment** component, as you can see in *Figure 6.7*, is very straightforward:

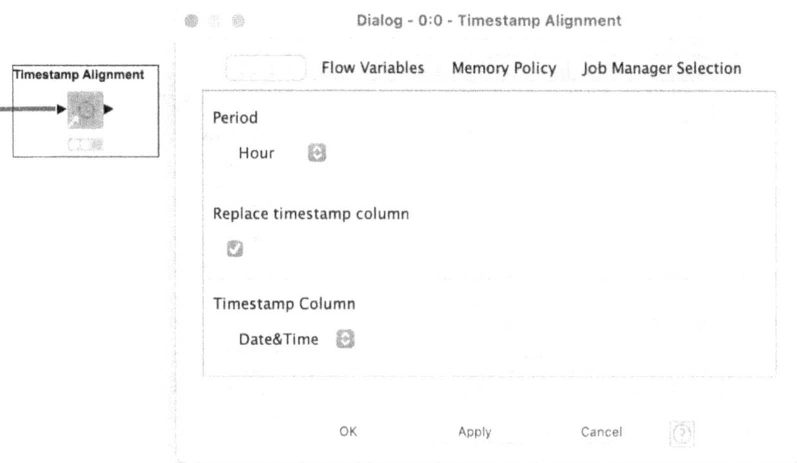


Figure 6.7 – The Timestamp Alignment component and configuration dialog

Select the granularity of your data in the **Period** dropdown box and select the column containing your timestamp data in the **Timestamp Column** dropdown box. Checking the **Replace timestamp column** box will replace the existing column with a new one that contains regularly spaced timestamps. If this box is left unchecked, a new column will be added with the regularly spaced timestamp.

After executing this node, your table will have one row per hour, minute, and second, and for any new timestamps that needed to be added to regularly space the Time Series, new rows will be in the table. These rows will have missing values for the remaining columns of the input table. We can now deal with the missing timestamps in the same way we would deal with missing values.

## Missing values

**Missing values** are also common when working with IoT data. Sometimes this is due to the correction of irregularly spaced data, as we discussed in the previous section, sometimes this is a momentary loss of connection to a sensor, or it could even be the sensor's way of sending a 0 value and working as intended.

To impute missing values properly will require some level of domain expertise. If you don't have this expertise, I strongly encourage you to reach out to whoever is in charge of data acquisition and check in with them.

For IoT data, or any data I expect to be continuous, my favorite method for interpolation is linear interpolation. **Linear interpolation** is the process of connecting a straight line from the last data point before the missing value to the first data point after it and using this line to extrapolate a value for the missing data point. In the event that only one sequential data point is missing and the Time Series is evenly spaced, this results in a value directly in the middle of the previous and next data point.

Be careful when choosing a method for missing value imputation, however; imagine for a moment you're working with a table containing daily sales data for a grocery store. There is a missing value for the revenue on November 13 and on December 25. It may be a bookkeeping error that resulted in a missing value on November 13 and linear interpolation or a mean value imputation may be OK, however, December 25 is Christmas and the store may have been closed; that missing value could be a zero in disguise.

To impute **missing values** in KNIME, we use the **Missing Value** node, which has several options for imputation methods based on the column's data type. The node supports doubles, integers, date and time, and strings with different methods. Let's look at how to configure and use the **Missing Value** node you can see in *Figure 6.8*:

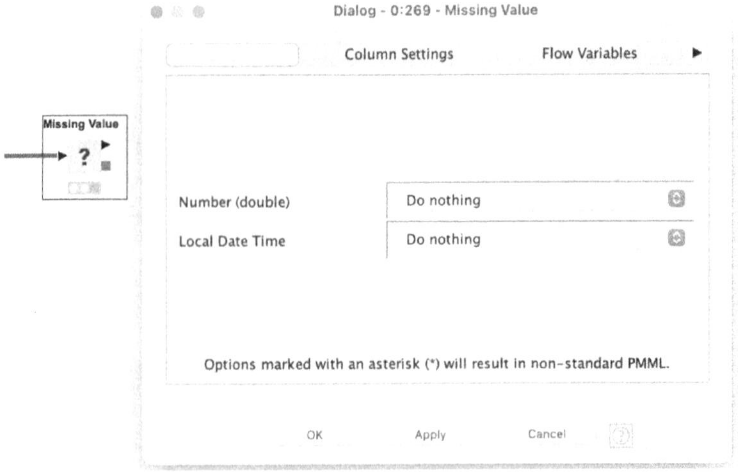


Figure 6.8 – The Missing Value node and configuration dialog

Start by selecting the type of interpolation you want to use for each data type. By default, they are set to **Do nothing**, leaving missing values as they are. Some other notable methods include the following:

- **Previous Value**
- **Mean value**
- **Fixed Value** (such as 0)
- **Moving Average**
- **Remove Row**

To build more specific methods of cleaning Time Series data, we look to windowing the data and aggregating these windows.

## Aggregation techniques

Beyond aligning timestamps and correcting missing values, it's often a good idea to aggregate Time Series data. This can be crucial when working with very high-frequency IoT data but is still a great way to prepare data for visual exploration of low-frequency data. For example, viewing average daily sales numbers by month can help make it easier to see seasonal patterns. Most of the **aggregation** techniques we'll apply are familiar ones: Max, Median, Mean, and Min. However, the question becomes: what does this mean in the context of a Time Series?

### *Windowing*

To perform aggregations on Time Series data, we first **window** the data. This is the process of taking a chunk of the series; perhaps if our data is by the second, we create a 5-minute window, or if it's hourly, we make a 1-day window. These windows can be entirely disjointed, meaning they do not overlap, or they can share data points. Using overlapping windows adds a smoothing effect to our Time Series but does less for reducing the size of the dataset. To facilitate this choice, sometimes it's best to think in terms of two values: window step size and window length.

> **Example**
>
> I want my newly aggregated Time Series to have values every 5 minutes, but I want these values to be based on a 10-minute wide average, which can be helpful if the Time Series is highly variable. I should use a step size of 5 minutes and a window length of 10 minutes. This will need to be translated to a number of rows.

We can perform windowing with the **Window Slider** node, but the **Moving Aggregation** node will produce the aggregations on our configured window in one pass. So we will use the Moving Aggregation node for now. Look to the Window Slider node if you want to use an aggregation technique that's not supported by the Moving Aggregation node. We do this to take advantage of the Fourier transform in *Chapter 8, Audio Signal Classification with an FFT and a Gradient Boosted Forests.*

There are a few settings to configure for the Moving Aggregation node; let's run through them, as in *Figure 6.9*:

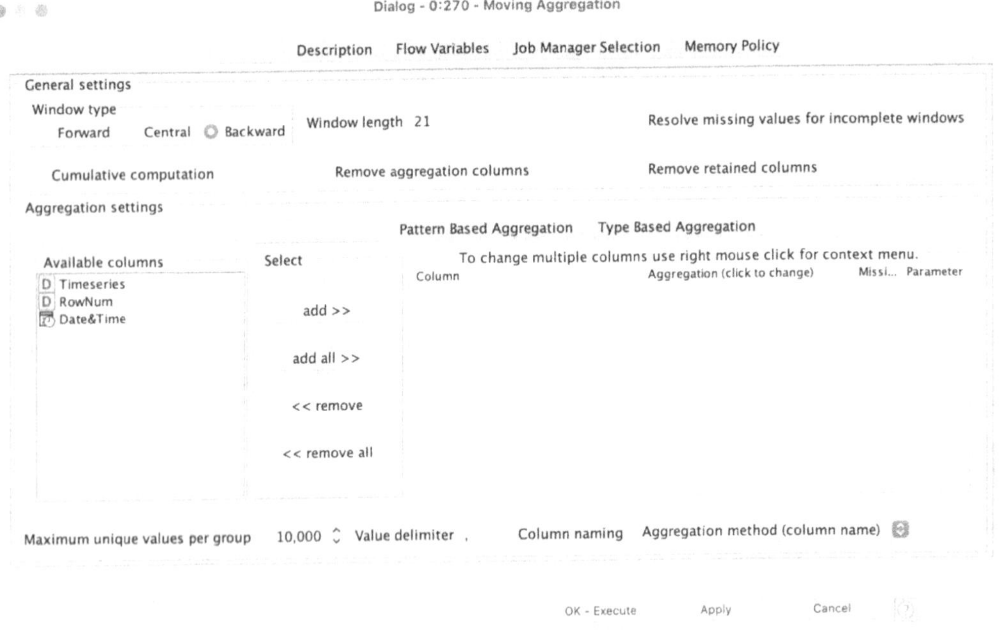


Figure 6.9 – Moving Aggregation node configuration dialog

To the top left, we see the **Window type** box; you can select **Forward**, **Central**, or **Backward**. Each row in the input table will have an output. The **Window type** option controls how the window is built around each row. **Forward** will include future rows in the calculation, **Central** will build the window with half of the records from before and half from after, and **Backward** will exclusively use records from before the row being processed. To the right of this setting is **Window length**, where the number of rows included in the window is set. Finally, the bottom columns from the table on the left show as **Available columns**, and adding them to the list on the right will enable the selection of an aggregation method. Each method will be added as a new column at the output of the node.

> **Window Type**
>
> **Central** may be the most intuitive option when selecting a window type, but there are some side effects to consider. Selecting **Forward** will produce missing values at the end of your table since there are no values after the final row, **Backward** will do the same at the start of the table, and **Central** will produce some missing values at both ends.

Windowing and aggregating are often the final stages of preprocessing we perform before modeling, but they aren't only useful for that end goal. Keep in mind that visualizing these various aggregation techniques can be important for building intuition before moving on to…

# Training and deployment

Training and deployment in KNIME Analytics Platform come in a variety of complexities; for this chapter, we'll look at some of the simpler options. No matter how you plan to train your model, it's good to first partition your data. To partition data in KNIME, we use the **Partitioning** node:

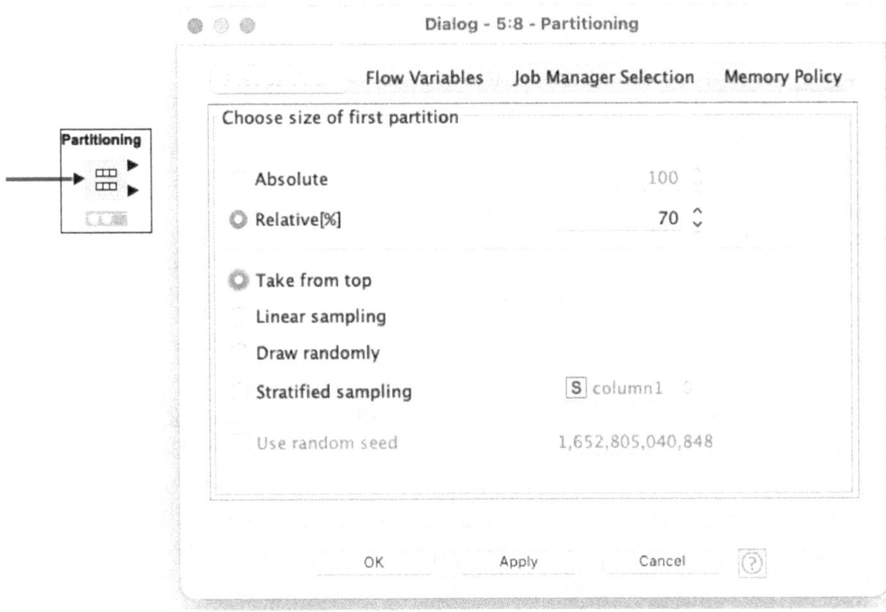


Figure 6.10 – The Partitioning node and configuration dialog

In *Figure 6.10*, we see the **Partitioning** node and its configuration dialog. You'll notice the node has one input port to the left and two output ports to the right. The input port is our full dataset, and the two outputs are the two splits based on our configuration choices. Note that the top port aligns with the options in the configuration dialog.

There are two things to configure for this node: the size of the first partition and how it is created. A 70/30 split with 70% being for the training set is common practice, but this can vary by use case. For example, if I'm only forecasting 100 records into the future, I get no benefit from a test set with 1,000 records. The more important option here is the bottom half, where we configure how the sets are created. By default, the Partitioning node will randomly sample the dataset to create the partitions, but when working with time series data, it is important to partition with the **Take from top** option. This ensures our training data all comes from before the test data, preventing data leakage and ensuring our testing setup resembles a real deployment of the model as much as possible.

Let's review some of the methods we use most frequently; they aren't the most powerful, but they are incredibly robust methods.

## Types of classic models available in KNIME

There is a myriad of models that can be used in Time Series analysis, some advanced and great for large datasets such as neural networks, and some simple and great for producing results with exceptionally small datasets. Let's look at some of these classic approaches to forecasting first, to get our feet wet with the process. We'll cover the following:

- Naïve forecast
- Mean value forecast
- Simple exponential smoothing
- Linear regression

The first of these classic techniques requires nearly no computation or data at all.

### *Naive forecast*

The **Naïve forecast** is the simplest of the forecasting tools we'll cover in this book and is aptly named *naïve* because it forecasts all future values as the same as the most recent known value. There's no machine learning to speak of and no model to fit when using a Naïve forecast. You may be surprised how often this can outperform even the most sophisticated of models (such as SARIMA or Neural Networks from later in this book) when being used for very short-term forecasts.

The reason the Naïve forecast is so effective at short-term forecasts, such as what the humidity will be 5 minutes from now, is because of continuity. Think of temperature, for example; if it's 24°C outside right now, the only way for it to get down to 22°C is if it first becomes 23°C. If your Time Series is continuous in this way, the Naïve forecast is a very powerful tool you shouldn't overlook. Let's look at an example of a Naïve forecast in the following figure:

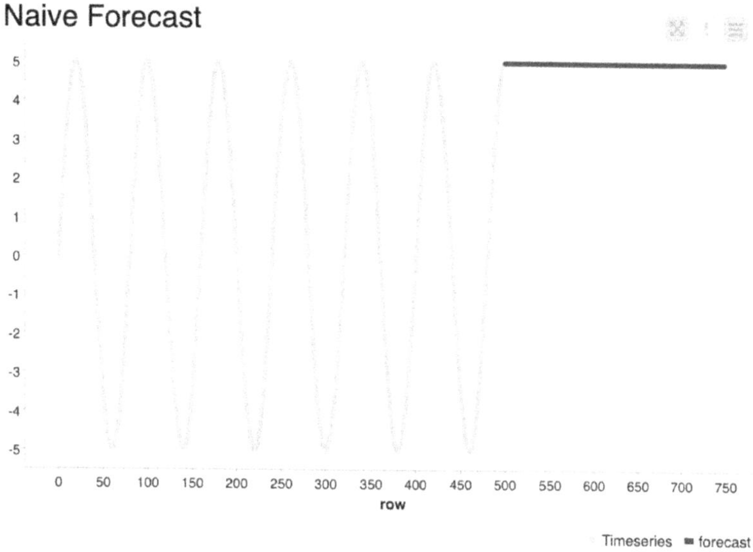


Figure 6.11 – Naïve forecast of a sine wave. The last value determines the prediction

Imagine you have a basic sine-wave-shaped Time Series, as you saw in the preceding figure; a naïve forecast would extend as a constant value line from the last recorded point. Because each individual value of the sine wave is very similar to the previous value, this naïve forecast will predict the value one unit into the future very effectively. However, the usefulness of this forecasting method decays very quickly as the forecast horizon grows longer.

### *Mean value forecast*

The **mean value forecast** is another very simple method of generating future predictions. Like the Naïve forecast, there is no *machine learning* and the forecast is a *constant value*. Unlike the naïve forecast, however, the constant value is not equal to the most recent recorded data point but to the mean value. The mean value forecast is ideal when you suspect there is no pattern to our data, or when you do not have enough data to determine a pattern.

> **Naïve Versus Mean Value Forecast**
>
> When deciding whether the mean value or the naïve value is the best forecast method for your use case, consider whether your data is continuous, and whether you only need to forecast a few units into the future. If the answer to both is yes, use the naïve forecast.

Let's look to the sine wave again for a simple illustration; as you can see in the next figure, the forecast is a constant value line. This time, however, it extends from the mean value of the wave. Because of this, we have far larger forecast errors in the first units of the forecast. This is again because of continuity; the mean value forecast does not preserve it.

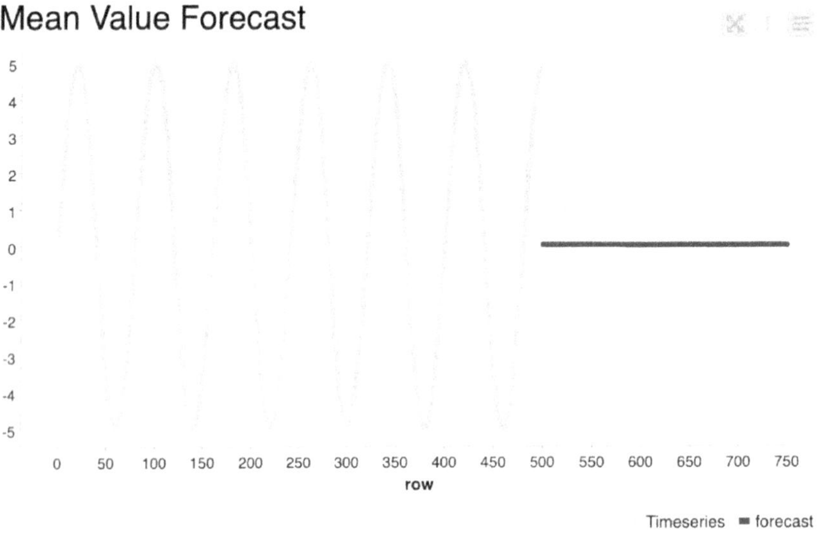


Figure 6.12 – Mean value forecast of a sine wave. The average value determines the prediction

The mean value forecast, for this reason, is typically used on discontinuous Time Series. Those are Time Series where the value now does not correlate to the value one observation into the past.

**White Noise**

White noise is a type of Time Series defined by its random oscillation around a mean. The mean value forecast is the best possible forecast for this type of data.

### *Simple exponential smoothing*

**Simple exponential smoothing** is the logical progression of the mean value forecast. Where the mean value forecast calculates the mean based on the entire available dataset, exponential smoothing calculates a weighted average. This weighted average values more highly recent terms in the Time Series. In a way, it's a blend of the best parts of the naïve and mean value forecasting methods. Let's review the equation for this one, first looking at $S_t$: the smoothing statistic.

$$s_t = \alpha x_t + (1 - \alpha)s_{t-1}$$

Formula 6.1

Where $s$ is the smoothing amount at time $t$, $\alpha$ is the smoothing factor, a value between `0` and `1`. Values of $\alpha$ closer to `1` will weigh more strongly recent values, and values closer to `0` will more heavily smooth the series by incorporating older terms more strongly. Let's unfold the previous equation to make it more clear:

$$s_t = \alpha x_t + (1-\alpha)\alpha x_{t-1} + (1-\alpha)^2\alpha^2 x_{t-2} + (1-\alpha)^3\alpha^3 x_{t-3} \ldots$$

Formula 6.2

There is no *best* way to pick the value of your $\alpha$ value; it can vary widely from use case to use case. The way we choose to think about selecting an $\alpha$ value is to first think, how many records do I suspect I need to get ~95% of the information about my Time Series? Then, by doing a little math, we can get to an $\alpha$! Here's a table to help you choose an $\alpha$ using this method:

| | |
|---|---|
| $\alpha = 0.40$ | ~95% of the information in the past 5 terms |
| $\alpha = 0.24$ | ~95% of the information in the past 10 terms |
| $\alpha = 0.13$ | ~95% of the information in the past 20 terms |
| $\alpha = 0.06$ | ~95% of the information in the past 50 terms |
| $\alpha = 0.01$ | ~95% of the information in the past 100 terms |

Table 6.1 – $\alpha$ term value versus number of terms to achieve 95% of the information

*Table 6.1* was produced based on the weighting terms back in the expanded equation. For example, with $\alpha = 0.4$, the first five terms are weights as follows: 0.4, 0.24, 0.14, 0.09, and 0.05. If you add up these terms, they equal 0.92. This means 92% of the average will be based on those five terms.

**α = 0 and α = 1**

When setting $\alpha$ equal to 0, you arrive at the mean value forecast, as the $(1 - \alpha)$ term equals 1 and, therefore, does not decay as we move farther into past records, removing any weighting from the average. In the case of $\alpha$ being equal to 1, we see the opposite; the only term given any weight when calculating the average is the most recent term. In this way, the simple exponential smoothing is really a combination of the naïve and the mean value forecasts.

As with the prior two types of forecasts, let's take a quick look at the Exponential Smoothing Forecast of the sine wave. It's also a constant value forecast but lies somewhere in between the mean value and naïve forecast lines. Let's look at an exponential smoothing forecast in the next figure; note that it is a flat line, like the naïve forecast, but doesn't extend from the end of the Time Series directly:

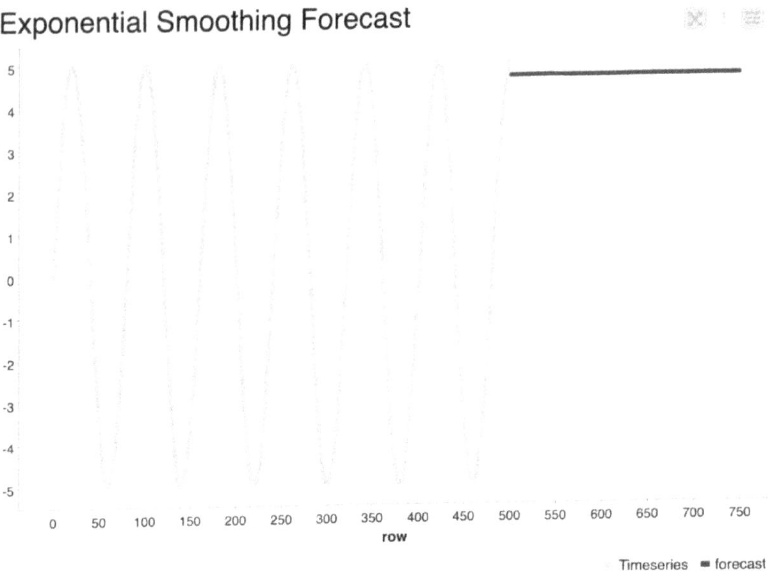


Figure 6.13 – Exponential Smoothing Forecast

The choice of $\alpha$ is really a choice between 0 for a mean value forecast and 1 for a naïve forecast. It enables us to land somewhere in the middle of the first two methods we observed. The next technique we'll look at will be the first for which an actual model is fit.

### *Linear regressions*

The first of the forecasting techniques that fit the model that we'll discuss is **linear regression**. Regression models come in a huge variety of shapes and sizes, but they all start from the same place. The first step in building a regression model is choosing the type of relationship you expect to find between input features and the target. In the case of linear regression, this is a linear function; think line, plane, and hyperplane. Once a class of mathematical equations is set, coefficients can be fit:

$$x_t = \beta_1 t + \beta_0$$

Formula 6.3

The most typical way to fit a linear regression model to a univariate Time Series is with an equation like the preceding one. We can read the equation as the regression of x on t. Note that t is the independent variable and x is the dependent.

**Other Regression Models**

The linear regression is easily expanded to a polynomial regression by adding additional terms, for example, a term where $t$ is squared. Now, instead of a straight-line forecast, we have a parabolic forecast:

$$x_t = \beta_1 t + \beta_2 t^2 + \beta_0$$

The SARIMA and ARIMA models we'll cover later in this book are also forms of regression models, but instead of regressing against $t$, they regress against previous values of $x$, and past forecast errors. More to come on that!

Linear regression is the first of the techniques we cover that does not generate a constant value forecast. It is a very effective model to use when performing explanatory analysis, specifically when investigating whether there is a trend in the data.

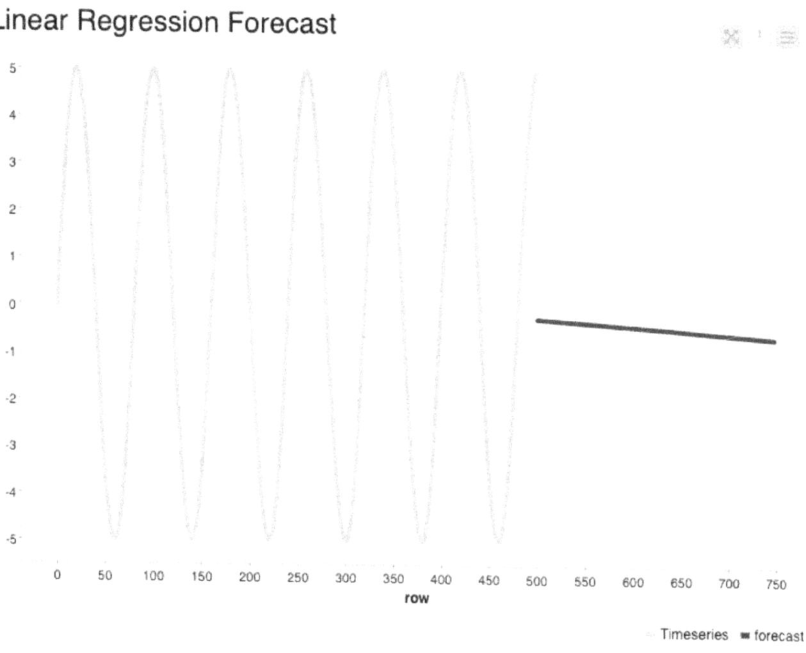


Figure 6.14 – Linear Regression Forecast

Looking at the linear regression forecast in *Figure 6.14*, we see that the model did detect a slight downward trend. We know, however, that this sine wave does not have a trend though...so what happened? Looking closely at the sine wave, we can see that its pattern repeats, but the initial pattern of the wave is an upward peak, and the final one recorded is a downward peak and the first half of an upward peak. For this reason, our data is primarily located above the mean at the start and below the mean at the end, and we see a forecasted downward trend. This is something to be aware of when applying a linear regression model to cyclic data.

Having discussed some of the models that we have available, let's move on to implementation, and talk about how exactly we use these models in KNIME Analytics Platform.

## Training a model in KNIME

With a few different types of forecasting techniques introduced, we'll use the linear regression model and our humidity data to demonstrate how to train a model in KNIME Analytics Platform. No matter what kind of model you train in KNIME, be it for classification, regression, or forecasting, the process is split into two nodes: a learner node to train the model, and a predictor node to apply it. In the case of Linear Regression, this is the Linear Regression Learner and the Regression Predictor nodes, as you can see in the following figure:

Figure 6.15 – Linear Regression Learner and Regression Predictor nodes

The learner node in *Figure 6.15* has one input port, which is the training data; any number of numeric columns can be used as model features to be selected when configuring the node, and additionally, one numeric column is needed for the target. This learner node also has two output ports; the top is a box that represents the trained model, which will attach to the box on the input side of the predictor node when you generate predictions with the model. The second output port contains information about the fit coefficients and some sample evaluation statistics such as R squared.

The predictor node, on the right, has two inputs and just one output. The top input, shaped like a box, connects back to the learner to load the fit model. The bottom input is the data you generate predictions for; this table should include all the columns with the same names as those used as input features in the learner node.

There is nothing of note to configure before using the predictor node, but let's recap the configuration dialog for the learner node before moving on:

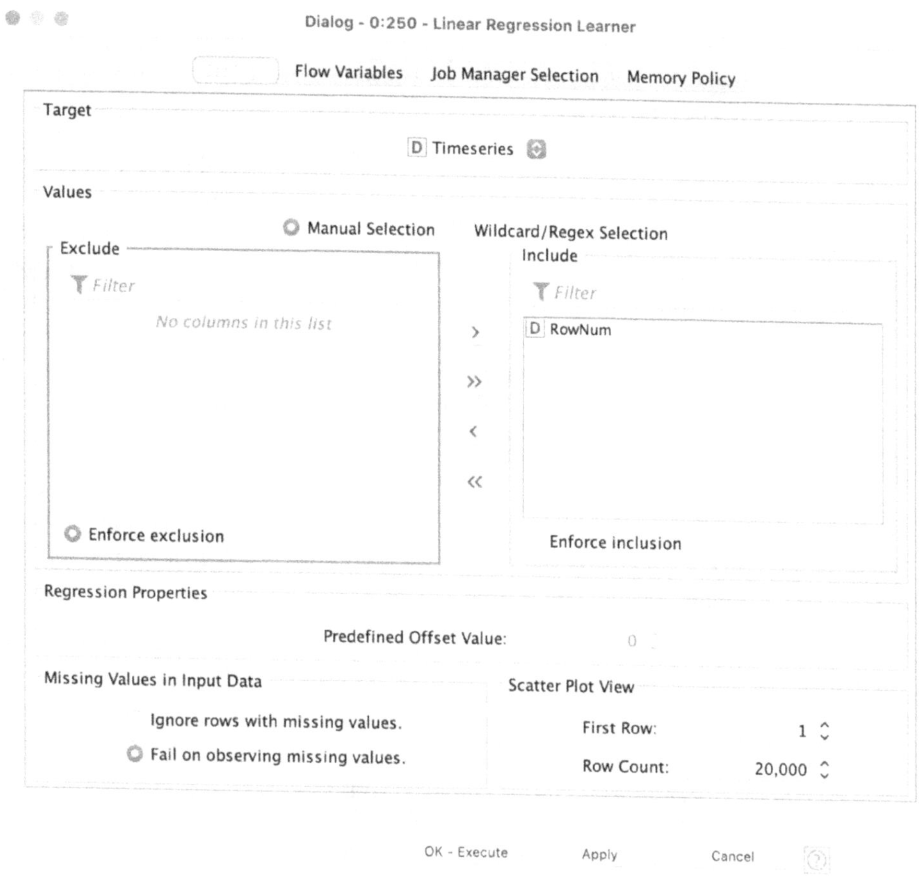

Figure 6.16 – Linear Regression Learner configuration dialog

*Figure 6.16* shows the configuration dialog for the Linear Regression Learner node. There are two areas we want to focus on when configuring this node and they're both quick and easy. At the very top of the configuration dialog is a drop-down box for selecting the target column; that's the dependent variable in other words. The second thing to configure is the input features. This is done by moving columns you *do* want to use as input features to the green box on the right, and columns you *do not* want to use as input features to the red box on the left. Only the columns used to fit the model, those in the right-hand box, will be needed as inputs for the Regression Predictor node.

The rest of the configuration options at the bottom of the window gives you choices for how to handle missing values in your training data, ignore missing rows, or fail the node's execution, and how many rows to include in the scatter plot, an extra view that the learner node produces to help you see how the model fits the data.

## Available deployment options

With the training workflow complete and a trained model now in our hands, the question becomes, what do we do with it? KNIME has a few different answers to this question, but since we started this chapter by talking about REST endpoints, let's start there again. Remember that any workflow loaded on to the KNIME Server automatically has these REST endpoints generated for it; these endpoints can be used to trigger the execution of the workflow or to retrieve metadata about it. If special nodes called input and output nodes are added to the workflow, these REST endpoints can also be used to pass data into a workflow when calling it or to retrieve data from the workflow after its execution. The easiest way to generate a deployment workflow with these special input and output nodes is with…

### *Integrated deployment*

Integrated deployment is a feature of KNIME Analytics Platform that enables us to capture specific portions of a workflow and combine them to create a new workflow. Often, that means copying a portion of the training workflow to automatically create a deployment workflow.

This works by the combined use of two main nodes, the **Capture Workflow Start** and **Capture Workflow End** nodes. As their names imply, you place the Start node at the beginning of the section of your data pipeline you wish to capture, and the End node at the end.

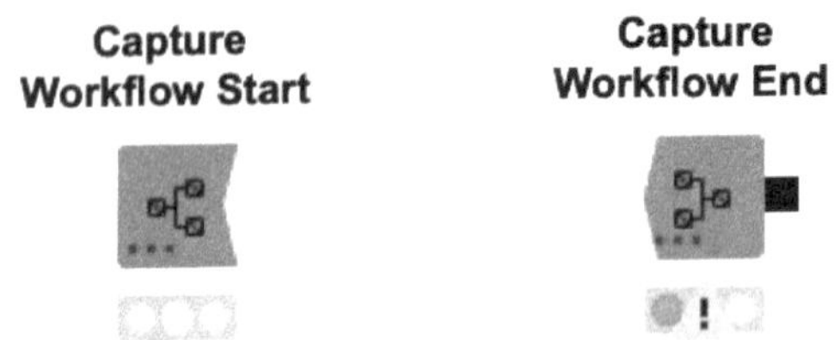


Figure 6.17 – Capture Workflow nodes for integrated deployment

Looking at the nodes in *Figure 6.17*, you'll see that the Capture Workflow Start node does not have any input or output ports, and the Capture Workflow End node only has one output port. These nodes have a configurable number of ports that can be added to them by clicking on the **...** in the bottom-left corner of the node. Clicking this icon will open a dialog asking what type of pass-through port you want to add; most of the time, this will be a **Data** port:

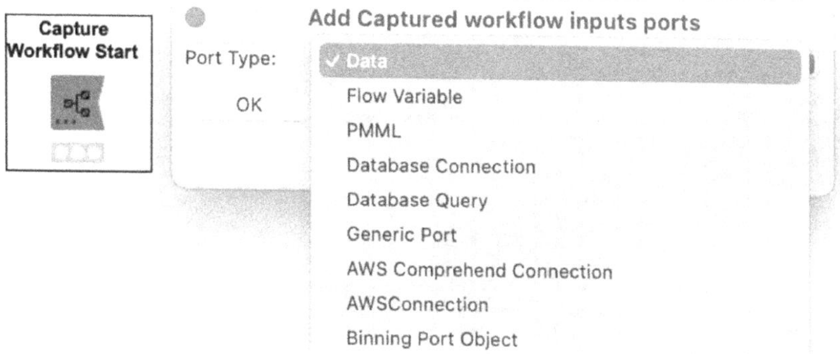


Figure 6.18 – Adding a port to the Capture Workflow Start node

The selection of these ports is important for more than just slotting the nodes into your existing workflow. They also determine what inputs from the Start node, and what output from the End node, will be expected by the workflow they will create. This means that if all we plan to pass into our deployment workflow when we hit its REST endpoints is a data table or a JSON, we should just add a data port. If we also plan to pass in a flow variable, PMML model, or some other connection, we need to add that here as well. The same holds true when choosing the ports for the Capture Workflow End node; be aware of what you want the workflow to return, if anything.

The typical sections of a training workflow we try to capture with integrated deployment are data preprocessing, the model predictor, and any post-processing there happens to be. In this chapter's example, that will just be preprocessing and the model prediction.

## Building the workflow

Now to assemble the data aggregating, cleansing, model training, and prediction into a workflow. A best practice that I talk about often is to do as much of your preprocessing as possible after partitioning your data into a train and test set. This prevents any accidental information leakage between the sets and makes it easier to trust your evaluation metrics when it is time to test your model. Let's look at a screenshot of the workflow to walk through how best to do this:

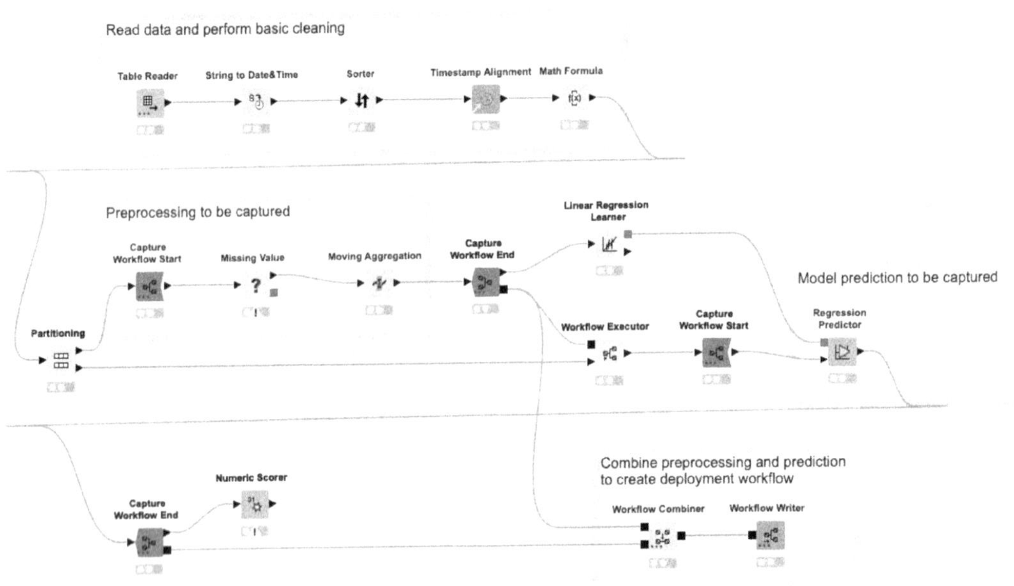


Figure 6.19 – Training workflow with integrated deployment to create deployment workflow

In the box at the very top of *Figure 6.19*, I read in the data and do some basic data cleansing. I differentiate this from preprocessing in that all the transformations on row by row, there is not linear interpolation of missing values or windowing of the data. For this reason, it is safe to perform before partitioning as there is no risk of information leakage. In this box, the timestamp is converted from a string to a proper date-time format with the **String to Date&Time** node, we verify the data is sorted with the **Sorter** node, and make sure the Time Series is regularly spaced with the **Timestamp Alignment** component. After this, the data is partitioned with the **Partitioning** node and the preprocessing that is not row-wise is performed. It's important to do these after partitioning to avoid data leakage. In this example there are only two steps: first, to impute missing values via linear interpolation with the **Missing Value** node, and second, to perform some smoothing with the **Moving Aggregation** node. With the latter, we do this by using a small window size of 3 and, in this window, calculate the mean value of the series, which helps smooth out anomalous spikes in the Time Series.

Notice that this section is surrounded by the **Capture Workflow Start** and **Capture Workflow End** nodes, and we use the integrated deployment feature for two purposes: to capture and reapply the preprocessing to the training set, which we do with the **Workflow Writer** node, and to save this portion of the workflow to use in the creation of the deployment workflow at the very end.

With the preprocessing sorted out, we use the **Linear Regression Learner** and **Regression Predictor** nodes to train the model on the training set and deploy it onto the test set. We also surround the Regression Predictor node with the Workflow Capture nodes; this is combined with the preprocessing section we just captured in the **Workflow Combiner** node before we save the deployment workflow with the Workflow Writer node.

## Writing model predictions to a database

Sometimes, you don't need your deployment solution to respond with anything, simply writing the prediction to a database is the end goal. KNIME Analytics Platform has the ability to connect to a huge variety of nodes right out of the box and can further connect to any database that has a JDBC driver.

### *Connecting to a database*

Before you can write to a database, you'll need to connect to it. In KNIME, this happens with one of the database connector nodes. If your database has a dedicated node, use that; if not, the generic DB connector node will allow the connection to any database for which you have a JDBC driver:

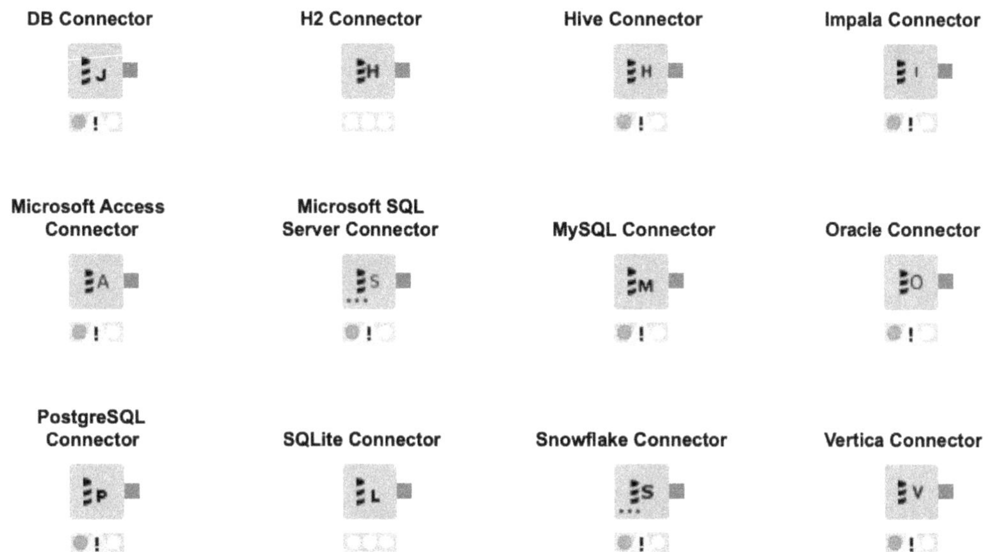


Figure 6.20 – Database connection nodes

In *Figure 6.20*, you can see the database **connectors** available in KNIME; note the DB Connector node to the top left, as this is the one you will use if you have a JDBC driver for a database that doesn't have a dedicated node of its own. These nodes will all have similar configuration dialogs prompting you for the database address as well as login credentials. Once you're connected, you can work with the tables inside the database.

### *Writing to a database*

Once connected to your database of choice, there is an entire section of nodes for reading, writing, updating, appending, and manipulating tables inside your database. To write to a database, we use the **DB Writer** node you'll see in *Figure 6.21* and connect its two input ports. The top port is the data we are writing to the database and the bottom port is the connector node for our database of choice:

Figure 6.21 – DB Writer node connected to SQLite Connector, and configuration dialog

To configure the DB Writer node, you'll need to configure just a couple of things. First, at the top right, select a table. You can type in the table name manually or you can click the **Select a table** button next to the text entry box to browse the database schema and select a table that way. Notice that there is also a **v** button next to this text entry box; this box allows you to use a flow variable to automatically update the table name if needed.

> **Database Permissions**
>
> It's often a good idea to only use credentials that have the permissions required for the task, especially if you save them in a workflow. For example, we only need read and write permissions for this use case, and no need for the ability to create or delete tables.

With your data forecasted and loaded in to your database, we move on to further use cases.

# Summary

In this chapter, we covered the first use application of forecasting in KNIME Analytics Platform; getting data from IoT sensors for modeling can be facilitated by KNIME workflows that have been loaded to KNIME Server and given REST endpoints. One workflow accepted this data and appended it to a database table until we had enough stored to train a model to generate humidity forecasts.

We introduced several classic methods for generating Time Series forecasts: the naïve forecast, which uses the most recent known value as its predictions; the mean value forecast that uses the mean of the known values as its predictions; exponential smoothing, which uses a weight average to generate its predictions, putting it somewhere in between the naïve and mean forecasts; and finally, the linear regression, the first model that is actually a fit. The ARIMA and SARIMA models later in this book will expand the regression format.

Finally, we talked about how to automatically generate a deployment workflow with KNIME's integrated deployment feature, which copies portions of the training workflow to automatically be recombined into a new deployment workflow. This is great because any changes we make to model training are automatically reflected in the deployment workflow.

This chapter should leave you with an understanding of the common steps in a Time Series application pipeline, from data recording to data cleansing to modeling and deployment. In the coming chapters, we will extend these ideas with more advanced data transformation techniques, such as the Fourier transform, as well as more complicated models, such as ARIMA and SARIMA, coming next in *Chapter 7*.

# Questions

1. What type of classic model gives the best results when forecasting white noise?

    A. Linear Regression

    B. Mean Value Forecast

    C. Naïve Forecast

    D. Exponential Smoothing

2. What type of classic model gives the best results when forecasting random walk data?

   A. Linear Regression

   B. Mean Value Forecast

   C. Naïve Forecast

   D. Exponential Smoothing

3. Which type of classic model is most useful when performing explanatory analysis?

   A. Linear Regression

   B. Mean Value Forecast

   C. Naïve Forecast

   D. Exponential Smoothing

4. Which type of classic model is most useful when generating sample forecasts?

   A. Linear Regression

   B. Mean Value Forecast

   C. Naïve Forecast

   D. Exponential Smoothing

# 7
# Forecasting the Temperature with ARIMA and SARIMA Models

In the previous chapter, we talked about our first forecasting use case, with fairly uncomplicated statistical techniques. In this chapter, we will continue to implore statistical techniques to generate forecasts, but we will move on to the very popular and robust **ARIMA** and **SARIMA** models. ARIMA, and its big brother SARIMA, are acronyms that stand for (**Seasonal**) **Auto-Regressive Integrated Moving-Average**. You can think of it in four parts:

- **AR**: Auto-regressive
- **I**: Integrated
- **MA**: Moving average
- **S**: Seasonal

Each one of these terms represents a separate technique that is combined with the (S)ARIMA model. In this chapter, you'll learn about strong and weak stationarity, how to induce this in your data, the ARIMA and SARIMA models, and how to derive their hyperparameters from auto-correlation and partial auto-correlation plots.

In this chapter, we'll cover the following topics:

- Recapping regression
- Introducing the (S)ARIMA models
- Fitting the model and generating forecasts

# Recapping regression

If you're reading this book, without a doubt, you've heard of regression, and maybe you're even quite versed in its application, but humor me for a moment all the same. I find a quick aside from this topic to be very helpful when framing a conversation about the (S)ARIMA models. In the following diagram, you can see a linear regression line fit through some data points. We'll start by recapping this concept and then expand into the ARIMA and SARIMA models from there:

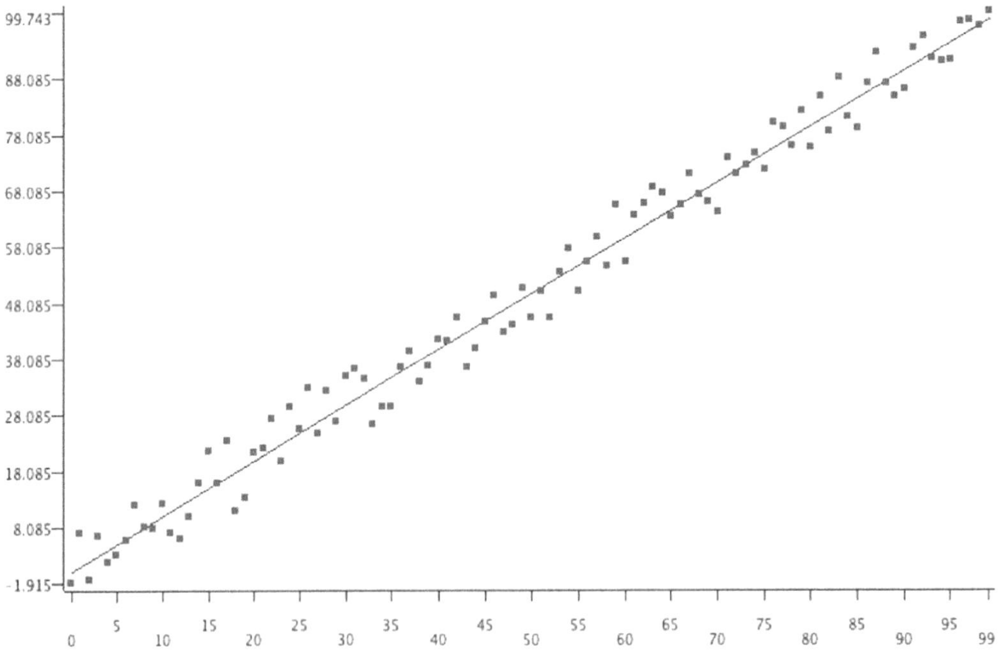


Figure 7.1 – A regression line fit in KNIME Analytics Platform

The line fit in the preceding regression is completely straight. We need the ability to capture seasonal patterns, cycles, and other auto-regressive features our time series data might contain. This is where the expansion into the ARIMA and SARIMA models will take us. Let's define this a bit more.

## Defining a regression

While you read this section, remember that what I want you to take away is simply that the ARIMA and SARIMA models are, at their core, elaborate regression models.

**Regression** models come in a multitude of shapes and sizes. However, for the most part, they all follow a couple of basic patterns:

- Numbers in. Numbers out.
- The output is a direct mathematical expression of the input.

OK, that's a massive generalization... so, what's next? Well, we pick the expression that connects the input to the output, adding in some parameters to make it flexible. Then, we fit it using one of many parameter estimation algorithms, for example, the method of least squares. Usually, that expression looks a bit like this:

$$Y = \sum \beta_i \cdot x_i + \beta_0$$

Formula 7.1

where,

- Y: The output or target
- $x_i$: The different input features
- $\beta_i$: The parameters we fit and multiply each by $x_i$
- $\beta_0$: A constant term and a parameter that we fit

> **Tip**
>
> This equation shows a linear model with multiple input variables and a single output variable. You can expand on this by adding extra terms, such as $x_i^2$, to break out of linearity or if you have multiple outputs by creating multiple equations to fit together or separately.

For a simple example, think of the good old $Y = m \cdot x + b$. We have two parameters, *m* and *b*, and we adjust them to change the vertical position and slope of our line so that it fits smoothly through some data.

We won't go into too much detail regarding the specifics of this parameter estimation or fitting algorithms.

# Introducing the (S)ARIMA models

With our little recap of regression taken care of, we can start talking about the requirements and different components of the ARIMA and SARIMA models, including how they're the same and how they're different. However, before we get into the formula and the two variations on the regression that make up the (S)ARIMA model, let's cover some of its requirements.

## Requirements of the (S)ARIMA model

While the (S)ARIMA model is famously an effective option for forecasting time series data and requires far less data than many alternative approaches, it does come with a little baggage. Unlike the techniques we'd likely bucket into the **Machine Learning** category, such as neural networks or even regression forests, the (S)ARIMA model requires a few things for our underlying data distribution, namely that our data is **stationary**. Let's dive into this topic a bit more.

### *What is stationarity?*

The primary requirement of the (S)ARIMA model is that the underlying data is stationary. Stationarity is a slightly loaded term; it might have slightly different meanings depending on the context. Similar to an average, stationarity comes in many varieties, but let's just introduce the two most common, **weak stationarity** and **strong stationarity**:

- **Strong stationarity**: A time series has strong stationarity if...
    - The probability distribution function is constant over time
- **Weak stationarity**: A time series has weak stationarity if...
    - The mean is constant over time
    - The variance is constant over time

Let's put this into perspective with a little example. Imagine our time series is as follows:

$$t_1, t_2, t_3, t_4, t_5, \ldots\ t_n$$

Formula 7.2

Each $t_i$ is a random variable pulled from a, frequently unknown, **Probability Distribution Function** (**PDF**). This function simply defines how probable different values are. Here are some common examples:

| PDF | Description | PDF |
|---|---|---|
| Uniform distribution | All values in a given range [a,b] have equal probability. |  Probability<br>1.4 1.2 1.0 0.8 0.6<br>0.0 0.2 0.4 0.6 0.8 1.0 |
| Bernoulli distribution | Takes value 1 with probability p and value 0 with probability 1 - p. |  Probability<br>0.6 0.4 0.2 0.0<br>2 4 6 8 10 12 14 16 18 20 |
| Geometric distribution | Describes the number of attempts before a success, p, is achieved in the Bernoulli distribution (in the preceding row). |  Probability<br>0.6 0.4 0.2 0.0<br>5 10 15 20 |
| Normal distribution | Sometimes, this is described as the bell curve. The normal distribution is popular when the actual distribution is unknown. | 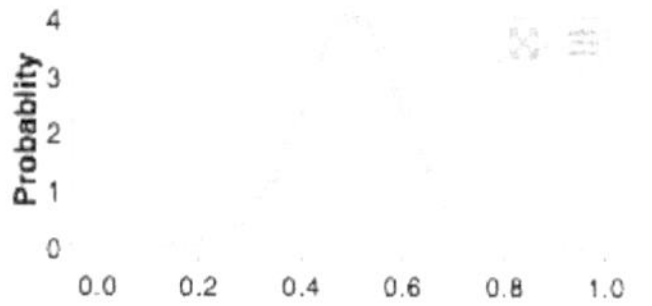 Probability<br>4 3 2 1 0<br>0.0 0.2 0.4 0.6 0.8 1.0 |
| Poisson distribution | This describes the number of times an event occurs in a given time window. |  Probability<br>8 6 4 2 0<br>2 4 6 8 10 12 14 16 18 20 |

Table 7.1 – A few common PDFs

I don't share this list with the purpose of going into detail, but I want to refresh our memories regarding what we mean when we talk about a PDF. Each of these PDFs can be *customized* by changing its parameters: with the Bernoulli distribution, that's $p$, the *probability* of success; with normal distribution, that's the mean, $\mu$; and the variance is $\sigma^2$. Strong stationarity, as we briefly defined earlier, requires the PDF to remain as the same distribution function with the same parameters. Weak stationarity does not always care if the PDF changes, or if some parameters change, as the mean and variance themselves stay the same. Let's look at some plots:

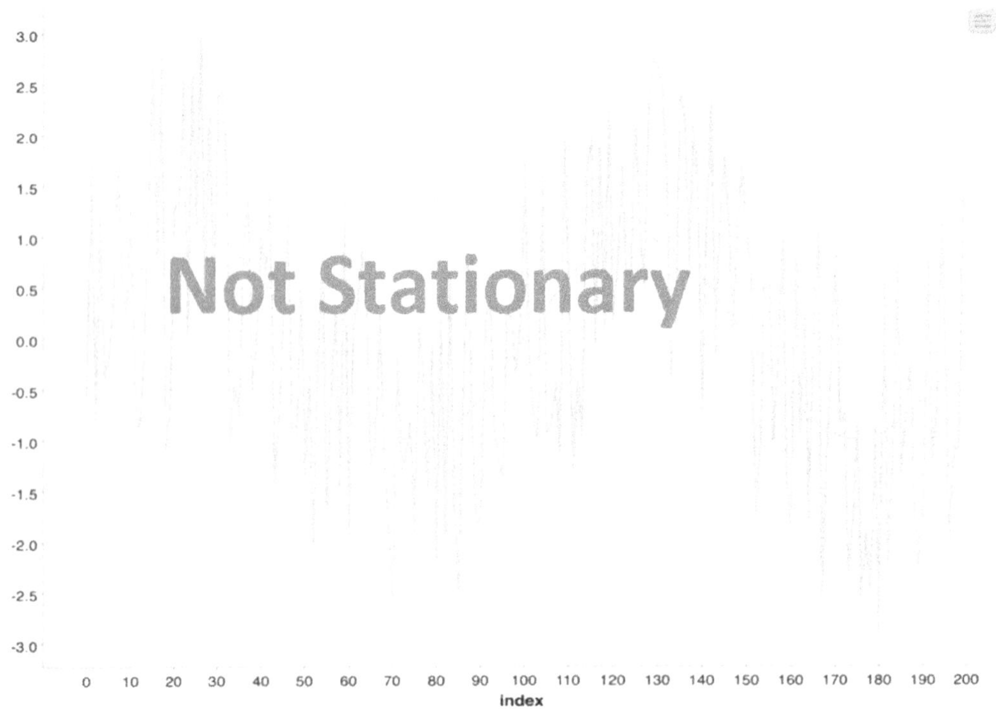


Figure 7.2 – Time series with changing mean

The time series in *Figure 7.2* fails to meet the weak stationarity requirement because its mean changes over time. We can see this as the series appears to randomly oscillate around a sine-like wave. We want to see a flat mean line, such as this:

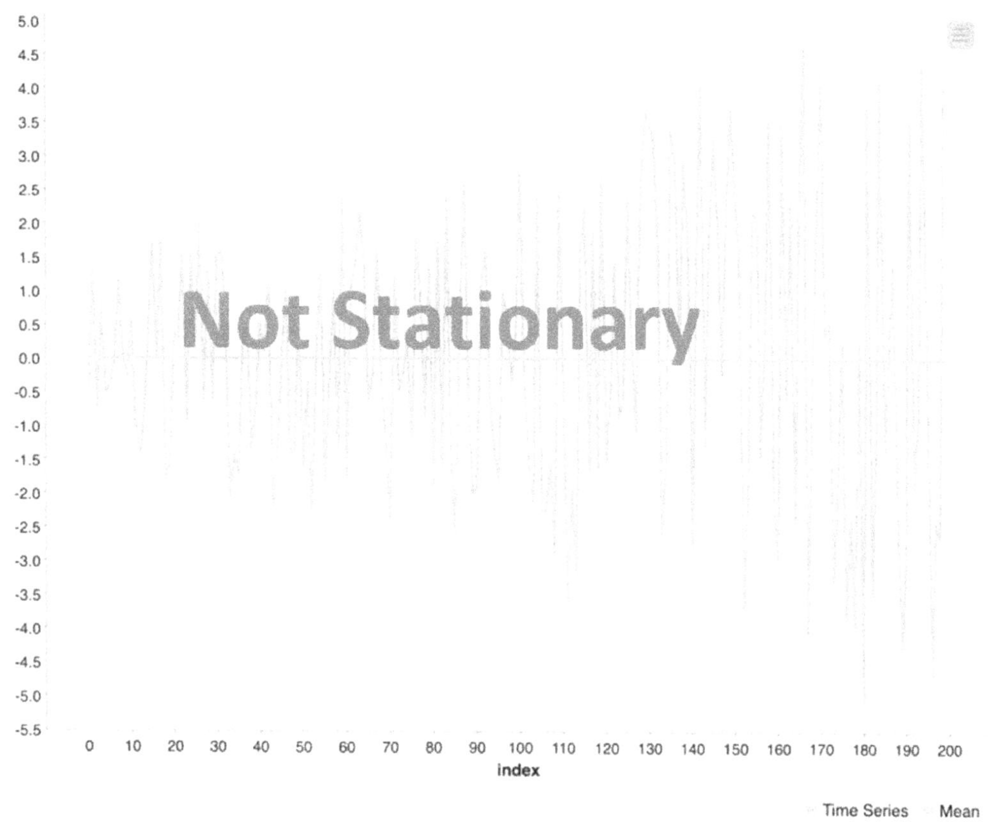


Figure 7.3 – Time series with changing variance

The time series in *Figure 7.3* fails to meet the weak stationarity requirement because its variance grows over time. We achieved the flat mean line that we were missing in *Figure 7.2*, but now we have a new problem. The amount of variation from this mean line changes over time and our data appears to grow increasingly random. We need this variation to be constant:

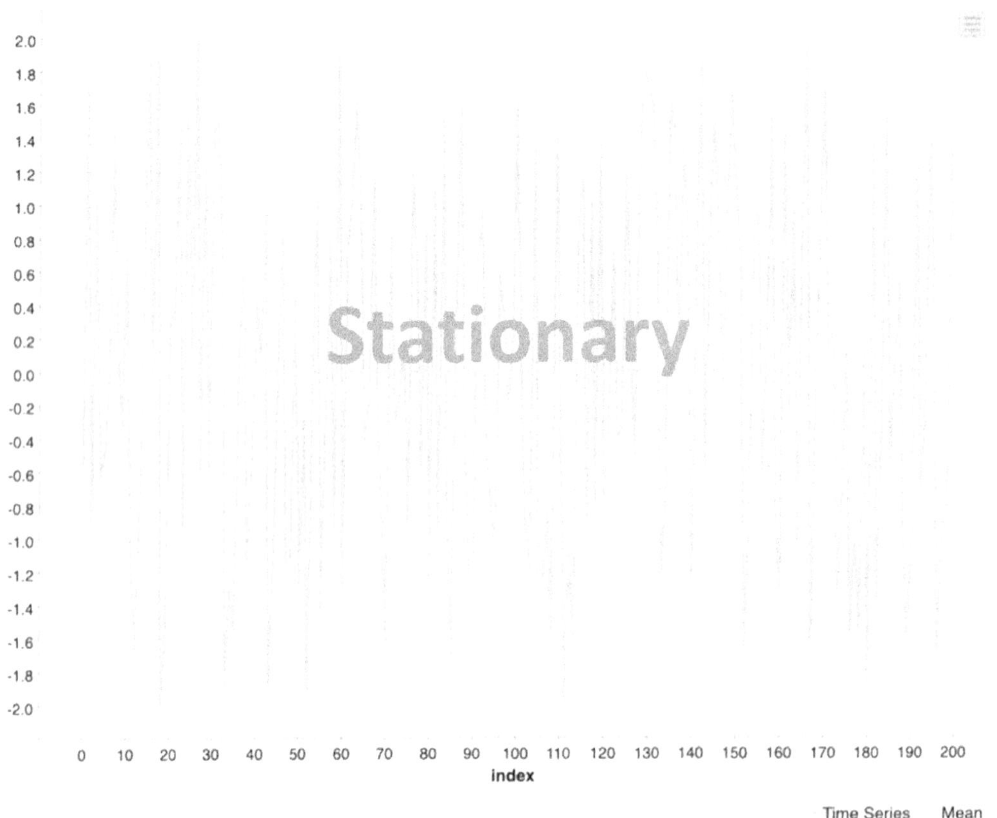


Figure 7.4 – Stationary time series

The time series in *Figure 7.4*, exhibits both of our required features for weak stationarity: a constant, or flat, mean line and a constant variance from that mean. Note that there are still some abnormalities due to random chance. This is expected, and we can move forward when our series looks like this! The ARIMA and SARIMA models only require weak stationarity.

### *Inducing stationarity*

Of course, most of the datasets we work with in real life are non-stationary. For example, look at *Figure 7.6*, which is a plot of daily minimum temperatures from 1980 to 1987. As expected, the mean value oscillates; it is warmer in the summer than the winter after all! Another way the mean might change is through a trend. For example, over a longer time span, we'd likely see an upward trend in this plot because of global warming:

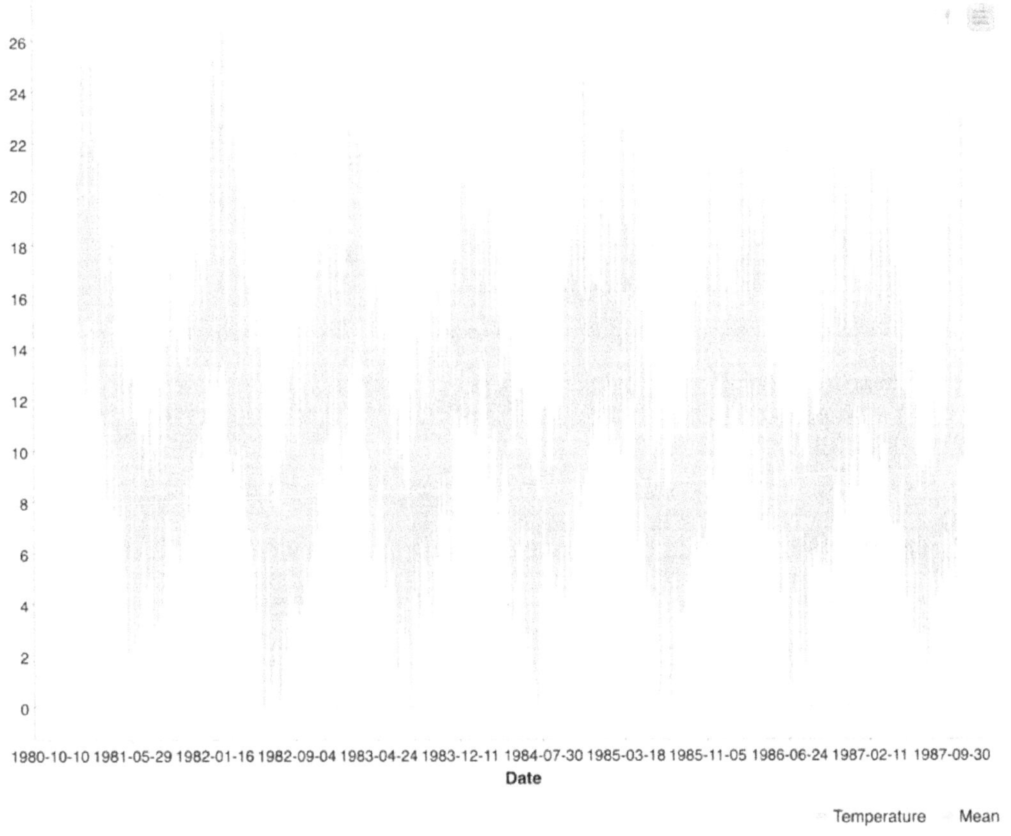


Figure 7.5 – Daily temperature data, non-stationary

These are not deal breakers for the (S)ARIMA model. We have several techniques at our disposal to account for these deviations from stationarity; some are built directly into the (S)ARIMA model, and some are not. First, let's look at the options baked right into the (S)ARIMA itself.

## Inducing stationarity within the (S)ARIMA model

At the beginning of the chapter, we introduced the terms that make up the (S)ARIMA model: Seasonal Auto-Regressive **Integrated** Moving-Average. In this section, we'll discuss the "I" term, integration. This is our first tool for correcting non-stationary data. It is an amazingly easy-to-apply-and-deploy method, as it is ultimately baked right into the model itself.

Integration, the "I" in (S)ARIMA, is simply differencing out time series. It comes in two varieties, the **Standard Differencing** in the ARIMA and the **Seasonal Differencing** that we get with the full SARIMA. Let's define them:

- **Standard Differencing**: Subtract the value of the prior term from each term in the time series:

  $x_t' = x_t - x_{t-1}$ for all $x_t$ in our time series.

- **Seasonal Differencing**: Subtract from each term in the time series, the value of the term one seasonal length (S) prior:

  $x_t' = x_t - x_{t-s}$ for all $x_t$ in our time series.

Here, $x_t$ is our original time series, $x_t'$ is our new time series, and *s* is our seasonal period.

Standard differencing is useful for removing trends, as one application can remove a linear trend. Look at this simple example series:

$$1, 2, 3, 4, 5, 7, 8, 9$$

Now, let's apply standard differencing by subtracting the value of the prior term from each term:

$$1-?, 2-1, 3-2, 4-3, 5-4, 6-5, 7-6, 8-7, 9-8$$

$$?, 1, 1, 1, 1, 1, 1, 1, 1$$

As you can see, the growth pattern has completely been removed. In the same way, we can remove a quadratic or higher power trend by applying this approach multiple times. However, the most wonderful part is that this differencing, and just as importantly, the restoration of the original values, is all done directly through the **I** (**Integration**) portion of the (S)ARIMA model. That's one of the reasons why this is the first approach to try!

Next, let's talk about seasonal differencing. Here, the key difference is that we do not subtract the previous term but a term from some length into the past. We denote this length s. Look at this simple example series:

$$1, 2, 3, 1, 2, 3, 1, 2, 3, 1, 2, 3$$

You can see that we have a repeating pattern. When this pattern is relatively short, we call it a seasonality. Since this seasonality is 3 items long, and shorter than likely in a real application, we say that the seasonal period is 3, or s = 3. Now, let's apply seasonal differencing with s = 3:

$$1-?, 2-?, 3-?, 1-1, 2-2, 3-3, 1-1, 2-2, 3-3, 1-1, 2-2, 3-3$$

$$?, ?, ?, 0, 0, 0, 0, 0, 0, 0, 0, 0$$

Just as the standard differencing technique removed a trend, the seasonal differencing technique has removed a seasonal pattern. Bear in mind that both trends and seasonalities can occur simultaneously in the same time series, in which case we can deploy both techniques!

Let's look at some line plots of actual time series to get a better understanding of how these differencing techniques transform our data. Note that we can perform this standard differencing outside of the (S)ARIMA model relatively easily by using the **Remove Stationarity** component in KNIME. This can be found either on KNIME Hub or in KNIME Explorer under **Examples | Components | Time Series | Remove Seasonality**. In *Figure 7.6*, we see the remove seasonality component and an example of how to configure it to apply differencing to remove seasonality:

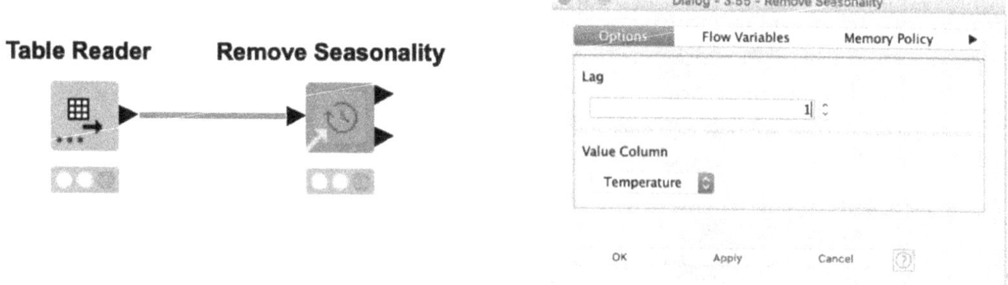


Figure 7.6 – The Remove Seasonality component and configuration dialog

Set the **Lag** value in the configuration dialog to `1` for standard differencing or higher for seasonal differencing, as we will discuss shortly. In *Figure 7.7*, we can see how this differencing affects our time series and help us reach the weak stationarity requirement:

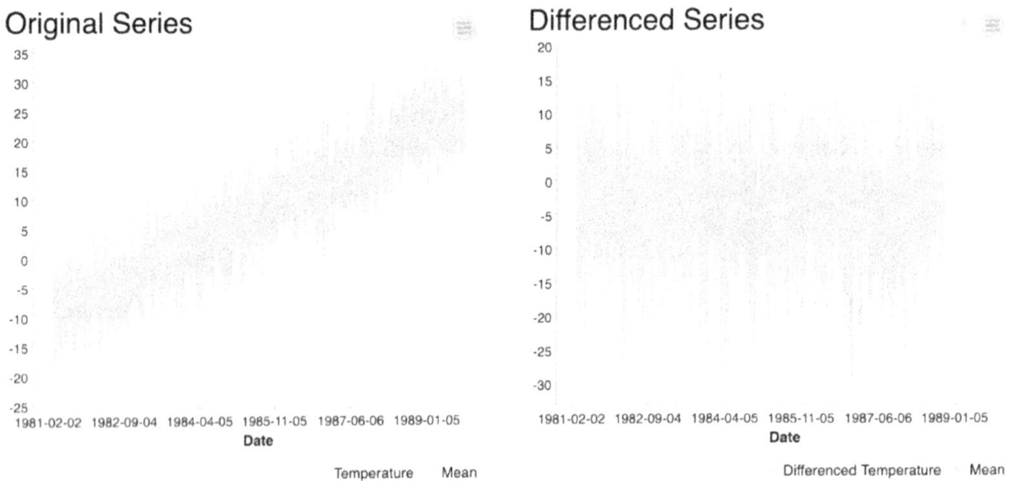


Figure 7.7 – Time series with an upward trend, corrected with standard differencing

On the left-hand side of *Figure 7.7*, we see a time series with a rather obvious upward trend (I've added this artificially for clarity). This breaks one of the requirements for weak stationarity, as the mean is clearly changing over time. Since our series is trending linearly, a single application of standard differencing was sufficient to remove the trend. If we had a quadratic trend, or something even more aggressive, an additional application of differencing would be required. In the next section, we'll see how easy this additional application is to implement:

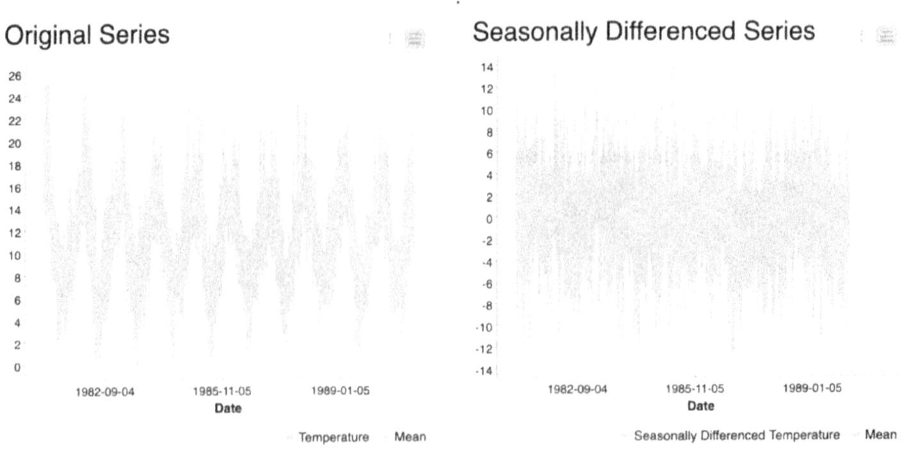


Figure 7.8 – Time series with seasonality, corrected with seasonal differencing

On the left-hand side of *Figure 7.8*, we can see a time series with a repeating seasonal pattern. You might recognize this as the daily temperature series from earlier. Once again, this breaks one of the requirements for weak stationarity in that our mean cannot change over time. In this example, our seasonal pattern is the result of actual yearly seasons: spring, summer, fall, and winter. With this in mind, we can apply seasonal differencing with a seasonal period of 365, or s = 365, as our data is daily, and there are 365 days in a year. As with standard differencing, we can apply seasonal differencing multiple times if the relationship to last year's value is non-linear, but this is less common. Recall from *Figure 7.7* that we can also perform this type of differencing outside the SARIMA model by using the **Remove Seasonality** component and setting the **Lag** value to our seasonal period; for example, 365.

### Inducing stationarity with other techniques

In the previous section, we talked about differencing inside the (S)ARIMA model; we used this to adjust for changing means with polynomial trends (1 differencing per degree of the polynomial). Additionally, we looked at seasonal differencing to correct repeating patterns, called **Seasonalities**, in our data. There are many other options, and really, any easily reversible transformation could be applied. Let's look at a few popular options next.

### Logging

Exponential patterns are everywhere in nature. Calculus tells us that anything with a rate of change directly proportional to its own value is exponential. That means lots and lots of our use cases! In the following table, you'll find some common types of growth that exhibit exponential trends:

| Exponential effects | Description |
|---|---|
| Population growth | Since populations are self-reproducing, more people means more reproduction. |
| Half-life | When we talk about the probability of items or particles being lost in a time window, we end up with a half-life. Exponential decay. |
| Wildfire spread | As with population growth, a fire starts a fire; the bigger it is the faster it grows. |
| Pandemics | Again, we draw a parallel to population growth. More infected individuals lead to more spread. |
| Investment accounts | Since investment accounts typically return a percentage of their value in interest payments, we also have a connection between the value and growth rate here. |

Table 7.2 – Examples of exponential trends

> **Remember**
>
> If the proportional rate of change is between `-1` and `0`, we have exponential decay instead of growth!

These exponential trends can be less obvious to see in a graph than some of the earlier types of patterns we've discussed, as they make look almost linear. However, typically, it's a good area in which to leverage some domain expertise. Simply ask yourself the question: *Does my growth depend on how much I have?* If the answer is yes, you should give logging a shot!

So far, we've been talking about exponential growth, but recall that the inverse function of an exponential function is a log. The goal is that if we apply a log transform to an exponential function, we will get something that's cleaner and easier to work with:

- Exponential function: $e^{k \cdot t + c}$
- Apply the log transform: $\ln\left(e^{k \cdot t + c}\right)$
- The transformed function: $k \cdot t + c$

In this case, we're now left with a far more approachable function. However, bear in mind that there is no guarantee that if there is an exponential pattern in our data, it will be after we apply a log transform. Additional processing might still be required.

Let's see an example of this transform being applied to some data:

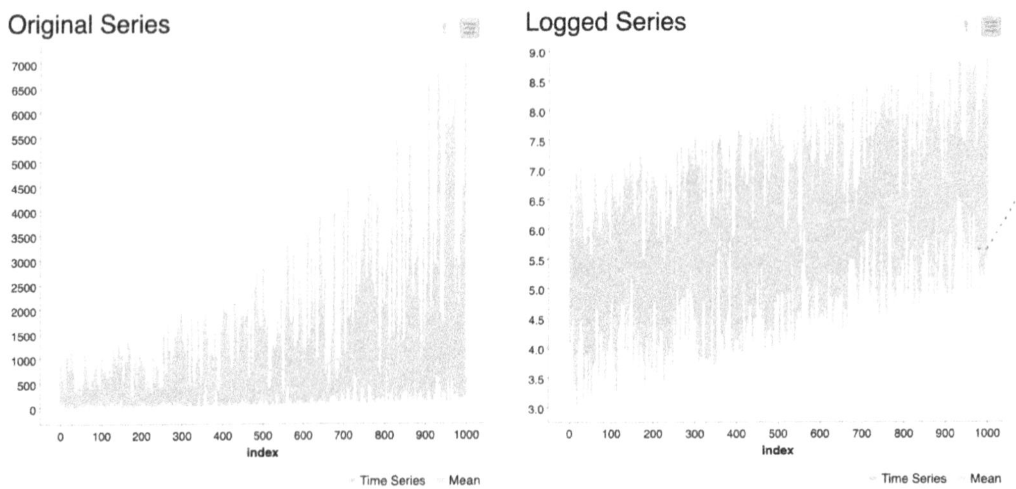


Figure 7.9 – Applying the log transform

Note that the left-hand series is far from stationary and not something we can readily apply the (S) ARIMA model to. Even worse, its problem is not strictly a trending mean or seasonality, as its variance behaves quite oddly, too. This is expected as the random variable that represents the time series scales up exponentially. On the right-hand side, we see the plot of the series after a log transform has been applied. In this case, a series with a trending mean and constant variance is revealed! From here, we can resort to the techniques in the prior section and use the differencing inside the (S)ARIMA model to correct this.

Remember that if you apply the log transform before the (S)ARIMA model, your forecast will be generated on that transformed series. Luckily the log, like the exponential, is quite easy to invert. We can apply the exponential function to our forecast and restore our data to its original shape:

$$Y_t = e^{Y_t'}$$

Formula 7.3

Here, $Y_t$ is or true or corrected forecast, and $Y_t'$ is the forecast that the (S)ARIMA model generated in the log-transformed series.

Now that our data has been cleaned up and we've done our best to induce the weak stationarity required for the ARIMA and SARIMA models, it's time to talk about…

## How to configure the ARIMA or SARIMA model

OK, inducing and verifying stationarity is the hardest part of forecasting with the (S)ARIMA model, but we're not quite done yet. As with many modeling techniques, the (S)ARIMA model has hyperparameters that we will want to select intelligently. These hyperparameters correspond with the order of the AR, I, MA, and seasonal variations laid out at the beginning of the chapter. We'll introduce two diagnostic plots, the **Auto-Correlation Function** (**ACF**) and the **Partial Auto-Correlation Function** (**PACF**). They, along with our knowledge of differencing, will enable us to choose these hyperparameters with intention.

> Tip
>
> Try minor variations of whatever hyperparameter combination you ultimately choose. You might find that our assumptions for these hyperparameters are best used as starting points.

## *The hyperparameters*

The basic ARIMA model has 3 hyperparameters (p, d, and q) corresponding to the order of the AR, I, and MA parts of the acronym, respectively. SARIMA adds 4 more: the seasonal versions of the original 3, (P, D, and Q), and finally, s denoting the seasonal length. We'll go into a little detail for each.

### p – the auto-regressive order

An auto-regressive model is, as the name suggests, a regression model whose input is the same series as its output. It is just lagged or delayed in time. In a simple example, we might say a model that uses yesterday's temperature to predict today's is auto-regressive. Formally, we can have a series such as the following:

$$Y_1, Y_2, Y_3, \dots Y_t$$

Formula 7.4

An auto-regressive model would be as follows:

$$\hat{Y}_t = \beta_0 + \beta_1 \cdot Y_{t-1} + \beta_2 \cdot Y_{t-2} \dots + \beta_p \cdot Y_{t-p} + \varepsilon$$

Formula 7.5

Here, $\beta_i$ are the fitted coefficients, and $\mathcal{E}$ is the error term. Notice that the number of past terms regressed against in the model is p. That's where our hyperparameter comes into play. It is simply the number of terms past terms we include in our model. This pattern will continue in most of the hyperparameters.

### *d – the order of integration*

The concept of differencing is something that we introduced in detail back in its own section. We discussed its use for removing trends by shifting our series into the difference domain with the following equation:

$$Y_t' = Y_t - Y_{t-1}$$

Formula 7.6

Here, $Y_t'$ is our new differenced series. The hyperparameter *d* indicates the number of times we perform this transformation before the model is fit.

> **Remember**
>
> Differencing once is sufficient to remove a linear trend, twice is sufficient for a quadratic trend, and so on.

### *q – the moving-average order*

Be careful not to confuse this term with exponential smoothing or similar techniques that slide a window along the series to calculate a literal *moving* average. In this context, a moving average is more akin to the auto-regressive model in hyperparameter p, with one major difference.

In this case, the moving-average model is a regression model trained on past forecast errors, which can be a little weird to wrap your head around at first. You might be wondering why that's useful at all. We can explain it in two words, **shock absorption**, but we'll discuss it in more detail later.

First, let's explicitly define a forecast error, $\varepsilon_t$:

$$\varepsilon_t = \hat{Y}_t - Y_t$$

Formula 7.7

Here, $\hat{Y}_t$ is the value forecasted for time t, and $Y_t$ is the true value.

Now we can define a regression model in terms of these past forecast errors:

$$\hat{Y}_t = \theta_0 + \theta_1 \cdot \varepsilon_{t-1} + \theta_2 \cdot \varepsilon_{t-2} \ldots + \theta_q \cdot \varepsilon_{t-q}$$

Formula 7.8

Here, $\theta_i$ are the fitted coefficients. You'll notice that, with the **auto-regressive section** (**AR**), the moving-average model incorporates a number of past error terms equal to our q hyperparameter.

Let's circle back to my comment about *shock absorption*. Maybe you have a model that is forecasting temperature, as we will later in this chapter, and it exclusively uses an auto-regressive model to generate forecasts. It wouldn't be a stretch of the imagination to find that the following model is fit:

$$\hat{Y}_t = Y_{t-1}$$

Formula 7.9

This is simply forecasting that today's temperature will be the same as yesterday. For where I live, in Austin, Texas, that's a very good model during the summer…most of the time. However, sometimes, a thunderstorm rolls in and the temperature drops dramatically! Without a more robust meteorological model, I wouldn't expect my forecast to catch that, of course, but what about the next day? Should my forecast revert to type and output 100 F, or should it do as before and just say the temperature will be the same as yesterday? This isn't a question we have to answer if we fit a moving-average model. The inclusion of that past forecast error term allows our model to perceive those anomalies and react in whichever way its training deems best. That is what I mean by shock absorption.

### *s – the seasonal period*

In the upcoming sections on the P, D, and Q seasonal hyperparameters, we will continually reference the value of s. This is simply the length of our seasonality; if we have hourly data and a daily pattern, that might be 24, while if we have daily data and expect a weekly pattern, that might be 7. This enables us to talk about the concepts from the basic ARIMA model in seasonal terms.

### *P, D, and Q – the seasonal variations*

So far, we've covered all the basic components of the ARIMA model. But how do we turn it into SARIMA? Well, we just slap on a few extra terms!

#### P – the seasonal auto-regressive order

In the case of P, just like before, it is the number of terms we add to our auto-regressive model with one exception. While P is still the number of seasonal terms, we do not count 1, 2,... P. We count *1·s, 2·s,...P·s*. If our data is hourly and we suspect a daily seasonality, s = 24, then that would look like the following:

$$\hat{Y}_t = \beta_0 + \beta_{24} \cdot Y_{t-24} + \beta_{48} \cdot Y_{t-48} \dots + \beta_{P\cdot 24} \cdot Y_{t-P\cdot 24} + \varepsilon$$

Formula 7.10

Or, in generic terms, it will look like the following:

$$\hat{Y}_t = \beta_0 + \beta_s \cdot Y_{t-s} + \beta_{2\cdot s} \cdot Y_{t-2\cdot s} \dots + \beta_{P\cdot s} \cdot Y_{t-P\cdot s} + \varepsilon$$

Formula 7.11

When it comes to training time, all we really have is a longer regression model, which is no problem at all! We'll see this clearly, in the next section, when we take everything we know and assemble the full SARIMA model.

#### D – the seasonal order of integration

As with standard differencing, we dissected this topic in some detail in its own section on inducing stationarity. Recall that we use seasonal differencing to remove seasonal patterns from our series in the same way that we use standard differencing to remove trends in the previous section. Seasonal differencing is defined by the following equation:

$$Y_t' = Y_t - Y_{t-s}$$

Formula 7.12

Here, $Y_t'$ is our new seasonally differenced series. Hyperparameter $D$ indicates the number of times we perform this transformation before the model is fit.

### Q – the seasonal moving-average order

Finally, hyperparameter number 7, the seasonal moving average. As with P, our seasonal auto-regressive hyperparameter, Q, is nothing more or less than the additional terms of our standard moving-average model in the basic ARIMA. To reiterate the example from P, we simply count up by s instead of by 1. We count *1·s, 2·s,…Q·s*. If our data is hourly and we suspect a daily seasonality, s = 24, that would look like the following:

$$\hat{Y}_t = \theta_0 + \theta_{24} \cdot Y_{t-24} + \theta_{48} \cdot Y_{t-48} \dots + \theta_{Q\cdot 24} \cdot Y_{t-Q\cdot 24}$$

Formula 7.13

Or, in generic terms, it will look like the following:

$$\hat{Y}_t = \theta_0 + \theta_s \cdot Y_{t-s} + \theta_{2\cdot s} \cdot Y_{t-2\cdot s} \dots + \theta_{Q\cdot s} \cdot Y_{t-Q\cdot s}$$

Formula 7.14

And just as with the seasonal auto-regressive part of the model, these are ultimately just additional terms that we have fit to the moving-average portion of SARIMA and will be fit together as part of a larger moving-average model. Finally, let's put it all together.

### Summarizing the hyperparameters

Use the following table as a reference to recall all 7 hyperparameters of the SARIMA model. The first three, p, d, and q, are the hyperparameters of the ARIMA model:

| | |
|---|---|
| p | The number of lagged terms in the auto-regressive model |
| d | The number of times standard differencing is applied |
| q | The number of past forecast errors in the moving-average model |
| P | The number of seasonally lagged terms in the auto-regressive model |
| D | The number of times seasonal differencing is applied |
| Q | The number of seasonal terms in the moving-average model |
| s | The length, in number of data points, of the seasonal period |

Table 7.3 – A recap of all the parameters of a SARIMA model

## *Assembling the full SARIMA model*

So, we've talked about regression from this angle and that angle, stationarity, differencing, and everything in between. Additionally, we've prepared our data for the SARIMA model. Now, let's put everything together.

First, we have the auto-regressive model, which when combined into its full seasonal form, looks like the following:

$$\hat{Y}_t = \beta_0 + \beta_1 \cdot Y_{t-1} + \beta_2 \cdot Y_{t-2} \dots + \beta_p \cdot Y_{t-p} + \beta_0 + \beta_s \cdot Y_{t-s} + \beta_{2\cdot s} \cdot Y_{t-2\cdot s} \dots + \beta_{P\cdot s} \cdot Y_{t-P\cdot s} + \varepsilon$$

Formula 7.15

This is simply a combination of the standard lagged terms and the seasonally lagged terms.

Second, we have the **Moving-Average model**, which, when combined with its full seasonal term, looks like the following:

$$\hat{Y}_t = \theta_0 + \theta_1 \cdot \varepsilon_{t-1} + \theta_2 \cdot \varepsilon_{t-2} \dots + \theta_q \cdot \varepsilon_{t-q} + \theta_s \cdot Y_{t-s} + \theta_{2\cdot s} \cdot Y_{t-2\cdot s} \dots + \theta_{Q\cdot s} \cdot Y_{t-Q\cdot s}$$

Formula 7.16

Again, this is just a concatenation of the standard and seasonal moving-average models that we introduced earlier.

This is where it gets ugly on paper, but bear in mind that all we're doing is creating a giant regression model with lots of terms pulled from different purposes. We concatenate the auto-regressive and the moving-average models into one giant regression; this is SARIMA! Take a look at the following:

$$\hat{Y}_t = \beta_0 + \beta_1 \cdot Y_{t-1} \dots + \beta_p \cdot Y_{t-p} + \beta_0 + \beta_s \cdot Y_{t-s} \dots + \beta_{P\cdot s} \cdot Y_{t-P\cdot s} + \theta_1 \cdot \varepsilon_{t-1} \dots + \theta_q \cdot \varepsilon_{t-q} + \theta_s \cdot Y_{t-s} \dots + \theta_{Q\cdot s} \cdot Y_{t-Q\cdot s} + \varepsilon$$

Formula 7.17

**Remember the "I" for Integration**

To be technically correct, the preceding equation only represents the SARMA model; note the missing "I" term. For it to be a SARIMA model, we need to include some form of integration or differencing. This happens outside the regression formula.

### *Choosing the best hyperparameters*

We've talked about the hyper-parameters each in some detail; they represent the size of the regression equation we ultimately fit, along with the number and types of differencing we apply to our data. But how should we choose their values? We'll introduce a pair of exploratory plots, the ACF and the PACF. They'll help us understand how far back is worth regressing against.

> **Tip**
>
> It's easy to say "just use a large number for your hyperparameters." That will pull information from as many places as possible. However, as is true in other endeavors within data science, simpler is better. Remember that simple models fit more quickly and generalize better than larger models.

### ACF

The ACF, as its name suggests, describes how a series correlates to itself, specifically, to the lagged version of itself:

$$Y_t \sim Y_{t-1}$$

$$Y_t \sim Y_{t-2}$$

$$Y_t \sim Y_{t-3}$$

$$Y_t \sim Y_{t-4}$$

Let's look at the auto-correlation plot calculated on a simple series. We can easily see a plot inside KNIME using the inspect seasonality component, which can either be found on KNIME Hub or in **KNIME Explorer** under **Examples** | **Components** | **Time Series** | **Inspect Seasonality**. The following diagram demonstrates what the KNIME workflow utilizing the **Inspect Seasonality** component could look like:

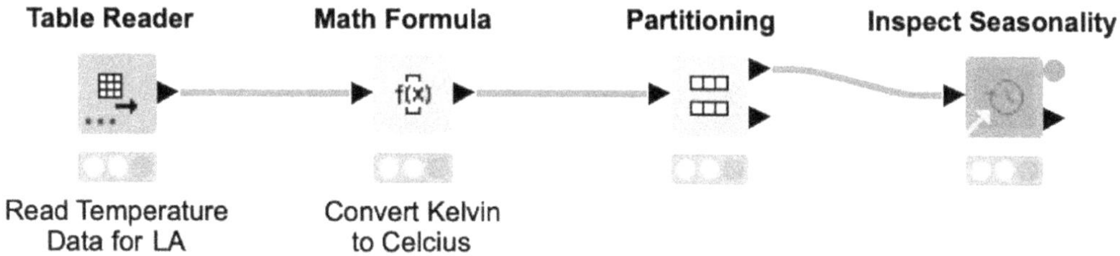


Figure 7.10 – The Inspect Seasonality component

To use the inspect seasonality component, as shown in *Figure 7.12*, we simply attach our data table, which includes our time series column, and make and select the appropriate column in the configuration dialog. If you suspect particularly long seasonal periods in your data, make a note to increase the maximum value your ACF and PACF plots stretch to sufficient lag values. Now, let's look at some of the plots that this component creates:

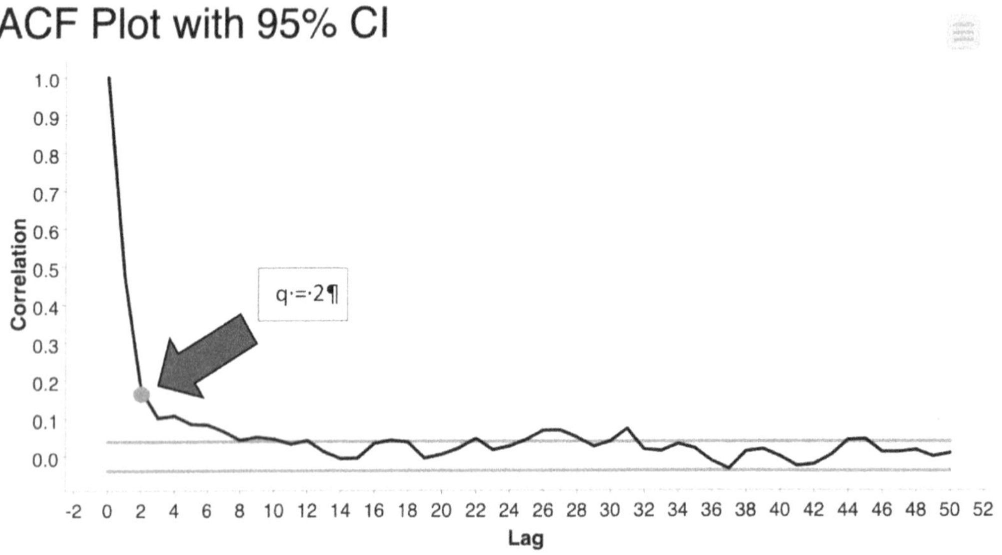


Figure 7.11 – The ACF of differenced temperature series

Looking at the preceding plot, you can see the correlation, or auto-correlation value, on the *y* axis and the lag value on the *x* axis.

**Auto-correlation**

When we talk about auto-correlation here, we are referring to the **Pearson correlation** of the lagged copies of our time series. Recall that Pearson correlation is defined as the covariance of the two series divided by the product of their variances. Here it is in mathematical notation:

$$p_{Y,Y'} = \frac{Cov(Y,Y')}{\sqrt{Var(Y)\cdot Var(Y')}}$$

Here, Y is our time series, and Y' is the lagged copy.

Consider the red dot on the plot in *Figure 7.12*; we read this by saying $Y_t$ correlates to $Y_{t-2}$ with a correlation value of 0.2. That is to say, the series, when lagged by 2, correlates with itself with a value of 0.2.

The goal of modeling with the (S)ARIMA is to encode as much of this auto-correlation into our regression as possible. For this reason, SARIMA is sometimes described as the most general class of model for a series that can be made stationary. With that in mind, we use the preceding plot to choose how far back the auto-regressive portion of the (S)ARIMA model needs to go. In the preceding plot, our correlation drops to zero very quickly, so a small value will suffice. There is no specific correlation value where I would recommend cutting our model. However, I see a definite flattening of the curve after 2 or so. This is our value for q!

## PACF

PACF is very similar to the previous plot. On one axis, it plots the partial correlation, and on the other axis, it plots the lag value. However, it has one key difference. Imagine, for a moment, a series where $Y_t$ correlates strongly with $Y_{t-1}$. This automatically means that $Y_{t-1}$ correlates strongly with $Y_{t-2}$. What do you suppose that means for $Y_t$ and $Y_{t-2}$? Well, they must also be correlated by proxy. The PACF accounts for this dependence and attempts to remove it from the plot, only displaying a direct correlation between the lagged variables.

**Partial auto-correlation**

I won't fully unpack the partial auto-correlation formula here. But if you're comfortable with your background in linear algebra, I encourage you to investigate that further. The partial auto-correlation is written as follows. It is, effectively, the auto-correlation given when all values between $Y_t$ and $Y_{t-h}$ are known:

$$pp_{Y,Y'} = \frac{Cov(Y_t, Y_{t-h} | Y_t, Y_{t-1} \ldots Y_{t-h+1})}{\sqrt{Var(Y_t | Y_t, Y_{t-1} \ldots Y_{t-h+1}) \cdot Var(Y_{t-h} | Y_t, Y_{t-1} \ldots Y_{t-h+1})}}$$

Here, Y is our time series, and Y' is the lagged copy.

Now, let's take a look at the plot again with the differenced temperature data from earlier:

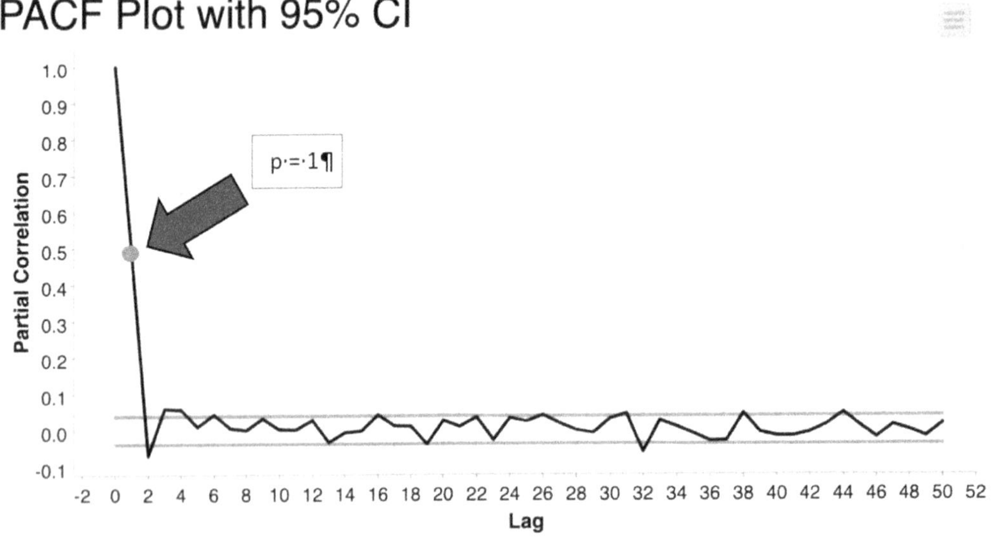


Figure 7.12 – PACF of differenced temperature series

The partial auto-correlation plot reads just like the auto-correlation plot before it. On the *y* axis, we have the correct correlation for the dependencies, called partial auto-correlation, and on the *x* axis, we have the lag value. For example, we read the red dot, as $Y_t$ partially correlates to $Y_{t-1}$ with a correlation value of 0.5. Beyond this point, essentially, our partial correlation decays to zero and the inclusion of these terms in our auto-regressive model is no longer helpful. This is our p value!

With our p's and q's out of the way and our differencing and stationarity dealt with, we're ready to train our model. So, let's put it all together.

Use the following reference table to recap where each term was derived:

| | |
|---|---|
| p | Chosen by observing how long the PACF plot takes to decay |
| d | Chosen by the polynomial degree of the trend in our original series |
| q | Chosen by observing how long the ACF plot takes to decay |
| P | Chosen by observing seasonal spikes in the PACF plot |
| D | Typically 1, but chosen by the polynomial degree of the seasonal relationship |
| Q | Chosen by observing seasonal spikes in the ACF plot |
| s | The Seasonal Period, for example, 24 for hourly data with a daily pattern |

Table 7.3 – SARIMA hyperparameters

Using this table and your ACF and PACF plots, you have all you need to derive your SARIMA hyperparameters.

# Fitting the model and generating forecasts

We've induced stationarity in our data, we've inspected the trend, we've investigated the seasonal patterns, and we've plotted the ACF and PACF. We're ready to fit the model to our data.

## The data

We'll be working with hourly temperature data to deploy a SARIMA model and generate our forecasts. The following data is hourly temperature data from Los Angeles, California, taken in 2013:

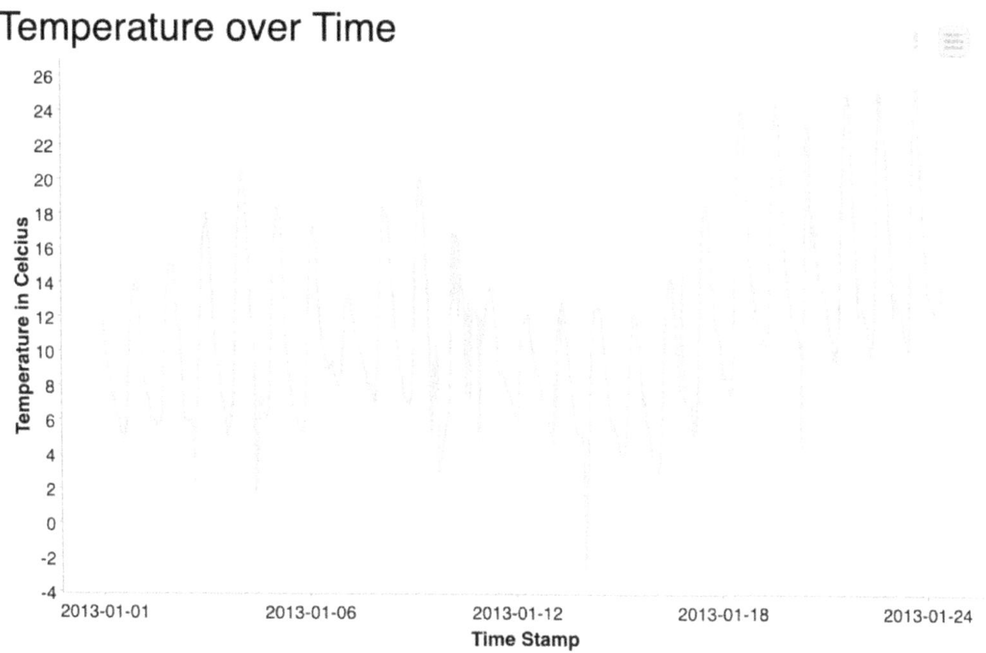


Figure 7.13 – Hourly temperature data from Los Angeles, California

From here, we'll move through the steps to explore our data and train an effective SARIMA model to generate a 5-day forecast of this temperature data. We will skip the data cleaning steps as they have been addressed in earlier chapters.

### *Does our data look stationary?*

Recall the very first topic that we discussed under the (S)ARIMA section, stationarity. To deploy an (S)ARIMA model, we require weak stationarity in our time series. This means that the mean and variance do not change over time. Evidently, our data does not meet the constant mean requirement, as we can see 24-hour seasonal patterns in the temperature. No shock there: it's cooler at night after all. Do you remember how to fix this? By using seasonal differencing. Another way to detect a seasonal pattern is by looking at the ACF plot of the raw series. Note the sinusoidal wave with period 24, as shown in the following screenshot:

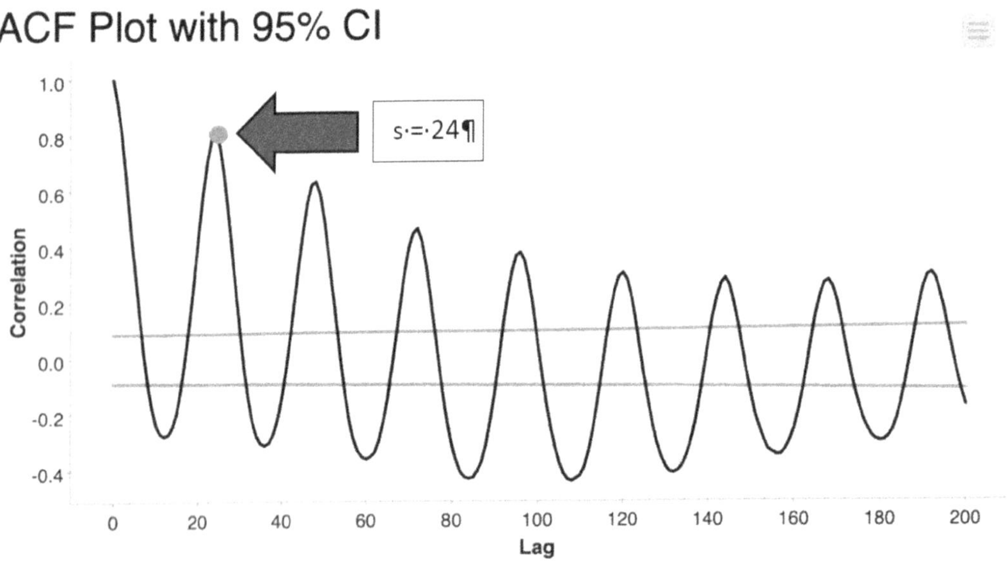


Figure 7.14 – An ACF plot of raw LA temperature data

Now that we know we have a 24-hour seasonality, we need to do two things. The first is to make note of our s value in the SARIMA configuration. This will be the seasonal period, 24. The second is to seasonally difference our data for...

### *Selecting the hyperparameters*

With our data seasonally differenced, we now have the series shown in *Figure 7.17*. Clearly, there are some things going on in this series. It's not white noise, but it does appear to have constant mean and variance, so we're clear to continue:

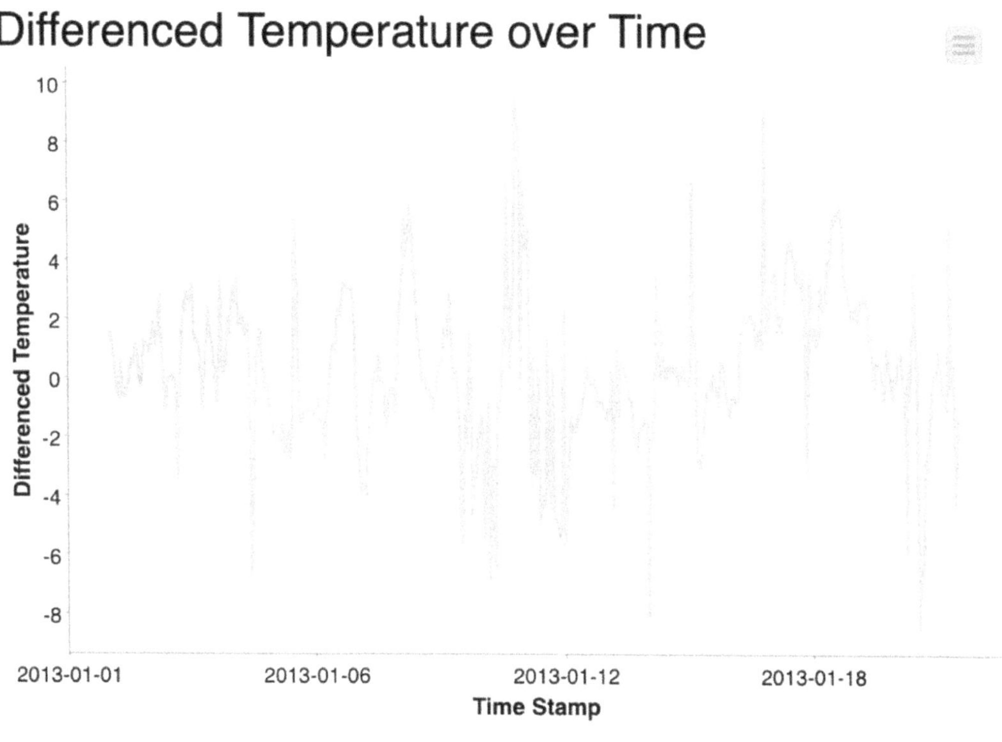


Figure 7.15 – Differenced temperature data, note stationarity

With this differenced data, we can again plot the ACF and PACF using the Inspect Seasonality component from *Figure 7.12* to determine the proper values of p, q, P, and Q. Let's look at those plots again and discuss the interesting points in them:

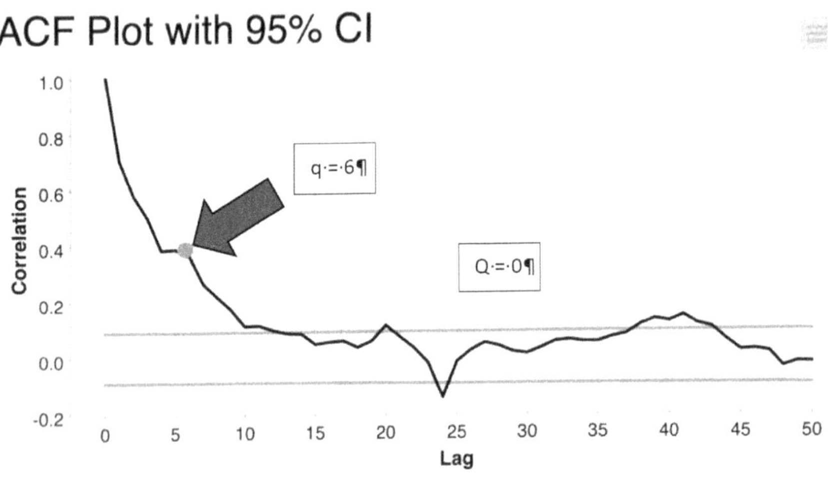


Figure 7.16 – An ACF plot of differenced data

We use the preceding ACF plot to select our q value. Since there are strongly diminishing correlation values after lag 6, I chose q = 6 as my hyperparameter. To choose our Q value, we look for seasonal spikes farther down the graph, for example, at 24 and 48. I do not see any, so we will say Q = 0:

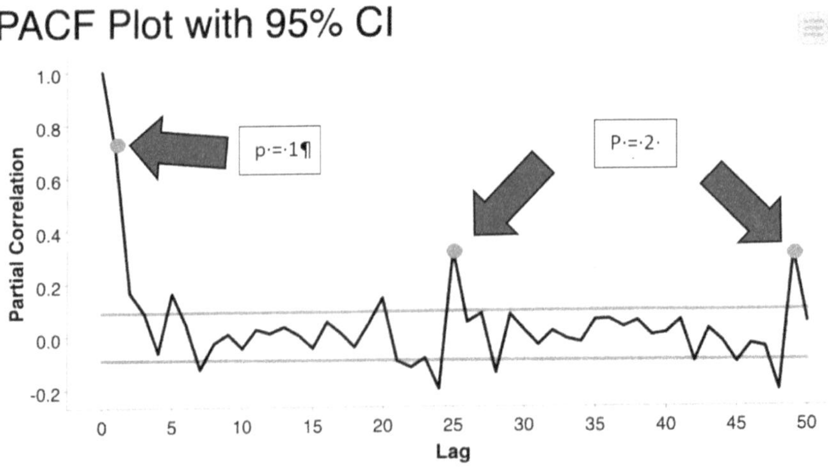


Figure 7.17 – A PACF plot of differenced data

Next, we look at the PACF plot to pick our p and P values. This plot decays extremely rapidly, and the correlation is very low after lag 1. We choose p = 1. However, unlike the ACF plot, we see correlation spikes at lags 24 and 48. This means that we want to include those auto-regressive terms in our model. So, we say P = 2 to include $Y_{t-24}$ and $Y_{t-48}$ in our model:

- p = 1
- d = 0
- q = 6
- P = 2
- D = 1
- Q = 0
- s = 24

### *Training SARIMA*

With the hyperparameters now chosen, all that remains is to run the training algorithm and observe and analyze our forecasts! This is super easy with the SARIMA Learner component in KNIME. You can see it assembled in *Figure 7.20*:

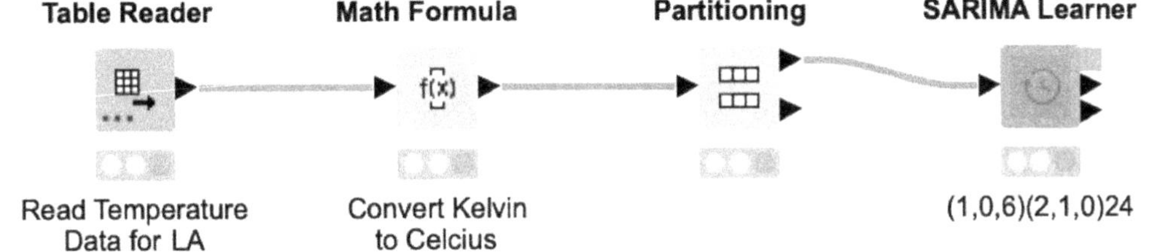


Figure 7.18 – Training SARIMA

We can simply drag and drop the SARIMA Learner component from either KNIME Hub into our workflow or from the example server in KNIME Explorer, where it can be found under **Examples | Components | Time Series SARIMA Learner**. Having chosen our hyperparameters, the configuration will be simple, as we will see later. However, keep in mind that, sometimes, fiddling with these values a bit is a good idea. What we've discussed so far is a great starting point:

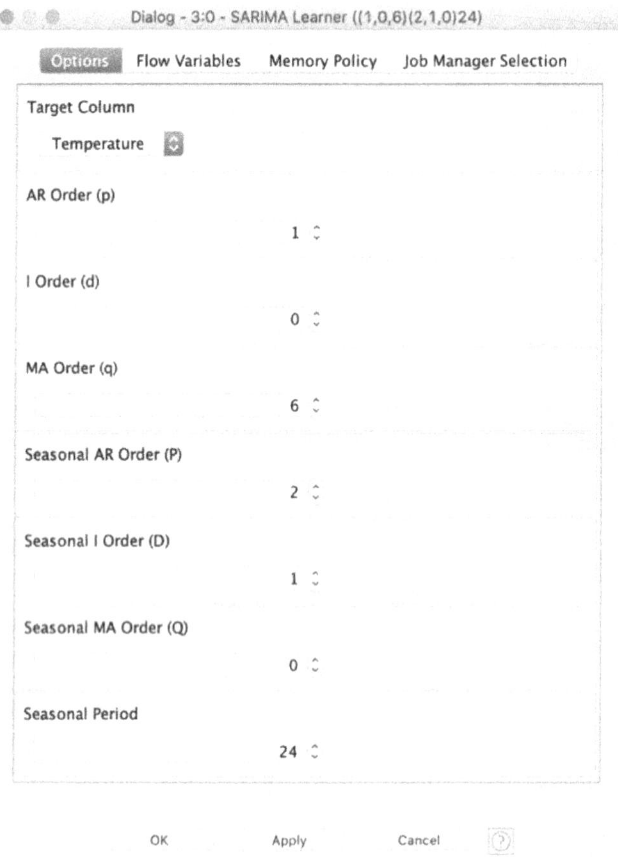


Figure 7.19 – The SARIMA Learner configuration

You'll see the configuration dialog for the SARIMA Learner component on the left-hand side of *Figure 7.22*. Here, we simply select the target column, the thing we're trying to forecast, such as the temperature, and then go down the list typing in each of our chosen hyperparameters.

Next, we connect the SARIMA Predictor component to the blue output port on the right-hand side of the SARIMA Learner component and chose how many forecasts to generate! Unlike many other models, the SARIMA model does not require any kind of data input at the prediction stage. This is handled internally since the model is auto-regressive. After running the workflow in *Figure 7.22*, we've fit our model and generated the forecasts:

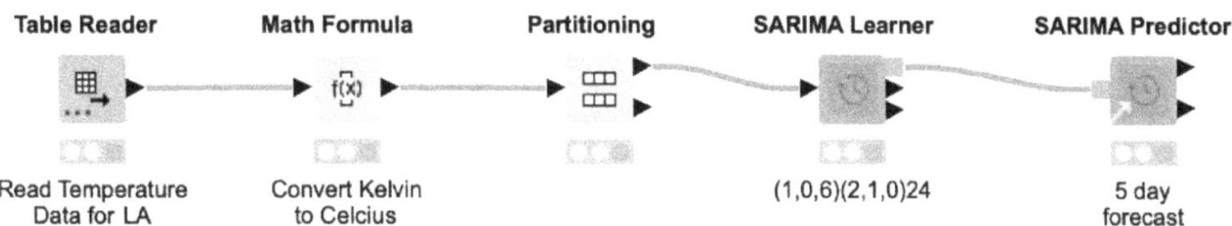


Figure 7.20 – Adding the SARIMA Predictor component

5-day forecasts are common enough requests when asking about the weather, so we'll aim for that. We can open up the configuration dialog for the SARIMA Predictor component, as shown in the following screenshot, and select 120 for our forecast length. This corresponds to our 5-day forecast when converted into hours:

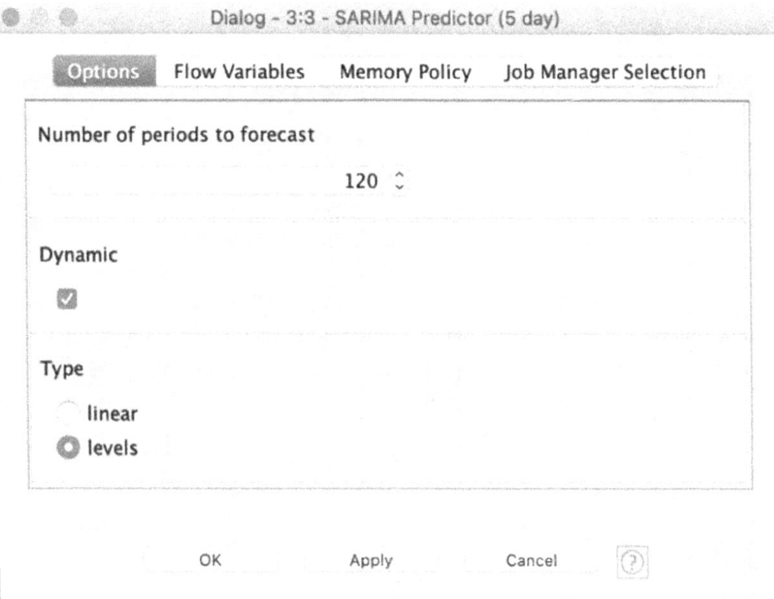


Figure 7.21 – The SARIMA Predictor configuration

Other than our forecast length, there are two configuration options. Checking the box for dynamic alters how in-sample forecasts are generated (we will not use this today) and **Type**. Selecting **levels** returns our data to its undifferenced state before outputting the forecast. That's super helpful! Choose this.

### *Plotting the forecasts*

That's it! We trained our SARIMA model and generated our forecasts! Let's take a quick look back at the workflow that took us through all the steps.

1. We started with some temperature readings from LA.
2. We performed a simple transform to make our data more relatable but it converts from Kelvin into Celsius.
3. We partitioned off some training data from the beginning of our time series. Remember this is important so that our testing looks like deployment as much as possible. We can only train our model on the past.
4. And we trained the SARIMA model with the parameters we picked from the ACF and PACF plots.
5. Finally, we use some line plots to visualize and compare our forecasts.

Let's see the workflow covering the preceding steps:

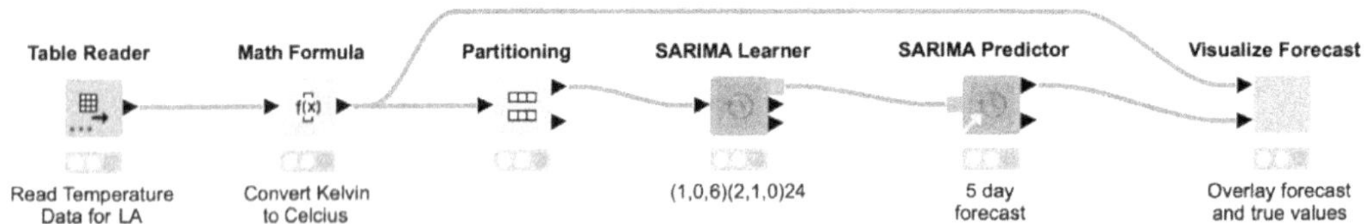


Figure 7.22 – Adding visualization to the end

You can find the workflow, as shown in *Figure 7.23*, by going to KNIME Hub (`hub.knime.com`) and searching for `SARIMA Temperature Forecasting` or by going directly to `https://hub.knime.com/corey/spaces/Public/latest/SARIMA_Example_TSA_Book~QFbQUOFdJcSMNVby`

There's just one more thing. Let's look at our forecasts and see how well they fit:

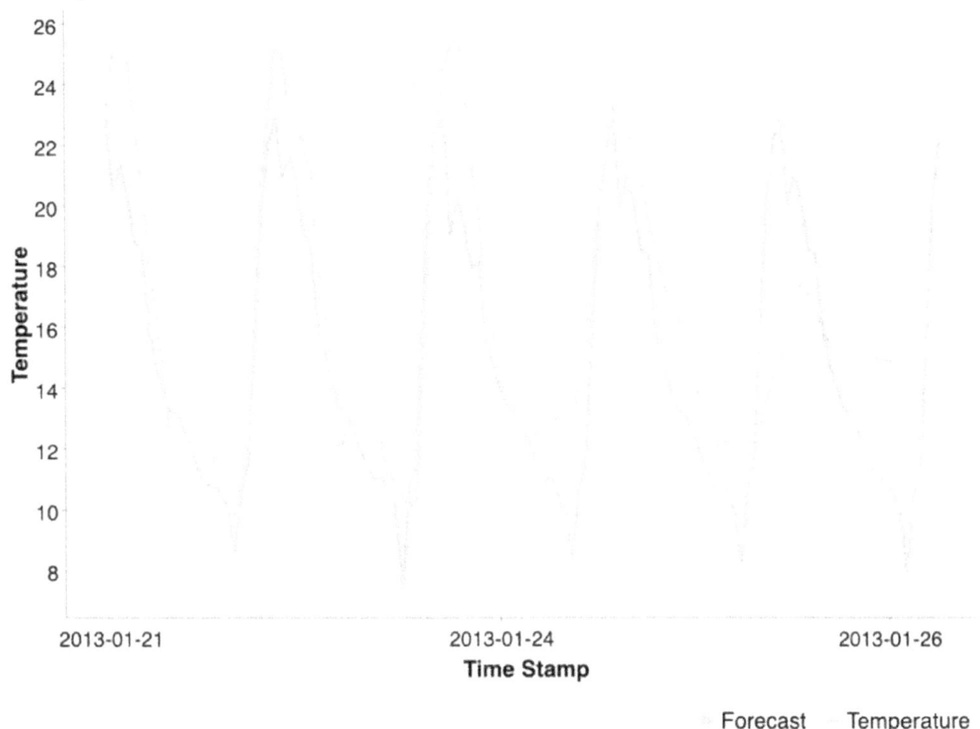


Figure 7.23 – The SARIMA forecast

I'd say our forecast fits very nicely, at least for the first 4 days or so. After that, the true temperature appears to drop while our forecast stays constant in its pattern. This is expected, as cold fronts blow in, thunderstorms drop the temperature, and some days are cloudy. For this reason, modern weather forecasting tools include meteorological simulations to account for these phenomena. We've generated a sophisticated forecast model with no code, and under 500 records, less than a month, of hourly temperature data. SARIMA is a powerful tool.

## Summary

There's so much to say about SARIMA. It's a wonderfully simple and elegant solution to forecasting in an era filled with increasingly complex modeling techniques. It requires very little data and generates powerful, interpretable forecasts. However, its assumptions can be intimidating.

We've removed trends and seasonality from our data via differencing, hopefully inducing a more stationary time series. We've investigated both the ACF and PACF in our search for the ideal hyperparameters. The preparation can be long, but the ease of training and deployment of this model is our reward.

In the next chapter, we'll continue exploring classic techniques, but this time, with a 200-year-old transform from mathematics and a classification use case.

## Further reading

In this chapter, we used several components. You can find them on KNIME Hub at the following links:

- SARIMA Learner: `https://kni.me/c/gVVjDkkaH79V-ju2`
- SARIMA Predictor: `https://kni.me/c/ZQhtGH_fOhzA_49_`
- Inspect seasonality: `https://kni.me/c/YStBnJ-9lhpx4txe`
- Remove seasonality: `https://kni.me/c/rrch-lyih6L4P9Hl`

## Questions

1. Which plot do we use to determine the p and P values of SARIMA?

   A. **Auto-Correlation Function** (ACF)

   B. **Partial Auto-Correlation Function** (PACF)

2. Which plot do we use to determine the q and Q values of SARIMA?

   A. **Auto-Correlation Function** (ACF)

   B. **Partial Auto-Correlation Function** (PACF)

3. Which plot do we use to determine the D value of SARIMA?

    A. **Auto-Correlation Function** (ACF)

    B. **Partial Auto-Correlation Function** (PACF)

4. Which type of stationarity is required by SARIMA?

    A. Strong stationarity: when the probability distribution has no changes over time

    B. Weak Stationarity: when the mean and variance do not change over time

# 8
# Audio Signal Classification with an FFT and a Gradient-Boosted Forest

In this chapter, we will break from forecasting to perform a different type of machine learning on time series data: **classification**. Using the **Fourier transform**, we will transform our data and perform dimensionality reduction, then train a familiar classification model with input and target columns to classify an audio source.

The Fourier transform, however, has a myriad of applications in time series analysis beyond classification. It is used to better explore time series data in search of patterns by shifting to the frequency domain where we can view component seasonal patterns. Furthermore, it is used to construct complex state space models capable of incorporating more seasonalities than the SARIMA.

Before we can reach that conclusion though, we will discuss why working with high-frequency time series data can be tricky, introduce the theory behind the Fourier transform, and discuss how window functions can help clean our data before the application of the Fourier transform.

We will cover the following topics to arrive at our goal:

- Why do we want to classify a signal?
- Windowing your data
- What is a transform?
- The Fourier transform
- Preparing data for modeling
- Training a Gradient Boosted Forest
- Deploying a Gradient Boosted Forest

By the end of the chapter, you will be prepared to use the Fourier transform on various types of signal data for the purpose of building a classification model.

## Technical requirements

The following are the prerequisites for this chapter:

- KNIME Analytics Platform with **KNIME Python Integration** installed (for the **Conda Environment Propagation** node)
- **Conda** package manager installed on your machine

All workflows introduced in the chapter are available on the KNIME Hub at `https://kni.me/s/GxjXX6WmLi-WjLNx`.

## Why do we want to classify a signal?

First things first, we'd like to introduce the use case and the data we'll work with in this chapter. Using a microphone, we recorded audio data from four different audio sources. We'll build a model to analyze short examples of these sounds and identify them automatically.

Our use case is focused on audio data, but the pipeline we will create works equally well with many other recordings from IoT devices. In a manufacturing setting, for example, you may use this approach to attach vibration sensors to a machine and classify the activity, or even predict anomalies for predictive maintenance tasks. The Fourier transform really can be used in any place where data has temporal, or even spatial, relations.

Let's look at what the raw audio signal from source one looks like in the following plot.

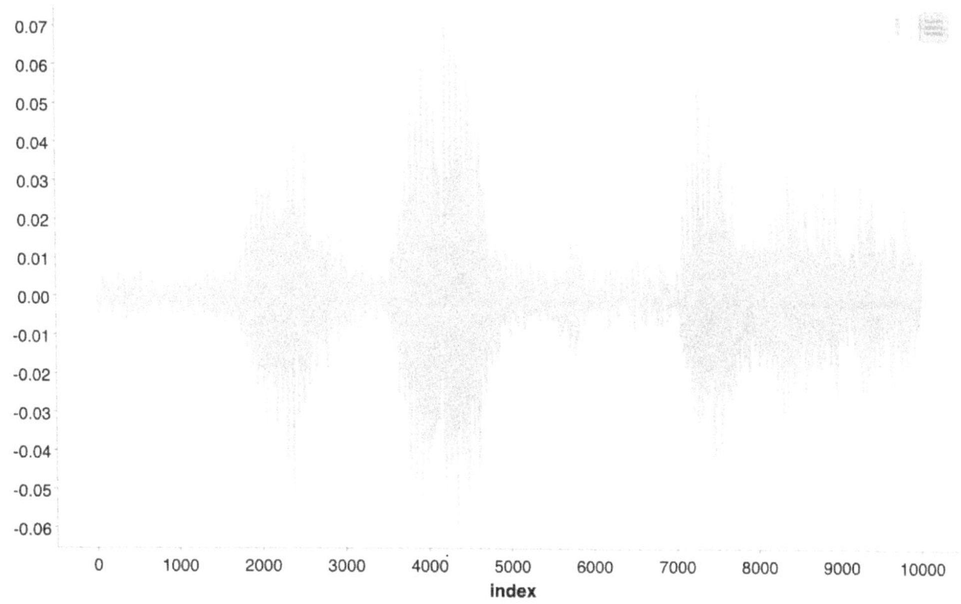


Figure 8.1 – Plot of raw audio data from source one

The preceding plot shows a short clip of the raw audio recording. Audio and other IoT data is sampled at such incredibly high frequencies that it's near impossible to classify in this raw state. Often it will take multiple seconds of audio data to hold enough info for classification; this would be many thousands of values. To circumvent this problem, we frequently create moving windows on top of our data and generate aggregation on those windows to extract information in fewer terms. Sometimes extracting familiar statistical properties such as mean, variance, max, min, and so on.

We don't want to apply the Fourier transform to our entire signal; we want to transform smaller sections of the signal and build a classification on those sections. Formally, we call those sections of the Time Series **Windows**.

## Windowing your data

Typically, before applying operations that extract features, we window our time series. For example, if our time series is daily sales information and we have a year of data, we may window our data into months before calculating the mean so we can understand how it changes over time. Likewise, the Fourier transform extracts frequency information that we can apply to windows of our time series to generate cross-sectional data to be used for classification or anomaly detection tasks. When using the Fourier transform for forecasting or curve fitting, which we don't cover in this chapter, we apply it to the entire series.

In the following figure, boxes represent windows of the signal. We'll apply our operation separately to these windows and each one will eventually become one cross-sectional data point composed of the extracted features.

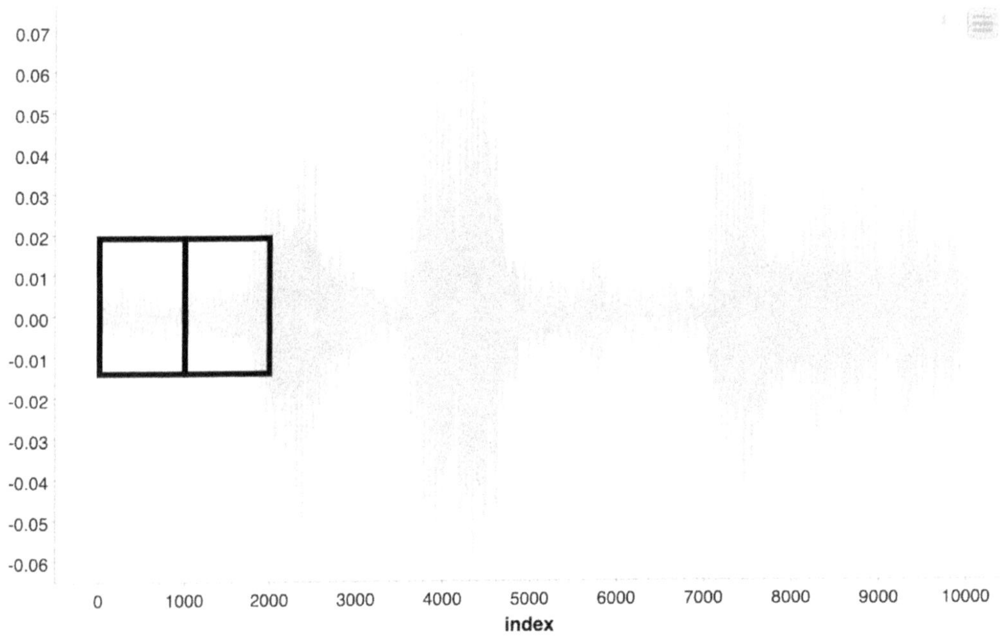


Figure 8.2 – Example window on raw audio data

In the preceding figure, you can see the first two windows of about 1,000 records. If we extract features such as the mean, variance, or powers of the Fourier transform, we generate the cross-sectional data we need for building a classification model. In *Figure 8.3*, you can see what these windows could look like if we extract the mean, min, max, and variance statistics from them, in this way, converting a single column of numeric data into a cross-sectional example extracted from it.

| Row ID | D Mean(... | D Min*(S... | D Max*(... | D Varian... | I Iteration |
|---|---|---|---|---|---|
| Row0#0 | 0.007 | 0 | 0.855 | 0.004 | 0 |
| Row0#1 | 0 | 0 | 0 | 0 | 1 |
| Row0#2 | 0.002 | -0.008 | 0.761 | 0.001 | 2 |
| Row0#3 | -0 | -0.006 | 0.007 | 0 | 3 |
| Row0#4 | 0 | -0.023 | 0.028 | 0 | 4 |
| Row0#5 | -0 | -0.05 | 0.042 | 0 | 5 |
| Row0#6 | 0 | -0.052 | 0.059 | 0 | 6 |
| Row0#7 | -0 | -0.059 | 0.07 | 0 | 7 |
| Row0#8 | -0 | -0.015 | 0.014 | 0 | 8 |
| Row0#9 | 0 | -0.01 | 0.009 | 0 | 9 |
| Row0#10 | 0 | -0.041 | 0.054 | 0 | 10 |
| Row0#11 | -0 | -0.032 | 0.032 | 0 | 11 |
| Row0#12 | -0 | -0.025 | 0.029 | 0 | 12 |
| Row0#13 | -0 | -0.038 | 0.039 | 0 | 13 |
| Row0#14 | -0 | -0.035 | 0.035 | 0 | 14 |
| Row0#15 | 0 | -0.016 | 0.015 | 0 | 15 |
| Row0#16 | -0 | -0.045 | 0.045 | 0 | 16 |
| Row0#17 | 0 | -0.03 | 0.038 | 0 | 17 |
| Row0#18 | -0 | -0.007 | 0.01 | 0 | 18 |
| Row0#19 | 0 | -0.009 | 0.01 | 0 | 19 |
| Row0#20 | -0 | -0.074 | 0.089 | 0 | 20 |
| Row0#21 | 0 | -0.06 | 0.082 | 0 | 21 |
| Row0#22 | -0 | -0.093 | 0.085 | 0.001 | 22 |
| Row0#23 | -0 | -0.094 | 0.092 | 0.001 | 23 |
| Row0#24 | 0 | -0.026 | 0.027 | 0 | 24 |

Figure 8.3 – Table containing 25 processed windows

Now that we have a general idea of what we're looking for with windows, let's talk about creating these windows in the KNIME Analytics Platform.

## Windowing your data in KNIME

There are a few options for windowing your data in KNIME, but we like to do it with loop functionality. This makes it super easy to apply the following logic to each window. Our favorite two options are the **Group Loop Start node** and the **Chunk Loop Start node**.

In the following figure, we look at the configuration dialog for the Group Loop Start node. Month is used as the grouping feature so each iteration of the loop contains a different month.

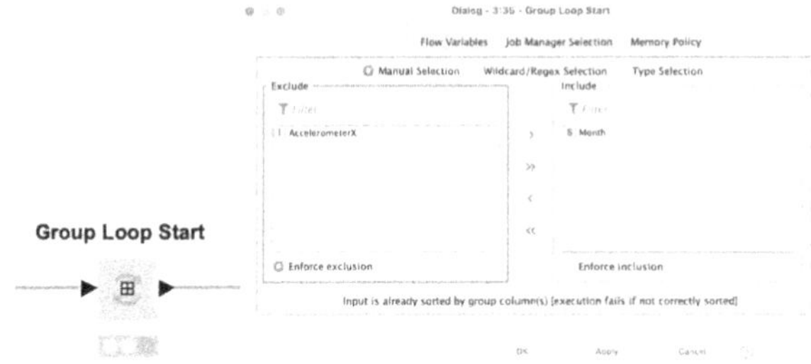


Figure 8.4 – Group Loop Start node and configuration dialog

Group Loop Start allows you to define groupings on your data in the same way as the **GroupBy node** by using other columns in your dataset. This is useful when you want to window your data month by month.

To configure this node, simply move the columns that define your grouping to the green box on the right, such as Month in the preceding figure. Next, we look at the configuration dialog for the Chunk Loop Start node in *Figure 8.5*. Instead of defining groupings, we specify the number of rows for each window in the dialog.

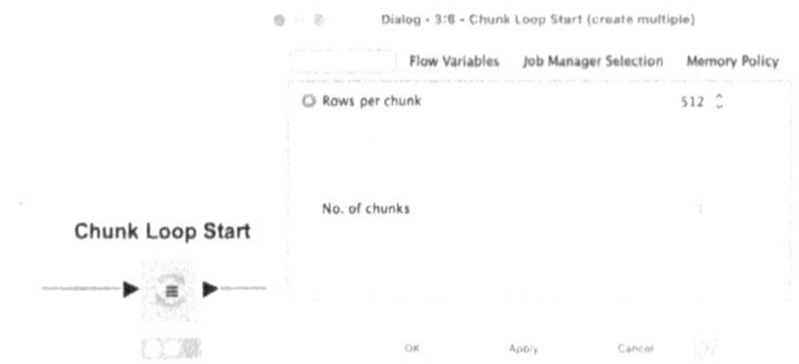


Figure 8.5 – Chunk Loop Start node and configuration dialog

This is great if we're just working with one column of data as we may be with IoT information, but it also allows us to keep our windows the same size. Having windows of a consistent size and data sampled at a consistent frequency is important for the Fourier transform. This is because the number of data points and the sampling rate dictate the frequencies at which we can extract information, as we'll see in the following sections.

When configuring the Chunk Loop Start node, you have two options: either set the number of rows per chunk or set the number of chunks. For our purposes in this chapter, the rows per chunk option is perfect. It allows us to create windows of our data of the same size, which is perfect for the Fourier transform, as we will see.

**Window Sizes**

Choosing the size of these windows can feel like trial and error, but there is an opportunity to apply domain expertise. For every two data points in the window, one frequency can be extracted. So, the finer detail you need, the larger the window must be. Moreover, the highest frequency that can be extracted is ½ the sampling rate.

With our data windowed, we have cross sections of the time series. Next, we will look at how to extract features from these windows. There are a variety of transforms that could be useful, but the Fourier transform is the most useful when working with audio, vibrational, or other periodic signals. Before we dive into the mechanics of the Fourier transform, let's explain what a transform is.

## What is a transform?

What is a transform in the first place? We define a transform as any operation that takes input data and outputs a new representation of it. That is vague, but we think it captures the spirit.

Some common examples are the log transform or an exponential transform as follows:

$$x' = Log(x)$$

$$x' = e^{x}$$

x is the original data and x' is the transformed data. Note that in this case, these transforms undo each other. So, our data is recoverable if we apply either of the preceding transformations. This is not always the case. We call these kinds of transformations **invertible**. The Fourier transform and its discrete counterpart, which we will also discuss, are also invertible transformations!

## The Fourier transform

The Fourier transform, in its raw form, is an operation performed on mathematical functions across a continuous band of frequencies. If you haven't worked with complex exponentials or even with integrals before, or you simply haven't worked with them recently as it often turns out, then don't worry. We won't be doing the calculations by hand. The following formula is how to apply the Fourier transform to a continuous function. This is used for analog data; any continuous periodic function can be perfectly represented as a sum of complex exponentials, or equivalent sine and cosine waves.

$$\hat{f}(\xi) = \int_{-\infty}^{\infty} f(x) \cdot e^{-2\pi i x \xi} dx$$

Formula 8.1 – Fourier transform

In effect, the Fourier transform sweeps across all possible frequency values, $\xi$, outputting a high value when the frequency in question correlates strongly to *f(x)* and a low value when it does not. Entire books have been written on the Fourier transform, when it works, why it works, and what can be done with it. However, that is largely beyond the scope of this book, but we can confidently say, from experience, that it works.

**Why the Complex Exponential?**

Euler's formula, $e^{ix} = \cos(x) + i\sin(x)$, tells us that the complex exponential is just a circle in the complex plane. Because of this, it can be broken into cosine waves representing the real-valued component and sine waves representing the complex value.

However, this is not the version of the Fourier transform that we choose to use in data science. It operates on a continuous signal, our data, no matter how fine in granularity, is discrete. For that, there is a second version of the Fourier transform simply called the **Discrete Fourier Transform** (**DFT**).

## Discrete Fourier Transform (DFT)

Most of the time as data scientists, we do not work with functions directly or analog data, no matter how high the frequency is or how discrete digital data is. We use the following formula instead.

$$x'_k = \sum_{0}^{N-1} x_k \cdot e^{\frac{-i2\pi}{N}kn}$$

Formula 8.2 – Discrete Fourier Transform

Now, instead of using an integral, we use its discrete predecessor, the summation. We can also think of this as sampling a continuous function, where $x_k$ is sampled data points from the function *f(x)* in *Formula 8.1*. Moreover, instead of extracting every possible frequency, $\xi$, we restrict the frequencies we consider down to $0, \frac{1}{N}, \frac{2}{N}, \frac{3}{N}, \ldots 1$ where N is the number of data points in our series. With this new discrete version of the Fourier transform, we start to understand a bit more about what we're doing to our data; we're fitting to it different sinusoidal waves. See the following example.

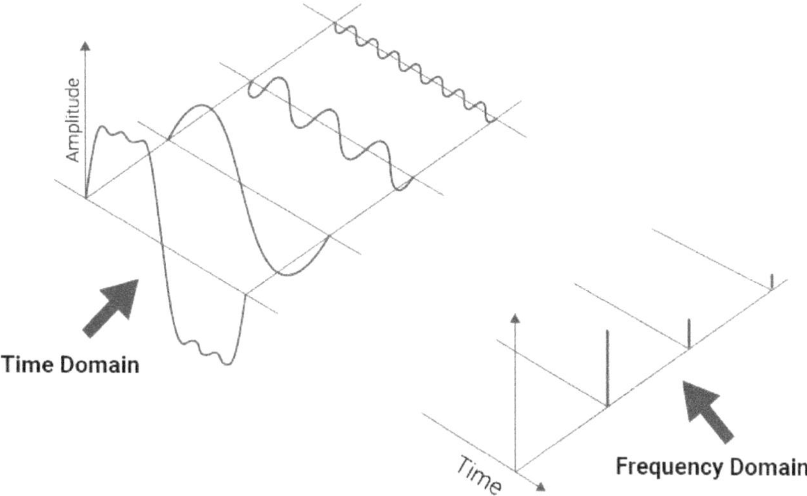


Figure 8.6 – The Fourier transform

If you think back to your calculus class, you may start to see some similarities between this Fourier stuff and the Taylor Series, which is a method for re-representing functions as polynomials. This is very similar except we use waves instead of powers of x.

Imagine for a moment that our signal looks like the first pattern on the left of the preceding figure. It can easily be broken down into a few basic waves of different amplitudes. When we convert that signal into the frequency domain via the discrete Fourier transform, we describe that same original signal in terms of the amplitudes of those component wave patterns. Now, most signals require far more than two or three waves to be accurately represented, but this serves as a simple illustration. This is also why vibrational and auditory data are such good targets for the use of the Fourier transform; they're natural combinations of auditory notes or vibrational patterns containing periodic patterns. You'll also hear about Fourier terms being added to forecasting models for the same reason; they're excellent at capturing repeating patterns.

Finally, we accelerate the speed at which a computer can perform these discrete calculations with one final algorithm: the **Fast Fourier Transform** (**FFT**).

## Fast Fourier Transform (FFT)

There are many distinct algorithmic applications of the FFT, but the most popular is the **Cooley-Tukey algorithm**. This algorithm, which decomposes large DFT summations into smaller factorizations, immensely speeds up the computation time of the Fourier transform. The algorithm was originally invented by Carl Friedrich Gauss in 1805 while he was studying asteroid trajectories. However, it was independently invented by James Cooley and John Tukey while researching methods to detect nuclear weapon tests in 1965. The latter popularized its use and supplied its name.

## Applying the Fourier transform in KNIME

Now that we understand what the Fourier transform is and what it is for, how do we apply it inside of the KNIME Analytics Platform? The easiest option is to use the FFT component found in the KNIME **EXAMPLES** server under **00_Components | Time Series**.

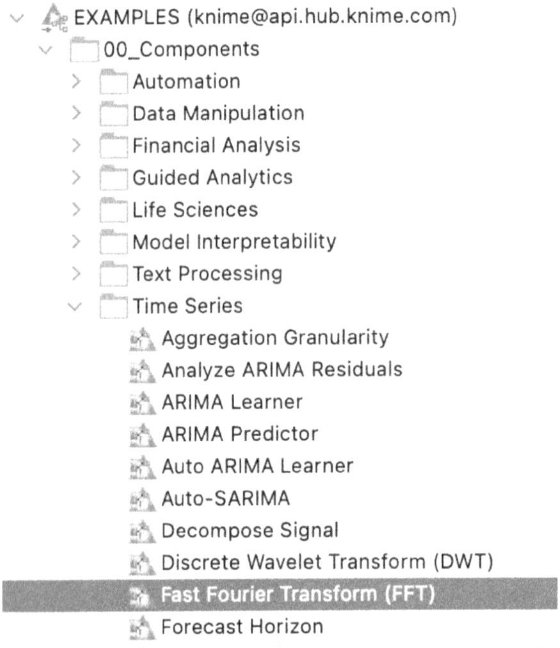

- EXAMPLES (knime@api.hub.knime.com)
  - 00_Components
    - Automation
    - Data Manipulation
    - Financial Analysis
    - Guided Analytics
    - Life Sciences
    - Model Interpretability
    - Text Processing
    - Time Series
      - Aggregation Granularity
      - Analyze ARIMA Residuals
      - ARIMA Learner
      - ARIMA Predictor
      - Auto ARIMA Learner
      - Auto-SARIMA
      - Decompose Signal
      - Discrete Wavelet Transform (DWT)
      - Fast Fourier Transform (FFT)
      - Forecast Horizon

Figure 8.7 – Location of the FFT component

From the examples server, we can simply drag and drop this component into our workflow as we would a node from the node repository. As with several other components in the **Time Series** category, we leverage Python under the hood to bring this additional functionality.

There are a few configuration options for us to set when using this component. Let's review them.

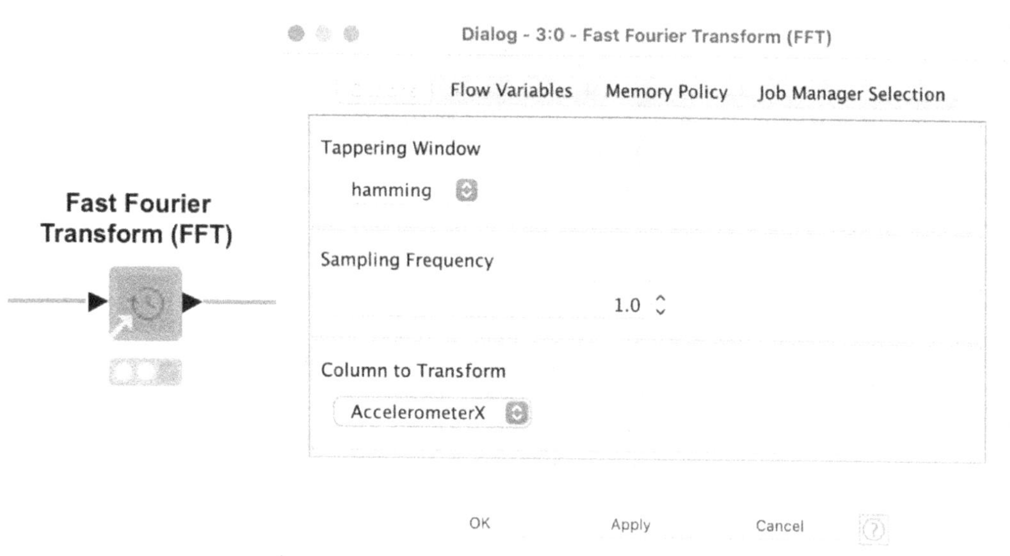


Figure 8.8 – The FFT component and configuration dialog

The first setting you'll see in the preceding configuration dialog is **Tapering Window**. The different options here are different smoothing functions that are applied to your time series before the Fourier transform is applied. The Fourier transform assumes that input data is periodic. The window functions all work by smoothing the beginning and end of the window of data to zero; this artificially creates the periodic data required. You can imagine how you could now copy and paste the window end to end in a repeating pattern. The different window functions perform this smoothing in different ways. While we won't cover this in detail in this chapter, it does allow the Fourier transform to fit better into the data. A quick Google search of `Window Functions` will bring up many options for further reading. In general, the `Hamming` function, the default option in the FFT component, is considered an excellent general use option and we encourage you to use it unless you have a specific reason to do otherwise.

The next option in the configuration dialog is **Sampling Frequency**. This is the frequency our data was recorded at and it is used to properly name the output columns. Our data was recorded at 16,000 Hz, so the maximum frequency in the output table will be half of that, 8,000 Hz. If you recall from the *Discrete Fourier Transform (DFT)* section, the frequencies we attempt to fit into our data are dictated by the number of data points we input into the Fourier transform. The more data points we supply, the more frequencies we can extract. This is important to a point, but keep in mind that there may be no need to extract information from many frequencies. We can simplify the output of our FFT by using appropriately sized windows to reduce frequency granularity or by downsampling our data to reduce the maximum frequencies.

Finally, there is the **Column to Transform** option. This column will be the input series that we transform and extract frequency information from.

In the previous sections, we learned how to take a single column of time series data and convert it into cross-sectional data by creating windows. We also applied the Fourier transform to extract useful features from these windows. Next, we'll discuss how we can prepare this high-dimensional, cross-sectional data for classification modeling.

# Preparing data for modeling

Now that we've converted our single column of high-frequency time series data into multiple columns of frequency amplitudes by windowing our data and applying the FFT, we're in more familiar territory. The way our data is shaped now contains columns we can use as inputs for modeling. However, there are far too many columns.

## Reducing dimensionality

Some modeling algorithms support very wide tables or very large input sets; neural networks come to mind. However, practicality is not the only reason to reduce dimensionality. Overfitting is a serious concern when working with wide datasets; we want our model to generalize well to new data and not just pick up on one frequency that, perhaps by random chance, turned out to be an amazing classifier.

In the following sections, we'll review different types of binning and filtering to reduce the dimensionality of our newly cross-sectional data to a manageable size without too much information loss.

### *Binning*

The first method we'll cover is **binning**. Normally, when we bin data, we talk about converting a numeric data column into a categorical one by defining numeric ranges and binning data into them. For this chapter, let's call that familiar method **row-wise binning**.

The data we're working with now, though, is prime for **column-wise binning**. We take a range of frequencies, gather up those columns, and combine them into one column by performing an aggregation, using the average is common.

| Table "default" - Rows: 884 | Spec - Columns: 8193 | Properties | Flow Variables | | | |
|---|---|---|---|---|---|---|
| Row ID | D Frequ... | D Frequ... | D Frequ... | D Frequ... | D Frequ... | D Frequ... |
| Row0 | 0.252 | 0.254 | 0.252 | 0.253 | 0.253 | 0.252 |
| Row1 | 0.001 | 0.001 | 0.001 | 0.001 | 0 | 0.001 |
| Row2 | 0.001 | 0.001 | 0.001 | 0 | 0 | 0.001 |
| Row3 | 0.001 | 0.001 | 0.001 | 0 | 0.001 | 0.001 |
| Row4 | 0.001 | 0.001 | 0.001 | 0.001 | 0 | 0 |
| Row5 | 0 | 0.001 | 0.001 | 0.001 | 0 | 0 |
| Row6 | 0.001 | 0.001 | 0 | 0 | 0 | 0.001 |
| Row7 | 0.001 | 0.001 | 0 | 0.001 | 0.001 | 0 |
| Row8 | 0.001 | 0.001 | 0.002 | 0.003 | 0.003 | 0.002 |
| Row9 | 0.003 | 0.006 | 0.007 | 0.003 | 0.003 | 0.004 |
| Row10 | 0.005 | 0.004 | 0.004 | 0.002 | 0 | 0.001 |

Figure 8.9 – Data table with many frequency columns

The preceding table shows the first six frequency columns in our transformed data table. Notice how each row has very similar amplitudes across these frequency columns. That's because these columns have very similar frequencies, so it makes sense that they should represent our original time series with similar strengths. This makes our data ripe for column-wise binning or aggregating those similar frequency columns into one.

Depending on our data, we may choose to use wide bins or narrow bins at different points in the frequency spectrum. For example, when we're working with audio data, specifically something perceptible to the human ear, we use wide bands at very low or high frequencies and narrow bands in the middle where we expect more information to be held.

### *High and low band filtering*

If you're a music or audio nerd or have a friend that is, you'll have heard the term high/low band filter, sometimes high/low-pass filter, before. A nice speaker system will often contain a tweeter for high pitched noises and a subwoofer for low pitches. The audio is separated by only passing the low frequencies extracted from the Fourier transform to the subwoofer where the desired part of the signal is reconstructed and played. You see, the Fourier transform is essential to so many aspects of digital signals.

For our use case in this chapter, we can also apply this filtering technique by removing sections of the frequency space we do not believe will be helpful when it's time for modeling. Since our data is auditory and intended for the human ear, we make the assumption that very high, or very low, frequencies are not likely to contain important information—we can't hear those sounds anymore.

The human hearing range is between 20 and 20,000 Hz. In this case, we are recording the audio data at 16,000 Hz; the frequencies we've extracted, then, range from ~1 Hz to 8,000 Hz. There's no filtering to do at the high end of our frequency spectrum, but there's a bit we can do at the low end.

> **Nyquist Frequency**
>
> Notice that the highest frequency we can capture with the Fourier transform is exactly 1/2 of the sampling rate of our recording. This is no coincidence; the Nyquist Frequency is the highest frequency extractable from a time series and it is 1/2 the sampling rate. This is effectively due to two sample points being required to see a turn in a signal.

It's also worth noting here that human hearing is strongest in the middle range of frequencies, typically around 1,000 Hz. For that reason, we may choose to look most closely at the frequencies in that space. See the following plot for a comparison of these ranges.

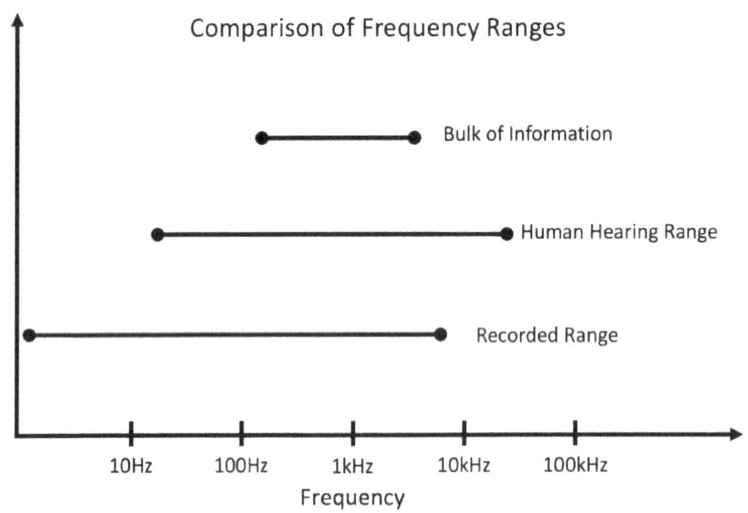


Figure 8.10 – Comparison of different frequency ranges

You'll notice that the recorded frequency stretches to 0 Hz. This would be just like extracting an average line from our signal data, and recall its maximum is 1/2 the sampling rate. To raise the recorded range, we could sample more quickly; high-fidelity audio recordings do exactly that. The human hearing range may not be relevant to all use cases, but it does give us an idea of where important information inside sounds designed for humans will lie, such as in this chapter's use case.

With our data processed by the Fourier transform, converting it into cross-sectional data in the frequency domain, and its dimensionality reduced to a more practical size via the binning of neighboring frequencies using narrower bands in sections of the frequency domain we suspect to contain more information, we're ready to train the model. Today, we will use the Gradient Boosted Forest. We find it very effective in extracting results from high-dimensional data.

# Training a Gradient Boosted Forest

To classify the four different audio signals so that we can tell them apart, we'll need to do more than just apply the Fourier transform; we need to build a model on our cross-sectional data. Training a Gradient Boosted Forest in KNIME is very easy. We'll use the Gradient Boosted Trees Learner node, which only has a few configurable options that we'll concern ourselves with. We've chosen to use the Gradient Boosted Forest model due to its ability to handle high-dimensional data and its impressive predictive power.

## Applying the Fourier transform in KNIME

The workflow we'll use to train the model and do all of our preprocessing with the Fourier transform can be seen in *Figure 8.11*. You'll notice it is a small workflow with some of the binning logic placed inside the FFT and Binning component.

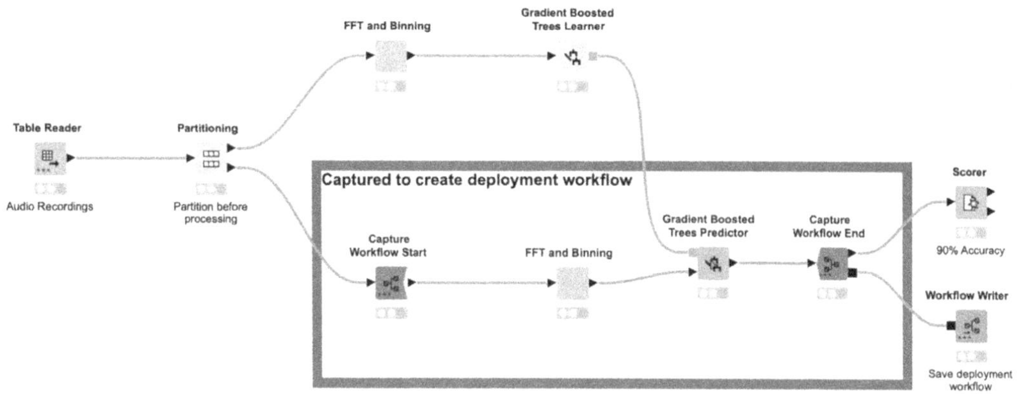


Figure 8.11 – Training workflow with FFT preprocessing

When constructing this workflow, the first node to the far left is the **Table Reader**. This is where we access the audio recordings data. For this example, the data has been embedded into the workflow for easy access, but for similar use cases, you may need to use KNIME's database connecters, Get Request nodes, cloud filesystem connectors, or even other flat file readers such as Parquet or CSV readers.

Once the data has been read into the workflow, we use the partitioning node to split the data into a training set and a testing set. When doing this, we make sure to select the **Take from top** option so that our training set represents data that comes before our testing data, chronologically. This is always important in time series analysis as we want to ensure our testing setup looks, as much as possible, like a real deployment scenario—where incoming data will be from the future. See *Figure 8.12* for the specific configuration used while partitioning; we also use a typical 70/30 percentage split.

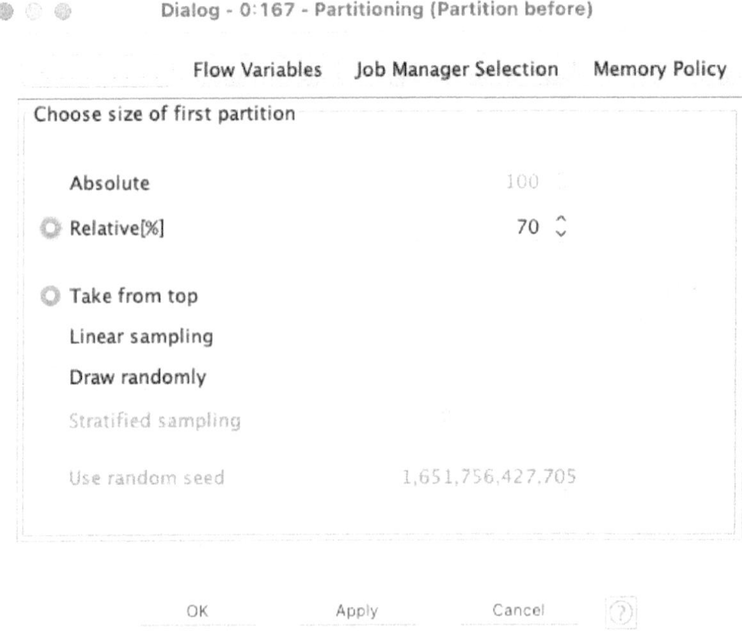


Figure 8.12 – Partitioning node configuration dialog using Take from top

Notice that we're applying the partitioning node before any of our preprocessing. This is intentional to remove the risk of information leakage between the train and test sets. The ability to package preprocessing steps into a component for easy reuse in both datasets makes this an easy precautionary step.

With our data partitioned, we move on to the Fourier transform that we discussed in the bulk of the earlier sections of this chapter. In the workflow from *Figure 8.11*, the windowing, Fourier transform, and binning are encapsulated in the FFT and Binning component. When exploring the example workflow, you can hold control, or command on a Mac, and double-click the component to move inside of it and explore the nodes used to construct it. This component does have some configuration options of its own, though. When we double-click to open the configuration dialog (as we would with a normal node), we see the option to set the number of bins in the low, middle, and high range of the frequencies.

Figure 8.13 – FFT and Binning component configuration dialog

The default setting for this component is to include **10** bins in the bottom 25% of the recorded frequency, **50** bins in the middle 50%, and **10** bins in the top 25%. This is in line with our assumptions that the bulk of the information will lie in the middle range, which is most relevant to human hearing. Try tuning the number of bins differently and see how it affects the results. These binned frequencies will be the input columns for our Gradient Boosted Forest model and the target will be the audio signal that the window originated from.

## Applying the Gradient Boosted Trees Learner

With the data loaded into the KNIME Analytics Platform and processed by the Fourier transform, we're ready to feed it into our learner node and fit the model. To train a Gradient Boosted Forest model, we use the Gradient Boosted Trees node. Simply connect the training dataset to the input port of the node as you saw in *Figure 8.10* and double-click to open the node's configuration dialog. There are a couple of settings we will tune or verify.

Figure 8.14 – Gradient Boosted Trees node configuration dialog

At the very top of the configuration dialog shown in *Figure 8.14*, you'll see the first configuration to set, **Target Column**. Set this to **Source** as it is our string column that represents the original audio recording the record is from; this is what our model will try to predict. Next, to set the input columns, we see two boxes towards the middle of the configuration dialog, one red to the left, and another green to the right. We want to move any columns we wish to use as inputs for our model to the green box on the right and leave the rest in the red box to the left. In this chapter's use case, we will use all available columns as inputs to our model, so simply click the double arrow pointing to the right box to move all columns.

Below those basic options that appear at the top of most learner configuration dialogs in KNIME, we also have a few options regarding the trees that make up the forest and how boosting is applied. The first of these options is **Limit number of levels** (tree depth), and this is enabled and set to **4** by default. What this does is limit the number of consecutive splits that will be made when fitting the individual trees that will compose the ensemble model. We'll leave this setting at its default, allowing each tree to be more generic and to train faster. Training speed is important to consider when building boosting-based models as the trees will be individually trained in sequence to target the errors of the previous trees. If each model is excessively slow, it will have a large effect on the total train time.

**Random Forest Models**

This is different from another common type of tree ensembles, Random Forests, which trains the trees entirely separate from each other and can, for that reason, leverage parallel algorithms to speed up the execution time.

The final two options are the **Number of models** and the **Learning rate**. We will leave the **Learning rate** at its default setting of **0.1**. This isn't a setting we recommend changing without a specific reason for doing so. However, we will change the **Number of models** from **100** to **200**. We choose to raise this setting because of the high number of input features. With only four splits per tree, some features may never be used with too few trees.

With the Gradient Boosted Forest model trained, we're ready to move on to discussing how to deploy it. You may have noticed the Capture Workflow Start and Capture Workflow End nodes back in *Figure 8.11*. They will be central to the creation of our deployment workflow as we'll see in the following section.

## Deploying a Gradient Boosted Forest

To deploy the classification model and preprocessing along with it, we'll use KNIME Analytics Platform's **Integrated Deployment** feature. As you will see in the following figure, the preprocessing of the test set along with the Gradient Boosted Trees Predictor node lie directly between the Capture Workflow Start and Capture Workflow End nodes. Any nodes between the capture start and end will be combined into an automatically generated deployment workflow as we will see.

In the following figure, we see how the Integrated Deployment nodes surround the preprocessing and model prediction.

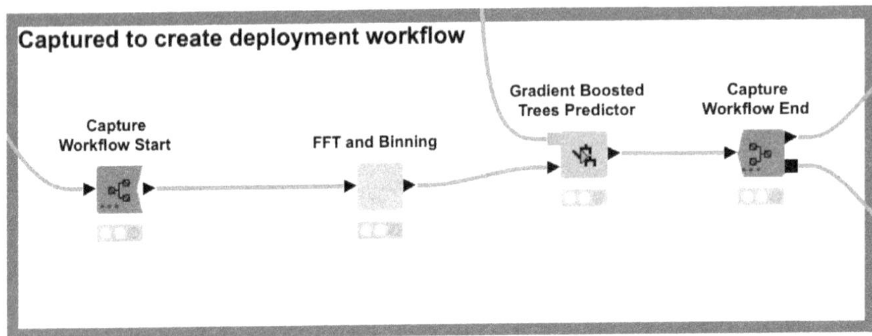


Figure 8.15 – Captured portion of training workflow

Looking at *Figure 8.15*, you'll notice that the trained Gradient Boosted Forest model that plugs into the Gradient Boosted Trees Predictor node is also required to execute this section of the training workflow. KNIME's Integrated Deployment functionality also accounts for this; any required inputs to the nodes being captured that do not pass through the Capture Workflow Start node will automatically be saved and embedded into the deployment workflow. The following figure shows the automatically created deployment workflow.

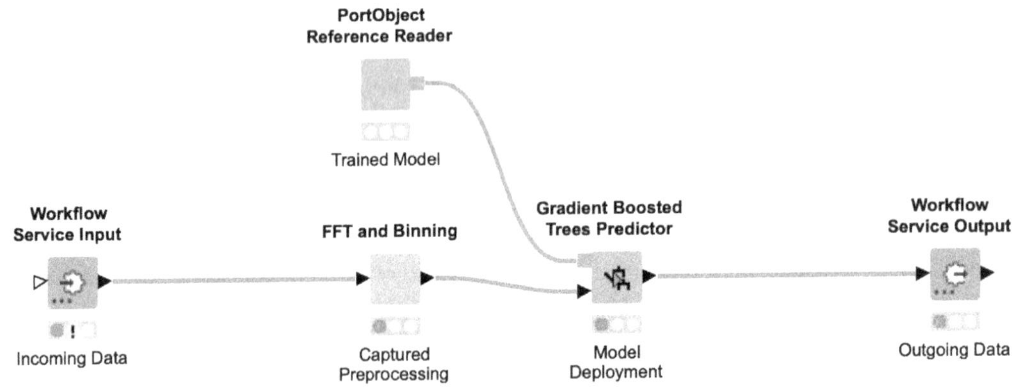


Figure 8.16 – Automatically generated deployment workflow

*Figure 8.16* should look familiar; the center of the workflow includes the FFT and Binning component that we used to preprocess the signal data as well as the Gradient Boosted Trees Predictor node that generates predictions using our trained model to classify the source of the audio signal. Above those two nodes, you see something new, the **PortObject Reference Reader**. This represents any required input objects from the captured section of the original workflow, which is in this case the trained model from the Gradient Boosted Trees Learner node. All are automatically copied from our training workflow.

Other than the captured portion of our workflow and any required objects, this newly generated deployment workflow has two more important nodes: the Workflow Service Input node to the left and the Workflow Service Output node to the right. These nodes allow the deployment workflow to accept input data and respond with output data when called either from inside other KNIME workflows or from **REST endpoints** if loaded to a KNIME Server. The REST endpoints are the perfect way to embed a deployed KNIME workflow into an external process.

Looking at the creation of the deployment workflow via KNIME's integrated deployment, we see how closely model training and deploying can be tied; any changes we make to data processing or model scoring in the training workflow are automatically realized in the deployment workflow. This doesn't even change the REST endpoints so other applications can access the deployment workflow identically as it evolves.

To view the REST endpoints of a workflow deployed to a KNIME Server, simply right-click on the workflow from KNIME Explore and select **Show API definition** as you can see in the following figure.

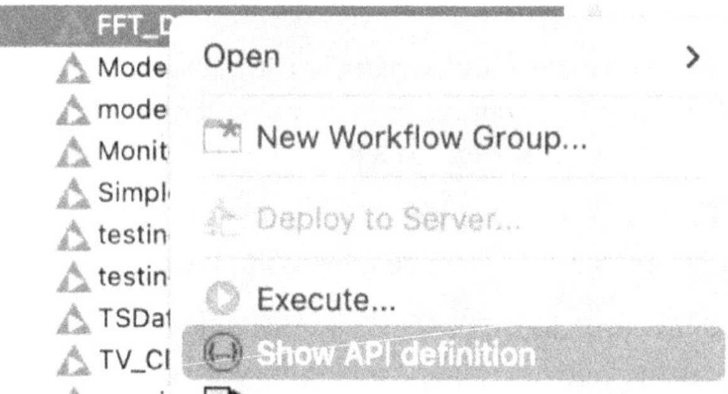


Figure 8.17 – Viewing the REST endpoints on a KNIME Server

Selecting this **Show API definition** button will direct you to the workflow on your KNIME Server and display its Swagger definition. With that being done, our audio signal classification is deployed and ready for use by whoever needs it.

With the deployment workflow captured and its REST endpoints shared with colleagues, our use case is deployed and signal data can be classified by our approach.

## Summary

In this chapter, we learned about the Fourier transform in its original form as well as its discrete counterpart, the discrete Fourier transform. We touched on the algorithm used to compute that discrete version, the Fast Fourier Transform, and detailed the application of data analysis from the perspective of the frequency domain.

With the audio signal data converted into cross-sectional data in the frequency domain, we built a classification model to predict the source of the signal. To do this, we employed a binning technique to aggregate adjacent frequencies from the output of the Fourier transform into average columns. This significantly reduced the dimensionality of the newly generated cross-sectional data without significant information. We further tuned these bins to be narrower in the center band of the frequency spectrum where we believe most information are held. This assumption was made because the audio signals were for human hearing and this middle section corresponded to the most sensitive range of our human hearing. This data was fed into a Gradient Boosted Forest model to generate a prediction as to the source of the signal.

Finally, with the data processed and modeled, we leveraged KNIME's Integrated Deployment functionality to capture the necessary portions of the training workflow to automatically generate a deployment workflow complete with REST endpoints when loaded to a KNIME Server.

This approach is useful beyond audio signal classification and can be tuned to classify other kinds of signals or time series data as well as detect anomalous behavior in either.

In the following chapters, we will introduce deep learning and how it can be applied to time series data for forecasting purposes, starting with how a standard feedforward network can be used to forecast glucose levels in the bloodstream.

## Questions

1. The Fourier transform moves data from the time domain to the ____ domain.

   A. frequency

   B. cosine

   C. cross section

2. How does the Fourier transform help reshape data for traditional classification modeling?

   A. It extracts relevant features.

   B. It generates cross-sectional data.

   C. All of the above.

3. Which aggregation technique did we apply when binning the frequency columns?

    A. Mean

    B. Median

    C. Minimum

    D. Maximum

4. In which section of the frequency domain did we use the narrowest bins?

    A. Bottom 25%

    B. Middle 50%

    C. Top 25%

# 9

# Training and Deploying a Neural Network to Predict Glucose Levels

In this chapter, we will look at a more critical prediction problem: forecasting glucose levels to provide diabetics with early warnings when their insulin or carbohydrates need to be balanced due to their blood sugar levels.

We will also introduce **neural networks**. We will start by learning how to use a neural network for time series prediction by using the simplest neural architecture: a classic **feedforward neural network** (**FFNN**) without any recurrent layers. Though simple, the results obtained by this neural network for glucose level prediction are already quite accurate. However, the network's performance could be improved by using a more complex network architecture, such as **long short-term memory** (**LSTM**), which we will introduce in the next chapter.

Thus, we will use this glucose level prediction case study to briefly explain how neural networks work and how they can be trained. Finally, we will learn how to automatically deploy the trained network via integrated deployment.

In this chapter, we will cover the following topics:

- Glucose prediction and the glucose dataset
- An introduction to neural networks
- Training a feedforward neural network to predict glucose levels
- Deploying an FFNN-based alarm system

By the end of this chapter, you'll have a basic understanding of neural networks and how to design custom neural architectures with KNIME's Keras integration. Let's start by exploring the problem of glucose prediction and the dataset we used for this case study.

# Technical requirements

The following are the prerequisites for this chapter:

- KNIME Analytics Platform with **KNIME Deep Learning – Keras Integration** installed, as well as **KNIME Python Integration** installed (for the **Conda Environment Propagation** node).
- The **Conda** package manager must be installed on your machine.

All the workflows that will be introduced in this chapter are available on KNIME Hub at `https://kni.me/s/GxjXX6WmLi-WjLNx`.

# Glucose prediction and the glucose dataset

In this chapter, we will look at glucose prediction to learn how to generate time series forecasts through a neural network model. This use case starts by predicting a physical variable that triggers a chain of actions. The physical variable could be anything that can be measured via a sensor: temperature, electricity, or, in this case, blood glucose level. This chain of actions ranges from a simple warning email to an alarm that shuts down the entire system and has numerous applications in manufacturing and machine maintenance. In the upcoming sections, we will review the dataset and techniques we will use to develop this alarm system, as well as why it is needed.

## Glucose prediction

**Diabetes** is an increasingly common disease that affects your ability to convert carbohydrates into energy. Food is broken down into **glucose** and released into your bloodstream. From here, a hormone called insulin moves the glucose to the cells that need it.

If you have diabetes, your insulin either doesn't quite function properly or enough isn't produced by the pancreas. In either case, glucose in your bloodstream is not being moved properly to the cells. This can cause tiredness in minor incidents or lead to issues such as heart disease, kidney disease, or vision loss in the long term.

In all cases, the body cannot metabolize enough of the glucose in the bloodstream, which leads to glucose spikes and a lack of energy.

Diabetes is not always severe. In some cases, a healthy diet and exercise are enough to keep the glucose level under control. In other cases, diabetes can be severe and additional amounts of insulin are necessary for the body to keep control of the glucose level.

For people affected by severe diabetes, keeping track of the glucose level in their bloodstream is an everyday task. In addition, the number of people suffering from diabetes is increasing worldwide, both due to modern nutrition imbalance and an aging population. This makes the problem of **glucose monitoring** and insulin production even more important. In this chapter, we will limit ourselves to the glucose monitoring issue and leave the problem of insulin production to others.

A common way to monitor glucose is to look at the current glucose measure (in mg/dl) and see if it deviates too much from *normal* values, as defined by medical statistics. However, this requires frequent tests, and you can't always be attached to a measuring device. So, a possible alternative could be to predict future glucose levels based on the recent glucose readings and see if those predicted levels exceed the recommended boundaries.

This is what we will implement in this chapter: an application for predicting future glucose levels and checking that their maximum and minimum values fall between the recommended boundaries. This application will consist of two parts:

- A workflow that will train a neural network to perform the forecasting
- A second deployment workflow that will make this model work in production by applying it to real glucose measures from sensor devices

In this use case, models are fit for each individual separately. The neural network is trained on the time series data of glucose levels of only one person, while the deployment workflow only works on the data from the **continuous glucose monitor** (**CGM**) device for that same person.

> **Transfer Learning**
>
> Training the model first on a group of people and then tuning the model via **transfer learning** could be a way to improve model performance and works very well with Keras networks like the one we will use in this chapter.

## The glucose dataset

To train the neural network, we used the time series data of glucose levels for selected patients from the `D1NAMO` dataset.

The `D1NAMO` dataset provides a variety of biological signals related to diabetes management in type 1 diabetes patients. The `D1NAMO` dataset is composed of two distinct subsets:

- A subset that contains data from 20 healthy people
- A subset that contains data from nine patients with diabetes

Both subsets contain ECG signals, breathing signals, accelerometer outputs, glucose measurements, and food pictures with annotations by a dietitian. Glucose levels have been sampled every few minutes.

More information about the `D1NAMO` dataset can be found at `https://zenodo.org/record/1421616` or *The open D1NAMO dataset: A multi-modal dataset for research on non-invasive type 1 diabetes management*, by Dubosson (`https://www.sciencedirect.com/science/article/pii/S2352914818301059`).

While the dataset contains other features, we will only focus on glucose levels. *Figure 9.1* shows a line plot of the glucose level of a selected diabetic patient over a few days:

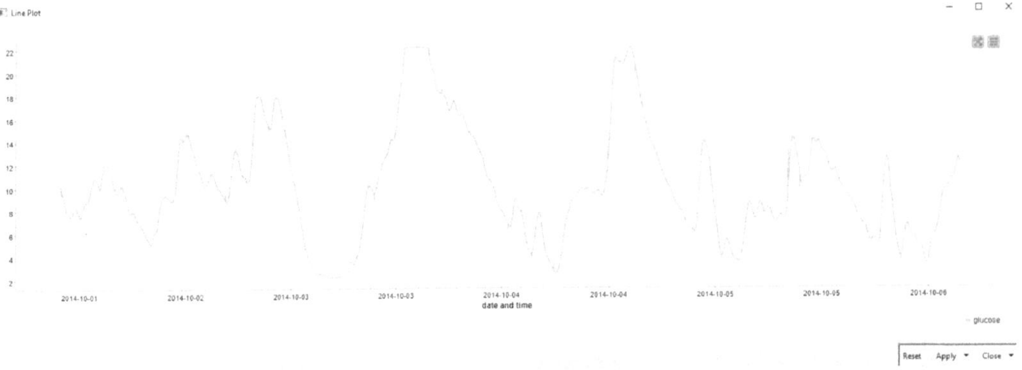


Figure 9.1 – Glucose level across time for a diabetic patient

To summarize, we would like to train a neural network to predict the future glucose levels of a selected patient from the `D1NAMO` dataset. The model will then be deployed to provide notifications if glucose levels are forecasted to rise too high or fall too low.

Before diving into a workflow in KNIME Analytics Platform, let's look at a few basic features of neural networks and their most common training methods.

# A quick introduction to neural networks

In this section, we will introduce the basics of neural networks – just enough to continue with this chapter. We leave it up to you to deepen this knowledge by exploring other types of neural architectures and neural training algorithms.

> **Codeless Deep Learning with KNIME**
>
> If you're interested in learning about deep learning in greater detail, I encourage you to check out KNIME's other book with Packt: *Codeless Deep Learning with KNIME*, which is available at `https://www.knime.com/codeless-deep-learning-book`.

Neural networks are not a new topic. They have gone through many ups and downs in popularity and are now back thanks to improvements in modern compute power. Let's start with a model of an artificial neuron and build our first multilayer neural architectures.

## Artificial neurons and artificial neural networks

The first model of a biological neuron represented input signals as a vector, $[x_1, x_{2,\dots,} x_n]$, the chemical synapses as weights, $[w_1, w_2, \dots, w_n]^T$T, and the total net input to the neuron as the weighted sum of the input signals, as follows:

$$net = \sum_{j=1}^{n} x_j w_j$$

Formula 9.1

The spiking character of the neuron output signal was simulated via a step function, *f()*. When the net input exceeds a given threshold, *b*, the neuron is active, *(y=1)*; otherwise, it is resting, *(y=0)*. *f()* is called the neuron's **activation function**:

$$f(net) = \begin{cases} 1 \ \ if \ net \geq b \\ 0 \ \ if \ net < b \end{cases}$$

Formula 9.2

Thus, the final formula for describing the behavior of an **artificial neuron** is as follows:

$$y = f\left(\sum_{j=0}^{n} x_j w_j\right) \qquad \text{with } b = w_0$$

Formula 9.3

To increase the computational power, many artificial neurons are used, instead of just one, and are organized in a layer-like architecture. Such neural architectures accept *n* inputs, $[x_1, x_2, \dots, x_n]$ through the input layer, produce *m* outputs, $[y_1, y_2, \dots, y_m]$ on the output layer, and process the data throughout a number, *k*, of hidden layers between the input and output layers.

Artificial neurons in the layers of a **neural network** can be connected in various ways, producing different **neural architectures**. Let's consider the direction of the data flow from input to output as the forward direction of the network structure, so that the input layer is the first layer and the output layer is the last. *Feedforward architectures* contain neurons that only connect to neurons in the next layer. *Recurrent networks* allow self-connections to be made on the same neuron or even for connections to be made to neurons in the previous layers. The following diagram shows how these layers connect. The neurons in the input layer are represented by $x_i$, the weights of the corresponding connections are represented by $w^n_{j,i}$, where *j* is the index of the former, *i* represents the index of the current layer, and *n* represents the layer in question:

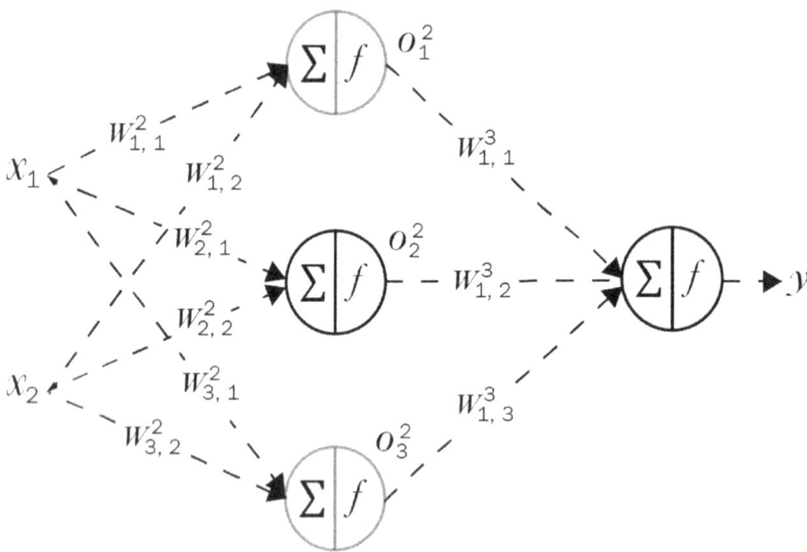


Figure 9.2 – Fully connected feedforward neural network with one hidden layer and one output unit

The preceding diagram shows a fully connected feedforward neural network with two inputs, one output, and one hidden layer with three hidden neurons. Notice the notations. $w^2_{1,2}$ indicates the weight connecting neuron 2 from the previous layer to neuron 1 in the next layer, which is layer 2 in the architecture. $o^2_1$ is the output value of neuron 1 in layer 2 of the architecture.

There are many types of activation functions, *f()*. The step function, the **Sigmoid Function**, the **Hyperbolic Tangent** tanh, and **Rectified Linear Unit** (**ReLU**) are the most common, as shown in *Figure 9.3*. Usually, neurons in the same layer have the same activation function, *f()*, while different layers can have different activation functions:

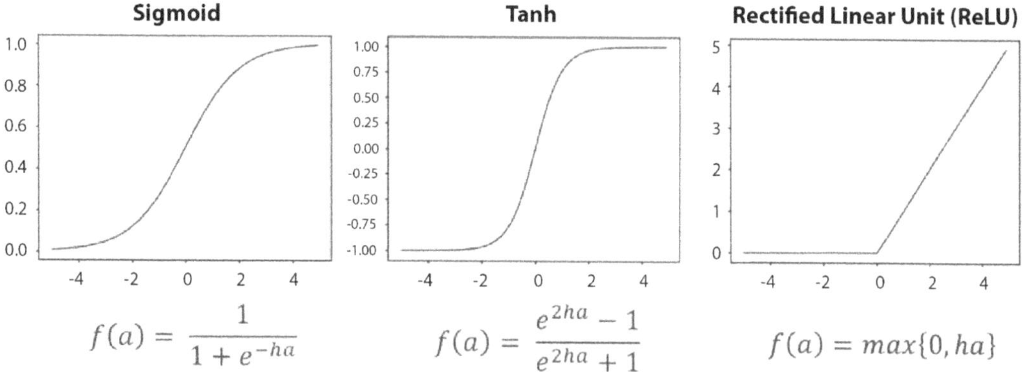


$$f(a) = \frac{1}{1 + e^{-ha}} \qquad f(a) = \frac{e^{2ha} - 1}{e^{2ha} + 1} \qquad f(a) = max\{0, ha\}$$

Figure 9.3 – Commonly used activation functions

In an FFNN, data is processed from the input toward the output, layer by layer, using a formula that simulates the artificial neuron. This happens as follows:

1. The outputs of the first layer are calculated from the inputs.
2. The outputs of the second layer are calculated using the outputs of the previous layer as input.
3. The outputs of the third layer are calculated using the outputs of the previous layer as inputs.
4. This process is repeated until we reach the output layer where the values become the literal outputs of the network.

Historically, the first and most popular training algorithm for fully connected feedforward neural networks is the **backpropagation algorithm**. We will look at how the weights are fit using this algorithm.

## The backpropagation algorithm

Training a neural network works by repeatedly applying the weight update as defined by the back propagation algorithm. Each time this happens, the training data is run through the network and its weights are updated to reduce the loss function. This is done until the loss function reaches a minimum, or a maximum number of training iterations has been reached.

Let's define the **loss function** to measure how close the network's output is to the target value across the training set, *T*. A classic loss function, *E*, is the total squared error:

$$E = \sum_{T} \sum_{j} \frac{1}{2}(t_j - y_j)^2$$

Formula 9.4

Here, $t_j$ and $y_j$ are the desired and real response values for the *j*th unit in the output layer of the network, respectively. The values are summed over all the outputs from all elements of the training set, *T*.

The backpropagation algorithm follows the **gradient descent strategy** to reach a minimum in the loss function. Once all the training examples have been processed, all the weights of the network are incremented in the opposite direction of the derivative of *E* in the weight space, as follows:

$$\Delta w_{ji} = -\eta \frac{\partial E}{\partial w_{ji}}$$

Formula 9.5

For the weights connecting to units in the output layer, the desired response is known, so such a derivative is easy to calculate, leading to the following weight update:

$$\Delta w_{ji} = \sum_{T} -\eta (t_j - y_j) f'(h_j) x_i = \sum_{T} -\eta \, \delta_j^{out} \, x_i$$

Formula 9.6

Here, we have the following:

- $\delta_j^{out} = (t_j - y_j) f'(h_j)$, $x_i$ for output node *j*.
- $x_i$ is the input, *i*, to output node *j*.
- $f'(h_j)$ is the first derivative of the neuron's activation function, *f()*.
- $h_j$ is the total net input to the same neuron, *j*.
- $\eta$ is a parameter called the **learning rate**.

> **Important Note**
>
> Note that the weight update is calculated across all the examples in the training set, *T*, after all the training examples have been processed by the network and the corresponding outputs and inputs have been stored.

The calculation of the derivative, $\frac{\partial E}{\partial w_{ji}}$, becomes more complicated for the weights to the units in the hidden layers of the network since, for them, the value of the desired response is not directly accessible. By applying the chain rule, however, a recursive formula allows the updates for such weights to be calculated as well, as follows:

$$\Delta w_{ij}^{hidden} = \sum_{x \in T} -\eta \cdot \delta_j^{hidden} \cdot x_i$$

Formula 9.7

Here, we have the following:

- $\delta_j^{hidden} = \sum_{k=1}^{c} \delta_k^{hidden+1} w_{jk}^{hidden+1} f'(a_j^{hidden})$, where *hidden* is the current hidden layer and *hidden +1* is the next hidden layer
- $w_{jk}^{hidden+1}$ is the weight connecting node *k* in the *hidden+1* layer to node *j* in the current *hidden* layer
- $f'(a_j^{hidden})$ is the first derivative of the *j*th neuron's activation function, *f()*
- $a_j^{hidden}$ is the total net input to the same neuron, *j*, and is, once again, the learning rate

So, $\delta_j^{hidden}$ for unit *j* in the *hidden* layer is calculated as the sum of $\delta_k^{hidden+1}$ for all units, *k*, in the *hidden+1* layer. That is, moving **backward** from the output layer toward the hidden layer, $\delta_j^{hidden}$, can be calculated

as the sum of all $\delta_k^{hidden+1}$ from the units in the previous layer.

> **Important Note**
>
> Moving backward from the output layer, $\delta_k^{hidden+1}$, to the first hidden layer is $\delta_k^{out}$, which we calculated for the output layer.

So, training an FFNN can be seen as a two-step process:

1. All the training samples are presented, one after the other, to the input layer of the network, and the signal is propagated through all network connections (and weights) to the output layer, where the square error is calculated. Once all the training examples have passed through the network, the total square error, *E*, is calculated as the sum of the single square errors. This is the **forward pass** (see *Figure 9.4* on the left).
2. All $\delta_k^{out}$ are calculated for all units, *k*, in the output layer. Then, $\delta$ is backpropagated from the output layer through all the network connections (and weights) until the input layer, and all $\delta_j^{hidden}$ are calculated. This is the **backward pass**. Finally, all the weights are updated (see *Figure 9.4* on the right).

This algorithm is called backpropagation because all $\delta$ are backpropagated through the network in the second pass. Remember how we defined the forward direction as starting from the input and moving to the output? *Figure 9.4* shows how the training set is passed forward through the network and then how the network weights are updated backward:

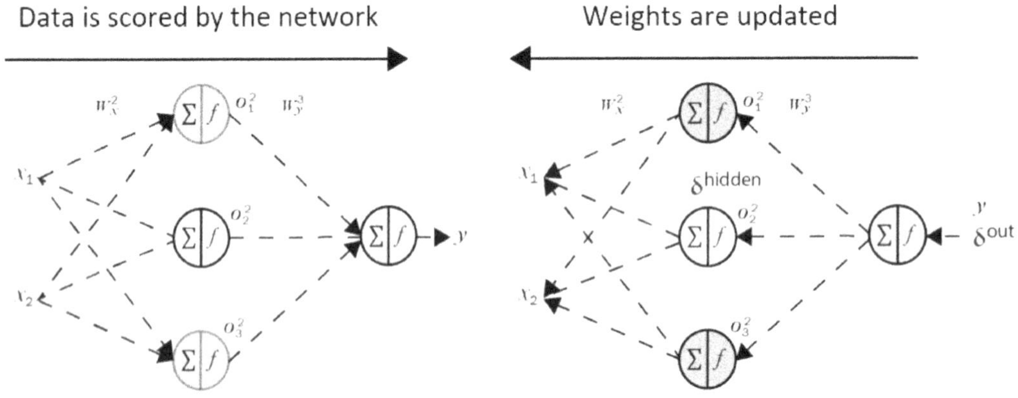


Figure 9.4 – The forward pass (left) and the backward pass (right) in the backpropagation algorithm

Given the frequent usage of derivatives of the activation functions in the backpropagation formulas, continuous derivable activation functions, such as sigmoid and tanh(), are preferred.

The backpropagation algorithm is not guaranteed to reach the global minimum of the loss function. If the local minimum does not ensure that the network provides satisfactory performance, the training process must be repeated with new initial conditions – new initial values for the weights of the network.

There are multiple ways to apply this method of fitting network weights. The first is called **batch training**, which updates the weights after all the examples of the training set have passed through the network, as described in this section. This is computationally expensive and often slow. It is possible to update the weights after each training example passes through the network (**online training**). This is computationally less expensive but is just an approximation of the original backpropagation algorithm and risks oscillations in the loss function. Usually, a compromise between the two strategies is used. A small batch of examples is presented to the network and after each batch is processed, the weights are updated. This strategy is faster than the original version of backpropagation and results in fewer oscillations in the loss function.

Finally, let's spend a few moments on the learning rate, $\eta$. The learning rate defines the magnitude of the update vector, which updates the network weights in the direction of the gradient on the error surface. A small $\eta$ produces small steps and takes a long time to reach a minimum in the error function. A large $\eta$ produces large steps that may overshoot and miss the minimum in the error function. The choice of the right $\eta$ is critical. Optimized versions of backpropagation include, among other things, an adaptive learning rate, starting with a large $\eta$ that decreases with the number of training iterations.

## Other types of neural networks

Feedforward architectures are not the only type of neural network. Many more have been proposed over the years. Special mentions go to **convolutional neural networks** (**CNNs**), which are often used for image analysis, and to **recurrent neural networks** (**RNNs**), which are often used for sequential data analysis.

Among RNNs, the most popular may be **long short-term memory** (**LSTM**), which employs a complex gating strategy to partially or completely remember or forget past values in the input sequences. RNNs and LSTMs are trained via a variant of the backpropagation algorithm, named **backpropagation through time** (**BPTT**). In this algorithm, the recurrent network is unrolled into multiple copies, with each being executed in sequence to accept the subsequent network's input. This unrolled larger network can be treated as a classic feedforward network and then trained with the backpropagation algorithm or one of its optimized versions.

The case study in this chapter can also be solved using an RNN or an LSTM network. However, for simplicity, we will use a classic fully connected FFNN. The same approach could be used with a different network, including an LSTM layer. You can try this yourself by modifying the example and including an LSTM layer in the network. Was there a considerable improvement in the model's performance?

Now, let's start implementing an FFNN to predict future glucose levels.

# Training a feedforward neural network to predict glucose levels

In this chapter, we aim to predict the next *n* values of the glucose level based on the previous *m* values via a fully connected feedforward neural network. To do this, we will do the following:

1. Introduce KNIME Deep Learning – Keras Integration.
2. Design the fully connected feedforward neural architecture.
3. Train the model.
4. Create an alarm that alerts the end user when glucose levels are predicted to exceed the safety threshold.

Let's start with **KNIME Deep Learning – Keras Integration**.

## KNIME Deep Learning Keras Integration

In this section, we will install and set up **KNIME Deep Learning – Keras Integration** to train neural networks in KNIME Analytics Platform.

KNIME Deep Learning – Keras Integration wraps Keras functions into KNIME nodes, giving them a configuration dialog to set the parameters. Such nodes allow you to read, write, build, train, and execute deep learning networks using the Keras libraries and without writing any code.

KNIME Deep Learning Keras Integration is supported by **KNIME Deep Learning – TensorFlow Integration**, which allows you to convert **Keras** models into **TensorFlow** models.

To use KNIME's Deep Learning Keras Integration, the following external software must be installed:

- The Keras and TensorFlow nodes via the following two extensions:
  - KNIME Deep Learning – Keras Integration
  - KNIME Deep Learning – TensorFlow Integration
- The required Python environment

To use the time series components in this book, you must have Conda connected to KNIME; after this, setting up the deep learning Python environment is easy. Select **File** | **Preferences** from the top menu. From the list on the left, select **KNIME** | **Python Deep Learning**. You should see the following **Preferences** page:

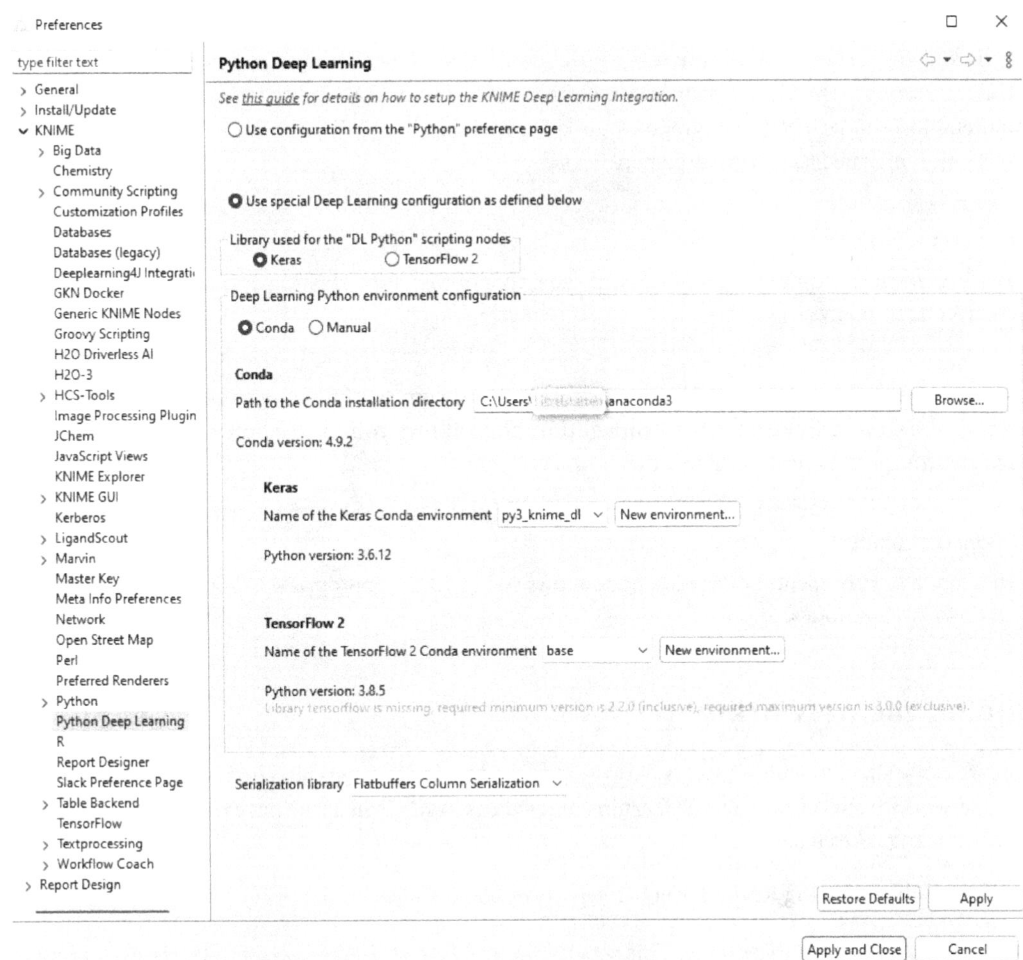


Figure 9.5 – The Preferences page

From this page, you can click the **New environment** button to create Python environments for Keras or Tensorflow. We will only need Keras for this example.

If you do not have Conda enabled already, click the **Browse** button under **Conda** and provide the path to your Conda installation directory. This enables KNIME to communicate with Conda and automatically create a Python environment with the required packages.

After clicking on the **New environment** button, choose **Create new CPU environment** or **Create new GPU environment**. The GPU option will require you have a **CUDA**-enabled graphics card on your computer. Most modern NVIDIA graphics cards support this. The GPU environment is not required but execution may be faster with large networks.

> **Important Note**
>
> The **Preferences** window is prefilled with the name of the latest existing appropriate Conda environment, if any.

If you are using multiple different Conda environments in your workflows or even within the same workflow, the **Conda Environment Propagation** node allows you to dynamically control which Conda environment a given node will use.

> **Important Node**
>
> The Conda Environment Propagation node allows you to set the appropriate Conda environment for downstream nodes.

## Building the network

Before we can train and deploy a Keras network, we need to design its architecture. This differentiates neural networks from other machine learning algorithms in KNIME as we have this additional step before modeling takes place.

We will need the following KNIME Keras integration nodes to design our architecture:

- The **Keras Input Layer** node. This sets the input layer of the network by accepting *n* input values under the **Shape** parameter in the configuration window.
- The **Keras Dense Layer** node. This implements a neural layer of *n* units that's fully connected to the previous layer via a selected activation function.

Our architecture can be built by the following sequence of nodes (*Figure 9.6*):

1. A Keras Input Layer node with **Shape** set to **36**. This represents the past 36 values of the time series that we will use as inputs.
2. A Keras Dense Layer node with **Units** set to **18**, the activation function set to **Softplus**, and an input tensor as the output tensor of the input layer. This is the first hidden layer.
3. A Keras Dense Layer node with **Units** set to **9** and the activation function set to **Softplus**. This is the second hidden layer.
4. A Keras Dense Layer node with **Units** set to **6** and the activation function set to **Softplus**. This is the output layer.

The following diagram shows nodes that are used to create this architecture in KNIME Analytics Platform:

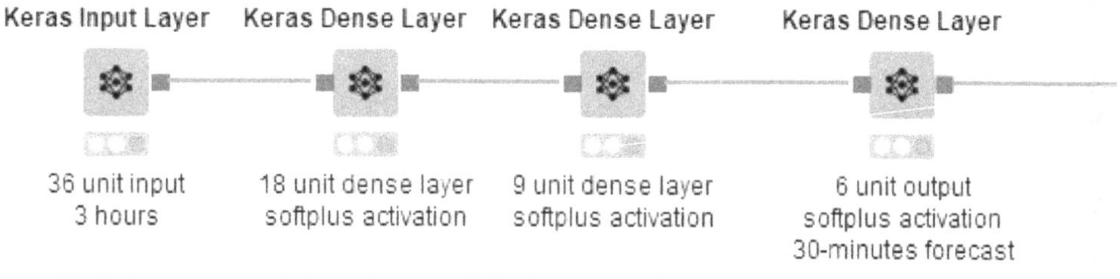


Figure 9.6 – An FFNN with KNIME Deep Learning – Keras Integration

We chose Softplus as the activation function for all the dense layers. Other activation functions are available from the menu in the configuration window. Softplus is a commonly used activation function that works well for most problems. Of course, you are welcome to experiment with other activation functions.

**Other Types of Networks**

The Keras Dense Layer node is your key to building a fully connected FFNN. However, you can build a different neural architecture using different nodes for the hidden layers, such as the Keras LSTM layer and the Keras convolution layer, or other nodes from KNIME Deep Learning – Keras Integration.

## Training the network

To train the network after designing its architecture, we will use the **Keras Network Learner** node.

The Keras Network Learner node has three inputs: a red square port for the architecture, a black triangle data port for the training data, and an optional white triangle data port for additional input information when using neural networks with more complex architectures.

The input data, as well as the target data, should be shaped as a **collection** of values for ease of use. Our input vector consists of the past 36 glucose level readings. The **Lag Column** and **Column Aggregator** nodes take care of creating the vector elements and combining them into a Collection object, as shown in *Figure 9.10*. The same applies to the six future values that will be used as targets when training the network.

> **Collection Data Type**
>
> The collection data type in KNIME Analytics Platform is similar to a list in common programming languages. It is a set of multiple values combined into one data cell. There are several nodes for manipulating them, all of which you can find by searching for *collection* in the node repository.

The Keras Network Learner node is powerful but complex. Its configuration window consists of five tabs for controlling the algorithm's settings:

- The **Input Data** and **Target Data** tabs control the columns to be used for the input and target vectors, respectively. They also control whether the vectors have been converted into or from integers, doubles, or one-hot encodings. The **Target Data** tab also lets you define the loss function to use during training.
- The **Options** and **Advanced Options** tabs control the algorithm's hyperparameters, such as batch size, learning rate, and optimizer. **RMSProp** is the classic backpropagation algorithm.
- The **Executable Selection** tab allows you to control the Python environment that's used via the Conda Environment Propagation node. If you're not using multiple Python environments, you don't need to worry about this.

The following screenshot shows how the input data is selected on the **Input Data** tab of the configuration dialog and how the target data is selected on the **Target Data** tab. This is slightly different than other learner nodes in KNIME since they put both in one tab as there is a bit more to configure:

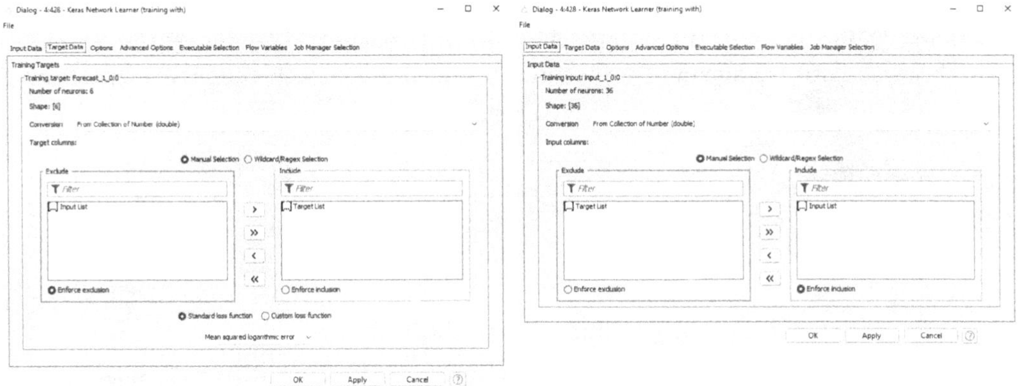

Figure 9.7 – The Input Data tab (left) and the Target Data tab (right) in the configuration dialog

Now, let's look at the **Options** and **Advanced Options** tabs. The most notable setting here is the number of epochs you'll train the model for; this is the number of times the complete training set is passed through the network. Many other options, such as which optimizer to use, can be found here as well:

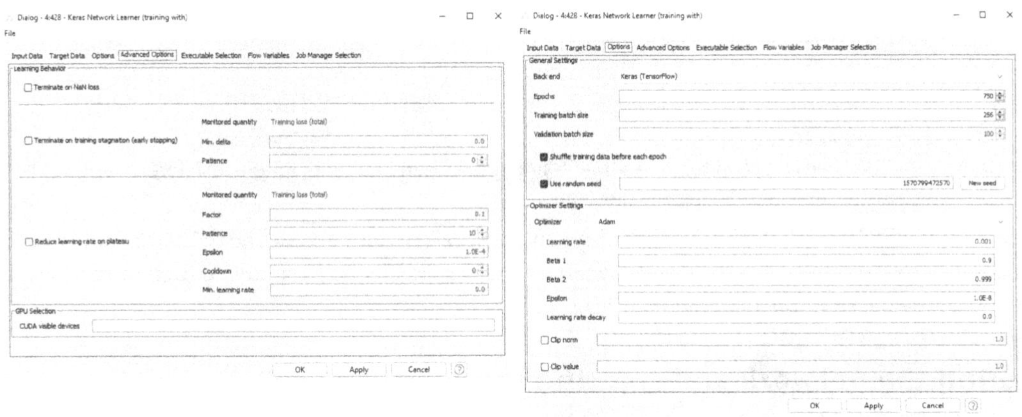

Figure 9.8 – The Options tab (left) and the Advanced Options tab (right) in the configuration window

The Keras Network Learner node also has a **Learning Monitor** view that can be accessed from the right-click menu. This view shows the accuracy and loss plots, which is extremely useful when you're monitoring the progress of the network to make sure that the algorithm is converging.

The following screenshot shows this **Learning Monitor** view; notice how the loss function drops rapidly at first. Did we need to train the model for as many epochs as we did here? Has the loss function already reached a minimum? Use the zoom options or the log scale options to investigate:

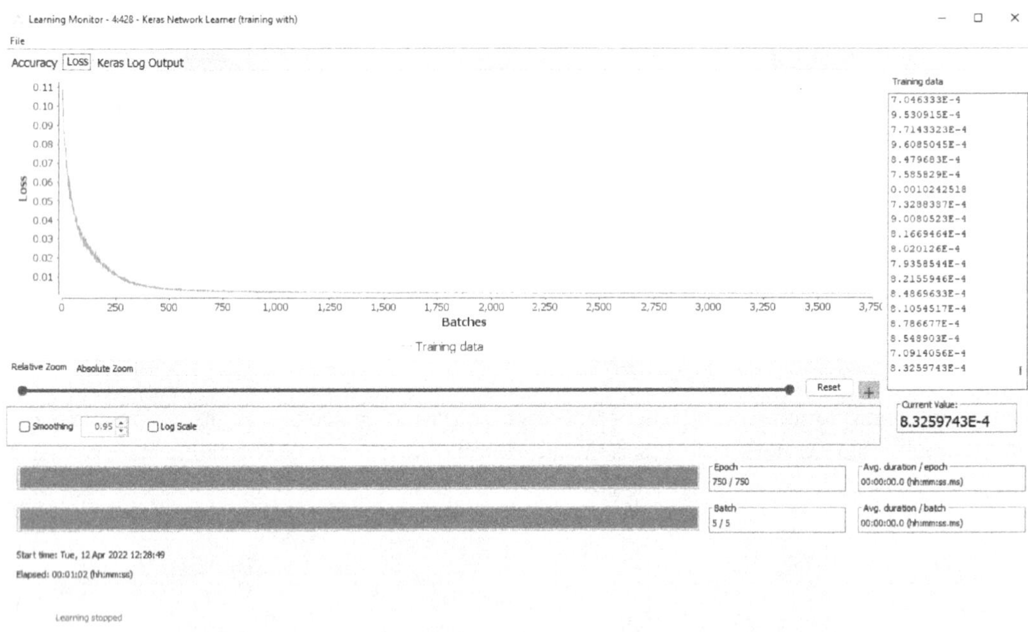


Figure 9.9 – The Learning Monitor view while training the neural network for glucose forecasting

Once the network has been trained, we need to score its performance and define the alarm rule. The workflow should send an alarm when the glucose level is predicted to become too high or too low, thus exceeding the recommended boundaries.

## Scoring the network and creating the output rule

The **Keras Network Executor** node accepts a trained network (red square port) and data as inputs. Then, it applies the network to the data and produces the network predictions at its output port. The configuration settings are similar to the configuration settings of the Keras Network Learner node, including the input vector as a Collection object and the expected conversion operation.

The output of the Keras Network Executor node that contains the network predictions is also formatted as a Collection column. After splitting the values in the Collection column and de-normalizing them to the original range, all that remains is to define the rule that sends an alarm when the predicted values of the glucose level exceed the suggested boundaries. This is implemented with two **Math Formula** nodes in the **Split Collections and Denormalize** component and one **Rule Engine** node, as shown here:

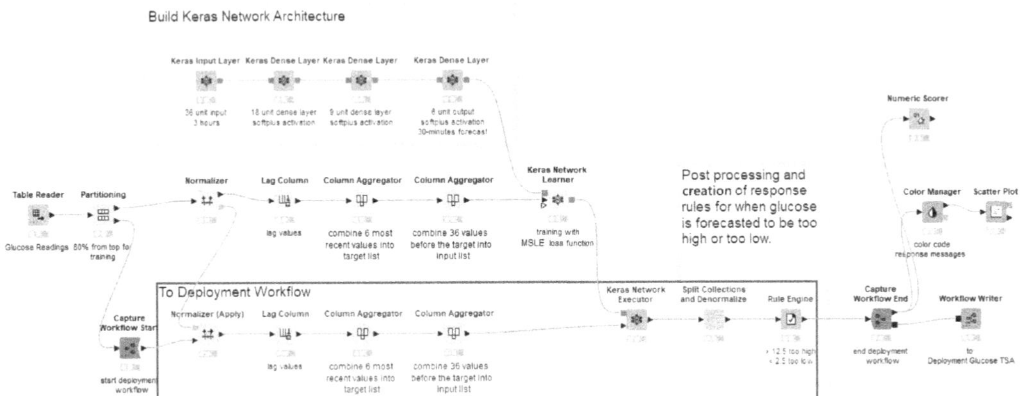


Figure 9.10 – The final workflow for training and evaluating a fully connected FFNN to predict the next six glucose level samples based on the previous 36

The two Math Formula nodes find the minimum and maximum value across the predicted values for the glucose level via the `max_in_args()` and `min_in_args()` functions, respectively. Then, the Rule Engine node sends the alarm according to the following rule:

```
$max$ > 12.5 => "Glucose forecast too high!"
$min$ < 2.5 => "Glucose forecast too low!"
TRUE => "All is well."
```

Here, `$max$` and `$min$` refer to the maximum and minimum values of the glucose forecast. The final workflow, including visualizations, is shown in *Figure 9.10*.

We can also apply a **Numeric Scorer** node to calculate the error between the first target value of the glucose level and the corresponding first predicted value. The **root mean square error** (**RMSE**) resulted in 1.24, which isn't too bad for values in the [0-14] range.

The Scatter Plot node visualizes the test dataset and shows which message the Rule Engine node responded with as it was fed new glucose readings. Here, we can see an early spike where the trained network and Rule Engine node warned the user that their glucose level was predicted to become too high and two valleys to the right where the glucose level was predicted to become too low:

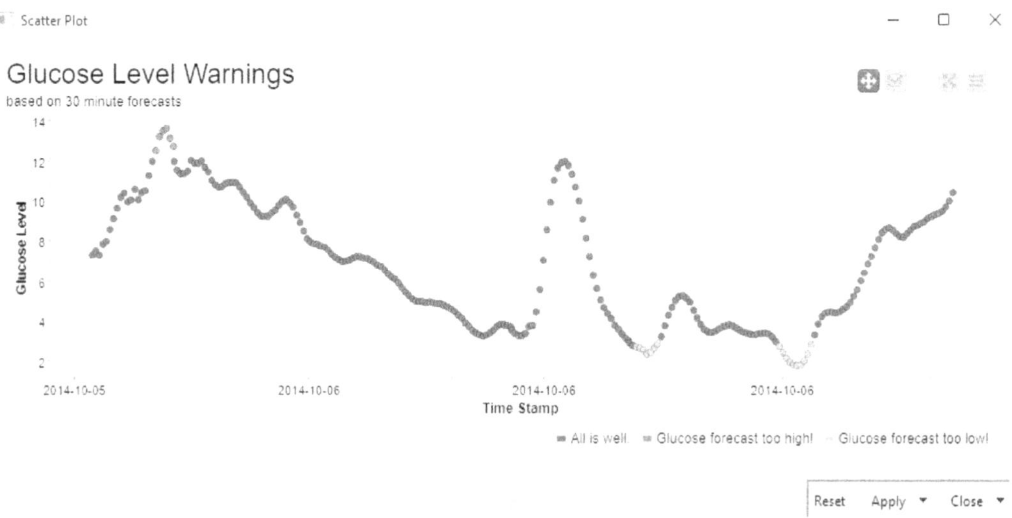


Figure 9.11 – Scatter plot showing the test dataset and message response from the KNIME workflow

Now that we have built the model, we need to deploy it. In the next section, we will review how this model can be deployed so that it can be used on real glucose data.

# Deploying an FFNN-based alarm system

In this section, you will deploy the previously trained alarm system within a dedicated workflow. This deployment workflow will need the following:

- The ability to accept new data in the same shape and format as the original data
- The normalization model to apply to the new data
- The same preprocessing steps as for the testing part of the workflow
- The trained FFNN model
- The Keras Network Executor node
- The same postprocessing of the results to create the alarm system

We can do this manually by using the workflow shown in *Figure 9.10*. However, we can also create the deployment workflow automatically by replicating the testing part of that workflow. KNIME's **Integrated Deployment** can do this and consists of three nodes: the **Capture Workflow Start** node, the **Capture Workflow End** node, and the **Workflow Writer** node.

The Capture Workflow Start and Capture Workflow End nodes are placed at the beginning and the end of the workflow segment we want to replicate, respectively. Integrated Deployment copies that workflow segment.

The Workflow Writer node turns a captured workflow segment into a complete workflow by adding nodes that accept the input and produce the output in the desired format. It does this by adding the **Workflow Service Input** and **Workflow Service Output** nodes at the beginning and end of the new workflow and embedding the two required models: the normalization model and the trained Keras network. All the other nodes are replicated from the captured segment.

*Figure 9.10* shows the nodes that are used for integrated deployment and, in the bottom purple annotation box, the workflow segment that has been captured. The automatically generated deployment workflow can be seen here:

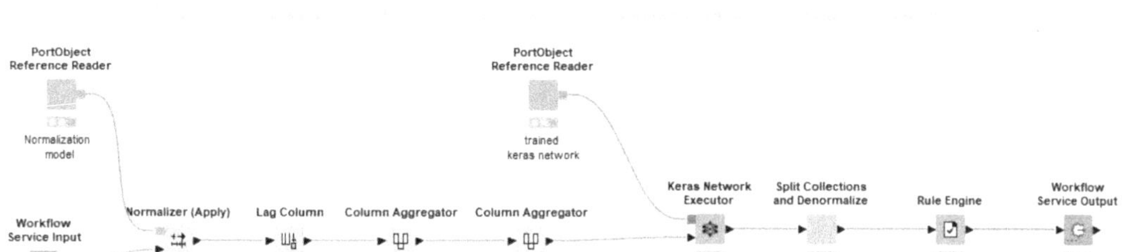


Figure 9.12 – The deployment workflow that was automatically generated from the workflow in Figure 9.10

> **Configurable Ports**
>
> The Capture Workflow Start/End nodes are created with no ports. To add a data port (or any other port), just click on the three dots in the bottom-left corner of the node. A menu where you can add new ports will appear.

With Integrated Deployment, deployment becomes pretty straightforward. Now, let's summarize what we've learned in this chapter.

# Summary

In this chapter, we explored how to use neural networks for time series prediction. We used a case study in healthcare: predicting future glucose levels.

Since this is a book on time series analysis and not on deep learning, we adopted a simple neural architecture: a fully connected feedforward neural network with two hidden layers. We used the past 36 values of glucose levels to predict the next six glucose values. Among the next six, we detected the maximum and minimum values and triggered an alarm if one of them exceeded the recommended boundaries.

Before showing the implementation of the neural network in KNIME Analytics Platform, we recapped the basics of neural networks and their original training algorithm: backpropagation.

Then, we looked at how to install and configure KNIME Deep Learning – Keras Integration, which allows us to use the Keras deep learning libraries from the familiar KNIME interface.

Then, we continued with the practical implementation and looked at the nodes that construct the neural architecture and train the network. In the training workflow, we added a Rule Engine node to check if the boundaries were broken.

Finally, we used KNIME's Integrated Deployment functionality to automatically create a deployment workflow based on the training and testing workflow.

You'll be able to use the skills you've learned in this chapter to build custom neural network architectures in the future, as well as apply integrated deployment to your workflows for easy deployment.

In the next chapter, we will introduce a more complex neural architecture that's powerful for **natural language processing** (**NLP**) as well as time series analysis: **long short-term memory** (**LSTM**).

# Questions

1. What is a neural network?

    A. A biological computing machine based on nervous cells

    B. A machine learning model that relies on many artificial neurons inspired by biological neurons

    C. A type of decision tree

    D. A networking strategy

2. How many passes does the backpropagation algorithm have?

   A. One

   B. Two

   C. Three

   D. Four

3. Why is integrated deployment helpful?

   A. It keeps the training and deployment workflows in sync

   B. It automatically saves any required input data or objects

   C. It appends input and output nodes that are compatible with KNIME Server's REST endpoints

   D. All of the above

# 10

# Predicting Energy Demand with an LSTM Model

In this chapter, we'll continue our brief foray into deep learning topics and employ a special neural unit called a **long short-term memory** (**LSTM**) unit. This will leverage the versatility of the **recursive neural network** (**RNN**) and expand on its ability to pull information from past events.

The goal of this chapter is to introduce a theoretical understanding of the LSTM unit, as well as build a forecasting model for Electrical Energy Consumption. Understanding the inner workings of the LSTM unit will be important when deciding if this model type is more appropriate than the standard feedforward network from the previous chapter.

In this chapter, we will cover the following topics:

- Introducing recurrent neural networks and LSTMs
- Encoding and tensors
- Training an LSTM-based neural network

By the end of the chapter, you will understand the inner workings of the LSTM unit and understand when to use it when designing a neural network architecture instead of using a simple feedforward setup.

## Technical requirements

The following are the prerequisites for this chapter:

- KNIME Analytics Platform with **KNIME Deep Learning – Keras Integration** installed
- KNIME Analytics Platform with **KNIME Python Integration** installed (for the **Conda Environment Propagation** node)
- **Conda** package manager installed on your machine

All the workflows in this chapter are available on KNIME Hub at `https://kni.me/s/GxjXX6WmLi-WjLNx`.

# Introducing recurrent neural networks and LSTMs

When we work with deep learning models, the first thing we typically do, after exploring our data, is choose a network architecture. In Keras and KNIME, we do this by designing, layer by layer, the shape of our network – perhaps starting with an input layer followed by a few dense layers and then an output layer. When these network architectures also take information from previous execution states, they are known to be **recurrent**.

In this section, we will recap on RNNs, discuss how LSTM units build on top of them, and show you how to use them to build a forecasting model for demand prediction.

## Recapping recurrent neural networks

As you may recall from the previous chapter, as shown in the following diagram, RNNs build on top of simple feedforward architectures by using the previous execution's output as an additional input. Beyond that additional input, the interior of the standard recurrent neural unit operates like a standard dense layer that acts on the combined input vector, *x(t)*, and the previous output vector, *h(t)*:

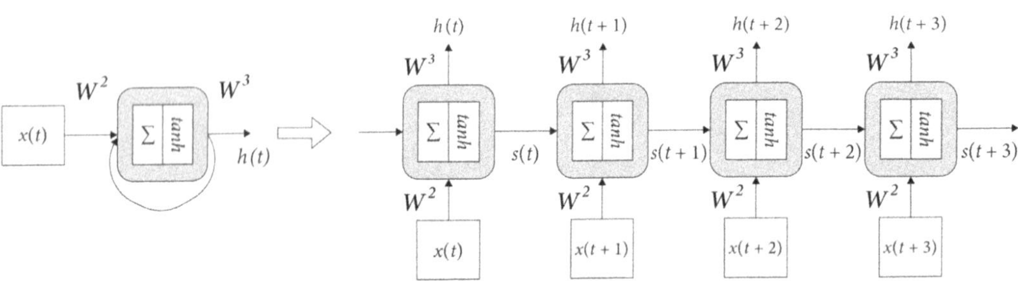


Figure 10.1 – Recurrent neural unit

In the next section, we'll introduce the LSTM unit, which will continue to apply the previous execution's output state as a new input. However, it will also add an internal memory store in the form of a tensor. We call this memory tensor the **Cell State**.

## The architecture of the LSTM unit

Before we set up our data and our use case for this chapter, let's review the inner workings of the LSTM unit. A clear understanding here will help you make your own decisions on when the LSTM unit is worth applying instead of a standard recurrent layer. It does make for a heavier architecture but it can be quite potent. The following diagram shows the internal structure of an LSTM unit:

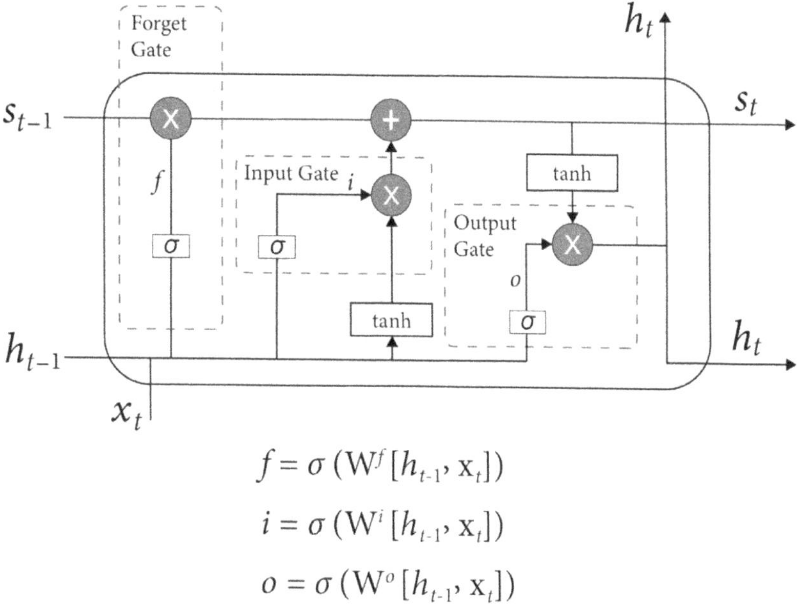


Figure 10.2 – The internal structure of an LSTM unit

Notice that we call it a neural unit and not a network layer, which is what we did with the other functional layers in our network architecture. This is because the LSTM unit is three separate *layers* combined into one intelligent unit! There's the **Forget Gate** to the left, the **Input Gate** in the middle, and the **Output Gate** to the right.

Before we discuss these three gates, let's define all the inputs and outputs; we'll reference these when we talk about them:

- **s(t)**: The cell state of the LSTM unit, this is a vector containing stored knowledge about the current state of the time series. For example, inside this vector, our model could denote that today is Wednesday.
- **h(t)**: The output tensor of the LSTM unit, this is passed along to the next layer in our overall network architecture for further processing, as well as to the next execution of the LSTM unit for use in the different logic gates.
- **x(t)**: The input tensor to our LSTM unit, this is the current tensor passing through our neural network.

The first gate to process the memory state, *s(t-1)*, is the Forget Gate.

## Forget Gate

The first gate in the LSTM unit is called the Forget Gate. It takes our old output tensor, *h(t-1)*, our old **cell state** tensor, *S(t-1)*, and our current input tensor, *X(t)*, and outputs something we call the Vector of Decision: *f(t)*. This Vector of Decision is comprised of values between 0 and 1. After forming this vector, we point-wise multiply *S(t-1)* with *f(t)* to *forget* some of the old information stored inside. Multiplying an element in the cell state vector by 0 effectively wipes that space in memory clean, while multiplying it by 1 keeps it:

$$f(t) = \sigma(W^f\ [h(t-1), x(t)])$$

Formula 10.1

The vector of decision is calculated based on the preceding formula. First, our old output tensor, *h(t-1)*, and our current input tensor, *x(t)*, are concatenated into one tensor. Then, they are simply multiplied by $W^f$, the Weight Matrix of this logic gate, and passed through a Sigmoid activation function, $\sigma$.

You may be wondering why we care about forgetting. Usually, we only talk about learning in data science. Well, it's important that our cell state, which may indicate that *now* is a Monday during the current execution, can *forget* that information when the clock strikes midnight and then *learn* that *now* is Tuesday. This gives the LSTM unit the ability to understand the changing conditions in our data and be more adaptive than a standard feedforward network.

So far, we have applied some *forget* logic to our cell state via pointwise multiplication:

$$s(t-1) * f(t)$$

Formula 10.2

This brings us to the Input Gate.

## Input Gate

The previous logic gate enabled our LSTM unit to forget things that are no longer relevant. However, the Input Gate will consider our new input and append new knowledge to the cell state tensor. Unlike the Forget Gate, the Input Gate comprises two distinct layers – you'll notice them as the $\sigma$ box and the *tanh* box in and around the Input Gate square in *Figure 10.2*.

First, let's talk about the tanh layer. Here, we will concatenate the previous output tensor, h(t-1), and the current input vector, x(t), and pass them through a tanh activation function to attain $s\tilde{}(t)$. This is a new candidate cell state:

$$s\tilde{}(t) = tanh(W^s\ [h(t-1), x(t)])$$

Formula 10.3

The new candidate cell state is calculated with the preceding formula. As always with a network layer, we multiply the input tensor by our weight matrix – in this instance, denoted $W^S$ – then pass that new tensor through the activation function, which is the hyperbolic tangent here.

Now, the LSTM unit won't just replace the old cell state tensor with this new candidate – it also passes the same tensor (the concatenation of *h(t-1)* and *x(t)*) through another layer. This time, it does so with our sigmoid activation function:

$$i(t) = \sigma(W^i\ [h(t-1), x(t)])$$

Formula 10.4

As you can see, once again, we multiply our input tensor by a Weight Matrix and then pass that value through our activation function, this time a sigmoid function. Now, we perform a pointwise multiplication of $\tilde{s}(t)$ and *i(t)*, then add this to the previous cell state to obtain our new cell state: *s(t)*.

Building on the operations in the Forget Gate, we have now performed pointwise multiplication to *forget* information in our previous cell state and pointwise addition to append new information, as follows:

$$s(t) = f(t) * s(t-1) + i(t) * \tilde{s}(t)$$

Formula 10.5

Now that we've created the new cell state, we're ready to move on to the Output Gate and generate our output tensor, *h(t)*.

## Output Gate

This is the final section of the LSTM unit! Now that we have a current cell state tensor that's been altered by the Forget and Input Gates, we can apply it in this final logic gate to generate the actual output of the LSTM unit: the *h(t)* tensor.

This gate behaves very much like the Input Gate in that it uses two activation functions – a *tanh* and a *sigmoid*. However, from there, things change a bit. First, we apply a tanh function to the newly created cell state: *s(t)*. Then, as we did previously, we will create a separate importance vector via the sigmoid layer based on our input, *x(t)*, and previous output, *h(t-1)*, to scale back our tanh output.

Let's look at the equation for creating our final importance vector:

$$o(t) = \sigma(W^o\ [h(t-1), x(t)])$$

Formula 10.6

This equation should be pretty familiar to you by now. As we did previously, we concatenate our input, *x(t)*, and previous output, *h(t-1)*, multiply them by a Weight Matrix, and pass that tensor through a sigmoid activation function.

We will use this new tensor, $o(t)$, in the following equation to finally generate our output tensor, $h(t)$, from the current cell state, $s(t)$:

$$h(t) = \tanh\big(s(t)\big) * o(t)$$

Formula 10.7

Here, we simply pass the current cell state tensor, $s(t)$, through a tanh activation function and pointwise multiply the output by our finally importance vector, $o(t)$!

Now, we have it: from Forget to Input to Output – the LSTM unit. Next, we'll talk about how to encode our time series data so that it can be used in an LSTM unit. This will differ slightly from the previous chapter's preprocessing, so pay attention!

# Encoding and tensors

Preparing time series data for deep learning models is already a bit different than working with more classic applications such as classification or regression. We twist and reshape our data by lagging our input series to create the input tensor. This pattern continues in our application of the base LSTM network. We'll also talk a little bit about how the cell state, $s(t)$, gets initiated as well.

We'll do this by recapping the shape of our input data, then introducing the nodes required for reshaping our data table, and finally producing the tensor, which we will input into the LSTM model.

## Input data

For this chapter and this use case, we'll assume we have a single variable time series to forecast. This is a single column representing data of the same type that's been recorded over time. We'll also assume the data has been cleaned properly, as detailed in *Chapter 3, Preparing Data for Time Series Analysis*.

> **Note**
> Unlike some of the early forecasting techniques that we have applied in this book, such as SARIMA, we do not need to concern ourselves with seasonality or trend removal in preprocessing. The LSTM network will be able to adapt to those features on its own!

For the example in this chapter, we will use an LSTM to forecast energy consumption data. The following diagram shows that our data shows strong seasonal patterns, which are visible in the repeated daily peaks that lessen on the weekends. Do you think the LSTM network will successfully account for these patterns?

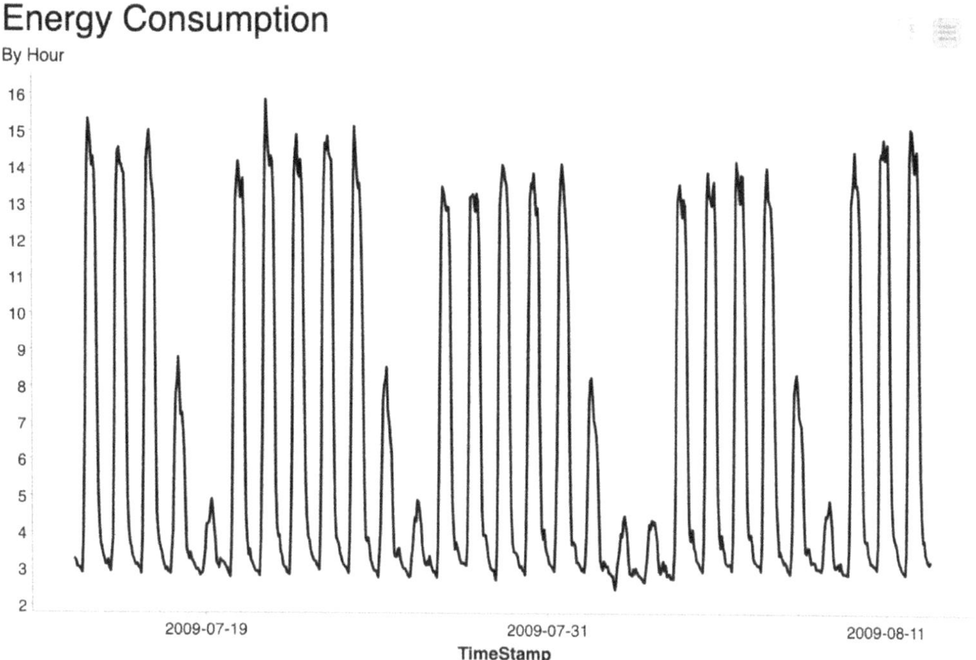


Figure 10.3 – Energy consumption data

Notice the seasonalities in the preceding line plot. With many forecasting methods, we need to manually interpret and account for these patterns, or at least account for them external to modeling. However, with the flexibility of neural networks, we can effectively ignore this common step and let the model handle the problem itself.

> **Note**
>
> Although neural networks are fantastically robust in their ability to interpret even the messiest of input series, they are weaker in an, often very important area: they require significantly more training data.

## Reshaping the data

Before we create the actual tensors that we will input into our LSTM network, we'll need to reshape our table a little. This will be very easy with KNIME's Lag Column node:

| Row ID | TimeStamp | D Energy Consumption |
|---|---|---|
| Row0 | 2009-07-15T00:00 | 3.254 |
| Row1 | 2009-07-15T01:00 | 3.198 |
| Row2 | 2009-07-15T02:00 | 3.038 |
| Row3 | 2009-07-15T03:00 | 3.03 |
| Row4 | 2009-07-15T04:00 | 3.006 |
| Row5 | 2009-07-15T05:00 | 2.944 |
| Row6 | 2009-07-15T06:00 | 2.882 |
| Row7 | 2009-07-15T07:00 | 4.024 |
| Row8 | 2009-07-15T08:00 | 6.9 |
| Row9 | 2009-07-15T09:00 | 11.495 |
| Row10 | 2009-07-15T10:00 | 14.18 |

Figure 10.4 – Energy consumption data before being reshaped

The preceding screenshot shows the cleaned time series data from our energy consumption use case: one column containing the time stamp information and one column containing the amount of energy that's been consumed. With the network model in this section, we do not want to supply a column like this. We need to create tensors of data.

Before we create the tensor inputs, we need to decide what shape they should take. This choice is tied to our network architecture design – specifically, to the shape and size of the input layer. This input tensor will be composed of the past values of the time series – in our case, that's the Energy Consumption column. We just need to choose which past values go into this tensor. Apply your domain expertise to try and include past values you think will be relevant. Including many of these values and letting the model *figure it out* can work, but it could lead to higher train times or overfitting. With that in mind, we will choose to include the past 200 values as our model input, thus creating a tensor of values from t-1 to t-200. This gives us just over a week of past data, so we will see a full past week's seasonal pattern.

### *Introducing the Lag Column and Column Aggregator nodes*

To reshape our table and generate the tensor we want, we'll use two KNIME nodes: the **Lag Column** node and the **Column Aggregator** node. We'll use this to generate new columns, one for each lagged copy of our time series, and then to combine all those lagged copy columns into one vector. A vector here is a collection of values, such as (1,2,3,4):

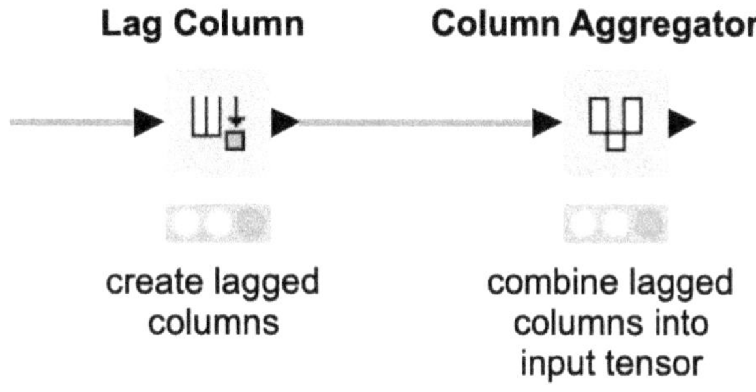


Figure 10.5 – The Lag Column and Column Aggregator nodes

As shown in the preceding diagram, you'll be combining these two nodes very frequently if you're using neural networks for time series analysis of any kind. Keep them handy!

Configuring both nodes is straightforward enough, with the Column Aggregator node having, admittedly, a few more boxes to check inside:

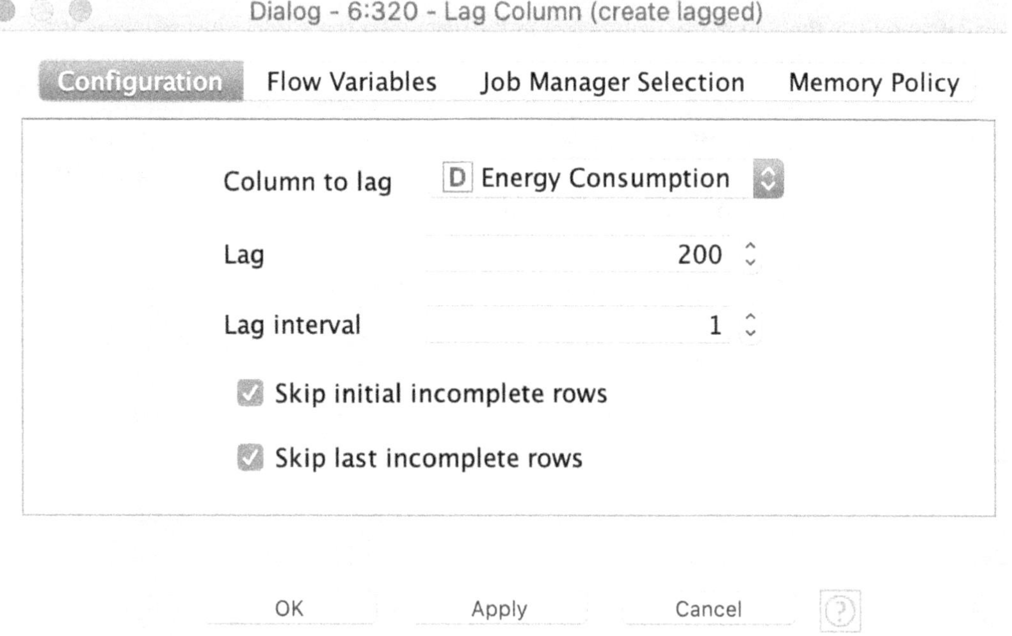


Figure 10.6 – Lag Column configuration dialog

In the Lag Column node's configuration dialog, you'll have a couple of options to work through. First, you must select the column to lag, the energy consumption, or whichever column represents your actual time series. Then, you'll come to **Lag** and **Lag Interval**:

- **Lag** is the number of actual lagged columns you'll create.
- **Lag Interval** is the spacing between these values. For example, with Lag Interval 1, we take the following:

$$x_{t-1}, x_{t-2}, x_{t-3}, \dots\ x_{t-200}$$

Notice how we count by one. We could also use Lag Interval 2 if we wanted to count by twos or Lag Interval 24 if we wanted to only include values from exactly 24 hours into the past. This is where we can get creative and leverage some domain expertise, or some of the exploratory analysis from *Chapter 7, Forecasting the Temperature with ARIMA and SARIMA Models*, to create a more intelligent model. This isn't strictly necessary, so we won't do this here. The neural network is quite competent on its own.

**Deep Learning Requires a Large Dataset**

Being more selective with the Lag Column node so that it includes fewer past values as inputs will help reduce the number of parameters in the deep learning model, thus reducing the amount of data needed to train it effectively.

The next node we will use to create our input tensors, which, like vectors, are a collection of values, is the *Column Aggregator* node. This node gathers some selected columns in our data tables and combines them into a list object. Let's look at its configuration:

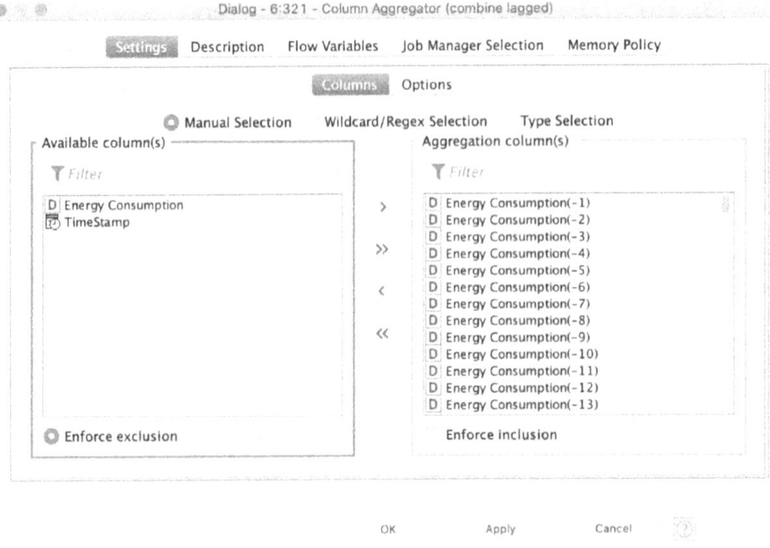


Figure 10.7 – Column Aggregator configuration dialog – the Columns tab

The configuration dialog of the Column Aggregator has two tabs we care about: the **Columns** tab and the **Options** tab. First, we select which columns will be aggregated into a single new column in the **Columns** tab, making sure to include all the lagged column copies but not the original column itself since we don't want to include the target as an input to our model. Now, let's talk about what we do with these collected columns in the **Options** tab:

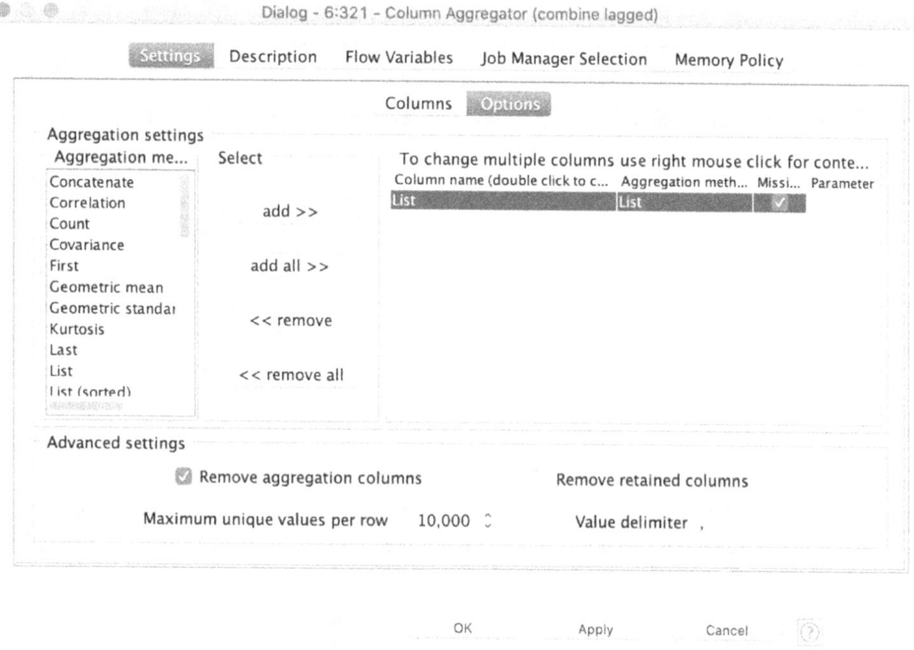


Figure 10.8 – Column Aggregator configuration dialog – the Options tab

Under the **Options** tab, we can configure what kind of aggregation(s) we want to perform on the previously selected columns. To combine our columns into a list for our neural network, we will use the **List** method. Simply double-click on the **List** option on the left to add it to the right-hand side. From here, I also like to check the **Remove aggregation columns** box at the bottom to remove all those lag columns and clean up our output table:

| Row ID | TimeStamp | D Energy Consumption | [...] List |
|---|---|---|---|
| Row200 | 2009-07-23T08:00 | 6.479 | [4.169060975609753,2.965,3.07491... |
| Row201 | 2009-07-23T09:00 | 11.558 | [6.478670731707316,4.1690609756... |
| Row202 | 2009-07-23T10:00 | 13.699 | [11.55781707317073,6.4786707317... |
| Row203 | 2009-07-23T11:00 | 14.649 | [13.698670731707315,11.55781707... |
| Row204 | 2009-07-23T12:00 | 14.466 | [14.649000000000003,13.69867073... |
| Row205 | 2009-07-23T13:00 | 14.841 | [14.466024390243902,14.64900000... |
| Row206 | 2009-07-23T14:00 | 14.385 | [14.840512195121955,14.46602439... |
| Row207 | 2009-07-23T15:00 | 14.248 | [14.384585365853662,14.84051219... |
| Row208 | 2009-07-23T16:00 | 14.187 | [14.24828048780488,14.384585365... |
| Row209 | 2009-07-23T17:00 | 12.055 | [14.187439024390242,14.24828048... |
| Row210 | 2009-07-23T18:00 | 7.595 | [12.054719512195124,14.18743902... |

Figure 10.9 – Table containing the input tensor column

To frame what we've done in a classical machine learning framework, we now have a column representing our target, the Energy Consumption column, and a column representing our model input, the List column. Let's set up the model architecture.

# Training an LSTM-based neural network

While neural networks are wonderfully flexible in regards to input data shapes and levels of cleanliness, they do require quite a bit more configuration than other model options before we even talk about model training. The first thing we'll do is define our network architecture:

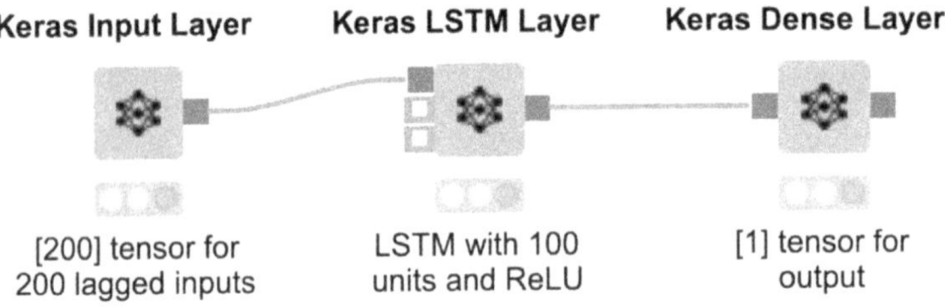


Figure 10.10 – LSTM model network architecture

The LSTM unit itself is a very powerful predictive tool. In many use cases, you may find LSTM units stacked on top of each other, running in parallel, or supplemented with additional dense layers to generate the desired output shape. Check out the book *Codeless Deep Learning* from Packt for more on LSTM networks.

In this example, we will consider a very simple architecture:

1. The first node in the preceding diagram adds an input layer whose shape matches that of our chosen input tensor – that is, a 200-unit one-dimensional vector representing our past 200 lagged temperature values.
2. The second node adds the LSTM unit, inside of which we will use a cell state vector of 100 units and a ReLU activation function.
3. Finally, the third node adds a single-valued dense layer to create our output shape, with one double value representing the Energy Consumption record at the current timestamp.

With that, we've set up a network architecture that consumes our past 200 lagged values and outputs the current value. Now, we're working with a standard input and target machine learning problem!

## The Keras Network Learner node

Now that we have our data in the proper shape, are supplying both the input and a target, and our model architecture has been designed, we can start the training step. Training the LSTM network will be exactly like training the FFNN from *Chapter 9, Training and Deploying a Neural Network to Predict Glucose Levels*, and much like any other *learner* node in KNIME.

The following diagram shows how to train a Keras network in KNIME, where we use the **Keras Network Learner** node:

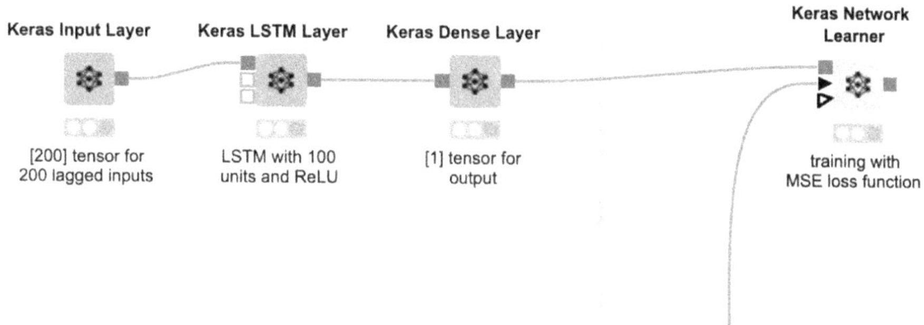


Figure 10.11 – Training the LSTM network

In addition to the usual data input port containing the training data, we also connect the Keras network port. Think of this as an additional configuration step where we define the type of model we're training. In this case, it is our simple LSTM network, which has an input layer, an LSTM unit, and an output layer. The Keras Network Learner node has many options available in its configuration dialog, but we'll just focus on the necessary ones to get started. The following screenshot shows how to configure the training for the network via the configuration dialog:

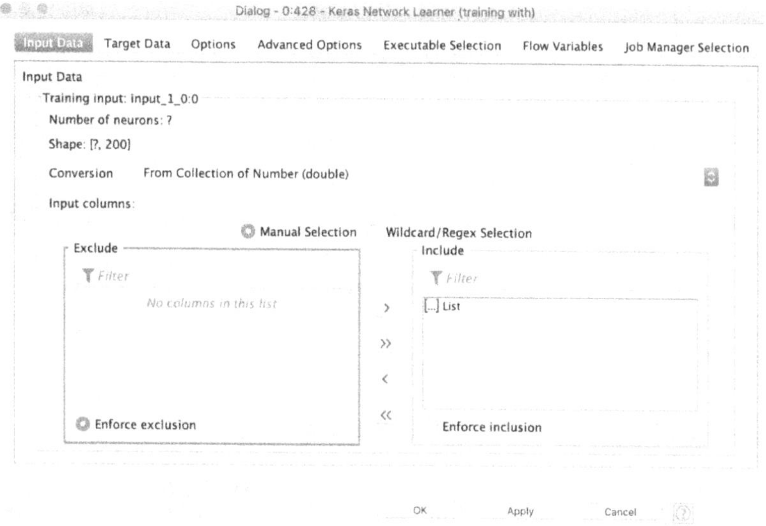


Figure 10.12 – Keras Network Learner configuration dialog – the Input Data tab

The very first tab in the configuration dialog is the **Input Data** tab. This is where we will select which table columns will be used to fill our input layer. Since we combined our 200 input columns into a collection or list, we must select **From Collection of Number (double)** from the dropdown at the top of the tab. We chose double because our data is of the double type. From there, we must make sure our **List** column is set to be included:

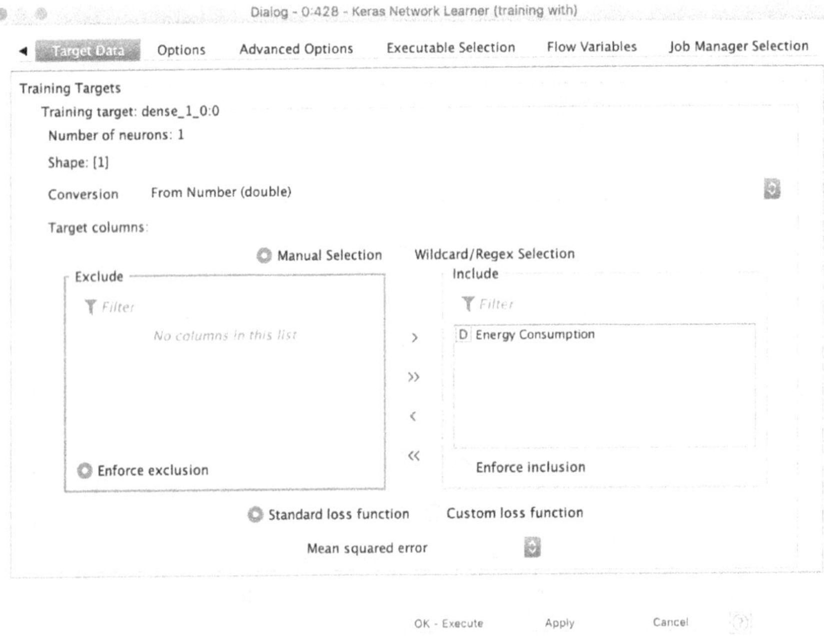


Figure 10.13 – Keras Network Learner configuration dialog – the Target Data tab

The next tab we need to configure is the **Target Data** tab. This is where we will select the data that will match our network's output shape. The LSTM network we configured earlier has a single-valued vector as an output, so we just need to include the one target column here. We can do so using the **From Number (double)** option from the conversation dropdown.

Finally, at the bottom of this tab, we must select our loss function or write a small script to create a custom one! You'll want to apply some domain expertise here to select the best loss function for your project, but it's hard to go wrong with the mean squared error. This loss function takes the difference between our predicted value and the true value, then squares it. Doing this allows us to penalize larger errors more heavily during training.

## Deploying an LSTM network for future prediction

With our LSTM network designed and trained, we can generate forecasts and deploy them. Remember that our network only generates one output forecast; the next value in the time series. To generate forecasts, we must recursively append our model's output to the model input collection. By doing this, we shift the timestamp 1 hour into the future with each iteration of the loop:

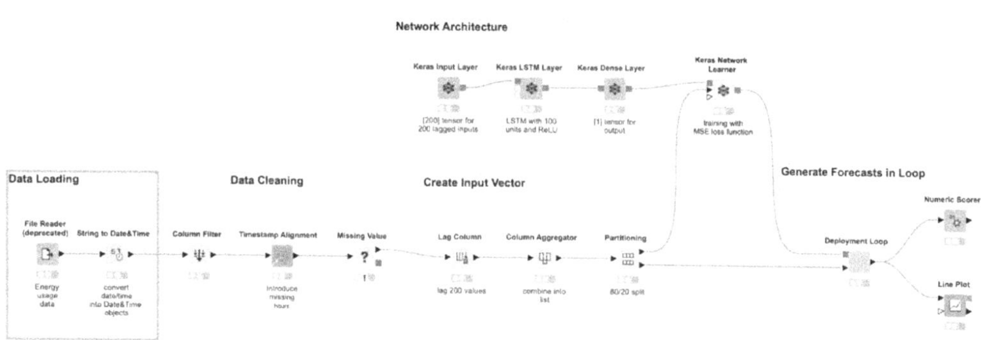


Figure 10.14 – LSTM network, train, and test workflow

You can find the preceding workflow at `https://kni.me/w/43u_UUTFcz-RAy4H`. I encourage you to play with different configurations of the Keras Network Learner, try different loss functions, and check out the inner workings of the Deployment Loop component.

To turn this workflow into a deployment-ready production workflow, we can remove the partitioning node and replace the Keras Network Learner and preceding Keras Layer nodes with a Keras Network Reader node. Then, we can simply read in a saved copy of our model and plug it directly into the Deployment Loop component.

## Scoring the forecasts

The workflow in *Figure 10.14* generates 4 weeks of hourly energy consumption forecasts. Let's explore how they performed!

First, we can use the familiar Numeric Scorer node; its configuration is quite simple. Just select the **Reference** and **Prediction** columns and click **Run**:

Statistics - 0:440 - Numeric Scorer

File

| | |
|---|---|
| $R^2$: | 0.99 |
| Mean absolute error: | 0.339 |
| Mean squared error: | 0.198 |
| Root mean squared error: | 0.445 |
| Mean signed difference: | 0.151 |
| Mean absolute percentage error: | 0.063 |

Figure 10.15 – Numeric Scorer metrics

Here, we can see the metrics that were output by the scorer. The incredibly high R2 value of 0.99 is sure to draw your attention. Normally, a value like this would make me very suspicious, but we know that our data has very strong daily and weekly seasonal patterns. The LSTM model is amazing at picking up on this automatically. This was something we had to account for manually with SARIMA.

We can also plot our forecast on top of the true values and compare how they perform visually:

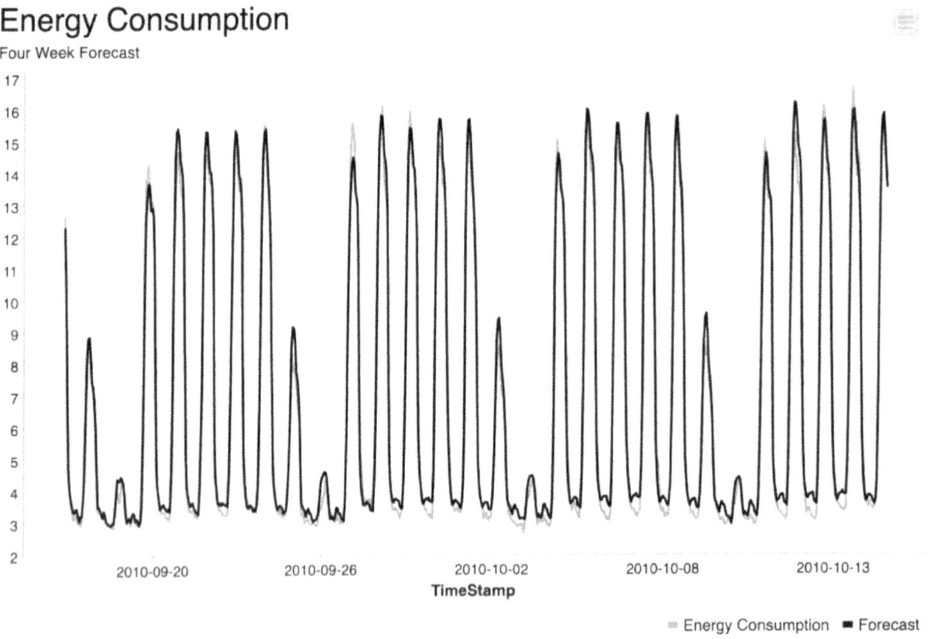


Figure 10.16 – Energy consumption forecast – line plot

Looking at the preceding line plot, it's even clearer that our forecasts fit very well. They overlap quite tightly with our true values and show no clear signs of drift. Keep in mind that we can attribute some of this success to the strong seasonal patterns in our data.

The massive success of the LSTM forecast may tempt you to use it as a solution for all your problems, which is one of the draws of deep learning, but keep in mind that neural networks require a lot more data than some of the other model types we've seen.

> **Tip**
>
> A limitation of the SARIMA model is its inability to handle more than one seasonality. You'll notice that this example has two: daily and weekly. This makes the use case a prime candidate for the flexibility of the LSTM.

## Summary

Deep learning is a massive topic, with entire books dedicated to it. This chapter on LSTM units ends our adventures into this topic, but I hope your interest has been piqued and that you leave feeling ready to experiment with these types of models on your own.

By completing this chapter, you should be able to reshape your time series data in ways that suit your model requirements according to your domain expertise. You'll find that architecture design is one of the hardest parts of forecasting with deep learning.

In *Chapter 11, Anomaly Detection – Predicting Failure with No Failure Examples*, you'll learn how to use some of the forecasting techniques we've learned so far to detect anomalous data points or data drift for use cases such as machine maintenance.

## Questions

1. How many season patterns can the LSTM model handle?

    A. One

    B. Two

    C. Any number

2. An LSTM unit is comprised of multiple neural layers. (True or False)

    A. True

    B. False

3. Which type of activation function is used in the Forget Gate?

    A. Sigmoid

    B. Tanh

    C. ReLU

# 11
# Anomaly Detection – Predicting Failure with No Failure Examples

The goal of this chapter is to be able to predict exceptional events with only normal data at hand. Here, "normal" refers to frequent events, and "exceptional" refers to rare events, such as signals with a low and high amplitude. However, if we cannot provide sufficient examples of exceptional events to train a model that predicts them, we need to exclude all **supervised learning** techniques such as classification models. This means we can use only **unsupervised learning** techniques that predict normal behavior and determine the exceptional events based on those prediction errors. Such prediction of exceptional events is called **anomaly detection**.

In this chapter, we will show you various techniques for anomaly detection from **Internet of Things** (**IoT**) data. IoT refers to data signals from sensors that monitor a physical object, such as a mechanical rotor, a smart home, or the human body. We will demonstrate the techniques through a real-world example of predictive maintenance, where a rotor breakdown is a rare, exceptional event. We will start with data access and preprocessing, continue with visualization, model building, and deployment, and then conclude with possible actions to trigger. Specifically, this chapter has the following parts:

- Introducing the problem of anomaly detection in predictive maintenance
- Detecting anomalies with a control chart
- Predicting the next sample in a correctly functioning system with an auto-regressive model

By the end of this chapter, you will understand how to preprocess and visualize IoT data for anomaly detection. Additionally, you will know how to build an anomaly detection application for predictive maintenance, which can then be extended to other anomaly detection applications.

# Technical requirements

In this chapter, you will need the following:

- KNIME Analytics Platform
- The KNIME Python Integration with the `statsmodels` package installed

If you currently don't have KNIME Analytics Platform installed, you can download it for free at `https://www.knime.com/downloads`. All of the workflows introduced within this chapter are available from the KNIME Hub at `https://kni.me/s/RbTmACK77IS4Aiv5` and GitHub at `https://github.com/PacktPublishing/Codeless-Time-Series-Analysis-with-KNIME/tree/main/Chapter11`.

# Introducing the problem of anomaly detection in predictive maintenance

Before we move on to the actual task of anomaly detection, we will explain the concept of an anomaly, discuss the challenges of anomaly detection, introduce IoT data for the application, and perform data preprocessing and exploration.

We'll complete this introduction with the upcoming subsections:

- Introducing the anomaly detection problem
- IoT data preprocessing
- Exploring anomalies visually

In the first subsection, we'll explain what characterizes an anomaly and introduce the anomaly detection application.

## Introducing the anomaly detection problem

Anomalies can be of two types, static and dynamic:

- **Static anomaly**: This is a data signal that is different from its neighbors; for example, a sudden rotor breakdown due to a power outage.
- **Dynamic anomaly**: This shows slowly changing patterns over time; for example, due to a deteriorating rotor, the mechanical pieces of a rotor affect the rotor's functioning until it eventually breaks.

In this chapter, we will focus on dynamic anomalies to monitor the deterioration of mechanical pieces over time. The goal of the anomaly detection application is to use data from a known breakdown episode to estimate the models' practicability in preventing future breakdowns, while all the models will only be trained on the data from the time of normal functioning. Additionally, we will check how far in advance the models start warning us about the upcoming breakdown. Based on that, we will determine a threshold for an automatic alarm system.

In this chapter, you will come to realize that dynamic anomalies have a couple of challenges compared to static anomalies:

- First, the subsequent signals change gradually, yet asynchronously on different frequency bands. This is because the frequency bands extracted from the same signal describe the deteriorating rotor differently.
- Second, defining an anomaly is not straightforward. On the one hand, we want to tolerate exceptional values as much as possible and save money on buying new mechanical pieces, but on the other hand, we want to react in time before the rotor breaks.

In the next subsection, we will describe the data and required preprocessing steps of the anomaly detection application.

## IoT data preprocessing

We use an IoT dataset from 28 sensors that monitor 8 parts of a mechanical rotor. The data shows signal values from January 2007 to April 2009, including one breakdown episode in July 2008. We access the data as already **Fast Fourier Transform** (**FFT**) preprocessed; therefore, we can start with standardizing and aggregating the data right away.

> **Note**
> In the examples of this chapter, we will only work on a subset of the data, which will be provided together with the workflows. If you want to work with the full dataset, you can download the ZIP file from `http://www.knime.org/files/AnomalyDetectionFullDataSet.zip`.

> **Note**
> When accessing raw IoT data, often, the first step in preprocessing is the **FFT**, which we covered in *Chapter 8, Audio Signal Classification with an FFT and a Gradient Boosted Forest.*

In the following subsection, we will describe the FFT preprocessed data as we access it, before implementing further preprocessing steps.

### Describing FFT preprocessed IoT data

The FFT preprocessed sensor data contains altogether 28 files, one file per sensor and a mechanical piece of the rotor. The parts of the rotor have their own codes: A1, A2, ..., A7, and M1. Additionally, the sensors monitoring them have different codes: SA1, SV3, and EA1.

The signals are then named after the rotor part and the sensor. For example, the signal called A7-SA1 refers to the A7 part of the rotor monitored by the SA1 sensor. A sample of this signal is shown in *Table 11.1*:

| Date | Time | FFT Frequency | FFT Amplitude |
|---|---|---|---|
| 05.01.2007 | 09:53:13 | 3.5156 | 0.002 |
| 05.01.2007 | 09:53:13 | 4.6875 | 0.0041 |
| 05.01.2007 | 09:53:13 | 5.8594 | 0.0059 |
| 05.01.2007 | 09:53:13 | 7.0312 | 0.0131 |
| 05.01.2007 | 09:53:13 | 8.2031 | 0.0265 |

Table 11.1 – A sample of the FFT preprocessed values of the signal named A7-SA1

The FFT preprocessed data contains a **timestamp**, an **FFT frequency value**, and an **FFT amplitude value**. The same timestamp is associated with multiple FFT frequency and amplitude values. In the example in *Table 11.1*, all five frequency and amplitude values refer to the same date and time. Furthermore, the time values are arbitrary: it's likely that another signal does not have values recorded every 13th second of a minute. We will tackle this issue in the next subsection, where we standardize the time and frequency references.

### Standardizing FFT preprocessed IoT data

Standardizing the data makes the signals from different rotor parts relatable to each other. Only with standardized data can we analyze what happens in all of the signals at the same time. We standardize IoT data via the following three steps:

1. By binning the frequency values
2. By aggregating the time and amplitude values
3. By time-aligning the timestamps

*Figure 11.1* shows the workflow that implements these steps:

Binning, aggregation, and time alignment

List Files/Folders

Table Row To Variable Loop Start

files

Filename

File Reader (Complex Format)

Frequency Binning

Timestamp Alignment

RowID

Loop End (Column Append)

Figure 11.1 – The workflow for standardizing the FFT pre-processed data

1. First, the workflow accesses the file paths of the 28 files for the different signals with the **List Files/Folders** node.
2. Next, the **Table Row to Variable Loop Start** node takes one file path (signal) at a time for reading and preprocessing.
3. Then, the **Frequency Binning** metanode aggregates the FFT amplitude values into average values by a 100 Hz-wide frequency band and day.
4. Following these tasks, the **Timestamp Alignment** component ensures that all data from the 28 files refers to the same dates. In the time-aligned data, the same row number in each table refers to the same date, which enables joining the amplitude values on different frequency bands row-wise by date.
5. Finally, the **Loop End (Column Append)** node collects the columns from all iterations, that is, all the preprocessed columns for all signals, and combines them into one table.

*Table 11.2* shows a sample of the output of the loop, that is, the standardized table:

| Date_time | [0, 100]+Amp A-1-EA1 | [100, 200]+Amp A-1-EA1 | | [900, 1000]+Amp A-7-SV3 |
|---|---|---|---|---|
| 05.01.2007 | 0.019 | 0.014 | ... | 0.003 |
| 06.01.2007 | 0.019 | 0.014 | | 0.003 |
| 07.01.2007 | 0.02 | 0.013 | | 0.003 |
| 08.01.2007 | 0.019 | 0.013 | | 0.003 |
| 09.01.2007 | 0.018 | 0.013 | | 0.003 |

Table 11.2 – A sample of the standardized FFT data

The standardized table is huge. It contains 313 columns representing the different frequency bands of the 28 original signals. The timestamps in the standardized table are single dates instead of random timestamps, and each date is referred to in only one row. Furthermore, each column is now represented by a single-frequency band of a single sensor. For example, the first column, named **[0,100]+Amp A-1-EA1**, refers to the average amplitude values on the 0–100 Hz frequency band of the EA1 sensor monitoring the A1 part of the rotor.

In the next subsection, we will inspect, via several views, how the IoT signals behave through the life cycle of the rotor.

## Exploring anomalies visually

Data exploration helps us to find out how much in advance the anomalous signals appear with respect to the rotor breakdown, and which sensors and frequency bands react to the rotor's condition the strongest.

We will explore the data for anomalies via five different views, each of them providing a different perspective of the data:

- Exploring the amplitude values over time with a **line plot**
- Exploring the relationships of frequency bands with a **scatter matrix**
- Comparing amplitudes on frequency bands with a **heatmap**
- Exploring the common variation of frequency bands with a **correlation matrix**
- Exploring the randomness of amplitude values with an **autocorrelation plot**

The visual exploration of anomalies is implemented in the same workflow as the data preprocessing (which is available from the KNIME Hub at `https://kni.me/w/D4MKIttYBLhaQClj`). The relevant part of that workflow is shown in the following screenshot:

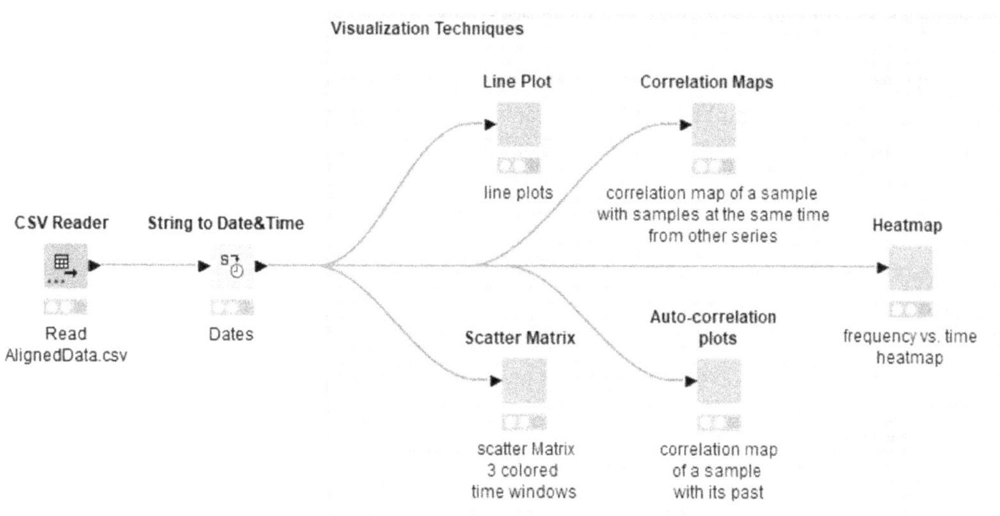


Figure 11.2 – The workflow for the visual exploration of the anomalous signals

In the following subsections, we will show the output views of the components and introduce details about them.

> **Note**
>
> For easier interpretation, in our demonstration, we have reduced the dimensions to the frequency band of only one signal (A-1-SV3). The same techniques could be applied to the signals in all other frequency bands, too.

## Exploring the amplitude values over time with a line plot

In a line plot, we can see whether the signal looks different for the old and new rotor pieces and, thus, get a hint of the timing and amplitude of the anomalous signals. *Figure 11.3* shows two line plots for two frequency bands (0–100 Hz and 500–600 Hz) of the A-1-SV3 signal:

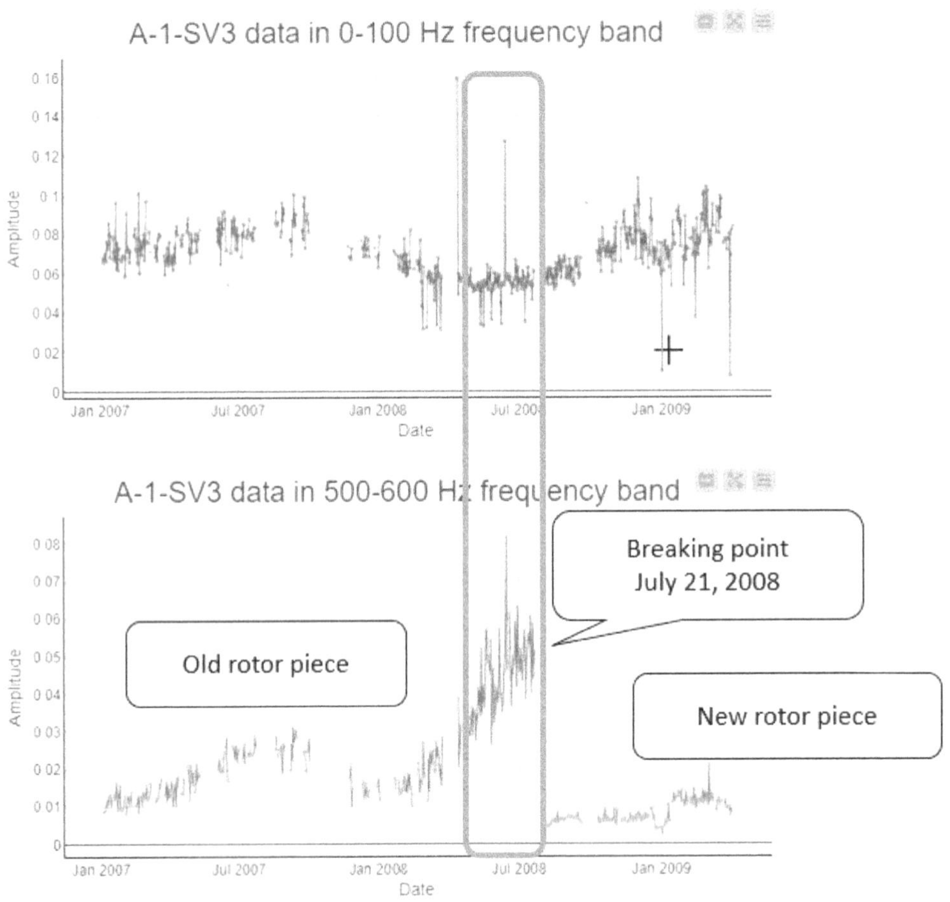


Figure 11.3 – Line plots for two frequency bands of the A-1-SV3 signal

The *x* axis of both line plots shows the time, and the *y* axis shows the amplitude values of the respective frequency band. The rotor breakdown from July 21, 2008, is highlighted in both plots. The top line plot for the 0–100 Hz frequency band doesn't show any remarkable change of pattern before or after the rotor breakdown. So, this frequency band doesn't seem to be sensitive to the deteriorating rotor. The static anomalies, the sudden exceptionally high values shown as sharp peaks in the top line plot, are not necessarily related to the breakdown event. In contrast, the bottom line plot for the 500–600 Hz frequency band shows exceptionally high amplitude values in the time before the rotor breakdown, and low amplitude values again after breakdown, with a new rotor piece.

Therefore, the 500–600 Hz frequency band is clearly indicating the rotor deterioration through higher amplitude values, and this is our first indicator of the rotor breakdown.

### Exploring the relationships of frequency bands with a scatter matrix

Next, we will look at the relationships of the frequency bands over time. In the preceding line plot, we saw that the frequency bands are describing the deteriorating rotor asynchronously, and this should obviously affect the correlation between the frequency bands. Therefore, we can build a scatter matrix with nine scatter plots, comparing the correlations between three different frequency bands.

> **Note**
>
> The scatter matrix mirrors the same information on both sides of the diagonal. The diagonal shows the correlation of the column versus itself. The scatter plots on both sides of the diagonal are the same, just with the `x` axis and `y` axis columns switched.

Additionally, we have divided the data into three time windows based on the time of the signal and the rotor breakdown, and these time windows are colored differently in the scatter matrix:

- **Training window** (dark gray): Signals from January to August 2007; one year before the rotor breakdown. This time window represents the time of normal functioning.
- **Maintenance window** (light gray): Signals from September 2007 to July 2008; the time when the rotor starts deteriorating and finally breaks.
- **Remaining window** (gray): Signals from August 2008 to April 2009; the time after rotor breakdown, with new mechanical pieces.

*Figure 11.4* shows one scatter plot from the scatter matrix. You can inspect all scatter plots in the original scatter matrix image, which is available from GitHub at `https://github.com/PacktPublishing/Codeless-Time-Series-Analysis-with-KNIME/blob/main/Chapter11/Scattermatrix_ORIG.png`:

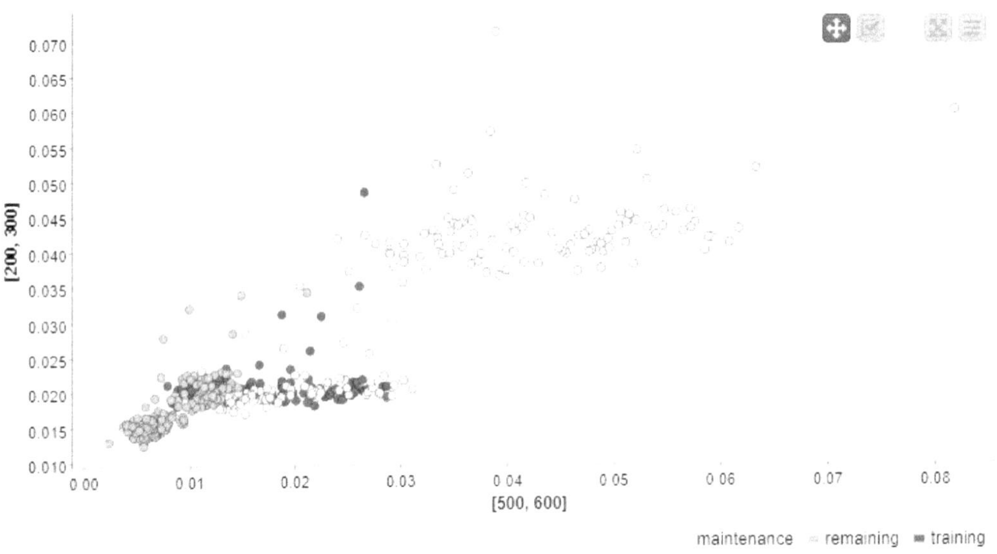


Figure 11.4 – A scatter plot showing the relationship between two frequency bands

The signal values from the maintenance window (the light gray dots) are scattered further toward the upper-right corner than the other signal values (the gray and dark gray dots). This means the deteriorating rotor seems to produce greater amplitude values. However, the amplitude values don't increase on all frequency bands simultaneously. This is because the 500–600 Hz frequency band on the *x* axis doesn't reach its highest value at the same time that the 200–300 Hz frequency band on the *y* axis does.

### Comparing amplitudes on frequency bands with a heatmap

We will continue the exploratory analysis with a heatmap. We want to find out which frequency bands show the maximum amplitude values before the rotor breakdown. *Figure 11.5* shows a heatmap of the signals, with dates as row IDs, frequency bands as column headers, and amplitude values as color-coded amplitude values between 0 and 1, during the training window (top) and during the maintenance window (bottom):

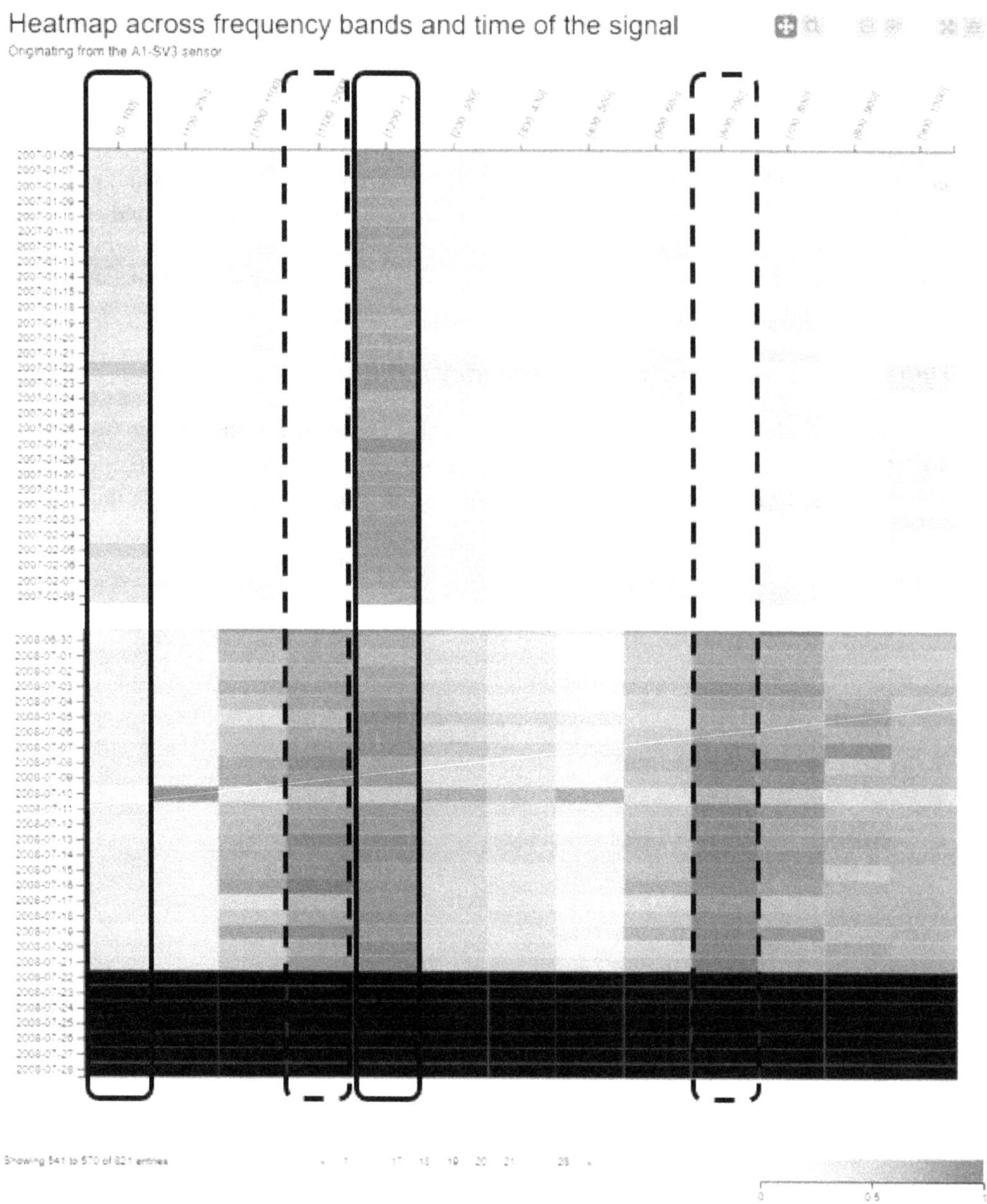


Figure 11.5 – A heatmap showing the amplitude values on different frequency bands by color progression

The heatmap shows light gray cells (low values) for the 0–100 Hz frequency band and dark gray cells (high values) for the 1,200+ Hz frequency band during both the training and maintenance windows. The columns for these frequency bands are highlighted by a solid line in *Figure 11.5*. That means these frequency bands do not show different signal amplitude values depending on the condition of the rotor piece, as we already found out for the 0–100 Hz frequency band in the line plot. Instead, the other frequency bands show darker gray cells (higher values) close to the rotor breakdown. The rotor breakdown is indicated by the black cells at the bottom. In the 1,100–1,200 Hz and 500–600 Hz frequency bands, the color progression from light gray to dark gray is the strongest between the training and maintenance windows, which means that these frequency bands describe the deteriorating rotor the strongest. These frequency bands are highlighted by a dashed line.

### Exploring the common variation of frequency bands with a correlation matrix

Next, we explore the relationships of frequency bands with a correlation matrix. If two frequency bands reach high values and low values at the same time, their correlation is *positive*. If one shows high values when the other shows low values, their correlation is *negative*. Zero correlation means that their dynamics are independent of each other.

*Figure 11.6* shows two correlation matrices between the frequency bands. The matrix on top corresponds to the training window, and the matrix at the bottom is for the maintenance window:

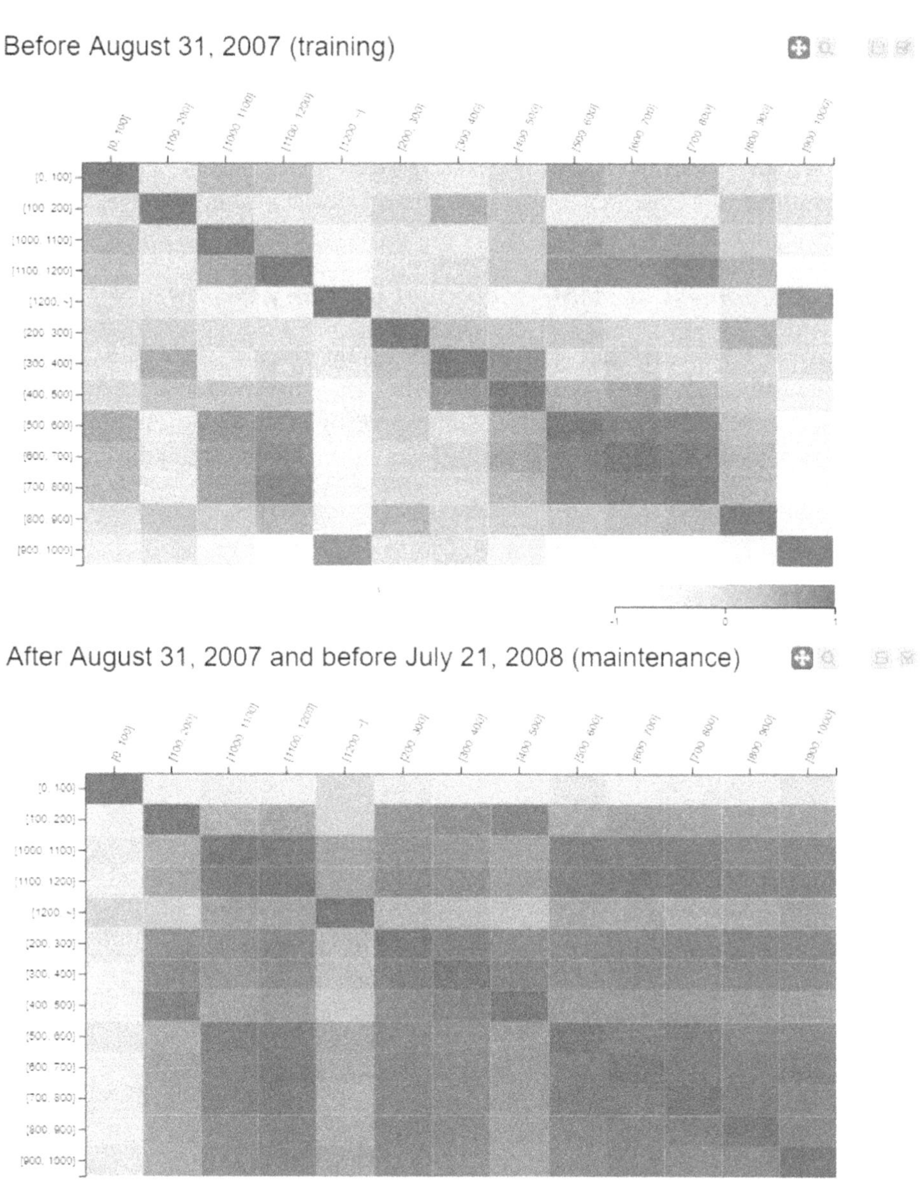


Figure 11.6 – A correlation matrix of frequency bands during the training (top) window and the maintenance (bottom) window

The colors in the cells of the correlation matrix indicate the strength of the correlation: light gray for a strong negative correlation and dark gray for a strong positive correlation. The top correlation matrix for the training window shows both light and dark colors. That means some frequency bands are positively correlated, some negatively, and others not at all when the rotor is functioning normally. On the opposite side, the bottom correlation matrix is far more monotonous. This means that all (except for one) frequency bands show a positive correlation when the rotor deteriorates. From the previous views, we know that the amplitude values increase on some frequency bands during the maintenance window. Now we know that this actually happens on all frequency bands except for the 0–100 Hz frequency band.

### Exploring the randomness of amplitude values with an ACF plot

At last, we will investigate the ACF plot of the signals. We want to see whether the signal values are fluctuating randomly or whether they are related to the past signals, and whether the behavior is different during the training and maintenance windows. *Figure 11.7* shows the **ACF** plots of the 300–400 Hz frequency band at lags 1–230 during the training window (top) and the maintenance window (bottom):

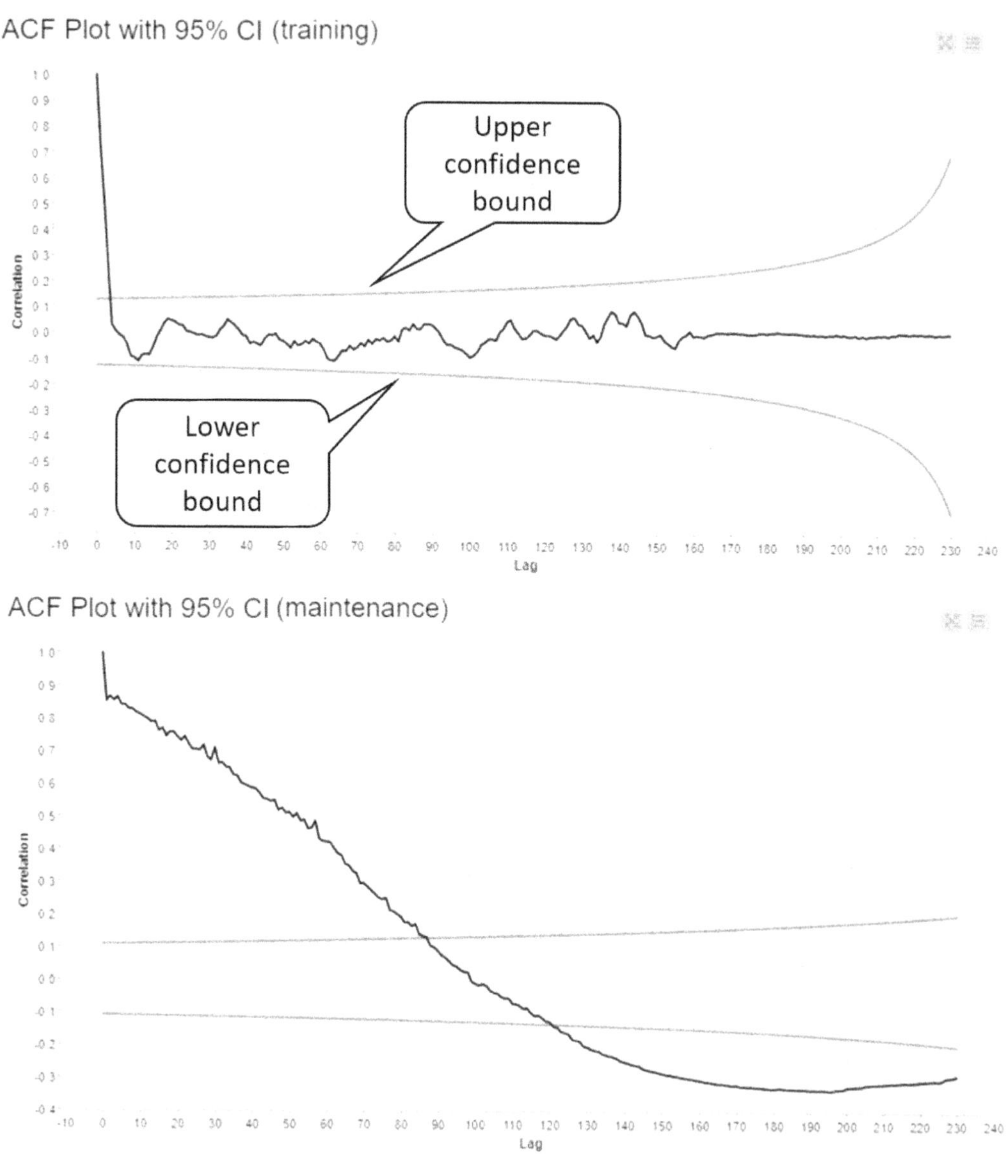


Figure 11.7 – ACF plots from lag 1 to lag 230 during the training (top) and maintenance window (bottom)

In the ACF plot at the top, for the training window, the ACF values decay quickly and fluctuate within the upper and lower **confidence bounds** at all lags, as annotated in *Figure 11.7*. The confidence bounds are the boundaries of the 95% **confidence interval** (**CI**) within which the ACF values are defined as statistically insignificant with 95% certainty. Therefore, we can assume that there is no significant ACF when the rotor is functioning normally, and we can say that the subsequent signals are not correlated.

On the opposite side, in the ACF plot at the bottom, for the maintenance window, the ACF is decaying very slowly and is outside the confidence bounds until lag 80. This means the signal values start increasing about 80 days before the rotor breakdown. From lag 120 onward, the ACF values are negative and they increase in magnitude. This is because the early *normal* signal values from the beginning of the maintenance window are negatively correlated with the high values at the end of the maintenance window.

Let's sum up our indicators of anomalies via a visual exploration:

- The amplitude values increase on most frequency bands during the maintenance window. You can see that in the heatmaps of *Figure 11.5* and in the correlation matrix of *Figure 11.6*.
- The amplitude values increase, especially on the 600–700 Hz and 1,100–1,200 Hz frequency bands. You can see that in the heatmaps of *Figure 11.5*.
- The amplitude values start increasing about 80 days before the rotor breakdown. You can see that in the ACF plots of *Figure 11.7*.

In the following sections, we are going to use these indicators to build an automatic alarm system. We will start with the control chart technique.

# Detecting anomalies with a control chart

A **control chart** defines boundaries for a *normal* signal based on the statistics of the training set, which, in this case, refers to values from a correctly working system. During deployment, an alarm system is built to warn when the signal is exceeding the boundaries.

We will introduce and build a control chart based on the IoT data using the following steps:

1. Introducing a control chart
2. Implementing a control chart
3. Deploying a control chart

In the first subsection, we will show you how to define and visualize a control chart.

## Introducing a control chart

A control chart defines the normal functioning of a process by a statistical range. We define this range by calculating the following statistics over the training window:

- **Upper limit**: *Mean+12*Standard Deviation*
- **Lower limit**: *Mean-12*Standard Deviation*

Once these boundaries have been set, we can visualize the control chart in a line plot. As an example, *Figure 11.8* visualizes the control chart for the 1,100–1,200 Hz frequency band:

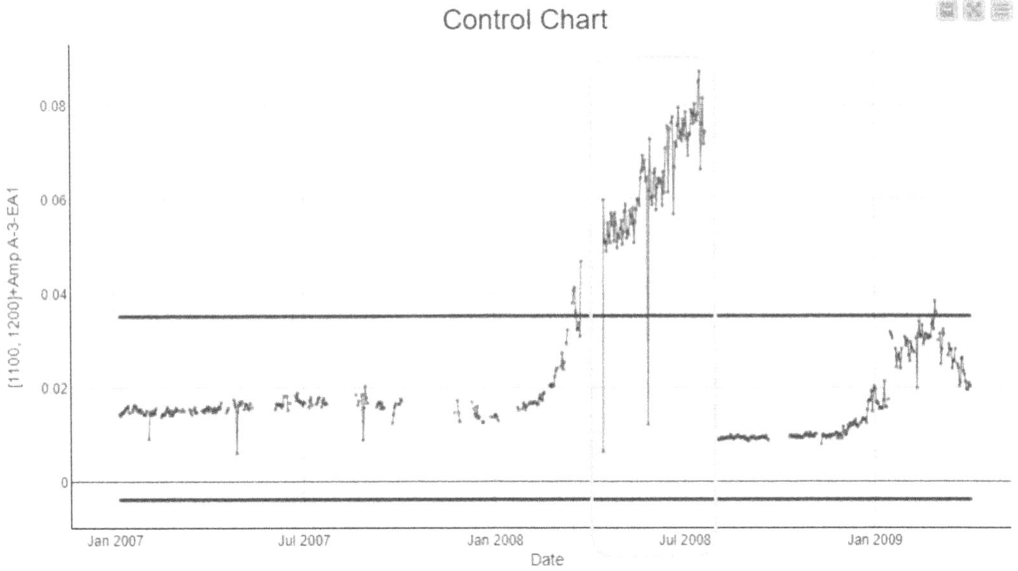


Figure 11.8 – An example of a control chart

The time on the *x* axis covers the training, maintenance, and remaining windows. The fluctuating line in the middle is the signal value. The horizontal lines show the upper and lower boundaries of normal functioning. These boundaries are calculated based on the signal values in the training window, where we are sure that the functioning is indeed normal. The signals that exceed the upper or lower limits are anomalous. The time of the rotor breakdown is highlighted in the control chart. Within this time, the signal values are frequently anomalous.

In the next subsection, we will explain the implementation of the control chart technique in KNIME Analytics Platform.

## Implementing a control chart

The implementation of a control chart consists of calculating the boundaries on the training data, comparing the boundaries with the signals on the deployment data, and raising an alarm if they are exceeded. These steps are implemented in the workflow shown in *Figure 11.9* (which is available from the KNIME Hub at `https://kni.me/w/MPCX6kEttoWAgs4p`):

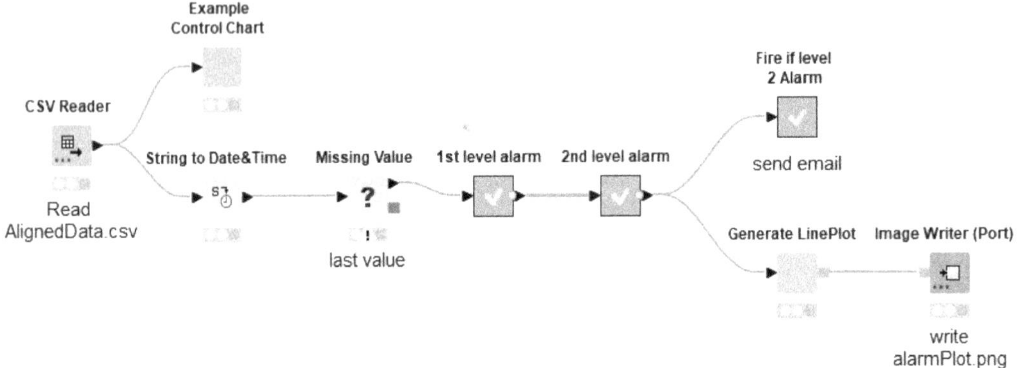


Figure 11.9 – The workflow for implementing a control chart

1. First, the **Example Control Chart** component in the top branch of the workflow visualizes the control chart for one frequency band. The line plot in *Figure 11.8* shows an example output of the component.
2. Next, the **String to Date&Time** node converts the dates into `Date&Time` format, and the **Missing Value** node replaces the missing signal values with the value of the last available signal.
3. After that, the **1st level alarm** metanode calculates the first-level alarms as deviations (1 for the outside boundaries, and 0 for the inside boundaries) from the normal functioning separately on the single-frequency bands. Visually, a first-level alarm occurs when the signal line crosses the upper or lower limit, as depicted in the control chart of *Figure 11.8*.
4. Next, the **2nd level alarm** metanode aggregates the first-level alarms across frequency bands into the second-level alarms. The second-level alarms range between 0 and 1, and they indicate the proportion of the frequency bands that raise a first-level alarm.
5. Finally, the **Generate LinePlot** component visualizes the alarms and the **Fire if level 2 Alarm** metanode triggers an action, which, in this case, is sending an email.

In the following subsection, we will show, in detail, how we calculate and apply the control boundaries for the first-level alarms.

### *Calculating the control boundaries*

The loop depicted in *Figure 11.10* shows the steps for calculating the control boundaries as implemented inside the first-level alarm metanode (*Figure 11.9*):

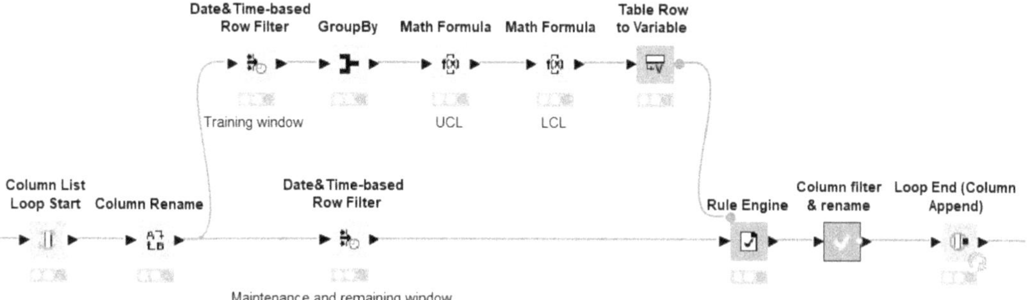


Figure 11.10 – A loop for calculating the first-level alarms separately on each frequency band

1. First, the **Column List Loop Start** node only handles one frequency column at a time, and the **Column Rename** node standardizes the names of the frequency columns for the calculations within the loop body.
2. Next, the top **Date&Time-based Row Filter** nodes filter the data for the training window, and the **GroupBy** and **Math Formula** nodes calculate the control boundaries.
3. After that, the **Table Row to Variable** node passes the boundary values for the checking the alarm status. These boundaries will be used by the **Rule Engine** node that checks the alarm status in the maintenance and remaining windows as filtered by the bottom **Date&Time-based Row Filter** node.

In the next subsection, we will explain the last step, deploying the control chart, and then we will continue with calculating and visualizing the second-level alarms.

### *Deploying the control chart*

We will deploy the control chart on the maintenance and remaining windows to find out the time difference between a second-level alarm and the rotor breakdown. Does the rotor need to be changed immediately or only in a few months? Acting too early is also expensive – as mechanical pieces are costly!

The **Rule Engine** node (*Figure 11.10*) deploys the control chart by activating the first-level alarm if the current signal value exceeds the control boundaries:

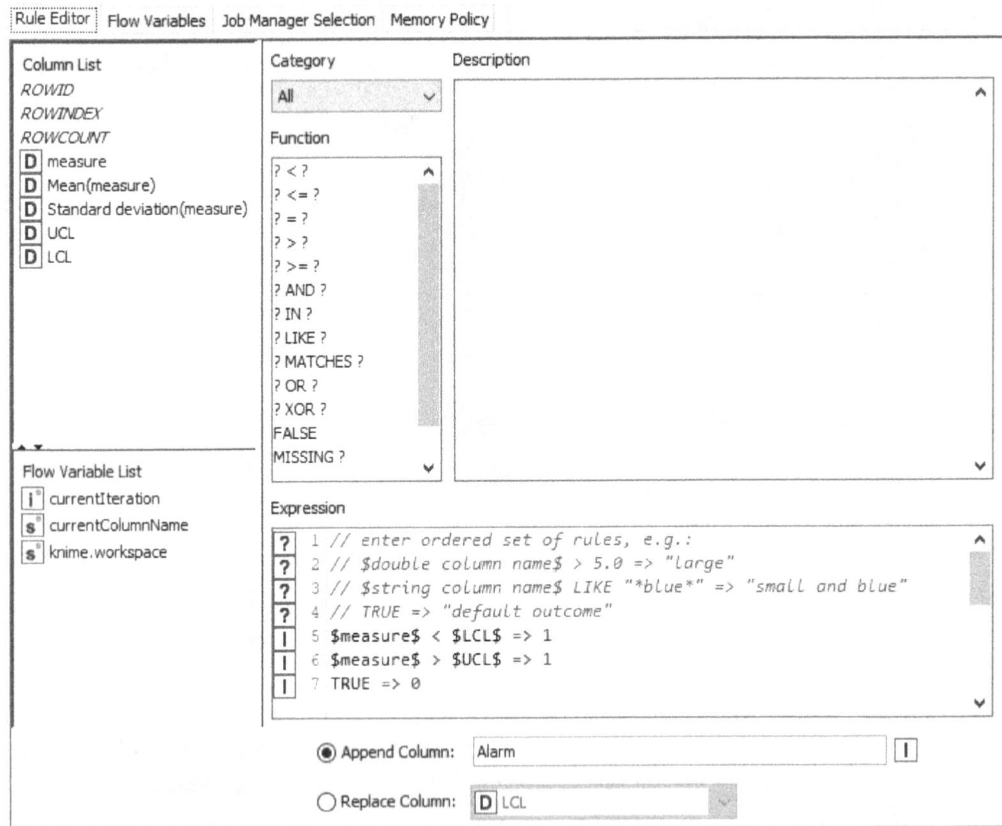


Figure 11.11 – The rule implemented in the Rule Engine node, activating the first-level alarm if the signal exceeds the range of normal functioning

The **Expression** editor in the configuration dialog of the **Rule Engine** node shows three rules. The top rule, `$measure$ < $LCL$ => 1`, sets the first-level alarm to 0 if the signal value is lower than the lower boundary. The middle rule, `$measure$ > $UCL$ => 1`, activates the first-level alarm if the signal value is greater than the upper boundary. The bottom rule, `TRUE => 0`, sets the alarm to 0 otherwise.

After that, the second-level alarms are calculated inside the second-level alarm metanode (*Figure 11.9*), as follows:

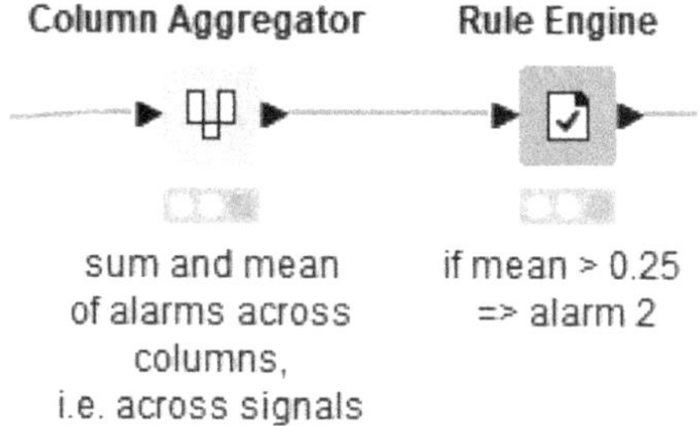


Figure 11.12 – A workflow for aggregating the first-level alarms into second-level alarms

1. First, the **Column Aggregator** node calculates the row average of the first-level alarm columns to see how many frequency bands on the first-level alarm occurred at the same time
2. After that, the **Rule Engine** node activates a second-level alarm based on a threshold of 0.25. A threshold of 0.25 means that if the first-level alarm occurs on at least 25% of the frequency bands, a second-level alarm activates.

Finally, we visualize the results. *Figure 11.13* shows a line plot with the first- and second-level alarms over the maintenance and remaining windows:

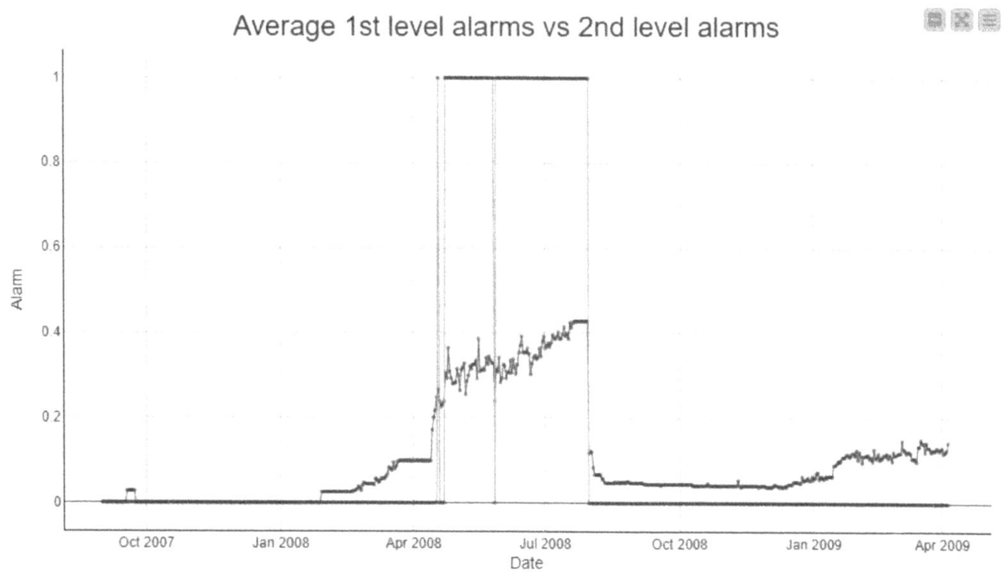


Figure 11.13 – A line plot displaying the first- and second-level alarms over the maintenance window

The line for the second-level alarms only shows two values, 0 and 1. The line for the first-level alarms shows values between 0 and 1 as the percentages of frequency bands where the first-level alarm occurred. If this line reaches a value higher than 0.25, the other line jumps from 0 to 1. This happens about 3 months before the rotor breakdown (May 2008) repeatedly as the line for the first-level alarms exceeds the threshold from everyday.

In the next subsection, we will finish this section regarding the control chart by explaining how to trigger an action based on an alarm check.

### *Triggering an action based on a control chart*

The final step of the anomaly detection application by a control chart is to implement the action that follows an alarm. We decided to send an email and implemented the action inside the *Fire if level 2 Alarm* metanode in the control chart workflow (*Figure 11.9*). This means that if the workflow executes and activates a second-level alarm, it triggers the email. Therefore, for a functional alarm system, ideally, the workflow should be executed and scheduled once a day. A scheduled execution is a feature of KNIME Server.

The workflow inside the *Fire if level 2 Alarm* metanode is shown in *Figure 11.14:*

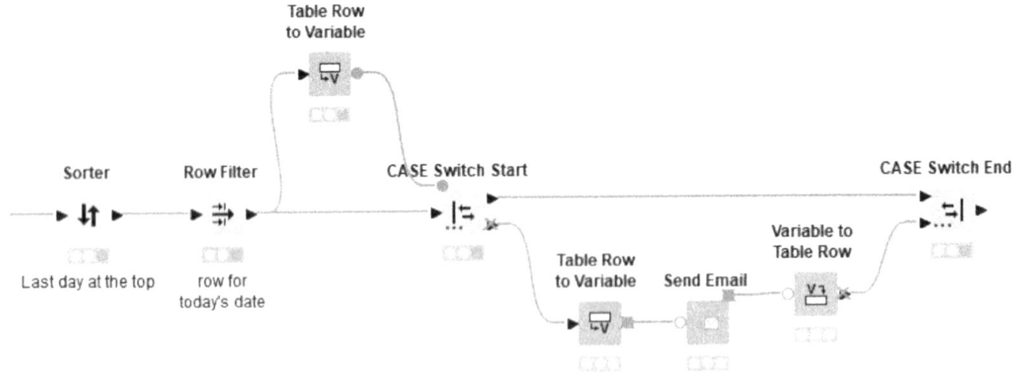


Figure 11.14 – Implementing a conditional execution of a task with the CASE Switch nodes

The workflow has two branches, one with the **Send Email** node and one without, separated by the **CASE Switch Start** node. The workflow controls the branch to execute as follows:

1. First, it extracts the latest alarm status with the **Sorter** and **Row Filter** nodes.

2. Then, it controls the action with the **Table Row to Variable** node, which produces a flow variable with a value of 1 if the second-level alarm is active and 0 otherwise.
3. It activates the bottom output of the **CASE Switch Start** node only if the second-level alarm is active, so if the **Table Row to Variable** node produces a value of 1.
4. Finally, it finishes the execution and collects the time and alarm information with the **CASE Switch End** node.

An example configuration of the **Send Email** node is shown in *Figure 11.15*:

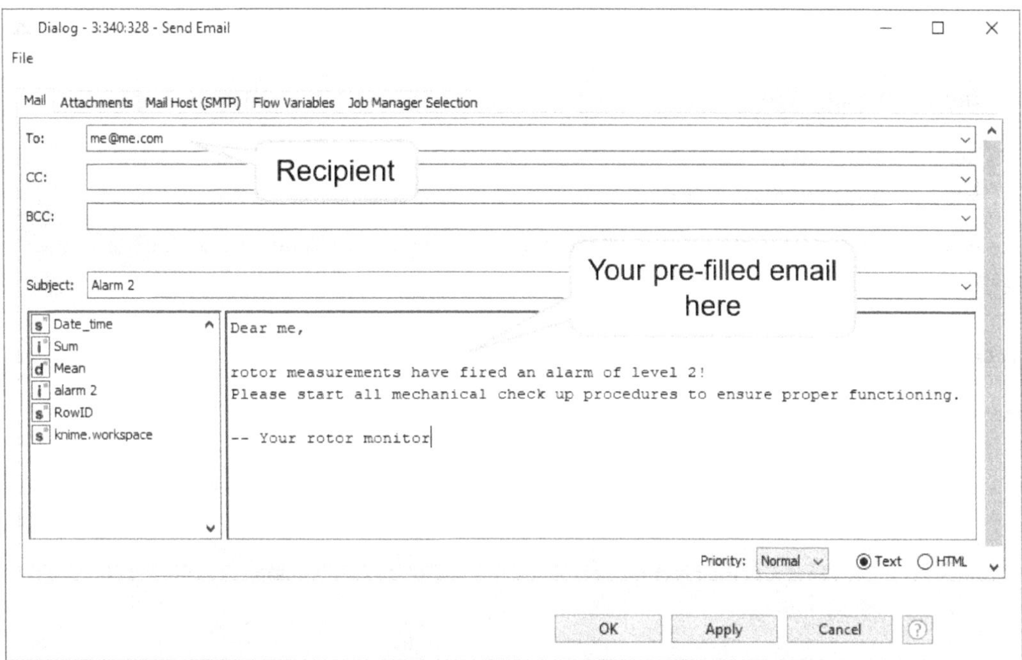


Figure 11.15 – Defining an email and its recipient in the Send Email node

In the configuration dialog, we define the recipient's email address in the **To** field and write in the text field below the email text, which will be sent automatically in the case of an alarm. In the **Mail Host (SMTP)** tab of the configuration dialog, we authorize the email account that sends the email.

In the next section, we will train an auto-regressive model to detect anomalous signals.

# Predicting the next sample in a correctly working system with an auto-regressive model

Since we only have normal values in the training set, we train and test an **auto-regressive model** to predict normal values. Then, during deployment, we set an alarm system based on the distance calculated between the real values and predicted values. The concept is that the auto-regressive model can only predict values reflecting a correctly functioning system. If the underlying functioning system starts deteriorating, then the predicted values and the real values will start diverging.

In the following steps, we will introduce the auto-regressive model approach and our implementation:

1. Introducing an auto-regressive model
2. Training an auto-regressive model with the linear regression algorithm
3. Deploying an auto-regressive model

In the first subsection, we'll introduce the linear regression algorithm as one option for training an auto-regressive model.

## Introducing an auto-regressive model

An auto-regressive model is a regression model that predicts a time series value by a linear combination of its past values. A simple example of an auto-regressive model is the *random walk* model, which predicts the next value in the time series by adding a random error sampled from a distribution with zero mean and fixed variance to the previous value.

The algorithm we selected for the auto-regressive model is the **linear regression algorithm**, which has the following equation:

$$y = a_0 + a_1 x_1 + a_2 x_2 + \ldots + a_n x_n + \varepsilon$$

Formula 11.1

Here, $y$ is the value to be predicted, $a_0, \ldots, a_n$ are the regression coefficients, $x_1, \ldots, x_n$ are the independent variables, and $\varepsilon$ is a random error. In the auto-regressive model, the $y$ value to be predicted has a time index of $y_t$, and the independent variables are the past values of $y_{t-1}, y_{t-2}, \ldots, y_{t-n}$.

> **Note**
>
> If you have already familiarized yourself with ARIMA models in *Chapter 7, Forecasting the Temperature with ARIMA and SARIMA Models*, you might remember that an ARIMA model is also an auto-regressive model and has a very similar equation to the preceding equation. However, the linear regression algorithm is not dedicated to time series analysis in the same way that ARIMA is; therefore, it doesn't assume a time relationship between the variables on both sides of the equation.

In the next subsection, we will introduce the implementation of the auto-regressive model in KNIME Analytics Platform, starting with data transformation and continuing with the model training.

## Training an auto-regressive model with the linear regression algorithm

First, we will transform the signal values into vectors of past values. Data transformation is required to use the selected algorithm, linear regression, in the form of an auto-regression. A linear regression algorithm predicts a **target variable** by one or more **predictor variables**. For example, the target variable could be the temperature, and the predictor variable could be the humidity. In such a scenario, we would have both features at hand. However, we must use the **Lag Column** node to create the vectors of past values, which, in our case, are the past 10 signal values:

| Date | Amp |
|---|---|
| 2007-01-05 | 0.019 |
| 2007-01-06 | 0.019 |
| 2007-01-07 | 0.02 |
| 2007-01-08 | 0.019 |

Lag Column

| Date | Amp | Amp (-1) | Amp (-2) |
|---|---|---|---|
| 2007-01-05 | 0.019 | ? | ? |
| 2007-01-06 | 0.019 | 0.019 | ? |
| 2007-01-07 | 0.02 | 0.019 | 0.019 |
| 2007-01-08 | 0.019 | 0.02 | 0.019 |

Figure 11.16 – Creating vectors of past values with the Lag Column node

As you can see in *Figure 11.16*, the **Lag Column** node transforms the data with one column (*Amp*) into a vector of past values at different lags, -1 (*Amp (-1)*), -2 (*Amp (-2)*), and so on. We need to define the following two parameters to create columns with past values with the **Lag Column** node:

- **Lag**: This indicates the number of past values to consider. 1 refers to one past value, 2 to two past values, and so on. We set the lag to 10.

- **Lag interval**: This indicates the number of steps that will be taken in the past to get a past value. If the lag interval is 1, then the previous value will be taken. If it is 2, the previous value will be ignored and the value before it will be taken. We set the lag interval to 1.

After the transformation, we continue to train the model using the training data obtained from the training window. *Figure 11.17* shows the **training** workflow (which is available from the KNIME Hub at `https://kni.me/w/z5pUwofr91o7OGOr`):

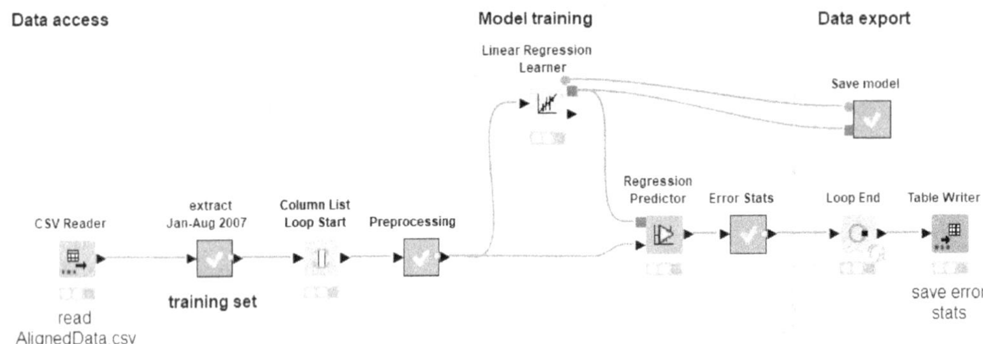


Figure 11.17 – The workflow for training an auto-regressive model (linear regression)

The workflow shows a loop because, first, we calculate the alarms separately on each frequency band and then aggregate the results. Overall, the training workflow covers the following steps on each frequency band:

1. It accesses the already preprocessed data with the **CSV Reader** node. Inside the next metanode, it extracts the training time window from all data for training.
2. Next, it generates the past columns with the **Lag Column** node inside the **Preprocessing** metanode.
3. After that, it trains the auto-regressive model on each column separately with the **Linear Regression Learner** node.
4. Next, it applies in-sample prediction on the training data with the **Regression Predictor** node and calculates the prediction errors.
5. Finally, it exports the prediction error statistics as a table file with the **Table Writer** node and writes the trained models as files inside the **Save model** metanode.

In the next subsection, we will move on to deployment. We will show you how to generate and visualize the prediction errors in the maintenance window. Additionally, we will show you how to trigger an action via REST.

## Deploying an auto-regressive model

We will deploy the pretrained auto-regressive models on the maintenance window to see what happens to the prediction errors when the rotor deteriorates – and as we already know, the amplitude values increase. We perform the deployment in two workflows, one that visualizes the results (which is available from the KNIME Hub at `https://kni.me/w/lou3haw35_mpc1GK`) and another that triggers an action (which is available from the KNIME Hub at `https://kni.me/w/MQ8JjydDub8OADVQ`). The model **deployment** part for both workflows is shown in *Figure 11.18*:

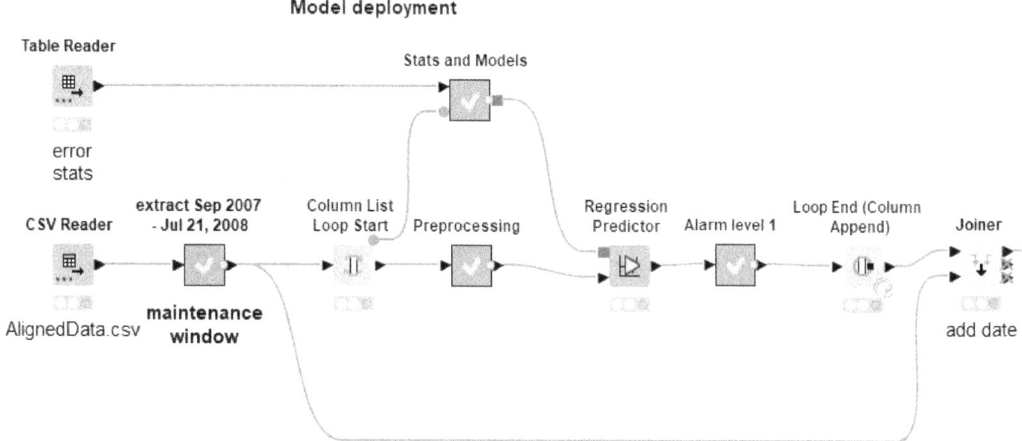


Figure 11.18 – A workflow for deploying the auto-regressive model

The deployment part of the workflow contains a loop that generates predictions separately on each frequency column of the maintenance window. The loop completes the following steps:

1. It generates the past columns inside the **Preprocessing** metanode.
2. It accesses the previously trained model and the prediction error statistics inside the **Stats and Models** metanode.
3. Then, it generates the predictions with the **Regression Predictor** node.
4. After that, it calculates the first-level alarms from the prediction errors inside the **Alarm level 1** metanode. Specifically, it truncates to 0 all prediction errors that are within the average prediction error from the training data $\pm$ 2 times its standard deviation.

In the following subsection, we will show you how to continue the deployment by calculating the second-level alarms.

## Calculating the second-level alarms

The first-level errors on all frequency bands are the output of the loop, and we aggregate them to the second-level alarms as the **moving average** of the first-level alarms over the past 21 days.

The moving average over the past 21 days means that each value is replaced by the average value over itself and 20 past signal values, smoothing out occasional first-level alarms and emphasizing the long-lasting ones. The steps to calculate the second-level alarms are shown in the workflow in *Figure 11.19*:

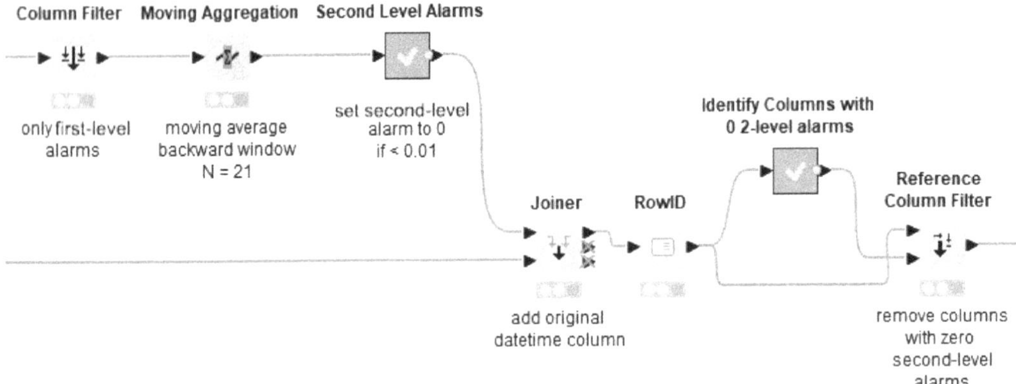


Figure 11.19 – Calculating the second-level alarms as the moving average of the first-level alarms

The workflow implements the following steps after the model deployment (*Figure 11.18*), which was introduced in the previous subsection:

1. First, it only filters the first-level alarm columns and calculates the simple moving average of them with the **Column Filter** and **Moving Aggregation** nodes.
2. After that, it sets the second-level alarm to 1 if the moving average value exceeds the threshold of 0.01 and to 0 otherwise inside the **Second Level Alarms** metanode.
3. Then, it joins the second-level alarm columns with the row IDs from the original data with the **Joiner** and **RowID** nodes. The row IDs indicate the timestamps of the second-level alarms.
4. Finally, it identifies all columns with no second-level alarms and excludes them from the following steps with the **Reference Column Filter** node.

In the next subsection, we show you how to visually explore the results of the anomaly detection application.

## Visualizing the alarms

We visualize the second-level alarms over time in a stacked area chart and a line plot. *Figure 11.20* shows the second-level alarms inside a stacked area chart:

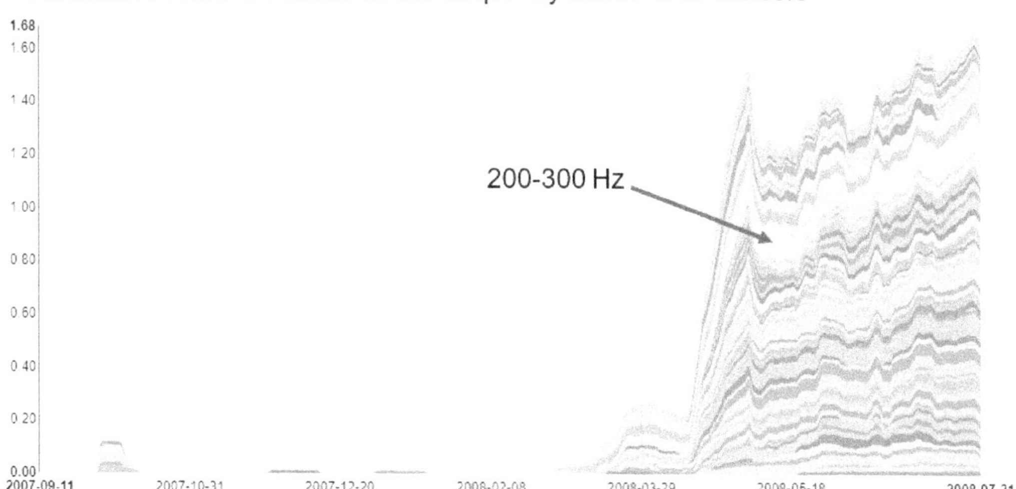


Figure 11.20 – Stacked area chart visualizing the second-level alarms through the maintenance window

The stacked area chart shows the cumulative second-level alarm on all frequency bands. The colored areas correspond to the magnitude of the second-level alarm on individual frequency bands. The cumulative value stays at a low level until April 2008, that is, 3 months before the rotor breakdown. After that, the second-level alarms start increasing on all frequency bands.

Also, note that some frequency bands contribute especially strongly to the second-level alarm, such as the 200–300 Hz frequency band of the A7-SA1 signal, as highlighted in *Figure 11.20*, which occupies the widest area. *Table 11.3* shows the corresponding second-level alarm values on that frequency band:

| Counter | D [200, 300] A-7-SA1 | D [300, 400] A-7-SA1 | D [400, 500] A-7-SA1 |
|---|---|---|---|
| 2008-05-01 | 0.138 | 0.058 | 0.053 |
| 2008-05-02 | 0.141 | 0.058 | 0.053 |
| 2008-05-03 | 0.145 | 0.059 | 0.054 |
| 2008-05-04 | 0.148 | 0.06 | 0.054 |
| 2008-05-05 | 0.15 | 0.054 | 0.05 |
| 2008-05-06 | 0.144 | 0.05 | 0.046 |
| 2008-05-07 | 0.14 | 0.048 | 0.045 |
| 2008-05-08 | 0.134 | 0.047 | 0.046 |
| 2008-05-09 | 0.132 | 0.045 | 0.045 |
| 2008-05-10 | 0.132 | 0.045 | 0.048 |
| 2008-05-11 | 0.132 | 0.045 | 0.049 |
| 2008-05-12 | 0.132 | 0.045 | 0.049 |
| 2008-05-13 | 0.134 | 0.044 | 0.049 |
| 2008-05-14 | 0.132 | 0.044 | 0.05 |
| 2008-05-15 | 0.129 | 0.042 | 0.048 |

Table 11.3 – Second-level alarms on three frequency bands of the A7-SA1 sensor during the maintenance window

For example, *Table 11.3* confirms that the second-level alarm values on the 200–300 Hz frequency band (the highlighted column) are greater than the 300–400 Hz and 400–500 Hz frequency bands of the same signal at the beginning of May 2008.

Finally, *Figure 11.21* shows the second-level alarms inside a line plot:

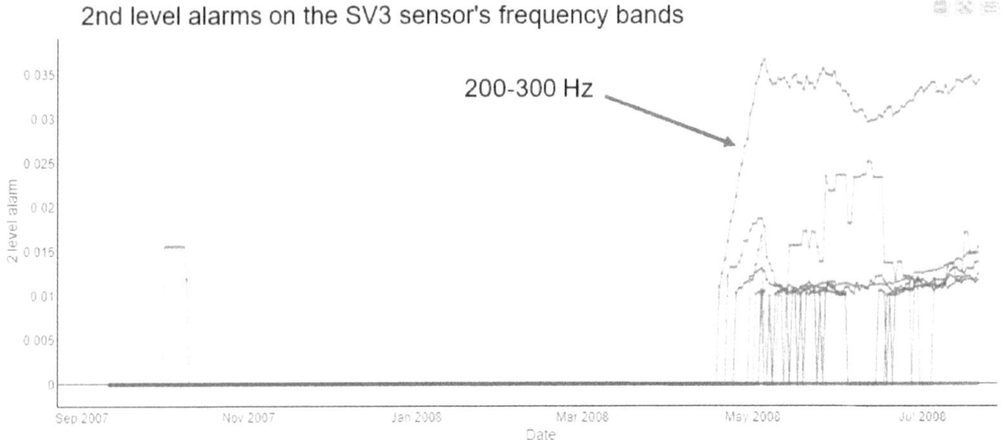


Figure 11.21 – Line plot showing the magnitudes of the second-level alarms on selected frequency bands through the maintenance window

The preceding line plot shows the exact second-level alarm values on single-frequency bands of the SV3 sensor. Although the second-level alarms are nonzero on all frequency bands close to the rotor breakdown, so all auto-regressive models throw remarkable errors, the 200–300 Hz frequency band shows the greatest errors, with second-level alarm values greater than 0.3. This confirms what we could see in the stacked area chart of *Figure 11.20* and in *Table 11.3*.

Furthermore, the line plot shows that the single-frequency bands show errors greater than 0.01 on all frequency bands close to the rotor breakdown. Therefore, we use 0.01 as the threshold in deployment. Additionally, we could tune the alarm system to be more or less tolerant. If we want to be more conservative and retire the rotor before it breaks at all costs, we can use a higher threshold. If we want to be more tolerant, and risk that the rotor breaks, then a lower threshold is fine. However, note that the latter approach might generate a number of false alarms, which we are already trying to reduce by calculating the second-level alarms. However, this conservative approach is used when examples of failures are not available and, thus, the models cannot be optimized, and this is the best we can do.

The next subsection finishes the anomaly detection application based on an auto-regressive model. It introduces the process of making a REST call from the deployment workflow to call any action.

## *Triggering an action via REST*

In the deployment workflow of the auto-regressive models, we make a **REST** call for an action instead of implementing the action inside it. This makes the deployment workflow more flexible: the same deployment workflow can trigger varying actions, and the same action can be triggered from multiple workflows.

> **Note**
>
> REST stands for *Representational State Transfer* and refers to the most predominant architecture for obtaining and managing data across web-based applications.

The deployment workflow performs the model deployment, as depicted in *Figure 11.18* (which is available from the KNIME Hub at `https://kni.me/w/MQ8JjydDub8OADVQ`), and the following steps that call the action:

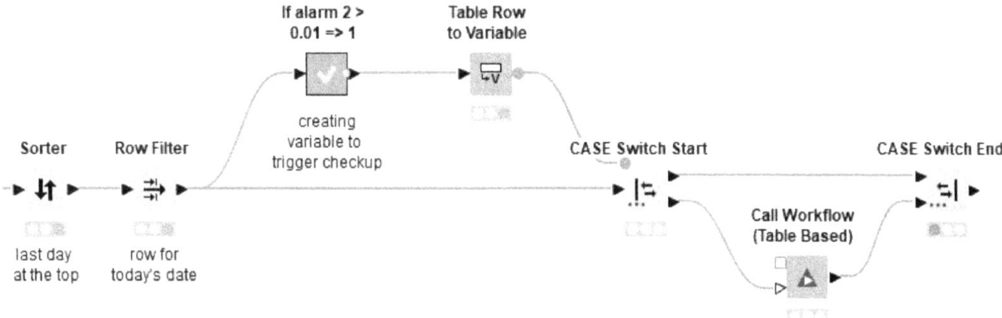


Figure 11.22 – A deployment workflow triggering an action via REST

The workflow activates the alarm if the latest available data exceeds the threshold for a second-level alarm (0.01) on sufficiently many (50%) of the frequency bands as implemented inside the `If alarm 2 > 0.01 => 1` metanode. If the alarm is active, the bottom branch of the *CASE Switch Start* node activates, and the **Call Workflow (Table Based)** node calls an action from another workflow via REST.

For example, the workflow could call a workflow that sends an email at advanced warning level. Alternatively, it could call a workflow that switches off the whole system, even in the middle of the night without human intervention. One example of a workflow that can be triggered via a REST call is shown in *Figure 11.23*:

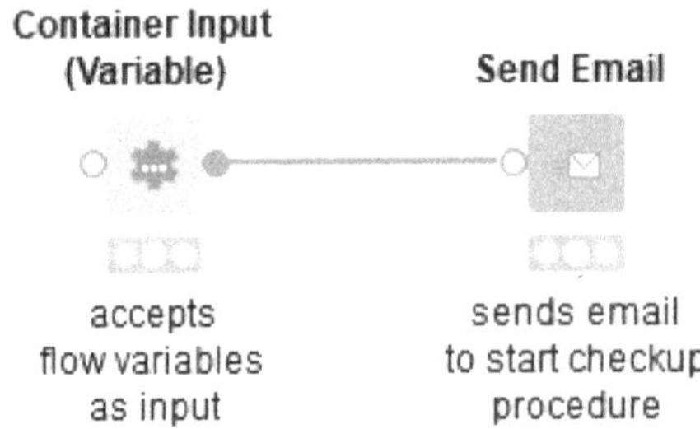


Figure 11.23 – An example of a workflow to call via REST

In this workflow, the action is sending an email. The **Send Email** node executes and sends the email to the mechanical support as soon as the deployment workflow calls this workflow. The **Container Input** node receives the input parameters from the **Call Workflow (Table Based)** node or any other external caller. If the workflow had an output, a **Container Output** node would appear at the end of the workflow and pass the output data or parameters to the external caller. You can find these **Container Input** and **Container Output** nodes in all workflows that can be called via REST, no matter what the action is.

# Summary

In this chapter, you completed a use case of anomaly detection for predictive maintenance. You gained a comprehensive toolkit for analyzing anomalies in IoT data, starting from a visual exploration and moving on to a control chart and an auto-regressive model. Finally, you learned how to trigger an action automatically via REST.

This example use case works as a reference for other anomaly detection use cases. Data standardization, looping over multiple frequency bands, building a control chart, training an auto-regressive model, calculating the first- and second-level alarms, and finally, triggering an action via REST are standard pieces of any anomaly detection application.

In the next chapter, we will continue working with a regression model for another common use case – demand prediction. Also, we will utilize the power of Spark in modeling.

## Questions

1. Which of the following features do you normally *not* find in IoT time series data?

   A. Timestamp

   B. FFT frequency

   C. FFT amplitude

   D. Class "anomaly"/"normal"

2. Why is the second-level alarm defined as the moving average of the first-level alarms?

   A. To account for anomalies that persist over time

   B. To remove the ACF on the frequency band

   C. To standardize the differences between the frequency bands

   D. To determine the threshold for deployment

3. How could you implement an anomaly detection system with a shorter warning time?

   A. Consider only the most sensitive frequency bands.

   B. Tolerate greater errors before raising an alarm.

   C. Train a more accurate auto-regressive model.

   D. Increase the number of past values as regressors.

# Part 3: Forecasting on Mixed Platforms

So far, we have seen solutions to the most common time series problems. In this part, we extend the previously described solutions to be more scalable, multivariate, and integrated and introduce advanced examples of demand prediction and stock price prediction. The following are the chapters included in this part:

- *Chapter 12, Predicting Taxi Demand on the Spark Platform*
- *Chapter 13, GPU Accelerated Model for Multivariate Forecasting*
- *Chapter 14, Combining KNIME and H2O to Predict Stock Prices*

# 12
# Predicting Taxi Demand on the Spark Platform

**Demand prediction** is one of the most popular applications of time series analysis. We can predict, for example, the demand for electricity in households, restock in the retail industry, and taxi drives in a large city. Regardless of the application, the idea is the same: use historical data and possibly some external information to predict the future demand. Then, use the predictions to optimize the supply chain or service management. What varies between the applications is the length of the forecast horizon and the granularity of the historical data. While restocks might be planned for the upcoming *months* based on *daily* data, the size of a taxi fleet might be adjusted for the next *days* or even *hours*, based on *hourly* data.

Therefore, different demand prediction applications work on very different *data volumes*. Historical data that adds up every hour or minute will likely result in a much larger volume than data that updates weekly or monthly. In the end, the volume determines whether you can run the application locally or not. The taxi demand prediction application represents the latter one. Recording every taxi trip in a large city easily produces millions, even billions, of rows over time, which are too much to process on a single computer. In such a case, we can utilize a cluster of several machines and a dedicated execution engine for big data such as **Apache Spark**.

In this chapter, we will complete a taxi demand prediction application while working through the following topics:

- Predicting taxi demand in **New York City** (**NYC**)
- Connecting to the Spark platform and preparing the data
- Training a random forest model on Spark
- Building the deployment application

You will learn how to connect to a remote big data environment and create and execute Spark applications from KNIME Analytics Platform. You will familiarize yourself with the Spark-compatible, code-free nodes for data preprocessing and data mining. Furthermore, you will learn how to complement your Spark applications with nodes for custom Spark queries and KNIME native nodes.

## Technical requirements

The following are the prerequisites for this chapter.

- KNIME Analytics Platform with KNIME Extension for Apache Spark to be installed
- For local execution: KNIME Extension for Local Big Data Environments to be installed
- For remote execution: The KNIME Big Data Connectors extension, or a dedicated extension for connecting to cloud storage to be installed

All the workflows introduced in the chapter are available on the KNIME Hub under `https://kni.me/s/XfLEQY_FHw3-CI1P` and on GitHub under `https://github.com/PacktPublishing/Codeless-Time-Series-Analysis-with-KNIME/tree/main/Chapter12`. The optional workflows for accessing and preprocessing big data are available on the KNIME Hub under `https://kni.me/w/yZI74OtdOBVajpsT`.

## Predicting taxi demand in NYC

Taxi demand prediction in large cities contributes to the satisfaction of a wide audience. The taxi fleet will be working more effectively, the customers will get their rides on time, and even city planners can benefit from knowing the taxi rush hours throughout the day and week.

We demonstrate the taxi demand prediction use case with the NYC taxi dataset (available at `https://www1.nyc.gov/site/tlc/about/tlc-trip-record-data.page`) provided by the NYC **Taxi and Limousine Commission** (**TLC**). The data contains altogether over 1 billion taxi trips from January 2009 forward. For each taxi trip, detailed information is recorded, such as the pick-up/drop-off date, time, and location, the type of the taxi (yellow/green/for-hire vehicle), passenger count, and fare.

The demand prediction means concretely predicting the expected count of taxi trips in the next hour based on the trip counts in the previous hours. The goal is to train the model on data from one year and predict the hourly trip counts in the next year. Because the trip counts of the different taxi types are different in their dynamics, and the time of the pandemic was characterized by reduced traffic, we limit the analysis to the *yellow taxis*, train the model on data from the year 2017, and apply it to data from the year 2018.

> **Note**
>
> The analysis can be extended to other/multiple years. Notice, though, that extra preprocessing might be needed because columns are removed, renamed, and/or added from year to year.

The size of the selected data sample is about 150 KB. This amount of data can be processed on a local machine, and we will use it to build a prototype of a big data workflow that will later execute remotely using all data. Therefore, access to a remote big data cluster is not required to complete the use case of this chapter.

In the next section, we will start with the implementation of the application on KNIME Analytics Platform and introduce you to the relevant concepts and nodes.

# Connecting to the Spark platform and preparing the data

In this section, we'll show you how to start the Spark application in KNIME by connecting to the cluster and loading data into it. We'll also introduce you to the Spark nodes, which you'll need in the prediction task in the next section. We'll cover these topics in the following subsections:

- Introducing the Hadoop ecosystem
- Accessing the data and loading it into Spark
- Introducing the Spark compatible nodes

In the first subsection, we explain what the Hadoop ecosystem is and show how to access it from a KNIME workflow.

## Introducing the Hadoop ecosystem

The **Apache Hadoop ecosystem** is an open source software framework that combines several computers into a computing cluster within which the processing tasks are split into smaller pieces and executed parallelly. *Figure 12.1* illustrates the Hadoop framework:

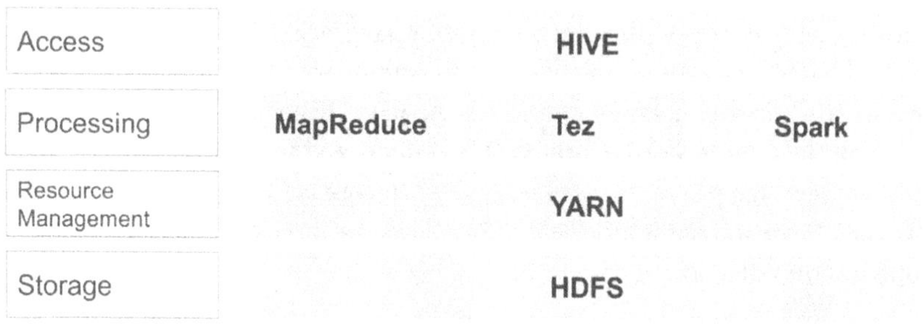

| | | | |
|---|---|---|---|
| Access | | **HIVE** | |
| Processing | **MapReduce** | **Tez** | **Spark** |
| Resource Management | | **YARN** | |
| Storage | | **HDFS** | |

Figure 12.1 – Illustrating the Hadoop software framework

The tasks and components in the Hadoop framework are the following:

- The **Hadoop Distributed File System (HDFS)** for storing large files
- The cluster's resource management system (*YARN*) for allocating and monitoring resources within the cluster
- The execution engine (*Apache Spark*, for example) for analytics tasks
- The data warehouse (*Apache Hive*, for example) for extracting and summarizing data with SQL-like queries

Next, we will explain how to connect to the distributed file system.

### Connecting to the HDFS

Follow these steps to connect to a remote file system:

1. Connect to a Spark compatible remote file system with the dedicated **connector** node, such as HDFS Connector, HTTP(S) Connector, or Amazon S3 Connector.
2. If required, use the relevant **authentication** node to access the remote service. For example, for Amazon S3, use the **Amazon Authentication** node. Notice that you will need your own credentials (for example, access key ID and secret key) at this step because the cloud storage is a paid service.

If you don't have access to a remote cluster, you can work with a sample of the real data in a local Hadoop ecosystem. Next, we will show how to create such a local big data environment.

### Creating a local big data environment

A local big data environment is a fully functional Hadoop ecosystem on your local machine, which lets you prototype big data workflows before eventually moving into remote, distributed processing. At that point, you will only need to replace the connector nodes at the beginning, while all other parts of the workflow stay the same.

You can create the local big data environment with the **Create Local Big Data Environment** node. It creates a fully functional big data environment with access to Apache Hive, Apache Spark, and HDFS. In the final big data workflow, you would connect to Apache Hive with the **Hive Connector** node, to Apache Spark with the **Create Spark Context (Livy)** node, and to the file storage with the **HDFS Connector** node, while in the prototype workflow, you can connect to all components with a single Create Local Big Data Environment node. *Figure 12.2* shows the three connection output ports of the node and its configuration dialog:

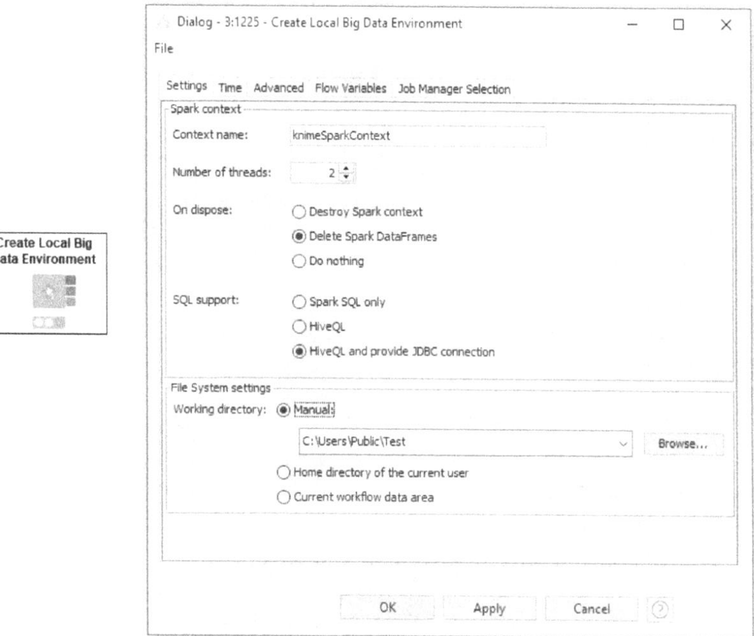


Figure 12.2 – Configuring the local big data environment

The three output ports of **Create Local Big Data Environment** are the top red square for the local Hive connection, the middle blue square for the local HDFS connection, and the bottom gray square for the local Spark context. The configuration dialog of the node provides a few setting options as follows:

- **Context name**: Using this field, you can change the name of the Spark context that the node creates.
- **On dispose**: Via this radio button, you can select how to handle the Spark data frames when closing the workflow.
- **SQL support**: Via this radio button, you can disable/enable data manipulation on the local Hive instance and determine which syntax the Spark SQL nodes support when connected downstream.
- **Working directory**: This field allows you to select the file system location on your machine.

If you have no preference for these settings, you can execute the node using the default configuration.

> **Note**
>
> By default, the Spark data frames will be deleted when you close the workflow, which frees up the resources allocated to the workflow.

In the next subsection, we will explain how to load data into Spark.

## Accessing the data and loading it into Spark

In this subsection, we show how to load the taxi trip data from file storage, where it is stored as a **Parquet** file, into a **Spark data frame**.

> **Note**
>
> `Parquet` is a dedicated file format for big data as it is optimized for performance. It stores the data in columns and not as rows such as, for example, a CSV file.

We access the Parquet file already pre-processed, and it is available in the **workflow data area** of the training workflow (available under `https://kni.me/w/13wY0Bz-2wUAxffc`). However, if you are accessing remote file storage, you should first upload the Parquet files from the `dataset2017` folder in the workflow data area to the remote file system with the `Transfer Files` node.

*Figure 12.3* shows a sample of the Parquet file in a local data table:

| Row ID | L pickup_timestamp | I pickup_year | I pickup_month | I pickup_dayofmonth | I pickup_hour | L trip_count | pickup_datetime | I pickup_day_num |
|---|---|---|---|---|---|---|---|---|
| Row0 | 1509073285 | 2017 | 10 | 27 | 3 | 3372 | 27.Oct.2017 05:01:25.000 | 6 |
| Row1 | 1509080385 | 2017 | 10 | 27 | 4 | 2755 | 27.Oct.2017 06:59:45.000 | 6 |
| Row2 | 1509081126 | 2017 | 10 | 27 | 5 | 3687 | 27.Oct.2017 07:12:06.000 | 6 |
| Row3 | 1509084299 | 2017 | 10 | 27 | 6 | 8716 | 27.Oct.2017 08:04:59.000 | 6 |
| Row4 | 1509088100 | 2017 | 10 | 27 | 7 | 15433 | 27.Oct.2017 09:08:20.000 | 6 |
| Row5 | 1509093447 | 2017 | 10 | 27 | 8 | 17670 | 27.Oct.2017 10:37:27.000 | 6 |
| Row6 | 1509098305 | 2017 | 10 | 27 | 9 | 17244 | 27.Oct.2017 11:58:25.000 | 6 |
| Row7 | 1509098893 | 2017 | 10 | 27 | 10 | 15997 | 27.Oct.2017 12:08:13.000 | 6 |
| Row8 | 1509105592 | 2017 | 10 | 27 | 11 | 15701 | 27.Oct.2017 13:59:52.000 | 6 |
| Row9 | 1509106598 | 2017 | 10 | 27 | 12 | 16457 | 27.Oct.2017 14:16:38.000 | 6 |
| Row10 | 1509109355 | 2017 | 10 | 27 | 13 | 16089 | 27.Oct.2017 15:02:35.000 | 6 |
| Row11 | 1509112948 | 2017 | 10 | 27 | 14 | 17672 | 27.Oct.2017 16:02:28.000 | 6 |
| Row12 | 1509116403 | 2017 | 10 | 27 | 15 | 16927 | 27.Oct.2017 17:00:03.000 | 6 |
| Row13 | 1509120054 | 2017 | 10 | 27 | 16 | 15019 | 27.Oct.2017 18:00:54.000 | 6 |
| Row14 | 1509126686 | 2017 | 10 | 27 | 17 | 18242 | 27.Oct.2017 19:51:26.000 | 6 |
| Row15 | 1509128183 | 2017 | 10 | 27 | 18 | 21073 | 27.Oct.2017 20:16:23.000 | 6 |

Figure 12.3 – A sample of the pre-processed training data

The pre-processed data contains the number of taxi trips per pickup timestamp and the additional date and time fields (year, month, day, and hour) extracted from the timestamp.

> **Note**
>
> If you are interested, you can also access the raw data from `https://www1.nyc.gov/site/tlc/about/tlc-trip-record-data.page` and pre-process it yourself. These steps are not discussed in this chapter, but they are implemented in the workflow available under `https://kni.me/w/yZI74OtdOBVajpsT`. Executing the workflow requires access to Amazon S3.

If you are connected to a remote file system, and the file already resides there, then the next step is to create a **Spark context** (connection to the Spark cluster) with the **Create Spark Context (Livy)** node. The node requires the following configurations:

- Select the *Spark version* (minimum Spark 2.2).
- Provide the *authentication*. If Livy requires Kerberos authentication, follow the steps outlined in the *Speaking Kerberos with KNIME Big Data Extensions* blog post available at `https://www.knime.com/blog/speaking-kerberos-with-knime-big-data-extensions` to set up your KNIME Analytics Platform accordingly.
- Specify the *staging area for Spark jobs* as a directory in the connected remote file system for transferring temporary files between KNIME and the Spark context. This configuration is only necessary if you are connected to Amazon S3 or Azure Blob Storage. Otherwise, the user home directory will be used by default.

> **Note**
>
> Apache Livy is an open source REST interface for interacting with Apache Spark to run all Spark jobs. Livy needs to be installed as a service in your cluster. Please consult the Apache Livy setup guide, available at `https://docs.knime.com/2018-12/bigdata_spark_installation_guide/index.html#livy_cdh`, for the instructions.

If you are working in a local Hadoop environment, then you only need to use the Create Local Big Data Environment node as introduced in the *Creating a local big data environment* subsection.

After establishing the connection, the final step is to create the Spark data frame with the **Parquet to Spark** node. After that, the data is ready for preprocessing and analyzing in Spark. Before we do, we will introduce the Spark nodes in the next subsection.

## Introducing the Spark compatible nodes

Creating and executing Spark applications from KNIME is possible with the **Spark compatible nodes** that are a part of the *KNIME Extension for Apache Spark*. The Spark nodes vary from simple data manipulation tasks to machine learning and nodes for advanced custom queries, such as Spark SQL Query and PySpark Script nodes. Most Spark nodes have a similar appearance and *visual configuration dialogs* as their KNIME native counterparts. *Figure 12.4* shows the **Spark GroupBy** node and its configuration dialog as an example:

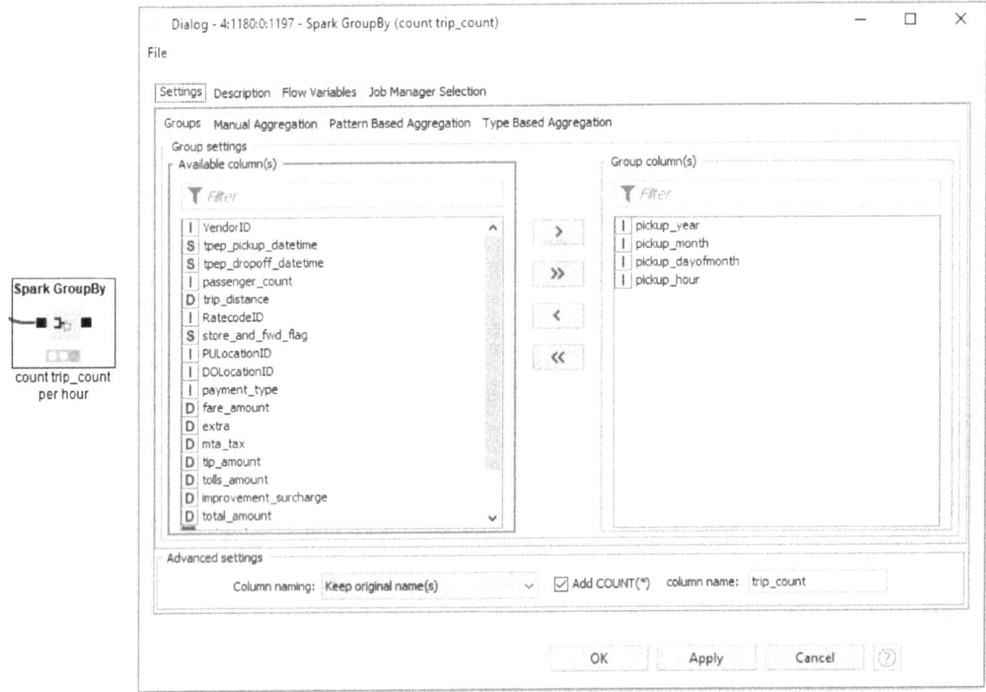


Figure 12.4 – Spark GroupBy node as an example of a Spark node with a visual configuration

The Spark GroupBy node has black rectangular input and output ports, which is a dedicated port type for a **Spark data frame**. Other than that, the configuration of the Spark GroupBy node works the same way as configuring the GroupBy node, and you can, therefore, switch to Spark execution without learning a new script.

For custom queries, *Figure 12.5* shows the script editor of the **Spark SQL Query** node as an example:

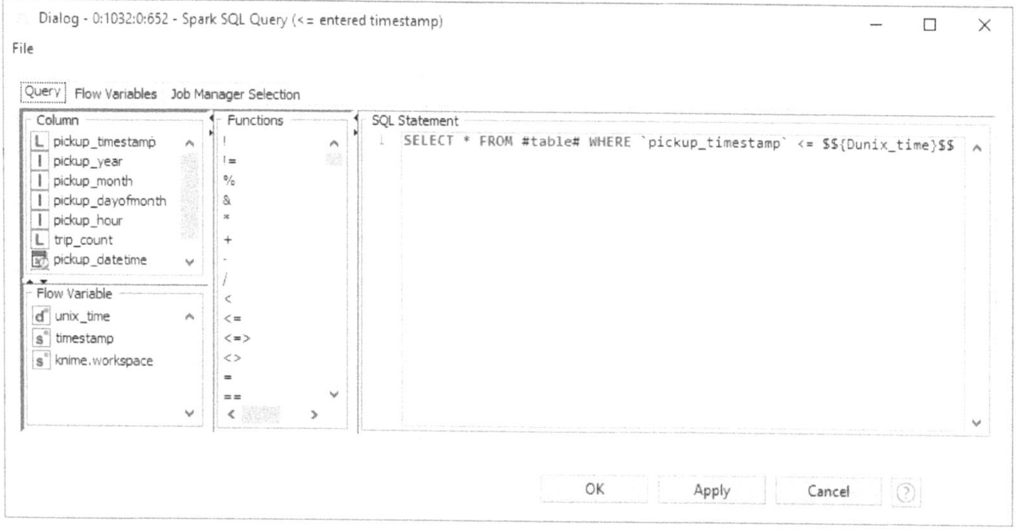

Figure 12.5 – The script editor of the Spark SQL query node

In the script editor, you can write any query in Spark SQL syntax and use elements from the **Column**, **Flow Variable**, and **Functions** panels in the script by double-clicking them. The `#table#` placeholder in the query corresponds to the input data frame of the node.

Furthermore, as with local KNIME nodes, you can inspect the intermediate results by retrieving a sample of the data in the node's output. You can also mix and match KNIME nodes with the Spark nodes in the same workflow. For example, you can pass flow variables to Spark nodes and retrieve data from Spark as local tables.

In the next section, we will show the Spark nodes in practice in the prediction application.

## Training a random forest model on Spark

In this section, we will explore and preprocess the historical taxi trip data and train and evaluate a random forest model for taxi demand prediction on Spark. We will introduce these steps in the following subsections:

1. Exploring the seasonalities via line plots and auto-correlation plots
2. Preprocessing the data
3. Training and testing the Spark random forest model

The steps in the application are also depicted in the training workflow in *Figure 12.6* (accessible on the KNIME Hub under `https://kni.me/w/13wY0Bz-2wUAxffc`):

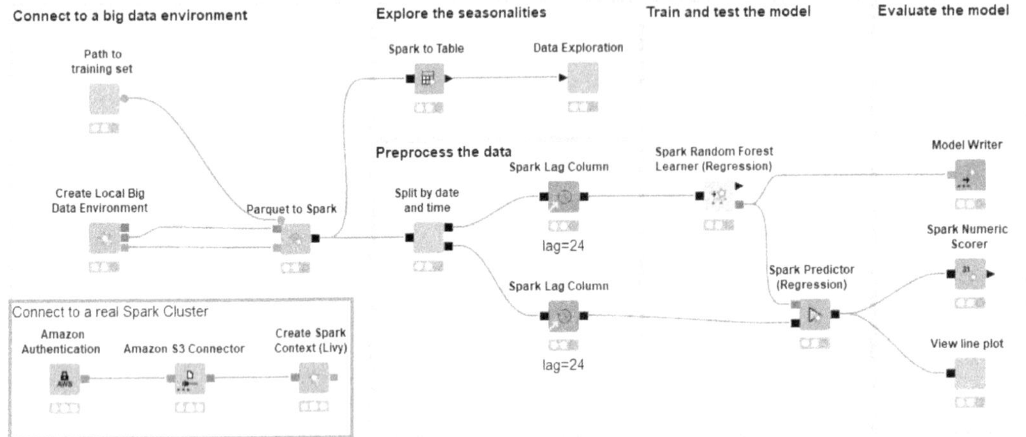


Figure 12.6 – The workflow training a Spark random forest model for demand prediction

The first part of the workflow loads the Parquet files onto Spark as introduced in the *Accessing the data and loading it into Spark* subsection. The downstream parts of the workflow – data exploration, preprocessing, model training and testing, and model evaluation – are introduced in the subsections that follow.

In the first subsection, we will explore the taxi trip data visually.

## Exploring seasonalities via line plots and auto-correlation plot

We explore the data in **line plots** and an **auto-correlation plot**. The line plots show how regularly the demand fluctuates, how much training data we need, and whether we can apply the model to new data from different years. An auto-correlation plot shows the dominant seasonality and determines the number of past values as predictors. The plots in this subsection are created inside the **Data Exploration** component in the training workflow (*Figure 12.6*) with the **Line Plot (Plotly)** node and **Inspect Seasonality** component.

The line plot in *Figure 12.7* shows the trip count per hour in the second half of the year 2017:

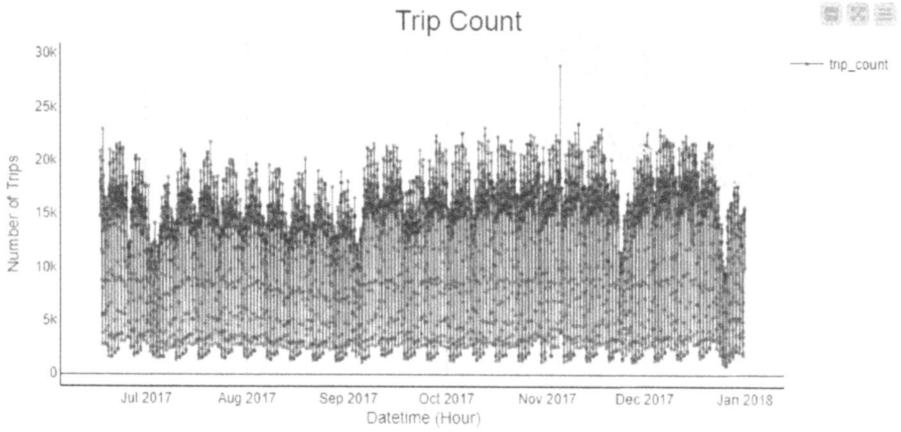

Figure 12.7 – A line plot showing the trip count per hour

The peaks and lows in the line plot repeat regularly, except for days with some special occasions, which are highlighted by arrows in the line plot. On these days, the patterns deviate from the other times as the trip count is exceptionally high or low. For example, the peak is exceptionally high on November 5, the day of the NYC Marathon, and exceptionally low at the end of November and December, at the time of the Thanksgiving and Christmas holidays.

The auto-correlation plot in *Figure 12.8* compares the regular dynamics at different lags:

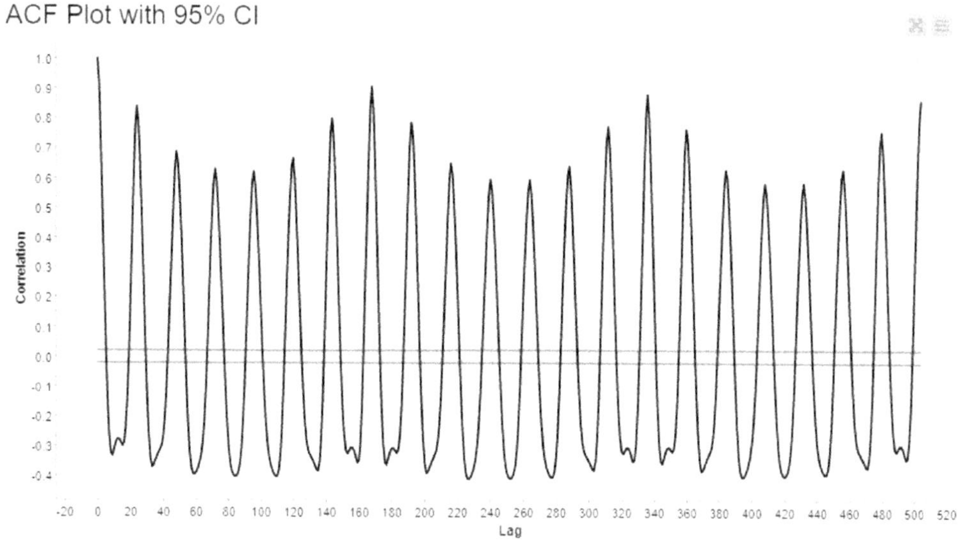


Figure 12.8 – The auto-correlation plot of the hourly taxi trips

The auto-correlation decays fast from the first lag to the twelfth lag. This means, the current trip count is a good estimate of the next hour's trip count, but when 2, 3, 4, up to 12 hours pass, the vaguer the relationship between the current and past hourly trip counts is, and the less informative the past values are for predicting the expected demand. However, after the twelfth lag, the auto-correlation values start increasing again reaching a peak at lag 24, so at the lag of 24 hours. The same pattern repeats up to the end of the plot. This indicates **daily seasonality** in the trip count. In addition, some peaks are higher than the others, and the highest peaks occur every 168 lags, so at a lag of 7 days. This indicates **weekly seasonality**.

Next, we plot a subset of the data in another line plot to inspect the daily seasonal pattern in more detail. The line plot in *Figure 12.9* shows the trip counts for only the first weeks of January:

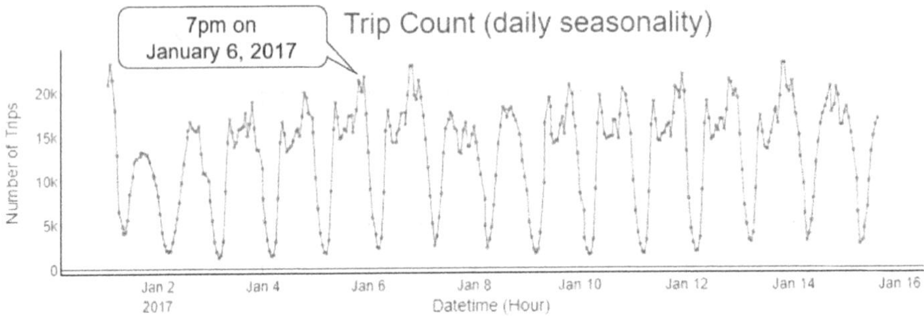


Fig 12.9 – The line plot showing the daily seasonality in taxi trips

The line plot shows the trip counts through the hours of the selected days at the beginning of January. On all days, there is a peak at 7 p.m., as shown by the annotation on the line plot. The daily low seems to occur about 8 hours after the peak, at 3 a.m. This means that the daily pattern consists of a wide peak covering the evening and afternoon hours, and a sharp low covering the early morning hours.

For the weekly pattern, we calculate the total number of taxi trips on each day and plot the aggregated data in a line plot:

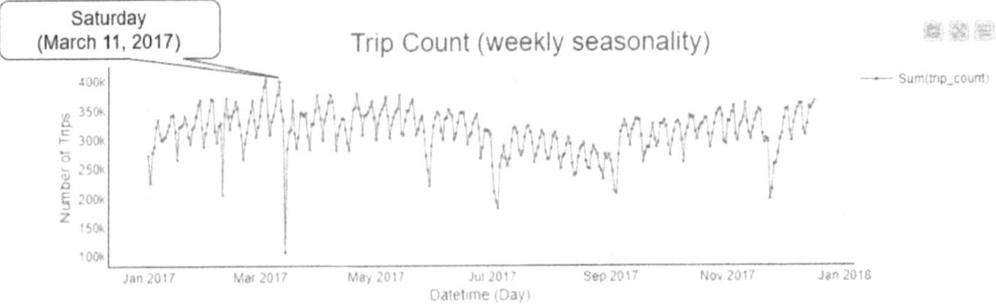


Figure 12.10 – A line plot showing the weekly seasonality in taxi trips

The weekly pattern is less regular than the daily pattern. What we can see, though, is that Saturday seems to be the busiest weekday in each week because the peaks occur every 7 days, as highlighted by the annotation on the plot. The lows always occur 2 days after the peak, so on Mondays. At the same time, the absolute counts are very different from week to week because the peaks and lows have different magnitudes.

The following is a summary of the insights gained from the visual exploration:

- The hourly taxi trips show a regular daily pattern with occasional outliers due to, for example, public holidays.
- Lag 1, and multiplications of lag 24 and lag 168, are the best predictors of the trip count.
- Daily seasonality is more regular than weekly seasonality.

In the next subsection, we will show how to perform the data preprocessing steps on Spark.

## Preprocessing the data

In this subsection, we will see how to pre-process the training data directly on the Spark platform by first, partitioning the data into training and test sets, and second, creating the vectors of past values as predictor columns.

### *Partitioning the data into training and test sets*

In **partitioning**, we reserve a part of the data for testing the model. From the previous section, we know that the data shows a *regular weekly pattern* and *irregularities occasionally*. We also know that the last month, December 2017, represents the data well because it contains irregularities due to the holidays in addition to the weekly pattern. We, therefore, use the data from January to November as the **training set** and December as the **test set**.

Because we want to split the data by a date value and this task doesn't have a dedicated Spark node, we use the Spark SQL Query node with the following query inside:

```
SELECT * FROM #table# WHERE 'pickup_timestamp' <= $${Dunix_
time}$$
```

Here, `pickup_timestamp` is the column containing the pickup timestamp of each taxi trip, and `unix_time` refers to November 30, 2017, which has been previously defined as a flow variable with the **Date&Time Configuration** node. You can find this Spark SQL Query node and the Date&Time Configuration node in the training workflow from inside the *Split by date and time* component in *Figure 12.6*.

> **Note**
>
> We cannot use the dedicated **Spark Partitioning** node in this case because the splitting is made by a date value.

In the next subsection, we will continue preprocessing by creating the predictor columns of past values.

### *Creating the predictor columns of past values*

We will create the predictor columns by transforming the one-dimensional time series into a multidimensional vector. We will transform the original column with hourly trip counts into multiple columns with the trip counts 1, 2, and so on, hours ago.

We can do this with the **Spark Lag Column** component (available on the KNIME Hub under `https://kni.me/c/vpE_LTbAOn96ZOg9`) shown in the workflow in *Figure 12.6*. In its configuration dialog, we can find the same settings as in the **Lag Column** node: the **lag** (the number of past values to consider) and the **lag interval** (the time difference between consecutive past values). Since we know from the data exploration that the length of the seasonal pattern is 24 hours, we apply `lag=24` and `lag interval=1`. This will produce 24 predictor columns that represent the trip counts in the previous 24 hours.

Furthermore, we use the hour of the day (`0` to `23`) and the day of the week (`1` to `7`) as additional predictor columns.

> **Note**
>
> You might ask why the predictor columns are created from the original data without handling the observed seasonality in the data. The reason here is that the random forest model is a highly parametric algorithm and doesn't necessarily profit from stationary training data. We tested this in an experiment, which is not discussed here but is available on the KNIME Hub under `https://kni.me/w/xD3HT1dyXH6jnmCb`.

In the next section, we will show how to train and test the prediction model on Spark.

## Training and testing the random forest model on Spark

In this subsection, we train and test a Spark random forest regression model on Spark. At the end of this subsection, we will also show how to retrieve the results locally and visualize them.

### *Training a Spark random forest (regression) model*

We train the model on the training set with the **Spark Random Forest Learner (Regression)** node as shown in the workflow in *Figure 12.6*. We selected the random forest as a powerful algorithm with a downside of large memory usage. To keep the execution time moderate in the local big data environment, we train a forest of only five trees with a maximum depth of 10. We select the `trip_count` column as the target column, the `pickup_hour` and `pickup_day_num` columns, and the 24 lagged columns as the predictor columns.

When we execute the node, the node produces the random forest model and a data table containing the **feature importance statistics**:

| Row ID | D Feature Importance |
|---|---|
| trip_count-1 | 0.533 |
| trip_count-24 | 0.249 |
| pickup_hour | 0.038 |
| trip_count-23 | 0.034 |
| trip_count-2 | 0.026 |
| trip_count-7 | 0.019 |
| trip_count-4 | 0.012 |
| trip_count-22 | 0.009 |
| trip_count-15 | 0.008 |
| trip_count-6 | 0.007 |

Figure 12.11 – A sample of the feature importance statistics of the Spark random forest regression model

The feature importance statistics table shows the most important features in descending order. For our demand prediction model, the most important predictor, apparently, is the trip count in the previous hour (`trip_count-1`), whose feature importance is `0.533`. The statistics are normalized so that they all (10 features shown in *Figure 12.11* plus 16 less important features) sum up to `1`. This means the trip count in the previous hour is a better predictor than all other features together! Another important feature is the trip count 24 hours ago (`trip_count-24`) with the value of `0.249`. All other features fall below `0.1`.

In the next subsection, we will apply and evaluate the model on the test set.

### *Testing and evaluating the model*

We apply the model to the test set with the **Spark Predictor (Regression)** node as shown at the right end of the training workflow in *Figure 12.6*. We will then calculate the numeric scoring metrics with the **Spark Numeric Scorer** node and compare the actual and predicted trip counts in a line plot.

For the numeric scoring metrics, Spark Numeric Scorer produces the following view:

Statistics - 4:1041 - Spark Numeric Scorer

File

| | |
|---|---|
| R²: | 0.976 |
| Mean absolute error: | 719.77 |
| Mean squared error: | 899,690.98 |
| Root mean squared error: | 948.52 |
| Mean signed difference: | 76.96 |

Figure 12.12 – The numeric scoring metrics of the Spark random forest model

In this view, the value of the **Mean absolute error** metric is about 720, which means that the predicted number of taxi trips deviates from the actual demand by 720 trips on average. With an hourly trip count of 10,000 to 20,000 taxis, this error indicates high accuracy. Furthermore, the value of the $\mathbf{R^2}$ metric is `0.976`. This means that the model can explain about 98% of the variation in the trip count in the next hour.

For a visual evaluation, we retrieve the test data into a local table with the **Spark to Table** node and visualize the predicted and actual trip counts in a line plot:

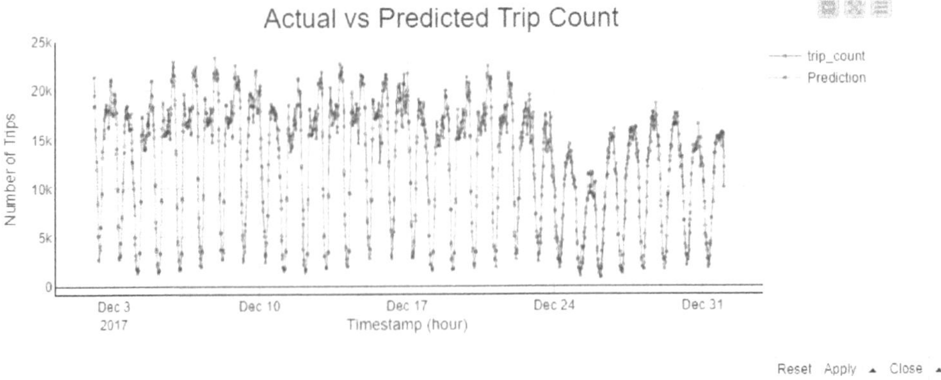


Figure 12.13 – The line plot for the actual and predicted trip counts in test data

The two lines for the actual and predicted trip counts are on top of each other, which indicates good prediction accuracy. Even the lower demand for taxis during Christmas time – as shown at the right end of the line plot – is predicted accurately.

As the last step of the training workflow, we save the model for deployment with the **Model Writer** node.

In the next section, we will show two ways of generating forecasts with the model.

# Building the deployment application

In this section, we introduce a deployment application that predicts the hourly trip counts on one day. We selected to predict the trip counts on July 1, 2018. We perform both static and dynamic deployment as introduced in the following subsections:

1. Predicting the trip count in the next hour (**static deployment**)
2. Predicting the trip count in the next 24 hours (**dynamic deployment**)

## Predicting the trip count in the next hour

The goal of this subsection is to predict the demand for taxis in the *first hour* on July 1, 2018, so at 00:00.

The required **seed data** for the prediction contains the 24 past values representing the hourly trip counts on June 30, 2018, and in addition, the hour of the day (`0`) and the day of the week (`1` since July 1, 2008, was a Sunday). We access the seed data already pre-processed as a Parquet file. The workflow containing the static deployment (accessible via `https://kni.me/w/wl2B4B5LNvj0Z4K9`) is shown in *Figure 12.14*:

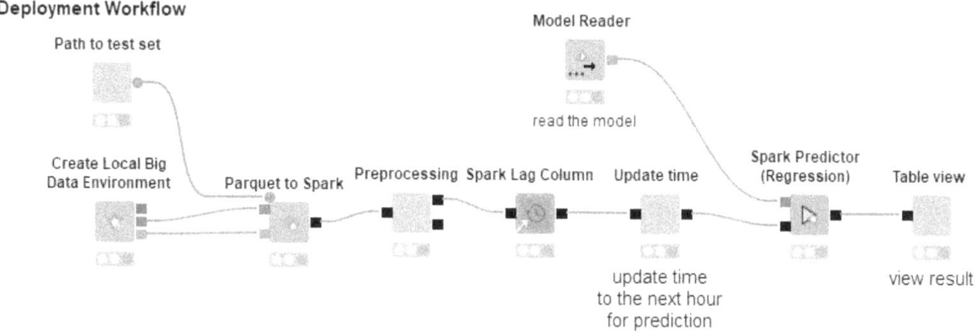


Figure 12.14 – The workflow for static deployment

The following are the steps included in the static deployment workflow:

1. First, it reads the preprocessed deployment file from the workflow data area and loads it into Spark with the Create Local Big Data Environment and Parquet to Spark nodes. Alternatively, you can also load the data into a remote big data environment and re-configure the workflow to read it from there as introduced in the *Accessing the data and loading it into Spark* subsection.
2. Next, it calculates the trip counts per hour and generates the vector of past values with the `Preprocessing` and Spark Lag Column components, respectively. Notice that the output of the Spark Lag Column component only outputs one row with 24 past values, that is, the 24 hours before July 1, 2018, at 00:00.
3. After that, it updates the timestamp in this row to the timestamp of the forecast (July 1, 2018, 00:00) with the `Update time` component.
4. Then, it reads the pre-trained Spark random forest regression model with the Model Reader node and applies the model to the row to predict with the Spark Predictor (Regression) node.
5. Finally, it displays the forecasted value in a local view with the `Table View` component.

The static deployment workflow predicts 10,741 trips in the first hour of July 1, 2018. While the prediction of one value might be useful for short-term planning, an estimate of the demand in the next 24 hours gives a more long-term perspective. We can achieve this via dynamic deployment, which we will introduce in the next subsection.

## Predicting the trip count in the next 24 hours

Dynamic deployment generates future *forecasts beyond the next value* by using the forecasted values as the past values of more future forecasts. We can implement the dynamic deployment with a recursive loop as shown in the workflow (accessible via `https://kni.me/w/wl2B4B5LNvj0Z4K9`) in *Figure 12.15*:

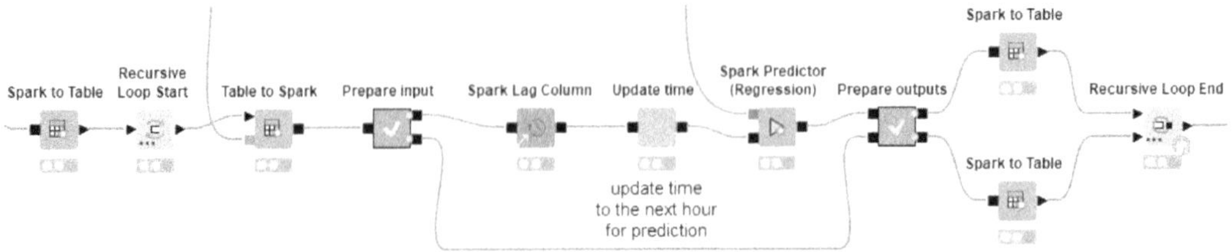


Figure 12.15 – The recursive loop for dynamic deployment

Before we start the recursive loop, we use the **Spark to Table** node, which converts a local data table to a Spark data frame. This is because the loop can only take a local data table as input. Besides that, the loop body completes the following steps 24 times – once for each hour to predict:

1. First, it reads the seed data containing the 24 past values with the **Recursive Loop Start** node and converts them into a Spark data frame with the **Table to Spark** node. These rows are used to generate the first prediction.
2. Next, inside the `Prepare input` meta node, it does the following:

   A. Duplicates the last row as a placeholder for the forecast with the **Spark Partitioning** and **Spark Concatenate** nodes

   B. Prepares the input (seed) data for the next prediction by removing the *first* (oldest) row from the input data with the Spark Partitioning node

3. After that, it generates the past columns as predictors with the Spark Lag Column component.
4. Then, it updates the timestamp of the forecasted value with the `Update time` component.
5. Next, it generates the forecast with the Spark Predictor (Regression) node.
6. Next, inside the `Prepare outputs` meta node, it does the following:

   A. Converts the prediction to a *long* data type with the Spark SQL Query node

   B. Adds the prediction as the *last* (newest) value into the seed data with the Spark Concatenate node

7. After that, it converts the outputs to Spark data frames with the Spark to Table nodes and passes the forecast into the top input and the updated seed data into the bottom input of the **Recursive Loop End** node.

When the loop has finished, we can collect the predictions from the output of the Recursive Loop End node, which we have set to stop after 24 iterations.

As the final step, we look into the actual hourly taxi trip counts on July 1, 2018, which we have downloaded from the TLC website (`https://www1.nyc.gov/site/tlc/about/tlc-trip-record-data.page`), and compare the dynamic forecasts and the actual values in the line plot and via numeric scoring metrics.

First, the line plot in *Figure 12.16* shows the actual and predicted hourly trip counts through July 1 in 2018:

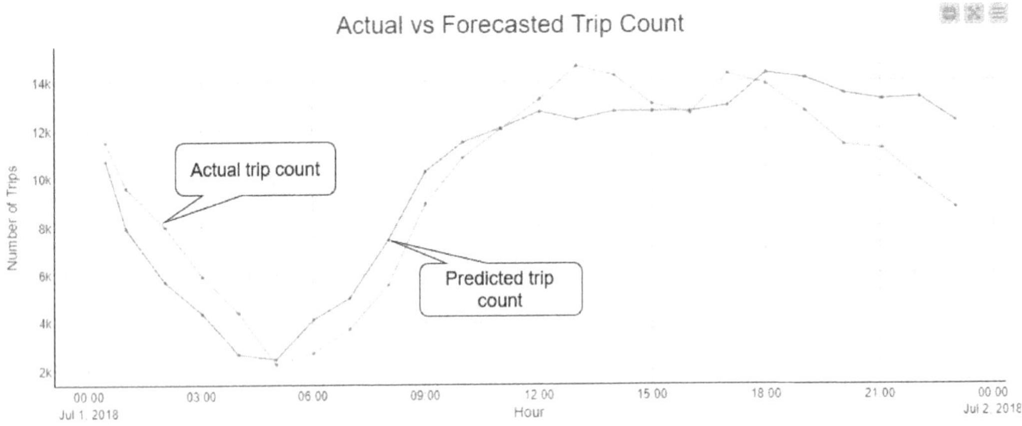


Figure 12.16 – The line plot of actual and predicted hourly trip counts in deployment data

In the line plot, the predicted trip count is slightly below the actual trip count for the first 6 hours and slightly above it for the next 6 hours, but in general, the counts are close to each other for the first 12 hours. After that, the gap between the lines becomes somewhat larger as the actual counts start decreasing faster than the predicted counts. This is expected, though, because the prediction accuracy decreases over time in dynamic deployment.

Second, the output view of the Numeric Scorer node shows the numeric scoring metrics:

Statistics - 0:1225 - Numeric Scorer

File

| | |
|---|---|
| $R^2$: | 0.8 |
| Mean absolute error: | 1,415.625 |
| Mean squared error: | 2,877,329.708 |
| Root mean squared error: | 1,696.269 |
| Mean signed difference: | 254.042 |
| Mean absolute percentage error: | 0.183 |

Figure 12.17 – The numeric scoring metrics of actual versus forecasted trip counts in deployment data

In this view, you can see that the **$R^2$** value of the forecasted versus actual values is `0.8`. It is lower than the **$R^2$** value reached in the static deployment setting (`0.976`, as shown in *Figure 12.12*). This means the explanatory power of the model decreases as the length of the forecast horizon increases. Furthermore, the mean absolute error is about 1,400 trips, which means that we will have an average uncertainty of about 1,400 trips per hour if we forecast the trip count maximum 24 hours ahead. This is double the number as in the static deployment where we only predict the next hour.

This concludes the deployment application, where we applied the trained and tested the model on real data – as is the final goal of the model. We leave it as an optional exercise for you to elaborate on the application, for example, via predicting a longer forecast horizon, via remote execution, or via automating the predictions with KNIME Server.

# Summary

In this chapter, you have completed a real-world taxi demand prediction application on the Spark platform.

We have shown you how to work with big data in KNIME and how to prototype big data workflows before accessing a remote cluster. You have, therefore, acquired a toolkit for accessing, preprocessing, and analyzing big data, which enables you with the full computational power of a remote cluster while working from the convenient visual environment in KNIME.

You have worked through training, testing, and deploying a demand prediction application using the random forest algorithm, enabling you with the necessary skills of building demand prediction applications in other fields as well, given that demand prediction is one of the classic applications of time series analysis.

In the next chapter, we extend the demand prediction problem into a multivariate case using an LSTM model.

# Questions

1. Which of the following does *not* contribute to more efficient data processing in a cluster environment?

   A. Connecting to a cluster of several machines

   B. Using Parquet file format

   C. Executing via Spark

   D. Retrieving data locall.

2. Performing Spark tasks in your workflows requires...

   A. Data as a Spark data frame

   B. A dedicated Spark node for the task

   C. A remote cluster

   D. Data in Parquet forma.

3. Which of the following often determines the appropriate granularity of the historical data?

   A. The available resources for the computation

   B. The forecast horizon

   C. The forecasting algorithm

   D. The number of predictor column.

4. Could you apply the same demand prediction model to forecast the trip count tomorrow?

   A. Yes, if the seasonality pattern is the same and there is no trend through the years.

   B. No, the model needs to be retrained as soon as enough historical data becomes available.

   C. Yes, if you increase the size of the seed data.

   D. No, because the model was trained on data with many outliers.

# 13
# GPU Accelerated Model for Multivariate Forecasting

**Time series analysis** models can become quite large, and their training can become computationally expensive. This is especially the case when moving from **univariate** to **multivariate** time series predictions. In some of these cases, GPUs can be used to accelerate the process.

So far, we have described univariate time series models, relying on past values of one time series to predict the future value of the same time series. Often, real-world problems and data are not that simple. If two time series correlate, the value of a variable at a given point in time can depend on the past values of the same variable and the past values of other variables from other series. Integrating such multiple variables into the input or output of the model is called multivariate time series analysis. A model for multivariate predictions can output just one value, which is the next value of one of the time series, or multiple values, which are the future values of multiple time series. The more values that are added to the input and the more values that are required at the output, the larger the model and the longer it takes to train.

When using a neural network model, it is possible to speed up the training execution by exploiting the computational power of **GPU**-powered machines. For the KNIME Deep Learning - Keras Integration, this requires a CUDA-enabled graphics card.

In this chapter, we will introduce a large feedforward fully connected neural network with 900 inputs and 30 outputs as an example of a complex model for multivariate time series prediction, and then we will show you how to enable its GPU execution on a GPU-powered machine. This chapter consists of the following sections:

- From univariate to multivariate – extending the prediction problem
- Building and training the multivariate neural architecture
- Enabling GPU execution for neural networks
- Building the deployment application

Here, you will learn how to prepare the input tensor for multivariate analysis, how to assemble a neural architecture to perform a multivariate prediction, and how to enable GPU execution for neural networks.

# Technical requirements

The following are the prerequisites for this chapter:

- A CUDA-enabled graphics card
- KNIME Analytics Platform with **KNIME Deep Learning – Keras Integration** installed
- KNIME Analytics Platform with **KNIME Python Integration** installed (for the **Conda Environment Propagation** node)
- **Conda** package manager installed on your machine

All of the workflows introduced in this chapter are available from the KNIME Hub at `https://kni.me/s/GxjXX6WmLi-WjLNx`.

# From univariate to multivariate – extending the prediction problem

Let's start by extending a univariate time series prediction problem to a multivariate time series prediction problem. To do that, we can go back to *Chapter 4 , Time Series Visualization*, where we discussed the visualization of the energy consumption time series dataset.

The raw energy consumption data originates from 6,000 households and businesses in Ireland, and it was collected by smart meters that recorded the energy consumption every half-hour in **kilowatts (kW)** between July 2009 and August 2010. The original data contains three columns: the timestamp, the ID of the smart meter, and the energy consumption. A few aggregated values have been calculated for every single ID to quantify the amount of energy used at different times of the day and week. Based on such aggregated values, the households have been clustered using a k-means algorithm, where k=30. Finally, the average time series for each one of the 30 clusters has been calculated. The final dataset contains 30 time series, with each representing the average energy consumption over time of a given cluster.

In *Chapter 10, Predicting Energy Demand with an LSTM Model*, we applied a neural network with an LSTM layer for the prediction of the next value given the past 30 values in the same time series, a univariate solution based on an LSTM neural network for the prediction of energy consumption for just one of the various clusters. In this chapter, we want to extend this univariate solution to a multivariate solution; to do this, we include past values of all clusters' time series inside the input tensor to predict the next value of multiple time series at once.

We will start with a solution that includes inputs from all the clusters' time series while only generating one prediction for the next value in a selected cluster's time series. Then, we will then expand the solution to predict the future values of all the clusters' time series at once.

**Correlated Features**

Adding additional data to the input tensor is only useful if the new features are not heavily correlated with existing input features. Adding features that strongly correlate with existing features will increase the amount of time the model takes to train without increasing the amount of information available to model. Also, it increases the risk of overfitting.

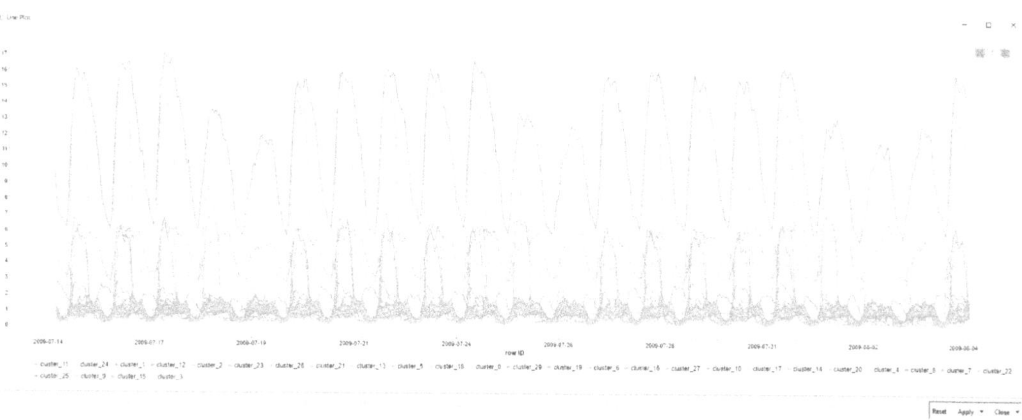

Figure 13.1 – All time series in the same plot; notice the daily and weekly seasonalities

In our case, the electricity consumption time series for the different clusters do show some degree of correlation, for example, they all follow the same weekly and daily seasonality (*Figure 13.1*). So, there might not be a huge gain in performance when moving from the univariate to the multivariate model. However, by adding many input features, we complicate the problem and increase the size of the network. Our attention will focus on improving the speed of the training algorithm to converge in a reasonably fast time.

# Building and training the multivariate neural architecture

Let's start with the simplest problem: only generating the predictions for one time series, *cluster_12*. To do this, we train a feedforward neural network to predict the next value of *cluster_12* given the past 30 values of all 30 time series in the dataset. The solution workflow, named *Multivariate_Training_one_output* and reported in *Figure 13.2*, covers the classic steps to import and prepare the data and then build, train, and evaluate the neural network:

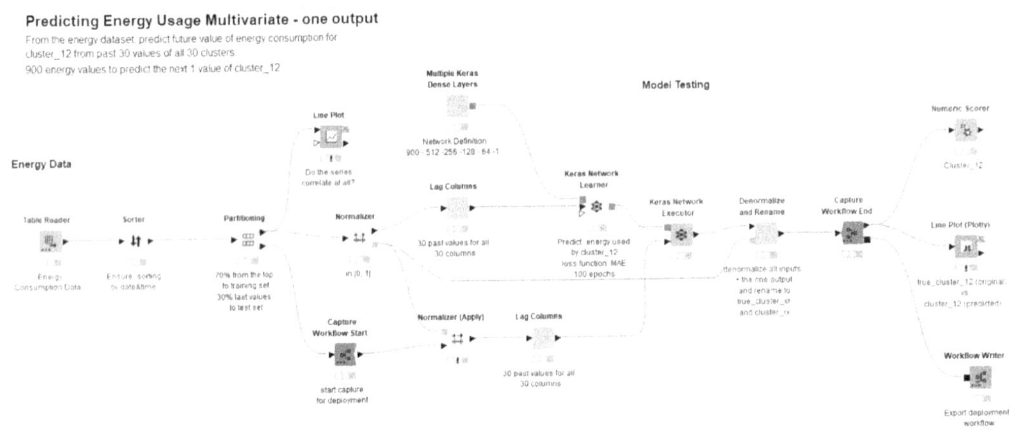


Figure 13.2 – The workflow for multivariate time series forecasting

After importing the data with the *Table Reader* node and sorting it to ensure its sequential order, all the time series are partitioned, using the first 70% for the training set and the remaining 30% for the test set. Next, all the values are normalized to the [0, 1] interval. So far, this is very similar to what we have done in the other chapters.

Now we want to build the input tensor on the network, including the 30 past values of the selected time series plus the 30 past values of all other time series. The construction of this input tensor happens within the *Lag Columns* component (*Figure 13.3*). This component loops over all 30 time series columns and, at each iteration, creates lagged copies of the time series till 1, 2, 3, … 30 steps back. All lagged and original time series are collected at the end of the loop. The final data table contains all time series at time t *xi (t)*, at time *t-1 xi (t-1)*, at time *t-2 xi (t-2)*, and so on until time *t-30 xi (t-30)*, for *i = 1, 2, 3, . . . 30*, where each *i* represents one of the 30 clusters' time series. The final data table includes 900 columns – 30 lagged copies for each of the 30 time series. Finally, the values in the columns of this data table are aggregated into a **Collection List** via the **Column Aggregator** node, which we did in the other deep learning chapters to create input tensors:

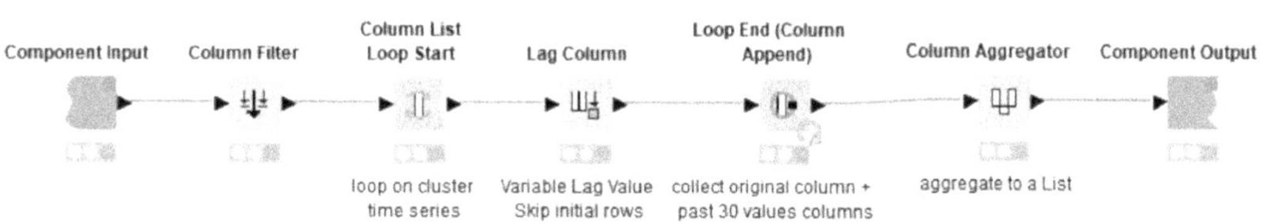


Figure 13.3 – Building the input vector for the network inside the Lag Columns component

The neural network is built inside the *Multiple Keras Dense Layer* component as a feedforward 900 - 512 - 256 -128 - 64 - 1 neural architecture, with ReLU activation functions (*Figure 13.4*). Notice the **Keras Dropout Layer** node after each **Keras Dense Layer** node. Since it is hard to properly dimension a neural architecture, dropout layers are often inserted inside large neural networks to randomly prevent the updating of some weights and, in this way, reduce overfitting.

The 900 values in the input layer of the network directly correspond to the 30 steps in the past for each one of the 30 time series. Therefore, at each time *t*, we have 900 inputs for the network.

The 1 output value represents one future value for one time series that we are currently forecasting. We will expand on this shortly:

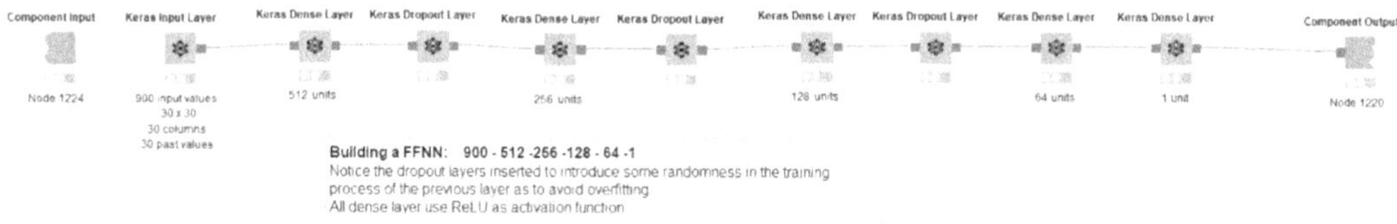


Figure 13.4 – Building a feedforward 900 - 512 - 256 -128 - 64 - 1 neural architecture

Now that the network architecture has been built and the data of the training set has been transformed to fit the input and output shapes of the network, we can train the Keras model with the **Keras Network Learner** node.

In the *Input Data* tab of the configuration dialog for the Keras Network Learner node, we select the collection column that we just created to be used in the network with the conversion type of *From Collection of Number (Double)*.

In the *Target Data* tab, we select the target column, which is the column that we want to generate forecasts for. In our case, this is *cluster_12* (*Figure 13.5*). We did not use a collection type column for this since it is a single value, so the conversion setting is *From Number (Double)*. We use the **Mean Absolute Error** (**MAE**) for our loss function, which is configurable beneath the target column selection.

In the *Options* tab, the **Adadelta** optimizer is selected with default parameters (the learning rate = 1.0, rho = 0.95, epsilon = 1.0E-8, and the learning rate decay = 0.05). We set the number of epochs to 100 with a batch size of 500 for the evaluation phase.

**Converting to a Multivariate Forecast**

To transform this model from the predictor of a single value to the predictor of multiple values, we simply change the number of units in the last layer of the network and add all time series columns in the **Target columns | Include** frame in the **Target Data** tab of the configuration dialog of the Keras Network Learner node.

To observe the training progress of the network, right-click on the **Keras Network Learner** node and select **Learning Monitor**. Then, inspect the *Loss* tab of the **Learning Monitor** to see the loss function over time. The accuracy plot is only useful when building a classification model:

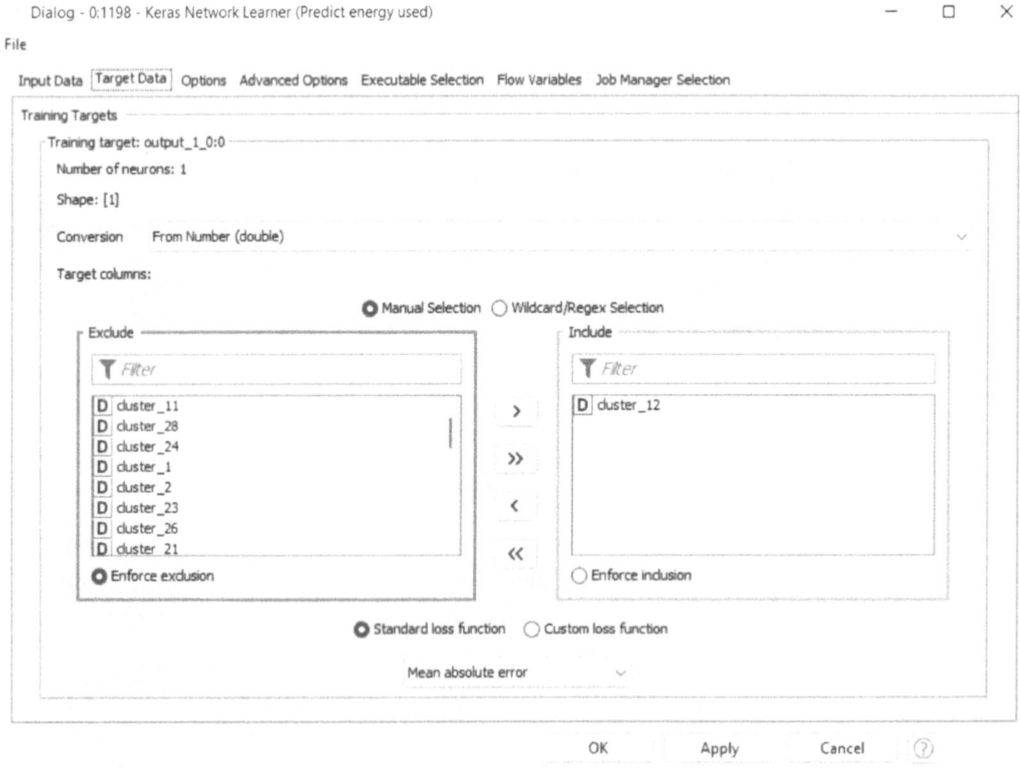


Figure 13.5 – The Target Data tab in the configuration dialog of the Keras Network Learner node

Now that we have trained the model, let's move and evaluate it on the test set. We apply the **Keras Network Executor** node, feeding it with the collection column including all 900 input values, as shown in the **Options** tab of its configuration dialog, again using the *From Collection to Number (Double)* conversion mode (*Figure 13.6*). In the same tab, the predicted value is set to be output as a number using the *To Number (double)* conversion and in a column named *output_1/BiasAdd:0_*. Note that we could not rename the output column to *cluster_12* just yet, since a *cluster_12* instance still exists in the input data table:

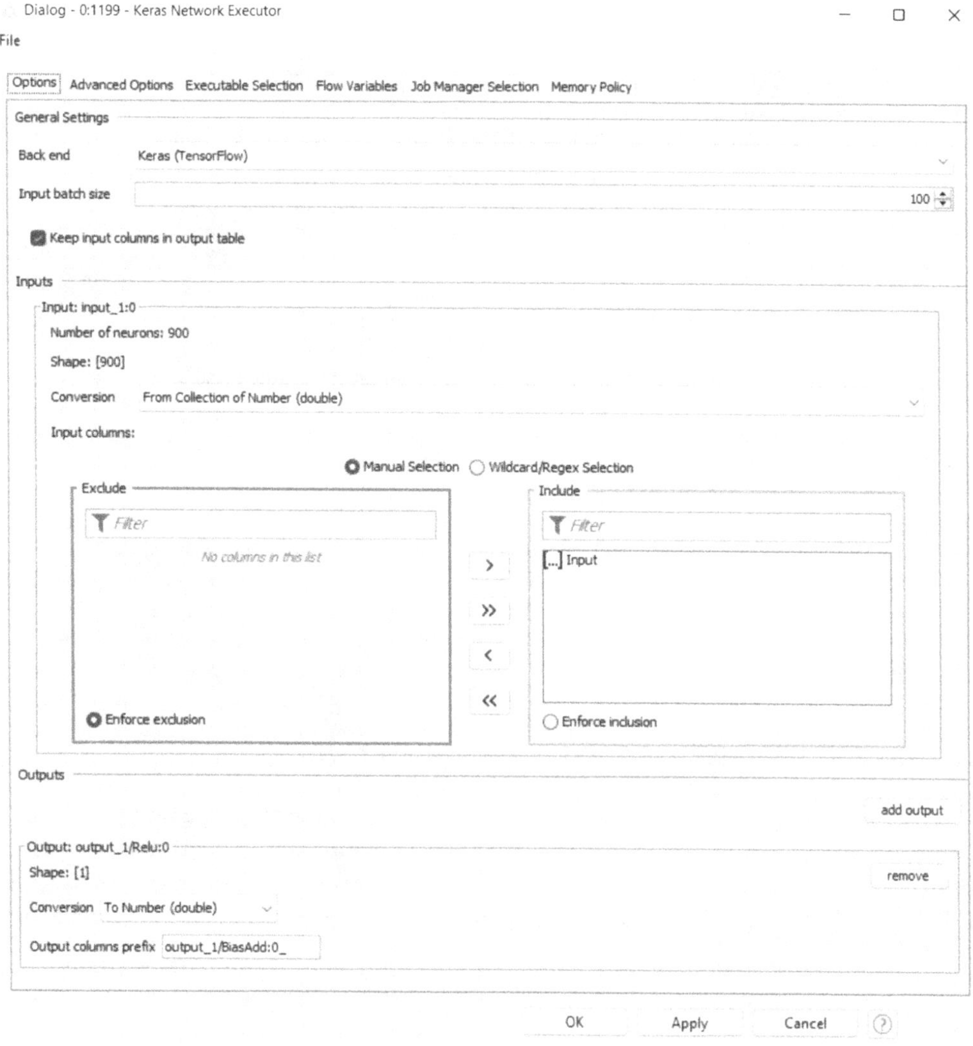


Figure 13.6 – The Options tab in the configuration window of the Keras Network Executor node to apply the trained network to new data

After renaming the original time series columns to `true_cluster_**`, renaming the column with the predicted values as `cluster_12`, and denormalizing all the columns, we can finally score the model performance with the **Numeric Scorer** node. The final error table includes MAE = 0.997 and **Root Mean Squared Error** (**RMSE**) = 1.29.

The plot in *Figure 13.7* illustrates the quality of the prediction according to the previously mentioned error values, by showing the predicted and original time series:

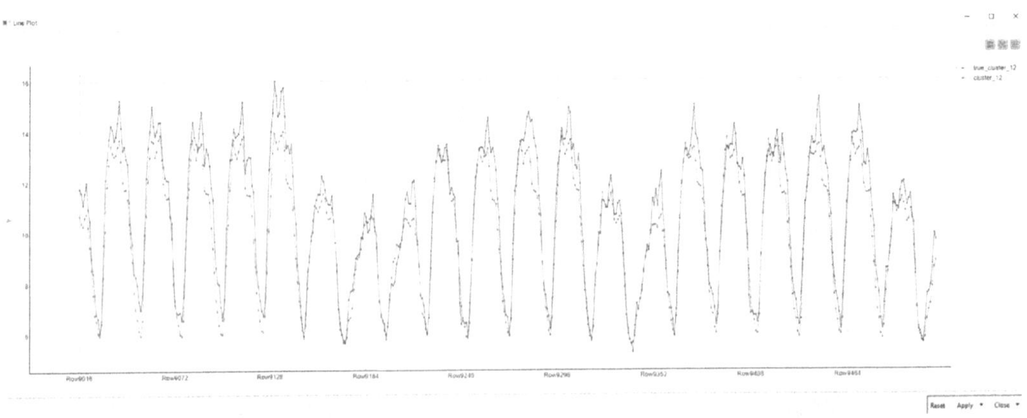

Figure 13.7 – The predicted cluster_12 time series in orange and the original cluster 12 time series in blue

This is a relatively simple architecture with a relatively small training set, and yet, the training takes quite a long time to execute, that is, about 10 minutes on my humble laptop. Imagine how easily it can become time-prohibitive by adding data and adopting an even more complex neural network.

In the next section, we will show you how it is possible to speed up the execution of the training algorithm by exploiting the computational power of a GPU-powered machine.

# Enabling GPU execution for neural networks

GPUs operate more slowly than CPUs but have the advantage of performing massive numbers of calculations in parallel. Libraries for the GPU execution of neural training algorithms have been developed and are included in the KNIME Deep Learning – Keras Integration. In this section, we will explore how to speed up the network execution, training, and application with GPU acceleration.

First of all, you need a CUDA-enabled **GPU**. Then, you need a Python environment that uses the GPU version of the Keras package.

> **Installing Conda**
>
> Conda can be installed easily and for free by going to `https://docs.conda.io/projects/conda/en/latest/index.html` and downloading the appropriate version for your machine.

First, we set up a GPU Python environment via the dedicated KNIME **Preferences** page. After that, we can use this Python environment in one of two ways:

- We set it up as the default environment and all workflows will use it for the execution of their Keras nodes unless specified differently.
- Alternatively, we can set up a CPU-based Python environment as the default environment and then overwrite it with the GPU environment only in selected workflows via the **Conda Environment Propagation** node. If we want to execute some networks on a CPU and some on a GPU, this is the way.

In the next session, let's walk through how to set up this GPU-specific Python environment, keeping in mind you'll need a CUDA GPU to do so. Don't worry though, all of the examples are still executable on a CPU.

## Setting up a new GPU Python environment

Let's assume that your machine has a CUDA-enabled GPU. Then, we can create a Python environment to run the Keras training algorithms on the GPU.

In KNIME Analytics Platform, from the main menu, navigate to **File** | **Preferences** | **KNIME** | **Python Deep Learning**.

On the **Python Deep Learning** preferences page (*Figure 13.8*), perform the following steps:

1. Select **Use special Deep Learning configuration as defined below**.
2. In the **Deep Learning Python environment configuration** section, select **Conda**.
3. Provide the path to the Conda installation directory.

4. In the **Keras** section, click on the **New environment…** button:

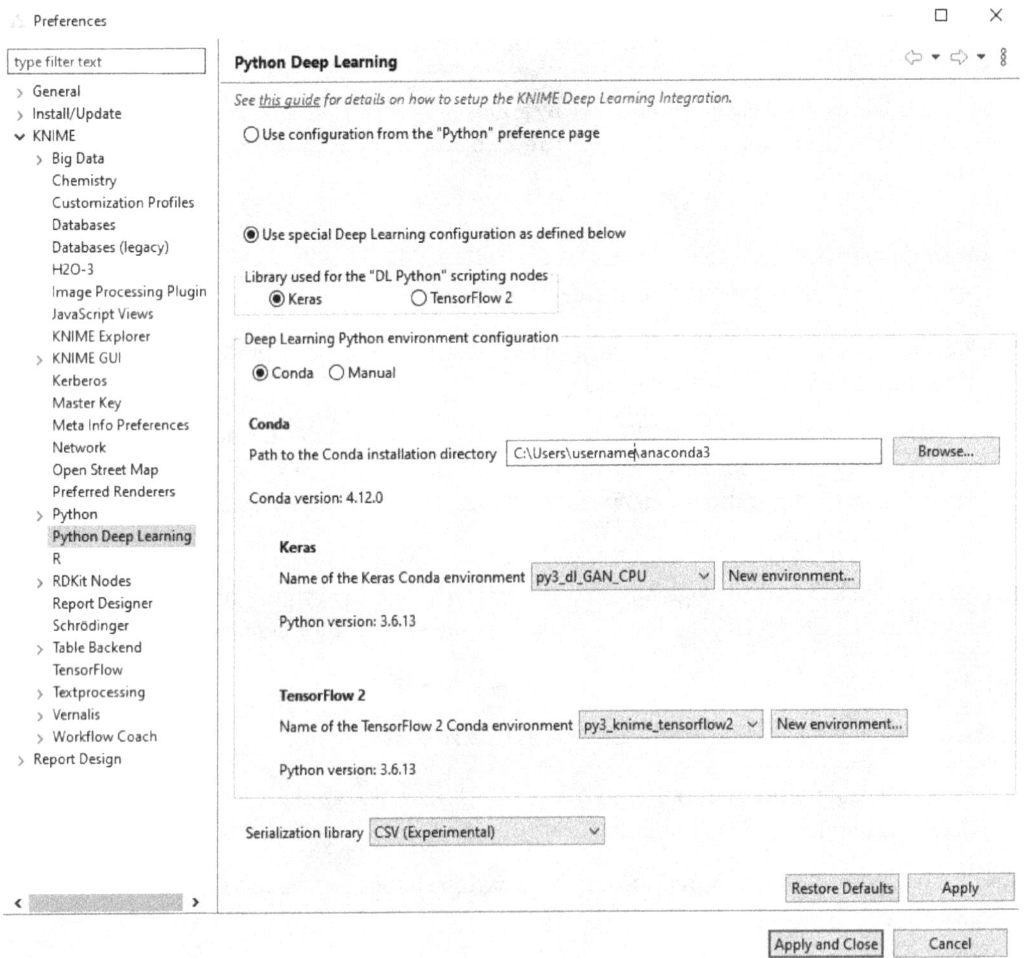


Figure 13.8 – The Python Deep Learning preferences page with all the options required to run the Keras libraries with and without a GPU

In the window that pops up (*Figure 13.9*), perform the following steps:

5. Give a name to the new environment.

6. Click on **Create new GPU environment**.

   With this set up, all Keras nodes in all workflows are executed in the new GPU environment via the Keras libraries of the KNIME Deep Learning – Keras Integration, unless configured otherwise:

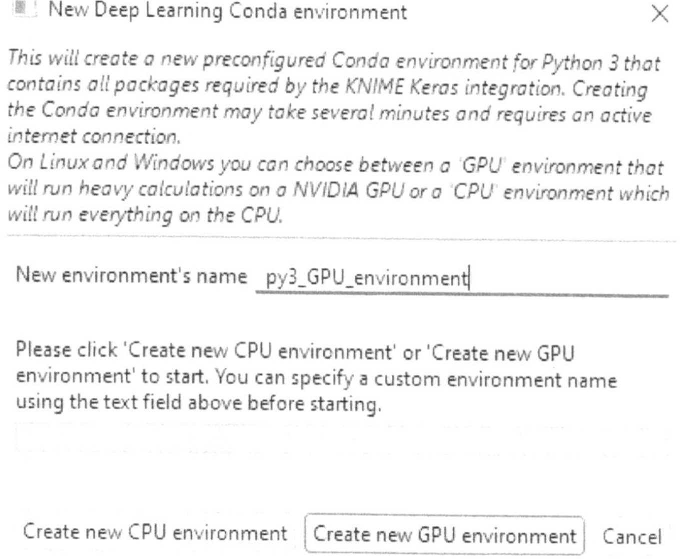


Figure 13.9 – The New Deep Learning Conda environment window used to create a new Conda environment with or without a GPU

Now, let's investigate how we can dynamically change the Keras Python environment from CPU to GPU, workflow by workflow, using the Conda Environment Propagation node.

## Switching Python environments dynamically

To set up the GPU Python environment for specific workflows, you can use the Conda Environment Propagation node. We have already seen that this node allows you to dynamically change the Python environment for the execution of subsequent nodes in a workflow. So, you can reference a Keras-GPU-enabled Python environment in the Conda Environment Propogation node and connect it to the Keras Network Learner. Then, when the Keras Network Executor executes, it will run with the GPU version of Keras on your graphics card. In my testing, I saw a 4x speed increase for the relatively small network we show in this chapter. On larger networks, the speed increase will only grow.

We already created a GPU Python environment on the **Preferences** page, as described in the first part of this section. Then, in the workflow developed in the previous section, perform the steps:

1. Add a **Conda Environment Propagation** node and connect it to the **Keras Network Learner** node (*Figure 13.10*).
2. In the configuration dialog of the **Conda Environment Propagation** node, select the Python environment that uses the GPU version of Keras:

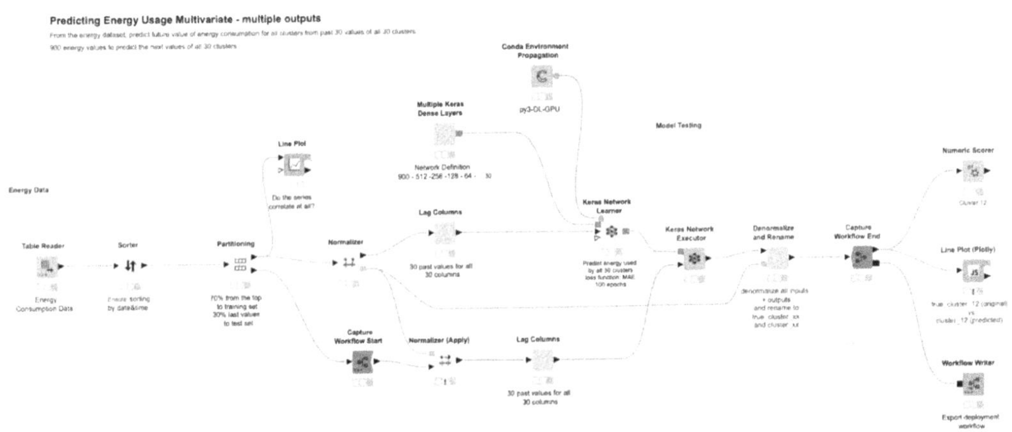


Figure 13.10 – Adding a Conda Environment Propagation node to the workflow

Now, you need to configure the Keras nodes to use the environment proposed by the **Conda Environment Propagation** node and not the default one:

3. Open the configuration of the **Keras Network Learner** (Keras Network Executor) node (*Figure 13.11*).

4. In the **Executable Selection** tab, select the **Use Conda flow variable** option. Then, select the **conda.environment** flow variable created by the **Conda Environment Propagation** node:

   Now the Keras node uses the configured Conda environment to execute on the GPU:

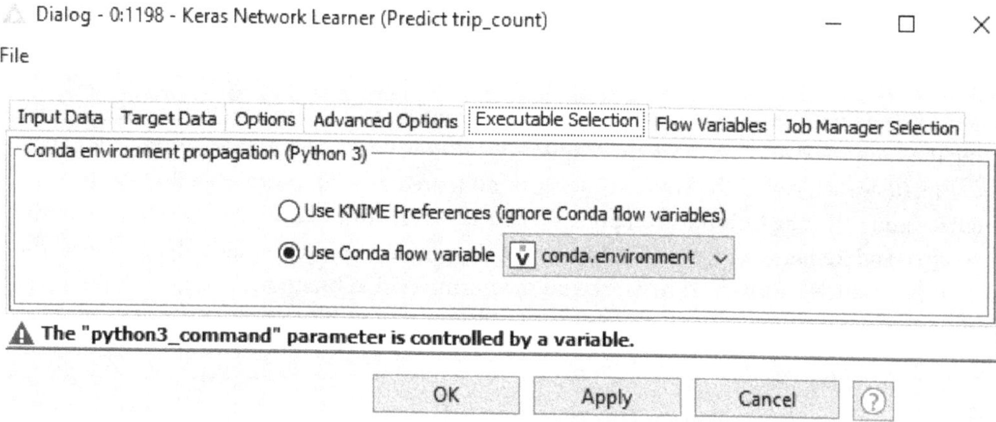


Figure 13.11 – The Executable Selection tab in the configuration dialog of Keras nodes, where you can select the Python environment to use for execution

Using our workflow as an example, with a neural network with multiple output predictions and trained for only 50 epochs, first, we ran it on a CPU only, using my desktop computer with an Intel Core i-7 CPU-9700k and 16 GB of RAM. Then, we ran it on the same desktop using my GPU, an NVIDIA GeForce RTX 2080 Super, instead. In the first scenario, the network trained in 10 minutes, while in the second scenario using the GPU, it trained in 2.5 minutes. This means a speed gain of 300% for the same prediction error!

> **Important Note**
>
> The Conda Environment Propagation node creates the selected Python environment if it does not already exist on the machine. This means that if you have a Conda environment working well on some other machine, you can replicate it locally by just copying and executing the Conda Environment Propagation node. Do note that to use the GPU version of Keras on a new machine, you will still need a CUDA-enabled graphics card.

Of course, our example is quite small. The number of epochs could be increased to 500, the network architecture could involve more complex, or larger, layers than just the feedforward layers we used today, and more. In a more complex situation, the gain in execution speed will be even more dramatic.

This is also true in the opposite direction. If your dataset is too small or your problem is not complex, the usage of a GPU might bring no gain in execution speed or even make it slower since there is an initial cost to set up the GPU. I do not recommend going straight to GPU executions if you do not have a large model, lots of data, or both!

## Building the deployment application

To create the deployment workflow we, once again, use the integrated deployment feature. Strategically inserting the **Capture Workflow Start** and **Capture Workflow End** nodes in the workflow, as shown in *Figure 13.10*, we can isolate the entire sequence of nodes required for processing the test data: the **Normalizer** node, the **Lag Columns** component, the **Keras Network Executor** node, and finally, the **Denormalize and Rename** component. Additionally, the capture nodes automatically include all the required input models (the trained network and the normalization functions) along with the input and output nodes according to the input and output data tables of the captured workflow segment (*Figure 13.12*):

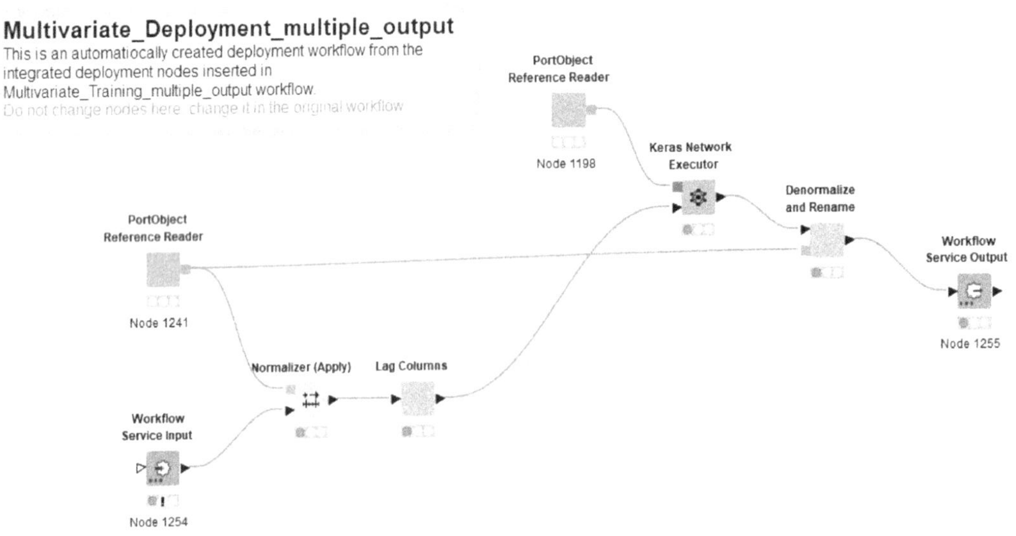


Figure 13.12 – The deployment workflow created via integrated deployment

This automatically created workflow is saved in the desired location via the **Workflow Writer** node and invoked via a **Call Workflow** node.

**REST Endpoints**

The automatically created deployment workflow in *Figure 13.12* can only be called from another workflow. Changing the input and output nodes to **Container (JSON)** allows the workflow to accept and return JSON data, making it easier to use as a web service called from an external application after being loaded to KNIME Server.

Additionally, we could include the Conda Environment Propagation node in the deployment segment to force a GPU execution. However, usually, deployment involves less data and fewer computational operations than a full training algorithm for neural networks. Because of that, the difference in execution time using a GPU or CPU is negligible for the deployment workflow and CPU execution was maintained.

# Summary

Arriving at the end of this chapter, we have demonstrated how to expand a prediction model from a one-dimensional time series (univariate) to a multi-dimensional time series (multivariate). We expanded the input from the past values of a single time series to include the past values of all 30 time series in the energy consumption dataset and learned how to build a model predicting the next value in one of the selected time series.

We approached the problem in steps. First, we trained a fully connected feedforward neural network to predict the next value in one time series based on the past values of all time series. Then, we trained a fully connected feedforward neural network to predict the next values in all 30 time series based on the past values of all 30 time series in the energy consumption dataset.

Finally, we observed that the more complex the problem and the model, the higher the computational load, and the longer the execution times, especially during the training phase. Therefore, we introduced a GPU-based environment to execute the neural network operations. The libraries for the GPU execution of neural training algorithms have been developed and are included in the KNIME Deep Learning – Keras Integration. In the second part of this chapter, we demonstrated how to enable GPU execution to make the execution of neural network operations much faster.

# Questions

1. Increasing the size of the neural network makes the training time…

   A. Shorter if the input values are correlated

   B. Longer

   C. Shorter

   D. Longer if the input values are not correlated

2. How can you enable a workflow to execute on GPU?

   A. Through the settings on the dedicated Preference page

   B. Via the BackPropagation algorithm

   C. Through normalization

   D. Through the CPU settings

3. Why should we use the Conda Environment Propagation node for GPU execution?

   A. To switch the default execution from CPU to GPU.

   B. We always have to use a Conda Environment Propagation node for GPU execution.

   C. If we want to execute the current workflow on a GPU while leaving default execution on the CPU.

   D. To reduce the number of weights in the network.

4. What is a Dropout layer for?

   A. To optimize the training algorithm for certain data types

   B. To increase the size of the network

   C. To increase the complexity of the network

   D. To help regularize the training of the network

# 14
# Combining KNIME and H2O to Predict Stock Prices

In every book about time series analysis, there must be at least one example application to predict stock prices, that is, the *forecasting problem*. So, we conclude this book with a final chapter describing a forecasting application and the integration of KNIME Analytics Platform with **H2O**, which is another open source platform.

The **stock price prediction problem** is infamously difficult to reach accurate results for as the data changes quickly, on a daily basis. Furthermore, the drivers of these changes vary from physical factors, such as environmental disasters, to socio-economic factors such as political elections, and even to random factors that cannot be predicted. Thus, we're dealing with data with complex structures and interrelationships, which, as a result of the increased number of exchanges in the globalized stock market, is produced at a high frequency and processed in real time.

At the same time, the massive amounts of data enable forecasting by using machine learning models, especially as they have become faster and more accurate, with increased computational capabilities. In this chapter, we'll train a machine learning model for stock price prediction on the H2O platform, which is optimized for speed and performance on big data.

We will introduce the stock prediction problem and the **machine learning-based stock price prediction** application in the following sections:

- Introducing the stock price prediction problem
- Describing the KNIME H2O Machine Learning Integration
- Accessing and preparing data within KNIME
- Training an H2O model from within KNIME
- Consuming the H2O model in the deployment application

In this chapter, you will learn about the specifics of the stock price prediction problem and how the characteristics of stock market data challenge making predictions. You will also learn how to train machine learning algorithms on the H2O platform from within your KNIME workflow. Finally, you will learn how to build a deployment workflow that consumes results from remote workflows.

# Technical requirements

The following are the prerequisites for this chapter:

- KNIME Analytics Platform with the KNIME H2O Machine Learning Integration installed
- The KNIME Python Integration with the `pandas-datareader` package installed

All of the workflows introduced in the chapter are available on KNIME Hub at `https://kni.me/s/O9gicrly8EJPN5mg` and on GitHub at `https://github.com/PacktPublishing/Codeless-Time-Series-Analysis-with-KNIME/tree/main/Chapter14`.

# Introducing the stock price prediction problem

Before we move on to the implementation of the application, we'll introduce what the stock price prediction problem is and what its challenges are.

Stock price prediction covers the practices – **qualitative** and **quantitative** – to predict the future value of a financial instrument traded on an *exchange*. The financial instruments are, for example, shares of publicly held companies whose prices change in real time and securities with a price not changing in real time. An *exchange* refers to a marketplace for buying and selling these instruments. The same stock market can contain multiple exchanges, such as the **New York Stock Exchange** (**NYSE**) and **National Association of Securities Dealers Automated Quotation** (**NASDAQ**) systems in the US stock market.

Qualitative prediction can refer to the evaluation of the business model, for example, and not necessarily on measurable data. Quantitative prediction instead relies only on measurable data. Furthermore, quantitative analysis can be divided into **fundamental** and **technical** analyses. The fundamental analysis predicts the stock prices by related microeconomic and macroeconomic variables, while the technical analysis only predicts the price via the price history. In this chapter, we will focus on **technical analysis** via machine learning methods.

The goals of stock price prediction include reacting to the changes in the stock market automatically, supporting decision making, increasing profits, and reducing the losses of the customers. The historical stock market data is also used for long-term analysis of prices and market risks. The stock prediction application implemented in this chapter addresses the challenge of time-sensitive predictions and complex interrelationships in large amounts of data. It is therefore based on a machine learning algorithm that is retrained regularly on the H2O platform.

In the next section, we will introduce the KNIME H2O Machine Learning Integration for accelerating machine learning processes.

## Describing the KNIME H2O Machine Learning Integration

The **KNIME H2O Machine Learning Integration** enables *fast* and *scalable* execution of machine learning tasks from within your KNIME workflows. When you execute tasks on H2O, you will build your workflows in much the same way as before – **codeless** – yet under the hood, the tasks are performed on **H2O data frames** in a cluster instance and processed via distributed in-memory computing. The H2O data frame is the main data structure for H2O, with numbered rows and named columns, located in an H2O cluster.

We will introduce the setup and functionalities of the H2O integration in the following subsections:

- Starting a workflow running on the H2O platform
- Introducing the H2O nodes for machine learning

In the first subsection, we show you how to get started with H2O workflows in KNIME.

## Starting a workflow running on the H2O platform

Building H2O workflows requires the extension called the KNIME H2O Machine Learning Integration (accessible via `https://kni.me/e/ahEvXl-NKGooJ7Od`), which gives you access to functionalities from the H2O libraries encapsulated as nodes. A thorough preview of the functionalities of the H2O open source machine learning platform is available on their website (accessible via `https://h2o.ai/platform/ai-cloud/make/h2o/`). Once you have successfully installed the extension, you will find all nodes via **Analytics** | **Integrations** | **H2O Machine Learning** as shown in *Figure 14.1*:

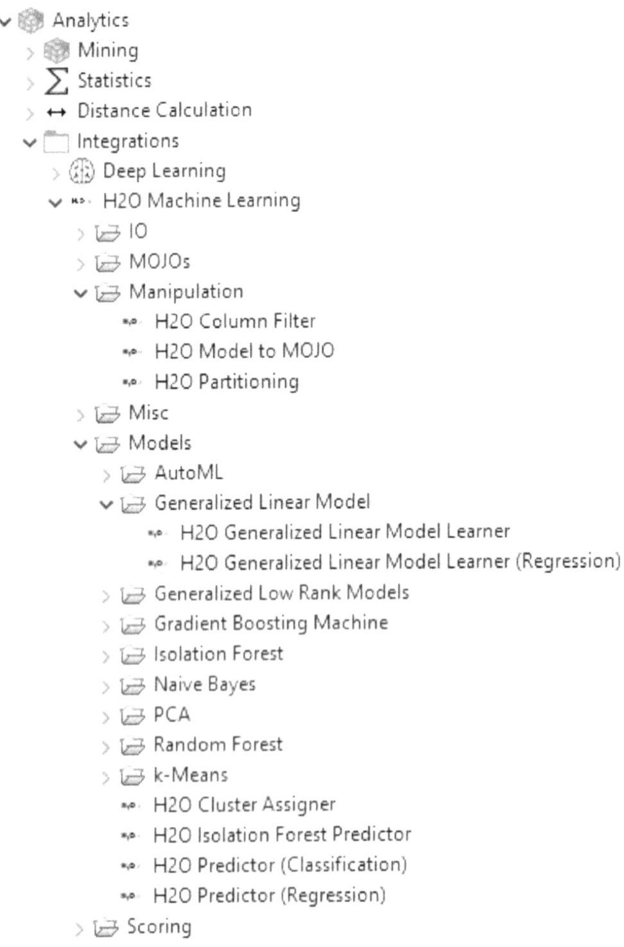


Figure 14.1 – Overview of H2O nodes in the node repository

The H2O nodes are distributed in categories, such as `IO` for reading and writing H2O data frames and `Manipulation` for performing data manipulation operations on the H2O data frames. The `Models` category provides a large variety of codeless nodes for training different machine learning algorithms. Some of the algorithms do not have a KNIME native implementation, such as a **generalized linear model** and **isolation forest**, while the others have a KNIME native implementation but can also be trained on H2O for better performance on big data, such as **Random Forest**.

When you start building a workflow with the H2O nodes, the first steps are to create the **local H2O cluster instance** and transform the KNIME data tables into H2O data frames, as shown in the following workflow:

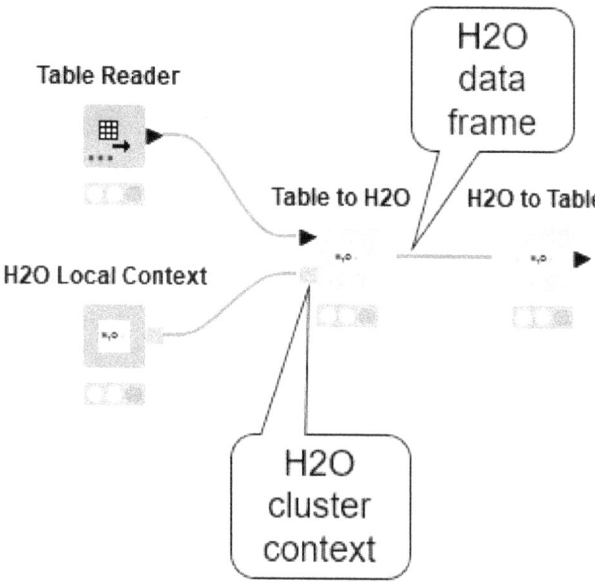


Figure 14.2 – Nodes for getting started with H2O workflows

The workflow starts with the **H2O Local Context** node. This node does not need to be configured since it only creates the instance of an H2O cluster on the local machine. Notice that the cluster will consume the resources allocated to KNIME Analytics Platform.

Once the local H2O context has been created, the next step is to convert data tables into H2O data frames with the **Table to H2O** node. This node takes the data table and **H2O cluster context** as input and produces an **H2O data frame** as output (highlighted in *Figure 14.2*). The **H2O data frame** can then be processed within the distributed memory of the H2O cluster instance. If needed, for example when you mix KNIME native nodes with H2O nodes in your workflows, you can convert an H2O data frame back to a local data table with the **H2O to Table** node.

In the next subsection, we will introduce the H2O nodes for machine learning.

## Introducing the H2O nodes for machine learning

The steps for data access and transformation introduced in the previous section are common for all workflows where you use H2O. After that, depending on your analysis task, you can use a wide range of nodes for machine learning algorithms, data preprocessing, and model evaluation, which all have a graphical user interface like the KNIME native nodes. See, for example, the configuration dialog of the **H2O Generalized Linear Model Learner (Regression)** node as follows:

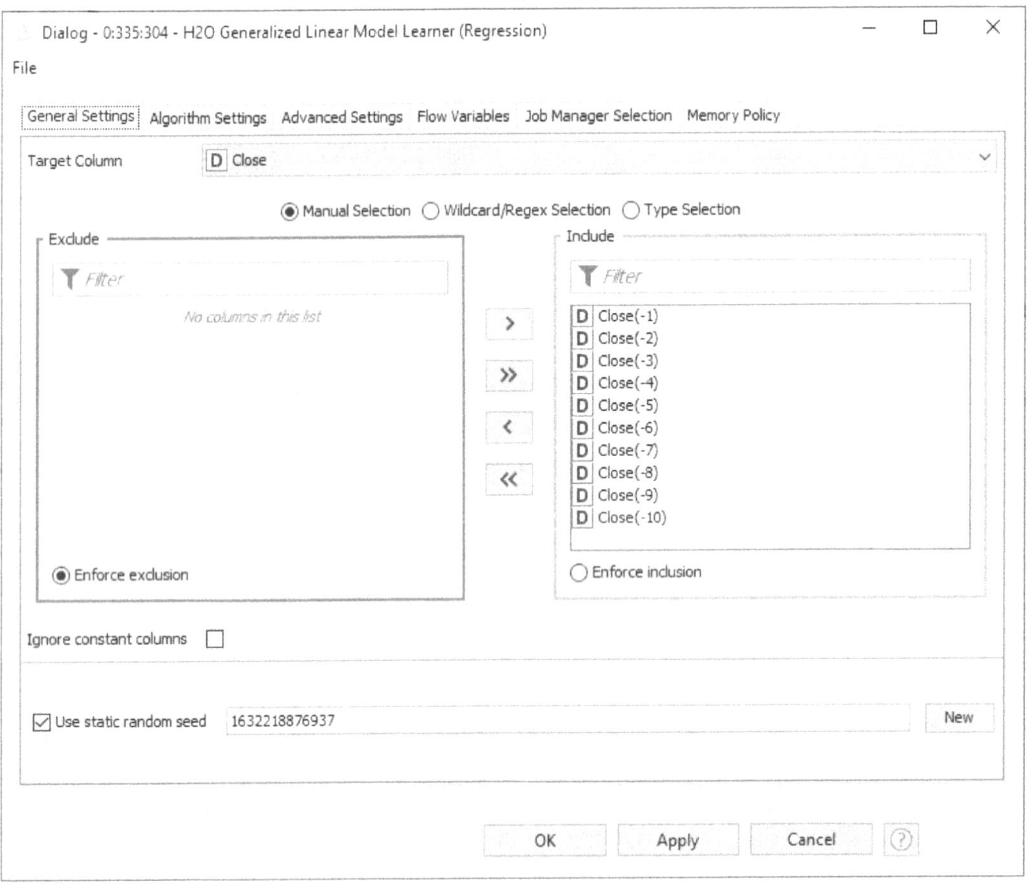


Figure 14.3 – The visual configuration of the H2O Generalized Linear Model Learner (Regression) node

In the configuration dialog, you can find similar options as in the KNIME native learner nodes: you can select the target column in the drop-down menu and the predictor columns in the **exclude/include** framework. In the **Algorithm Settings** and **Advanced Settings** tabs, you can define additional model configuration options.

In the same graphical way, you can configure other H2O nodes and connect them to each other via their H2O data frame input and output ports.

In the next section, we will introduce the stock prediction application, and in particular, how to access and prepare the data locally within KNIME.

## Accessing and preparing data within KNIME

The stock prediction application consists of three parts: **data access**, **model training**, and **deployment**. The deployment workflow orchestrates the data access and model training steps by calling them from separate workflows. Thus, the same data preparation and model training steps could also be called from other deployment workflows. *Figure 14.4* shows the part of the deployment workflow that calls the remote workflows (available on KNIME Hub at `https://kni.me/w/4JrfiNV6NrqE7VKo`). Further details of the deployment workflow will be introduced in the *Consuming the H2O model in the deployment application* section:

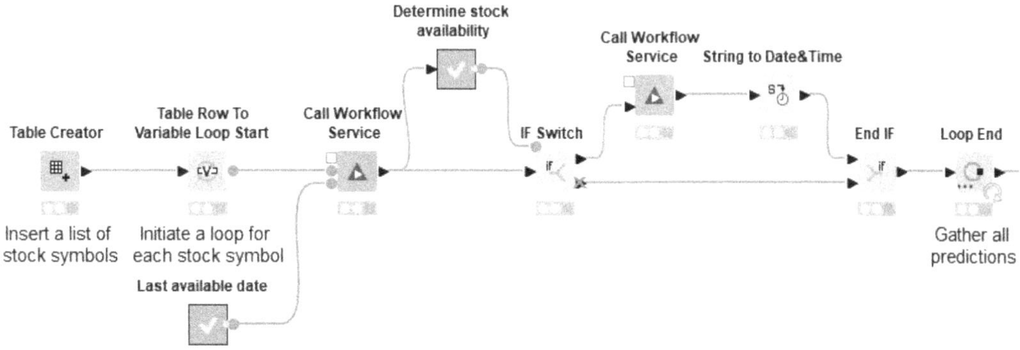


Figure 14.4 – Calling data preprocessing and forecasting steps from the deployment workflow

The deployment workflow generates the forecasts as follows:

1. The workflow loops over one *stock symbol* at a time with the **Table Row To Variable Loop Start** node.
2. Next, it calls the data access and preprocessing workflow with the **Call Workflow Service** node. This node sends the stock symbol and the *last available date* (the day before the execution date) as flow variables to the data access workflow and retrieves the output (the preprocessed historical prices) for this stock symbol up to this date.

3. After that, it checks whether the historical prices were available for the selected stock symbol with the **Determine stock availability** metanode. If the prices are available, it activates the top output of the **IF Switch** node and triggers the execution of the model-training workflow with the second **Call Workflow Service** node. This node sends the preprocessed historical prices in its data input to the model training workflow, retrieves the forecasted price and the model accuracy metrics from that workflow, and produces them in its data output.

**Important Note**

The **Call Workflow Service** node automatically adjusts its input and output ports according to the input and output in the workflow to call.

4. Finally, it collects the forecasted prices and accuracy metrics for all stock symbols with the **Loop End** node to continue with the selected deployment actions.

**Important Note**

We deviated from the static forecasting model to ensure that the model is retrained *daily* according to new data.

Next, we'll introduce the data access and preprocessing steps in the data access workflow. They were originally implemented in the **Stock Prediction** application available on KNIME Hub (accessible via `https://kni.me/s/_uV1ed73_uOJW5jz`). We have adjusted the implementation according to our use case.

First, we'll show how to access data from Yahoo Finance.

## Accessing stock market data from Yahoo Finance

In our stock price prediction application, we use data provided by **Yahoo Finance** (`https://finance.yahoo.com/`), which is a business news platform providing historical stock prices for free. We access the data directly from the KNIME workflow for selected stock symbols with the `pandas_datareader.data.DataReader(symbol, 'yahoo', start, end)` function in the **Python Source** node. You can find this node in the data access workflow introduced in *Figure 14.6*. *Figure 14.5* shows a sample of the accessed data for **Deutsche Bank AG** (**DB**):

| Row ID | D High | D Low | D Open | D Close | I Volume | D Adj Close | S symbol |
|---|---|---|---|---|---|---|---|
| 2016-01-04 ... | 23.49 | 23.02 | 23.17 | 23.49 | 2753900 | 22.589 | DB |
| 2016-01-05 ... | 23.62 | 23.24 | 23.61 | 23.48 | 1264700 | 22.58 | DB |
| 2016-01-06 ... | 23.28 | 23.03 | 23.12 | 23.14 | 1393300 | 22.253 | DB |
| 2016-01-07 ... | 23.1 | 22.67 | 22.75 | 22.72 | 2470100 | 21.849 | DB |
| 2016-01-08 ... | 22.86 | 22.08 | 22.82 | 22.1 | 2341500 | 21.252 | DB |
| 2016-01-11 ... | 22.77 | 22.4 | 22.75 | 22.68 | 2476100 | 21.81 | DB |
| 2016-01-12 ... | 23.13 | 22.64 | 23.03 | 22.93 | 1777300 | 22.051 | DB |
| 2016-01-13 ... | 23.15 | 22.15 | 23.1 | 22.17 | 2838200 | 21.32 | DB |
| 2016-01-14 ... | 22.17 | 21.49 | 21.83 | 22.01 | 3469000 | 21.166 | DB |
| 2016-01-15 ... | 21.18 | 20.73 | 20.96 | 20.96 | 3595100 | 20.156 | DB |
| 2016-01-19 ... | 20.73 | 20.23 | 20.68 | 20.42 | 3305900 | 19.637 | DB |
| 2016-01-20 ... | 19.83 | 19.09 | 19.74 | 19.33 | 7184100 | 18.589 | DB |
| 2016-01-21 ... | 18.79 | 18.05 | 18.18 | 18.58 | 8222300 | 17.867 | DB |

Figure 14.5 – The historical stock price data

The data contains the daily high, low, opening, and closing prices, the volume, and the adjusted closing price for the selected stock symbol. In our application, we will predict the *adjusted closing price* on the next day based on this historical data for each stock symbol separately. The included stock symbols are **DB**, **Lennar Corporation** (**LEN**), **Energy Transfer LP Unit** (**ET**), **Iqvia Holdings Inc** (**IQV**), **Johnson Controls International PLC** (**JCI**), and **Bausch Health Companies Inc** (**BHC**), which represent six companies listed in the NYSE.

> **Important Note**
>
> These companies were selected for the analysis arbitrarily, and you could perform the analysis on any other stock symbols as well.

The function calling the data is a part of the `pandas-datareader` Python package, and this package needs to be installed separately. The package contains functions for accessing real-time data sources from the internet, and in our case, we use it to access real-time stock market data from Yahoo Finance. You can install it by typing the following command in the **Anaconda** prompt:

```
conda install -n [your environment name] pandas-datareader
```

> **Important Note**
>
> Please check *Chapter 2, Introduction to KNIME Analytics Platform*, for more instructions on how to install additional Python packages.

After that, you can access the stock prices by executing the data access workflow (accessible on KNIME Hub at `https://kni.me/w/RhP9Fy3GGBSJDROy`) shown in *Figure 14.6*, and specifically the Python Source node within it:

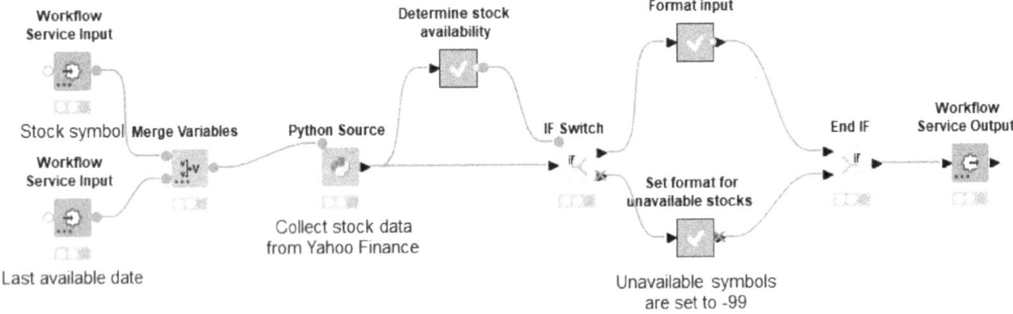


Figure 14.6 – Workflow for accessing and preprocessing the stock prices for selected stock symbols

This workflow accesses and preprocesses the stock market data in the following steps:

1. First, it accesses a stock symbol as a flow variable with the top **Workflow Service Input** node and the last available date as another flow variable with the bottom **Workflow Service Input** node, as sent by the **Call Workflow Service** node in the deployment workflow (*Figure 14.4*).
2. Next, it retrieves the historical price data for the stock symbol from 2016 up to the last available date with the **Python Source** node. The `symbol` and `end` parameters of the function (see the beginning of this section) are customized according to the input of the node.

3. Then, it checks whether the data retrieval was successful with the **Determine stock availability** metanode. It steers the execution to the **Format input** metanode if the data was accessed successfully and to the **Set format for unavailable stocks** metanode otherwise.
4. Finally, it sends the preprocessed data to the deployment workflow with the **Workflow Service Output** node.

In the next subsection, we'll introduce the data preprocessing steps.

## Preparing the data for modeling on H2O

After accessing the data from Yahoo Finance, we preprocess the data for modeling. The following workflow shows the preprocessing steps implemented inside the **Format input** metanode in the data access and preprocessing workflow (*Figure 14.6*):

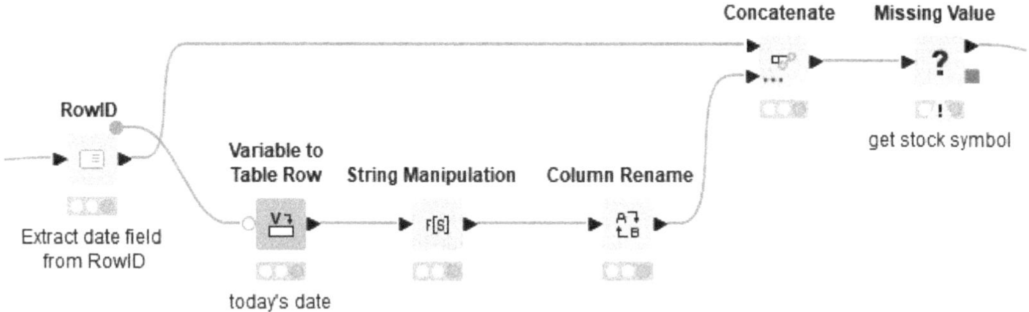


Figure 14.7 – The data preprocessing steps of stock price data

The workflow performs these preprocessing steps:

1. It extracts the date values from the row IDs into a string column with the **RowID** node.
2. Next, it converts today's date from a flow variable into a string cell with the **Variable to Table Row** node.
3. After that, it concatenates the execution date as a string with the dates extracted from the row ID with the **Concatenate** node. Also, at this point, it replaces the missing stock symbol name in the last row (forecast) by the stock symbol in the previous row (last available record) with the **Missing Value** node. The missing value in the price column will be populated by the forecasted price later.

If the prices for the stock symbol couldn't be retrieved, we skip these preceding preprocessing steps and just return one row with the value `-99` and the execution date inside the **Set format for unavailable stocks** metanode (*Figure 14.6*).

The data is now ready to be consumed by the deployment workflow to call the next action, modeling. In the next section, we explain how to train a model on H2O for forecasting.

# Training an H2O model from within KNIME

In this section, we will introduce the forecasting part of the application. We'll show how to train, optimize, evaluate, and deploy a stock price prediction model on H2O.

We selected the **linear regression model** as the stock price prediction model, which predicts the adjusted closing price based on the prices on the previous days. We can train the model as an **H2O generalized linear model** with **Gaussian** as the *distribution family* and **Identity** as the *link function*. This means we assume that the prices are approximately normally distributed and linearly related to the combination of the previous day's prices, as indicated by the following regression equation:

$$y = X\beta + e$$

Formula 14.1

Where $y$ is the target variable, $X$ is the vector of the previous day's prices, $\beta$ is the vector of regression coefficients, and $e$ is the normally distributed residual term.

If we assumed a non-linear relationship between the target and predictor variables, we could use the generalized linear model with a non-linear link function, such as the log function:

$$y = \alpha * \exp\,(X\gamma) + e$$

Formula 14.2

Where $\alpha$ and $\gamma$ are the coefficients of the non-linear equation.

The model training workflow (accessible on KNIME Hub at `https://kni.me/w/aJ7Z4Jm46oVGapIR`) is shown in *Figure 14.8*:

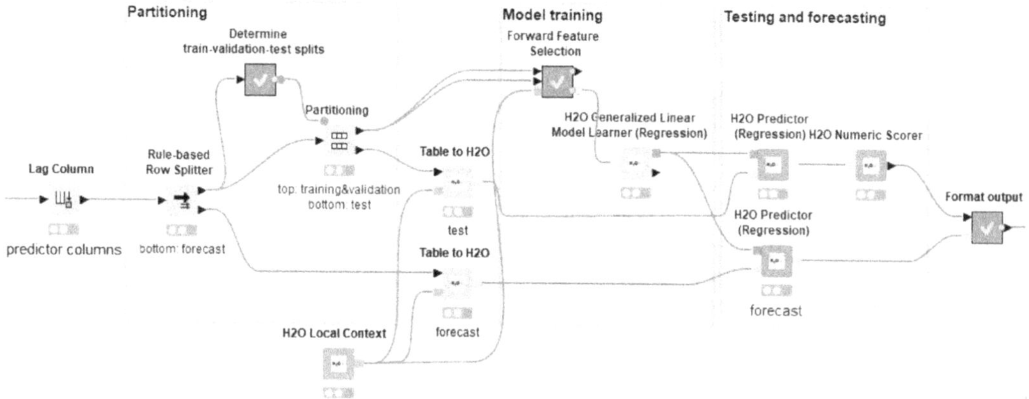


Figure 14.8 – The workflow training and applying a stock prediction model on H2O

The workflow covers the following steps on the data coming from the deployment workflow:

1. First, the workflow creates the predictor columns with the **Lag Column** node.
2. Next, it separates the last row for the forecast with the **Rule-based Row Splitter** node.
3. Then, it partitions the remaining data into training and test sets with the **Partitioning** node.
4. After that, it performs feature selection inside the **Forward Feature Selection** metanode.
5. Then, it trains the linear regression model on the training data using the best-performing features with the **H2O Generalized Linear Model Learner (Regression)** node.
6. Next, it applies the model to the test set and evaluates its performance with the **H2O Predictor (Regression)** and **H2O Numeric Scorer** nodes respectively.
7. Lastly, it creates a forecast of the adjusted price on the execution date with the **H2O Predictor (Regression)** node.

In the following subsection, we explain how to create and select the predictor columns.

## Optimizing the number of predictor columns

We start the model training workflow by creating 10 lagged columns with the **Lag Column** node as candidates for the predictor columns. We decide on a maximum of 10 past columns because we assume that the prices don't show regular dependencies in a term longer than 10 days. These columns will be used in the **feature selection** phase. This means that we will generate a fixed number of lagged columns, but not all will necessarily be used in the prediction.

> **Important Note**
>
> Feature selection discards predictor columns to obtain a better model performance. Too many predictor columns can lead to overfitting of the model and thus decrease the forecasting performance.

We perform the feature selection inside the **Forward Feature Selection** metanode (*Figure 14.8*) with a **feature selection loop**. The loop inside the metanode is shown as follows:

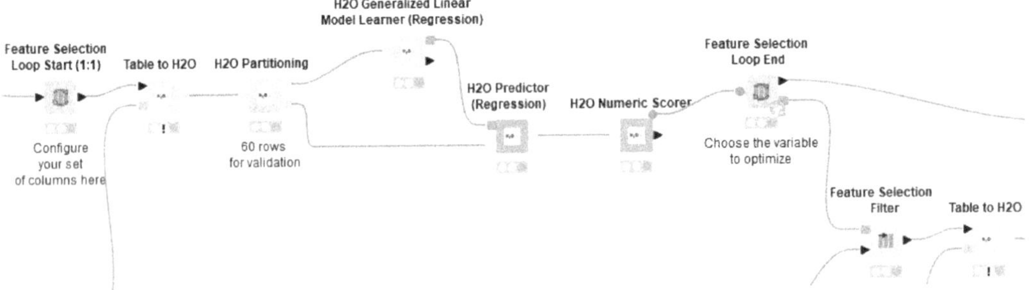


Figure 14.9 – A feature selection loop to find the best-performing predictor columns

The feature selection loop tests the performance on a varying number of prediction columns as follows:

1. First, it filters a subset of columns for each iteration with the **Feature Selection Loop Start (1:1)** node. Altogether it trains the model 10 times with one prediction column, *10+9* times with two columns, *10+9+8* times with three prediction columns, and so on, leaving always the best-performing column into the filtered set of prediction columns and thus excluding it from the training data in the next iteration..
2. At the start of each iteration, it partitions the last 60 rows from the training data into a validation set using the **Table to H2O** and **H2O Partitioning** nodes.
3. Next, it trains the model on the set of prediction columns with the **H2O Generalized Linear Model Learner (Regression)** node.

4. After that, it applies the model to the validation set with the **H2O Predictor (Regression)** node and evaluates it with the **H2O Numeric Scorer** node.
5. Finally, it collects the selected scoring metric – in our case **R-squared** – for each model with the **Feature Selection Loop End** node.
6. When the loop has finished, it filters the columns from the training and validation sets with the **Feature Selection Filter** node based on the output of the **Feature Selection Loop End** node.
7. As the last step, it converts the filtered columns into an H2O data frame with the **Table to H2O** node to perform the final model training.

In the next subsection, we'll introduce the remaining steps: training, applying, and testing the final forecasting model.

## Training, applying, and testing the optimized model

In this subsection, we'll describe how to train and test the final model after feature selection, generate a forecast with the model, and evaluate its performance. You can find the implementation of these steps at the end of the model training workflow in *Figure 14.8*:

1. Firstly, the top **H2O Predictor (Regression)** node applies the forecasting model to the test set, which we have defined as the latest 30 days of historical data.
2. After that, the **H2O Numeric Scorer** node produces the evaluation metrics to assess the performance of the forecasting model over these 30 days.
3. At the same time, the bottom **H2O Predictor (Regression)** node generates the forecast of the price on the execution day.
4. Finally, these two results are combined into a table (see *Figure 14.10*) and sent to the deployment workflow:

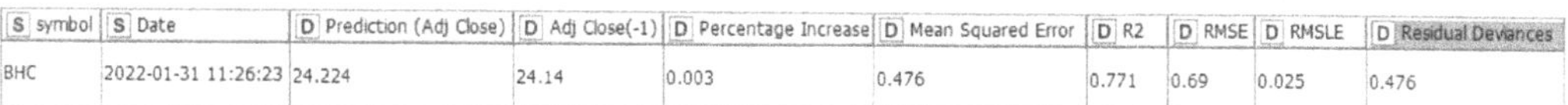

| S symbol | S Date | D Prediction (Adj Close) | D Adj Close(-1) | D Percentage Increase | D Mean Squared Error | D R2 | D RMSE | D RMSLE | D Residual Deviances |
|---|---|---|---|---|---|---|---|---|---|
| BHC | 2022-01-31 11:26:23 | 24.224 | 24.14 | 0.003 | 0.476 | 0.771 | 0.69 | 0.025 | 0.476 |

Figure 14.10 – The output table of the model training workflow

The table produced by the model training workflow and consumed by the deployment workflow contains the stock symbol for which the forecast is generated, the date, the prediction of the adjusted closing price, and the last available adjusted closing price. It also shows the forecasted percentage change in the **Percentage Increase** column.

In addition, it shows columns that report the forecasting model's performance in the past 30 days. For example, the value **0.771** in the **R2** column in *Figure 14.10* indicates that the model could explain about 77% of the variability in the prices from the previous 30 days.

In the next section, we'll see how to complete the application with deployment actions.

## Consuming the H2O model in the deployment application

In this section, we'll see how to visualize and export the forecasts in the deployment workflow. We'll see how to send the price prediction information via email and log it in a `.csv` file.

These steps are implemented in the deployment workflow (*Figure 14.4*, accessible on KNIME Hub at `https://kni.me/w/4JrfiNV6NrqE7VKo`). The last steps in the workflow are shown here. Like the data preparation steps, the steps of data exportation are referencing the original Stock Prediction application available on KNIME Hub (accessible via `https://kni.me/s/_uV1ed73_uOJW5jz`).

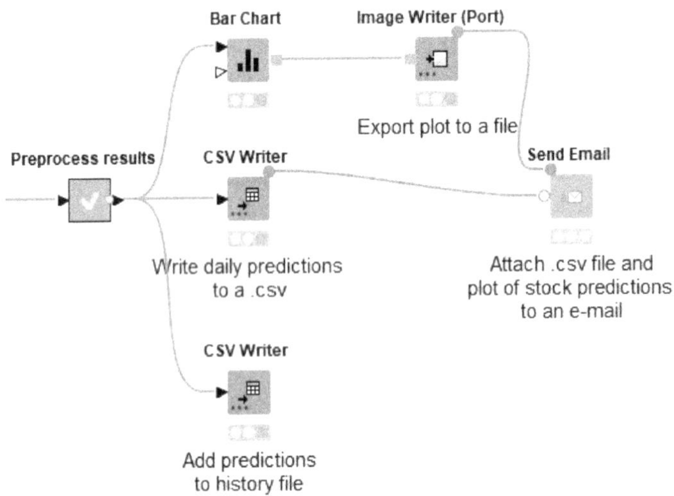


Figure 14.11 – Visualizing and exporting forecasts in the deployment workflow

The final steps in the deployment workflow are the following:

1. Firstly, the workflow filter out the missing values that exist if the price history could not be accessed for a stock symbol, and sorts the stock symbols in descending order based on the percentage return inside the **Preprocess results** metanode.
2. Next, it exports the preprocessed predictions data in the following four ways:

    - It builds a bar chart of percentage returns with the **Bar Chart** node and exports it into a `.svg` file and **Image Writer (Port)** node.
    - It writes the daily predictions into a `.csv` file with the top **CSV Writer** node.
    - It appends the daily predictions into previous days' predictions with the bottom **CSV Writer** node.
    - It sends an email with the bar chart image and the `.csv` file for the daily predictions as attachments with the **Send Email** node.

The following bar chart shows the predicted percentage returns for the selected stocks in descending order:

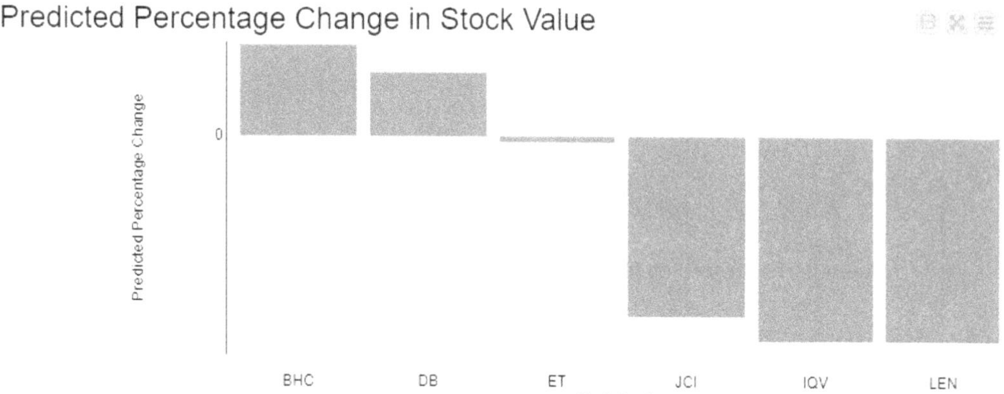


Figure 14.12 – Bar chart showing the predicted percentage changes of selected stock symbols

The two bars on the left show the stocks for which the return is predicted to be positive on the execution day (November 12, 2021). For the other four stocks, the return is expected to be negative. Notice, though, that the returns (and thus the bar chart) will vary from day to day and show different results.

The bar chart will be attached as a `.svg` image to an email that is sent automatically every time the workflow is executed. Also, a `.csv` file with the daily predictions will be attached. Therefore, we first save the bar chart as an `image.svg` file with the **Image Writer (Port)** node and the predictions as a `daily_predictions.csv` file with the **CSV Writer** node. After that, we configure the **Send Email** node as follows:

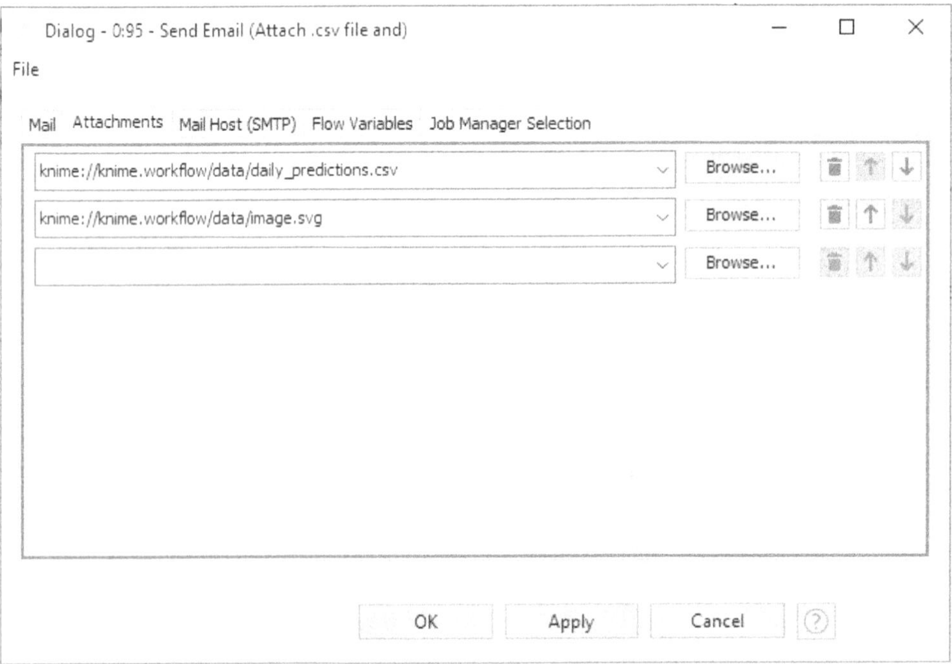


Figure 14.13 – Attaching files into an email sent by the Send Email node

In the **Attachments** tab of the **Send Email** node, we select the files by browsing the location in which they were saved in the previous step. In the **Mail** tab, we define the recipient, subject, and the email text. In the **Mail Host (SMTP)** tab, we define the email address that is sending the automatic email.

The deployment workflow can be executed on a regular basis to access predictions for varying days. On each day, it will access the latest data, update the model, and generate forecasts for the execution day, which will then be reported via email. The workflow can also be executed regularly on KNIME Server to produce the daily predictions automatically. Notice, though, that the predictions based on historical prices do not guarantee any trading success.

## Summary

In this chapter, we have demonstrated how to train a stock price prediction model on the H2O platform. We have explained how to build a deployment workflow that calls two separate workflows: one to access historical prices and another to generate a price forecast. Finally, we have shown how to export the results into a `.svg` image file and a `.csv` file and send them via email automatically.

You have learned about the challenges of stock price prediction and ways to adjust the application accordingly. You have also learned how to connect to the H2O platform and how to use H2O nodes for the fast and accurate processing of machine learning tasks. You have also learned how to access stock market prices from the internet via the Python `pandas-datareader` package. Finally, you have learned how to orchestrate multiple workflows from one caller workflow that consumes their results.

You have acquired the necessary skills to build workflows running on the H2O platform. They work the same way regardless of which of the available algorithms you choose – H2O Random Forest, H2O Isolation Forest, H2O K-Means, and more. You can also elaborate on the stock price prediction workflow by, for example, selecting different stock symbols, changing the forecasting algorithm, or implementing other deployment options.

## Questions

1. Which of the following advantages do you reap by using the KNIME H2O Machine Learning Integration?

    A. You can build custom ensemble models.

    B. You can process data faster.

    C. You can access data from online data sources.

    D. You can write custom scripts.

2. Which of the following characteristics best describes stock market data?

    A. Regular patterns

    B. Rapid changes

    C. Many missing values

    D. Always multivariate

3. How can you perform feature selection on H2O?

    A. By connecting the H2O Partitioning node directly to the Feature Selection Loop Start node
    B. Using the H2O Feature Selection loop nodes
    C. By converting the data into an H2O data frame at the start of the loop body
    D. By checking the feature importance statistics of the H2O generalized linear model

4. How can you adapt the application to execute an H2O Random Forest regression model instead?

    A. By switching all learner nodes to H2O Random Forest Learner (Regression) nodes in the model training workflow
    B. By switching all learner and predictor nodes to H2O Random Forest Learner (Regression) and H2O Random Forest Predictor (Regression) nodes, respectively
    C. By switching the learner node inside the feature selection loop to the H2O Random Forest Learner (Regression) node
    D. By switching the learner node after the feature selection to the H2O Random Forest Learner (Regression) node

# Final note

This chapter finishes the introduction to time series analysis with KNIME Analytics Platform, covering both theory and use cases. We hope you've had fun reading and learning through this book!

If you want to learn more about forecasting and time series, there are several publications, dedicated web pages, and academic papers that extend the topics covered in this book. For example, we recommend that you take a look at these:

- *Forecasting: Principles and Practice, Third Edition*, by Rob J Hyndman and George Athanasopoulos (`https://otexts.com/fpp3/`): an amazing free book on time series analysis, full of tips and methodologies to face most of the challenges related to forecasting.
- M Competitions (`https://mofc.unic.ac.cy/history-of-competitions/`): A series of competitions on forecasting methods that focus on which models have produced good forecasts on real data to solve specific everyday problems; they are very useful for understanding which methods are state of the art of forecasting and when it is useful to use one approach over another.

If you'd like to learn more about KNIME, please visit the following links:

- KNIME Hub (`https://hub.knime.com/`) for example workflows.
- The KNIME Forum (`https://forum.knime.com/`) for questions and answers.
- The learning page (`https://www.knime.com/learning`) for KNIME courses, books, and other support material. You'll also find the L4-TS Introduction to Time Series Analysis course here, created and instructed regularly by the three authors of this book!
- The newest KNIME contributions are also shared on social media, so stay connected via these platforms:
  - LinkedIn (`https://www.linkedin.com/company/knime.com/`)
  - Twitter (`https://twitter.com/knime`)
  - Facebook (`https://www.facebook.com/KNIMEanalytics/`)
  - Instagram (`https://www.instagram.com/knime_official`).

# Answers

## Chapter 1

1. A collection of observations that are sampled regularly at specific times, typically equally spaced.
2. Function approximation.
3. Obtain an adequate number of historical observations.
4. Direct clustering algorithms.

## Chapter 2

1. The smallest processing unit in KNIME
2. Edit outside the KNIME workbench
3. The tasks are implemented using functionalities from Python libraries and combining them with the KNIME native nodes

## Chapter 3

1. The time interval between subsequent observations
2. To replace missing values not missing at random
3. Less than 365
4. Temperature data is missing because the thermometer breaks at minus temperatures.

## Chapter 4

1. It allows for displaying fewer data columns.
2. Line plot
3. Line plot and seasonal plot

## Chapter 5

1. Applying the logarithmic transformation.
2. Once the moving average is applied, the resulting time series will have less observations than the original series.
3. Additive and multiplicative seasonality.
4. Applying the Box-Cox transformation.
5. Trend estimation, calculation of the detrended series, calculation of seasonal factors, determination of the residual component.

## Chapter 6

1. Mean Value Forecast
2. Naïve Forecast
3. Linear Regression
4. Exponential Smoothing

## Chapter 7

1. Partial Auto-Correlation Function (PACF)
2. Auto-Correlation Function (ACF)
3. Auto-Correlation Function (ACF)
4. Weak Stationarity: when the mean and variance do not change over time

## Chapter 8

1. Frequency
2. All of the above
3. Mean
4. Middle 50%

## Chapter 9

1. A machine learning model that relies on many artificial neurons inspired by biological neurons
2. Two
3. All of the above

## Chapter 10

1. Any number
2. True
3. Sigmoid

## Chapter 11

1. Class "anomaly"/"normal"
2. To account for anomalies that persist over time
3. Tolerate greater errors before raising an alarm.

## Chapter 12

1. Retrieving data locally.
2. Data as a Spark data frame.
3. The forecast horizon.
4. Yes, if the seasonality pattern is the same and there is no trend through the years.

## Chapter 13

1. Longer
2. Through the settings on the dedicated Preference page
3. If we want to execute the current workflow on a GPU while leaving default execution on the CPU.
4. To help regularize the training of the network

## Chapter 14

1. You can process data faster
2. Rapid changes
3. By converting the data into an H2O data frame at the start of the loop body
4. By switching all learner and predictor nodes to H2O Random Forest Learner (Regression) and H2O Random Forest Predictor (Regression) nodes, respectively

# Index

## Symbols



## A

## B



## C

## D

# E



# F

## L

## Q



## R



## S

## U



## V



## W



## Y



## Z

Packt.com

Subscribe to our online digital library for full access to over 7,000 books and videos, as well as industry leading tools to help you plan your personal development and advance your career. For more information, please visit our website.

## Why subscribe?

- Spend less time learning and more time coding with practical eBooks and Videos from over 4,000 industry professionals
- Improve your learning with Skill Plans built especially for you
- Get a free eBook or video every month
- Fully searchable for easy access to vital information
- Copy and paste, print, and bookmark content

Did you know that Packt offers eBook versions of every book published, with PDF and ePub files available? You can upgrade to the eBook version at packt.com and as a print book customer, you are entitled to a discount on the eBook copy. Get in touch with us at customercare@packtpub.com for more details.

At www.packt.com, you can also read a collection of free technical articles, sign up for a range of free newsletters, and receive exclusive discounts and offers on Packt books and eBooks.

# Other Books You May Enjoy

If you enjoyed this book, you may be interested in these other books by Packt:

**Time Series Analysis with Python Cookbook**

Tarek A. Atwan

ISBN: 9781801075541

- Understand what makes time series data different from other data
- Apply various imputation and interpolation strategies for missing data
- Implement different models for univariate and multivariate time series
- Use different deep learning libraries such as TensorFlow, Keras, and PyTorch
- Plot interactive time series visualizations using hvPlot
- Explore state-space models and the unobserved components model (UCM)
- Detect anomalies using statistical and machine learning methods
- Forecast complex time series with multiple seasonal patterns

**Time Series Analysis on AWS**

Michaël Hoarau

ISBN: 9781801816847

- Understand how time series data differs from other types of data
- Explore the key challenges that can be solved using time series data
- Forecast future values of business metrics using Amazon Forecast
- Detect anomalies and deliver forewarnings using Lookout for Equipment
- Detect anomalies in business metrics using Amazon Lookout for Metrics
- Visualize your predictions to reduce the time to extract insights

## Packt is searching for authors like you

If you're interested in becoming an author for Packt, please visit `authors.packtpub.com` and apply today. We have worked with thousands of developers and tech professionals, just like you, to help them share their insight with the global tech community. You can make a general application, apply for a specific hot topic that we are recruiting an author for, or submit your own idea.

## Share Your Thoughts

Now you've finished *Codeless Time Series Analysis with KNIME*, we'd love to hear your thoughts! Scan the QR code below to go straight to the Amazon review page for this book and share your feedback or leave a review on the site that you purchased it from.

`https://packt.link/r/1803232064`

Your review is important to us and the tech community and will help us make sure we're delivering excellent quality content.

CPSIA information can be obtained
at www.ICGtesting.com
Printed in the USA
BVHW061940290722
643376BV00012B/235